Legal Research Methods
in the U.S. & Europe

Also by Henrik Spang-Hanssen:

*Cyberspace & International Law on Jurisdiction*
1. ed. 2004
ISBN 978-87-574-0890-4

*Public International Computer Network Law Issues*
1. ed. 2006
ISBN 978-87-574-1486-8

J. Paul Lomio
Henrik Spang-Hanssen

# Legal Research Methods in the U.S. & Europe

## 2. edition

DJØF Publishing Copenhagen
2009

*Legal Research Methods in the U.S. & Europe*
2. edition

© 2009 by DJØF Publishing Copenhagen

DJØF Publishing is a company of the
Association of Danish Lawyers and Economists

Cover: Tor Morisse
Print: Narayana Press, Gylling
Binding: Damm's Forlagsbogbinderi, Randers

Printed in Denmark 2009
ISBN 978-87-574-1936-8

DJØF Publishing
17, Lyngbyvej
P.O.Box 2702
DK-2100 Copenhagen
Denmark

Phone: +45 39 13 55 00
Fax: +45 39 13 55 55
E-mail: forlag@djoef.dk
www.djoef-forlag.dk

The reason for why judges and lawyers should divert to the principles and decisions of foreign and international law is globalization. No institution of government can afford any longer to ignore the rest of the world.

*Former Associate Justice of the U.S. Supreme Court Sandra Day O'Connor, Southern Center for International Studies, Atlanta , Georgia, October 28, 2003*

Lawyers today need to be educated more broadly if they are to serve their clients and society well.

*Stanford Law School Dean Larry Kramer*

Legal education has changed little over the past century. Yet the challenges today's lawyers must meet are wholly new and different. Lawyers can contribute creative and effective solutions if we prepare them to do so … with innovative interdisciplinary and international programs, expand clinical education, and a deepened, nonpartisan commitment to public service.

*John L. Hennessy, Stanford University President*

It has become more and more obvious that an international operating lawyer cannot rely anymore on his knowledge of the national system only. He must be trained in comparative legal methodology and open minded to legal solutions of other jurisdictions. …Consequently, the national legal education systems have to adapt to this new generation of lawyers who are not anymore only concentrated on the[ir] own jurisdiction[s] but are global players on the international legal market.

*Universiteit Maastricht, The Future of Legal Education (June 2007)*

Comparative Legal Studies [should] indeed inspire students to learn more about and rethink the biases of their own cultural and legal education.

*Günter Frankenberg, Critical Comparisons: Re-Thinking Comparative Law, 26 Harvard International Law Journal 411, 412 (Spring 1985)*

The interest in comparative studies in American law schools is a response to the increasing relevance of foreign law to the concerns of laywers and their clients on a shrunken, interdependent globe. Both as professionals and as leaders in the public and private sectors, laywers in the West participate in a continual institutional reconstruction of the relevant world. Now that their relevant world embraces both the common law and the civil law … a familiarity with other people's law is indispensible to an adequate legal education.

*Mauro Cappelletti, Preface to J. Merryman & D. Clark, Comparative Law: Western European and Latin American Legal Systems (Indianapolis: Bobbs-Merrill 1978), at vii*

[The] common-law lawyer and [civil-law lawyer] each [has] assumed the modes of thought in which he had been trained to be fundamental and universal … [leading to] horrible examples of legal provincialism….

*Roscoe Pound, The Place of Comparative Law in the American Law School Curriculum, 8 Tulane Law Review 161, 167 (Feb. 1934)*

The case-study method paints a wrong picture of the legal profession for law students because of its reliance on using appellate cases to teach legal thoughts or reasoning based on the Langdell (Socratic) method.

*Professor Douglas A. Berman, Ohio State University, ABA Journal (July 2007), at page 44*

Vanderbilt University Law School is adding law classes based on statutes and regulations.

*ABA Journal (July 2007), at page 44*

Tomorrow's lawyers will be plucking increasingly valuable data from exponentially-growing fields of information; working with colleagues and clients spanning the globe, and establishing automated systems to leverage scarce legal resources more efficiently.

*Gene Koo, New Skills, New Learning, at page 24*

Law plays a foundational role in American society, and increasingly in articulating our global community.

*Gene Koo, New Skills, New Learning, at page 24*


The global economy is becoming more interconnected, so thinking how to teach comparative and international law becomes more and more important every year.

*Columbia Dean David Schizer, The National Law Journal (September 10, 2007)*


A comparatist should not limit to the staid and dry juxtaposition of the regulations of one legal system with those of another, with little or no critical analysis, as such comparatists do not compare, they contrast. What is required is analysis.

*Werner F. Menski, Comparative Law In A Global Context (2007)*


Otto von Bismarck famously compared laws to sausages – it is better not to see either being made. But while you can probably spend your life avoiding any sort of industrial food process, a life in the law will sometimes require you to scour what is known as legislative history. Legislative history, a term that is at once intimidating and boring, is the story of a law's creation.

*Travis McDade, Student Lawyer (December 2006)*

# Preface

It is nearly impossible for foreign students, scholars and lawyers/jurists, on visits of some months to either an American university or other research institution, to learn how to do legal research effectively on U.S. material. One has to have experienced American society and, moreover, the U.S. legal research environment, for quite some time to be able to truly understand the way American legal research is conducted.

The same can be said about Americans visiting Europe and its different legal families.[1]

This book is an attempt to outline usefully the basic research methods in the United States (overall common-law) and in Europe (overall civil-law). In addition, it tries to point out the salient issues the "visiting" scholar in particular should remember.

The two chapters on European Union resources (Chapter 4) and public international resources (Chapter 5) were deemed by the authors to be pertinent in the context of earlier chapters on U.S. and European sources and legal methods. The subsequent, shorter chapters on legal families (Chapter 6) and on comparative law (Chapter 7) also seemed appropriate.

We have tried to make the content of this book proportionate to the amount of lecture material that would ordinarily be provided in a course on legal research methods.

The process of writing the book has been a collaborative effort between Paul

---

[1] The American law graduate will likewise find that at least two years is necessary for studying abroad in Europe effectively, and that "the first year is likely to be wasted." Max Rheinstein, *Comparative Law – Its Functions, Methods and Usages*, 22 ARK. L. REV. 415, 424 (Fall 1968). The organization of legal studies in Europe is "so different" from what it is in the U.S. that "an American student is likely to be lost unless he is individually guided." *Idem.* at 424-25.

Lomio and Henrik Spang-Hanssen. The former took responsibility for Chapter 2. The latter composed the bulk of the draft manuscript and assumed responsibility for Chapters 3-7. The authors has reviewed and discussed each others contributions.

The authors devoted special attention to Sections 2.1. and 3.1. from the perspective of their national legal systems so as to make sure the different "cultures" in the U.S. and Europe are emphasized for the book's readers.

We anticipate receiving many suggestions for improvement and we hope, in turn, to be able to bring out improved later editions of the book.

We are extremely grateful to George D. Wilson, reference librarian, attorney-at-law and lecturer in law at Stanford Law School, for his invaluable comments on and contributions to the manuscript and for his careful proofreading. Also, we would like to thank Alba Holgado at the Robert Crown Law Library for her expert help in making the front-page and several graphics/tables.

If this book will help prevent even just a few students, scholars and lawyers/jurists from making the most common mistakes, our goal will have been fulfilled.

In addition, we hope it will assist students around the world who participate in such activities as the annual Philip C. Jessup International Law Moot Court Competition in Washington D.C. (arranged by the International Law Student Association (ILSA)), who have gained access to Westlaw and LexisNexis databases for international legal materials but who still must gain understanding of how these databases work. To such individuals especially, section 2.3 , Chapter 5, and Appendix 2 & 5 should be of help

We would like to emphasize that in this book we use the term "law" in the sense it is used in the U.S. (covering the broad body of judicial decisions, legislative enactments, and administrative/executive regulations/rules) and not as in civil law countries, where the term is mostly only regarded as the law made by parliaments. For the latter meaning, we generally use the terms "act" or "statute."

Because the URLs of websites often change, we have chosen only to give references to main/home webpages. Pinpoint URLs can be found at *our special website for the book* at <**www.geocities.com/legalrm**>, which will be kept current updated from time to time. As Chapter 2 points out, currency is an obsession with the American lawyer.

Citations in footnotes have generally been made on the basis of the American legal citations system. The bibliography in the appendix has been constructed in accordance with the European system, including full spelling of American law reviews. As this book does not deal with case law decisions in detail, it does not contain a case list.

Robert Crown Law Library, Stanford University, September 2007

J. Paul Lomio & Henrik Spang-Hanssen

*******

This **Second edition** is primarily an update of Chapter 4 due to the expected changes in the European Union caused by the Lisbon Treaty of December 2007.

Some errors in the first edition have been corrected.

Tips and notes in grey shadings have been included in chapters 1, 3-7.

I would like to thank Professor and Library Director Lee F. Peoples, Oklahoma City University, very much for his suggestion to make a "manual" for teaching European civil law. A first draft was published in March 2008 with approval of Professor Peoples and made available through a link from the book's corresponding website. A new version of this document is attached this second edition as an Addendum of the book (without copyright for DJØF).[2]

As my co-author has unfortunately been too much burden with other tasks, a real revision-edition must come later.

The updates – with few exceptions - have been made in chapters of which

---

[2] This "manual" can also be found as "The Modern Law School's *Uriaspost* - the Post of Danger" at <http://ssrn.com/abstract_id=1102293> (where it might have been updated from the text printed in this book).

I am the sole author and I have the full responsibility for any faults made in this second edition.

Because the book's paragraphs are written with justified alignment, text therefore sometimes will occur with large space between words in connection with a longer URL for a website, but I have chosen not to cut the (true) URL, which would be the only way to eliminate the large space.

I am extremely grateful to George D. Wilson for his once again careful proofreading.

Great thanks also go to Alba Holgado at the Robert Crown Law Library for her expert help in making several graphics.

Also, should be noted that websites are often changed, wherefore we have chosen not to give pinpoint references to websites' URLs in the book, but rather to announce them at *this book's corresponding website* at <**www.geocities.com/legalrm**> which will be kept updated from time to time.

Leland Stanford Junior University, August 2008

Henrik Spang-Hanssen

We have received many good suggestion for which we are extremely grateful to a revision of the first edition – which truly only was the authors' first attempt to construct a first and simple "bridge across the Atlantic ocean" - and we still hope to receive many comments or suggestions, which will be highly appreciated and should be sent to:

Paul Lomio:  plomio@stanford.edu and/or

Henrik Spang-Hanssen:  hssph@yahoo.com

# About the Authors

*J. Paul Lomio* is Library Director and Lecturer in Law at Stanford Law School. He holds both a U.S. Juris Doctor degree and an LL.M. degree in Law and Marine Affairs as well as a Masters of Library and Information Science. He was admitted to the Washington State Bar Association and was a member of the Gonzaga Law Review and has published several law review articles. He taught Resources in the Law at San Jose State University for ten years and currently teaches Advanced Legal Research at Stanford Law School. He was appointed to the Law Librarians Advisory Committee for the California Office of Administrative Law, served a three-year term on the Association of American Law Schools Committee on Libraries and Technology and is a member of the Electronic Court Filing Task Force for the United States District Court, Northern District of California and currently serves as a member of the West Academic Advisory Board. He has received several distinguished awards, including the Marshall D. O'Neill Award for "exceptional and enduring support of Stanford University's Research Enterprise." This is his first book. See www.law.stanford.edu/library

*Henrik Spang-Hanssen* is a Danish Supreme Court Attorney-at-law. Since 1998, he has worked as an independent senior researcher, including five years in the United States. He holds masters degrees in law from Copenhagen University in Denmark and Santa Clara University in California. He has clerked for the Chief Justice of the Supreme Court of Denmark. He has taught courses/seminars for paralegals, students and attorneys. He practiced law in his own law firm for over 15 years and worked as an external District Attorney in Appeals Courts in Denmark. He has been an elected member of the Attorney Disciplinary Board for the Copenhagen District. He has served as chairperson of a special committee on debt-collecting businesses and been a member of the Danish Law Society's committee concerning foreclosure auctions, debt-collecting businesses, bankruptcies and moratora. He has several times served as a judge at the international final rounds of the Phillip C. Jessup International Law Moot Court Competition in Washington, D.C. He is member of The American Society of International Law (ASIL) and an associated member of the American Bar Association. In addition, he has, written (in Danish ) the two fundamental books used by the Danish Law Society

(Denmark's bar association) and the Danish Attorney Disciplinary Board – "Advokatnævnet" (chaired by a Justice of the Supreme Court of Denmark) - and three books (in English) on issues of public international law and cyberspace. He is regarded by many as an expert on the intersection of public international law and public international computer networks. See www.geocities.com/hssph.

Both authors have taught university courses on legal research.

# Table of Contents

# CHAPTER 1

# Introduction

The different approaches of Common Law and Civil Law have once been described as follows: continental jurists "have attempted to go too far, to define and fix that which cannot, in the nature of things, be defined and fixed."[1] Indeed, "[t]hey seem to have forgotten

- that they wrote on a question which touched the comity of nations, and that that comity is, and ever must be, uncertain;
- that it must necessarily depend on a variety of circumstances which cannot be reduced to any certain rule;
- that no nation will suffer the laws of another to interfere with her own to the injury of her citizens;
- that whether they do or not must depend on the condition of the country in which the foreign law is sought to be enforced, the particular nature of her legislation, her policy, and the character of her institutions;
- that in the conflict of laws, it must often be a matter of doubt, which should prevail; and
- that, whenever a doubt does exist, the court, which decides, will prefer the laws of its own country to that of the stranger."[2]

However, it would certainly be wrong to make out that there was an unbridgeable opposition between Common Law's method of inductive prob-

---

[1] *Hilton v. Guyot*, 159 US 113, 144 (US 1895). The words are from U.S. Supreme Court Justice Joseph Story's treatise *Commentaries on the Conflict of Laws, Foreign and Domestic*, quoting Louisiana Supreme Court Justice Porter about the difficulty of applying the positive rules laid down by the European jurists .

[2] *Idem.*

lem-solving and Civil Law's method of systematic conceptualism.[3]

In Europe today, Civil Law and Common Law show several signs of convergence. In the United Kingdom, statutory law increasingly overrides common law traditions of judicial law-making, while on the continent, legal theory increasingly acknowledges the fact and necessity of judicial precedent and law-making. Important areas of the law are unified under international treaties. British judges faithfully implement European Union law that is based primarily on Civil Law notions. The Court of Justice of the E.U. creatively applies principles from both legal worlds. Nevertheless, despite refreshing Common Law input, the dominant legal culture of the European Union and the emerging *ius commune Europaeum*[4] remain very much in the Civil Law tradition.[5]

European scholars often criticize the way Americans do legal research. However, they seem to forget that it is a question of doing legal research in a country where there is a body of law that to a large extent is built on cases, which means one must compare different judges' opinions and decisions.

In addition, even if one can find a statutory provision, it is necessary to compare it with case law to see whether the latter has invalidated, or changed, or added to the statute's content - or vice versa ["*Shepardize* or *KeyCite*"].

Thus, the European scholars who criticize American legal research methods seem not to understand the U.S. legal system..

It appears to be the widely-followed rule in the United States that if one wants to make a legal point or advance a legal thesis and validate it, one must cite copiously to authoritative sources (with exact page references – "pinpoint citations") that support one's view;[6] compare Article 38(1)(d) in the Statute of the International Court of Justice ("ICJ Statute"), which in general means

---

[3] K. Zweigert & H.Kötz, INTRODUCTION TO COMPARATIVE LAW 33, 251 (3rd ed.)(Tony Weir trans., Clarendon Press, Oxford 1998).

[4] See Glossary in Appendix 1.

[5] Herbert Hausmaninger, THE AUSTRIAN LEGAL SYSTEM 320 (Vienna: Manzsche Verlags- und Universitätsbuchhandlung, 2003).

[6] The scholar has no other power than the one that comes from his capacity to persuade. Rodolfo Sacco, *Legal Formant:, A Dynamic Approach to Comparative Law* (Installment II of II), 39 AM. J. COMP. L 343, 349 (Spring 1991) [hereinafter SACCO II].

simply to cite either to case law or to other scholars' articles.[7]

It is arguably a phantom or a failure of Civil Law scholars to assert that any claimed idea (thesis) is of their own invention. In the modern context of the World Wide Web it is more than likely that someone somewhere else already has dealt with the same thing and opined on it in an article, law review, book or blog. Thus, to some extent, it is even unethical for Civil Law scholars not to cite to foreign publications and scholars and instead claim they are the inventors of an idea or thesis.

Furthermore, in literature on public international law it is common practice among the "most highly qualified publicists of the various nations" – a source itself in ICJ Statute 38(d)(1) – to cite and refer to other scholars in footnotes.

The aim of Chapter 2 of this book is to educate scholars outside the U.S. on how to do research on American legal material and how to then draw some useful comparisons and contrasts for analysis in order to gain at least a modicum of understanding. Chapter 2 also seeks to illuminate the vital differences between the American and, for example, the European continental legal research methods. If one is making comparison or reference to American material, one will have to use the American legal method; only then can one truly compare it with European material and thoughts, using the continental legal method.

It is an often seen failure of European scholars, and a dreadful mistake, to cite an American case or statute without doing proper *Shepardizing* or *Key-Citing*, that is, checking the present validity of the case or statute using a legal citator. Such check should be done just before printing or delivering articles or manuscripts to publishers. Otherwise, for example, a dissertation involving American material should be denied eligibility for a doctoral defense in Europe. The problem of validation is probably grounded on the European scholar's lack of education in and knowledge of using by and large up-to-the-minute legal resources such as Westlaw and LexisNexis for cite checking rather than merely as library search tools.

---

[7] European scholars should note that most U.S. professors appear to be of the opinion that if an article does not have at least 100 citations (including of the pinpoint variety), it is not worth publishing.

It should be noted here in this discussion of Civil-Common Law differences, at least in passing, that the American State of Louisiana is a Civil Law state,[8] and that the State of California, for example, is described at times as a "statute" state because of the large number of acts passed by the California Legislature (and signed by the Governor).

As for the difference between American and European scholars' work, one should note that an American dissertation for a law-related doctoral degree (equivalent to a European PhD) may typically be a minimum of 500 hundred pages long, with myriad footnotes (pinpointing the page of each reference citation), a table of cases and also a bibliography. American legal scholars regard an article or book without large amounts of footnotes (and, again, specifying the page of each reference citation) as essentially without value. This is due to the widespread opinion that an author's point of view becomes stronger when he or she can make abundant reference to case law or other scholars of like opinion.

In Europe, the stepping stone for legal students and scholars is the text of the law in question. There is very little unwritten law; case law is overall without importance. Thus, the basic building block, and starting point for analysis, of the law in Europe is the wording of a particular paragraph of a statute (In Europe, the symbol "§" can be used for a paragraph, section, and even a single statute; in the United States the symbol "¶" is used solely for a paragraph, while the "§" is employed only for a section).

A European dissertation for a PhD will usually be no more than 300 pages long, with very few footnotes; but it will contain an appendix with a bibliography (without pinpointing of the pages of reference citations) and no case list.

Some European scholars regard extensive use of footnotes (with pinpoint citations) as a kind of plague and, moreover, as an expression or evidence of

---

[8] *Reynolds v. Swain*, 13 La. 193 (Louisiana Supreme Court 1839). As to differences between Louisiana law and the law of other U.S. states, see Robert A. Pascal, *Louisiana Civil Law and Its Study*, 60 LA L. REV. 1 (Fall 1999).

the author only having compiled other people's opinions and ideas without any personal contribution, ideas, and opinion. Therefore, European legal scholars should not be astonished why their works are often rejected for publication by American law reviews.

Chapter 2 is written as an American will present and write the subject. Furthermore, it is written to be used for American courses on legal research methods.

Chapters 3-7 are written as an European will present and write the subject.

Thus, this book present the reader with the different ways of presenting and writing. Therefore, the difference in styles between chapter 2 and 3-7 will present the reader of the different legal writing cultures, which also is an aim with the book, as it illustrates the differences in styles on literature related to law between America and Europe.

Europeans (civil law lawyers) have to learn that information in footnotes in American legal literature is regarded having great value and should be studied.

Americans have to learn that in Europe cited literature and bibliography should be studied to find articles or books of importance – and that they will generally not find exact page-references in footnotes.

The main reason for this difference is that in Europe publication-cost are high, thus publishers want to limit the amount of words/pages and physical paper consumption.[9]

The differences between the two cultures will probably never find a common denominator as neither American or European scholars will denounce their vital way of doing legal scholarship, including the way of using footnotes and make citations.

---

[9] The latter is not originally based on eco-culture reasons, but the use of cutting trees/wood for publication purposes has become an environment concern in Europe.

Thus, each culture have to learn to use each others way of doing things – and how to present their scholarly works on the other side of the bridge.

A rough overview of the comparison between Common Law and Civil Law thinking can be set forth as follows:

| Common Law | Civil Law |
|---|---|
| The law is a gradual development from court decision to court decision | The law is the codification – nation by nation – of abstract rules |
| A decision is never made until it has to be made – and only concrete experience counts | Decisions are made in advance in the abstract and they systematize the applicable rules |
| All aspects of a unitary legal transaction should be dealt with in the same place in the legal system (e.g., "law of sale" should deal with both the question of delivery and the question of the change in ownership from a sales transaction) | Aspects of a unitary legal transaction are separated into their discrete parts (e.g., a separate law of sale and claim of ownership) |
|  |  |
| Lawyers look at things in concrete practice | Lawyers look at things in the abstract |
| The frame of mind is to prefer to proceed cautiously, on the basis of experience, from this case or that case to the next case, as justice in each case seems to require | The frame of mind seeks to refer everything back to supposed universals |
| The approach is not to try to deduce the decision for the case at hand from any universally formulated proposition |  |
| The underlying approach is based on the surefooted Anglo-Saxon habit of dealing with things ad hoc as they arise | The underlying approach is one based on anticipating things by abstract universal formulas |
| The Common Law lawyer reasons from instances to principles | The Civil Law lawyer reasons from principles to instances |
| The Common Law lawyer puts his or her faith in precedents | The Civil Law lawyer puts his or her faith in syllogisms[10] |
| The Common Law lawyer asks aloud in the same situation: "What did we do last time?" | The Civil Law lawyer silently asks in each situation: "What should we do this time?" |
| The working rule of the Common-Law lawyer is solvitur ambulando[11] | The instinct of a Civil Law lawyer is to systematize |

---

[10] A "syllogism" can be defined as: (1) a deductive scheme of a formal argument consisting of a major and a minor premise and a conclusion (as in "every virtue is laudable; kindness is a virtue; therefore kindness is laudable"); (2) a subtle, specious, or crafty argument; (3) deductive reasoning (MERRIAM-WEBSTER DICTIONARY ONLINE <http://www.m-w.com/>).

| | |
|---|---|
| The Common Law lawyer thinks concretely in terms of cases, the relationship of the parties, and "right and duties" | The Civil Law lawyer thinks abstractly in terms of institutions |
| Common Law lawyers feel their way gradually from case to case | The Civil Law system is conceived as being complete and free of gaps |
| Common Law lawyers are skeptical of every generalization | Civil-Law lawyers delight in the systematic |
| Common Law lawyers think in pictures | Civil Law lawyers operate with ideas that often take on a life of their own |
| | |
| Case law | Enacted law |
| The law is concrete and comes from courts | The law is abstract and comes from study |
| Judges are recruited from among great lawyers | Judges are recruited from among professors |
| Judges were previously private attorneys | Judges were previously government officials |
| | |
| There is no division into private and commercial law | The law is divided into private and commercial law |

*Table 1: Comparison between Common Law and Civil Law Thinking*

---

[11] Latin for: "It is solved by walking," that is, the problem is solved by a practical experiment.

# CHAPTER 2

# Methods in the U.S. – A Common Law Method

The year 2007 saw a revolution in legal education in the United States. Early in 2007, Harvard announced "the most sweeping changes to its first-year curriculum in 100 years, requiring first-year law students to take ... a class on legislation and regulation, another covering global legal systems, and a third focusing on problems and theories."[1] Other leading law schools are likewise revising their curriculums to reflect the new world legal order. Stanford Law School "is in the process of rolling out joint-degree programs and 12 cross-disciplinary courses ..." with a special emphasis on international law.[2] The Columbia Law School dean remarked that "the global economy is becoming more interconnected, so thinking how to teach comparative and international law becomes more and more important every year."[3]

The lawyer of today cannot only rely upon his or her own national legislation or rules but has to take into consideration foreign law, and this is especially true between Europe and the United States. What happens on one side of the Atlantic Ocean is quickly felt upon the other. An article in Harpers Magazine makes an interesting observation about how law making on one side of the Atlantic effects (not just affects) law making on the other:

---

[1] Tresa Baldas, *Several Schools Adjust Their Curriculums*, THE NATIONAL LAW JOURNAL, Monday, September 10, 2007, p. S1.

[2] *Idem.*

[3] *Idem.*

[I]n 1976, the U.S. Congress passed the Toxic Substances Control Act . . . which granted the government the authority to track industrial chemicals and to place restrictions on any that proved harmful to humans or the environment. Because the United States was the world's preeminent economic power, other major chemical producers Germany, France, and Britain soon brought their national regulations into line with United States law.[4]

The purpose of this book is to introduce American legal research to Europeans and European legal research to Americans so that they can speak the same legal research language, a necessary first step for cross-Atlantic collaborations. The book is also the first legal research text to address the internationalization of the American law school curriculum.

## 2.1. U.S. Common Law Basics for Non-Americans

### 2.1.1. Introduction

The United States is a startling vast country, 3,000 miles (4.828 km) coast to coast, and that does not include its two detached states, Alaska and Hawaii.[5] Everything in the United States is "super sized." Americans drive enormous automobiles[6] and the American Dream is to live in a large single-family

---

[4] Mark Schapiro, *Toxic Inaction*, HARPER'S MAGAZINE, October 2007, p. 78, 79. However, the European Union has taken over the leading role by signing the following international agreements: Air Pollution, Air Pollution-Nitrogen Oxides, Air Pollution-Persistent Organic Pollutants, Air Pollution-Sulphur 94, Antarctic-Marine Living Resources, Biodiversity, Climate Change, Climate Change-Kyoto Protocol, Desertification, Hazardous Wastes, Law of the Sea, Ozone Layer Protection, Tropical Timber 82, Tropical Timber 94, CIA's The World Factbook European Union, <www.cia.gov/library/publications/the-world-factbook/print/ee.html>.

[5] For comparison: The European Union area is 4,324,782 Square Km (one-half the size of the U.S.) and has a population of 490,426,060 (190,000,000 more than the U.S.), <www.cia.gov/library/publications/the-world-factbook/print/ee.html>. The E.U. is the largest single market in the world with a $15.4 trillion economy and the largest trading partner of the U.S. Trade flows across the Atlantic are running at around €1.7 billion a day.

[6] The gasoline prices in the U.S. are only 1/3 of the prices in most of the rest of the world.

house.[7] Everything in America, it seems, is done on a grand scale, including law-making. It has been said that the United States is a litigious society and this is reflected in court statistics.[8] Most of this litigation occurs in the states, and not at the federal level,[9] and it is the state courts that apply and create the Common Law.

To the lawyer from the continent of Europe, Common Law has always been something rich and strange. At every step, the European lawyer comes across legal institutions, procedures, and traditions, which have no exact counterpart in the Continental legal world. The European lawyer scans the common legal scene in vain for much that seems to him or her to be an absolute necessity in any functioning legal system, such as a civil code, a commercial code, a code of civil procedure, and an integrated structure of legal concepts rationally ordered. The European finds that legal technique, instead of being directed primarily to interpreting statutory texts or analyzing concrete problems so as to "fit them into the system" conceptually, is principally interested in precedents and types of court cases.

It is nearly impossible for any scholar to do proper research on United States law without the use of computer-assisted legal research (CALR) databases, such as the ubiquitous LexisNexis and Westlaw research systems (although, as noted below, more and more competitors are appearing on the scene). Being able to sift, search, cull, and skim from millions and millions of reported, and, with greater frequency, unreported court decisions is what American lawyers and law students do, and they do it all of the time.

---

[7] According to HARPER'S MAGAZINE, the "percentage change since 1990 in the average size of an American master bathroom" is 50%. Harper's Index, Harper's (October 2007), p. 15 (citing National Association of Home Builders (Washington)).

[8] During the 12-month fiscal year 2005-2006, more than 9.2 million cases were filed in the California court system. Judicial Council of California, 2007 COURT STATISTICS REPORT. California is an important state, with a large population, but, still, that is just the number of court filings for one of fifty states and the District of Columbia.

[9] By comparison, in 2006 there were a little over 300,000 cases filed in the United States District courts (the federal trial level court of general jurisdiction). Of these, 259,541 were civil filings and 56,532 were criminal filings. See: Administrative Office of the United States Courts, FEDERAL COURT MANAGEMENT STATISTICS 2006, <www.uscourts.gov/fcmstat>.

## 2.1.2. State sovereignty

When one performs American legal research, one should regard the United States as a federal union of fifty fairly independent states, each with their own constitution. Thus, one could think of it as not so much as one nation, but actually more like the European Union of twenty-seven member states.

The United States Congress in Washington D.C. has limitations upon what issues it may legislate upon, and the federal courts in the United States similarly have limitations upon what cases they may hear.

While there exists no federal general Common Law,[10] all American lawyers and law students search for federal law precedents.

The United States can be regarded as a gigantic laboratory for legal policy and the critical method of comparative law is important for any lawyer and student in the U.S.[11]

Even though the U.S is regarded as a Common Law country and traces its origins to England, its Common Law varies from the Common Law found in England and the Commonwealth nations. English Common Law is inapplicable if conditions in America make it inappropriate. Nor is there such a thing as "a common American law" (even though it is to a certain degree taught in law schools).

England does not have a constitution, whereas the United States has a constitution creating civil rights[12] and giving the U.S. Supreme Court and lower federal courts the power to declare whether a federal statute is unconstitutional. The Constitution of the United States gives only the U.S. Congress competence in limited and special areas, whereas England has a Par-

---

[10] See *Erie Railroad Company v. Tompkins*, 304 U.S. 64 (1938) and 28 U.S.C. § 725 (2000).

[11] Modern comparative law is a critical method of legal science…a discipline where a detailed method cannot be laid down in advance, K. Zweigert & H.Kötz, INTRODUCTION TO COMPARATIVE LAW 33, 251 (3rd ed.)(Tony Weir trans., Clarendon Press, Oxford 1998).

[12] However, England has the so-called "Magna Carta Libertatum" ("Great Charter of Freedoms") of 1215, which led to the rule of constitutional law today. It influenced many common law and other documents, such as the United States Constitution and Bill of Rights, and is considered one of the most important legal documents in the history of democracy.

liament which can legislate for the entire nation without any limitation and
has courts that cannot declare a statute unlawful.

### 2.1.3. Life for the American law student

Cases, cases, cases. That is what American law students read morning, noon
and night.[13] Their textbooks are even called "casebooks."[14] By one estima-
tion, a typical United States law student will read  between forty and fifty
cases a week,[15] every week of their first year of law school (in the United
States full time law students take three years to earn their Juris Doctor
(J.D.)[16] degree, which is the degree most lawyers in the United States have).

---

[13] However, this is changing in regards to upper level courses with the new curriculum of
the leading law schools in the U.S.

[14] "In the first year of law school, much of the focus of law is on courses arising from
common law rules ... Rather than using traditional textbooks that talk about the law,
these courses expose students directly to the law itself through reading assigned in
casebooks. A traditional casebook focuses on only one area of law (for example, Torts
or Criminal Law) ... the casebook contains clusters of edited cases – actual opinions
written and published by judges in various jurisdictions. These cases have been carefully selected and carefully edited by the casebook based on what the author wants you
to learn ... Some of these cases may contradict one another (they are collected from
different jurisdictions that may apply different common law rules), some show evolution in the law, ... some show exceptions to a dominant rule ... and some are just
poorly decided (included to make you think about what does and doesn't make
sense)." Ruth Ann McKinney, READING LIKE A LAWYER: TIME-SAVING STRATEGIES
FOR READING LAW LIKE AN EXPERT (Durham, North Carolina: Carolina Academic
Press 2005).

[15] Professor Ruth Ann McKinney, Clinical Professor of Law and Director of the Legal
Writing & Learning Resources Center at the University of North Carolina School of
Law has researched the law school experience and estimates that "the average American law student is assigned about three to four cases a night in three classes a night.
So, on average, the average law student is reading between eight and twelve cases a
night, five nights a week. I estimate they are reading between forty and fifty cases a
week." E-mail correspondence from Ruth McKinney, dated September 18, 2007, on
file with the authors.

[16] This is a much lower degree than the European "Doctor Juris" degree, which is the
highest law degree and requires writing a large dissertation, getting it accepted by a
law scholar committee and finally passing a "defense" of the thesis asserted in the dissertation.

Indeed, one of the very first assignments for Stanford Law Students in their first-year Legal Research and Writing course is to read Owen Kerr's very excellent "How to Read a Judicial Opinion: A Guide for New Law Students".[17]

Students devour, discuss, and dissect a stream of these cases, seemingly without end. Federal cases, state cases, English cases, really old cases, bad cases, elegant cases, cases written in verse, unpublished cases, cases decided just today. Case analysis – that is the life of an American law student.

So what is a case? It is an opinion written by a judge - state or federal - and usually, but certainly not always, an appellate judge. Judges apply law to fact situations and, on appeal, only the questions of law are reviewed. Unlike in Europe, where all is de novo, appellate courts in the United States will not overturn facts that were decided by the trier-of-fact (which could be a jury or a judge if the defendant waived a jury trial). Appellate courts only consider questions of law. It is this exposition of law that American law students study. More on this later when we discuss case law research.

This case-centric approach to legal studies carries over to all three years of the American law students' education. Indeed, it is not unusual to see a second or third year student hunched over at the computer, searching, for hours – in vain – for the "white horse" case[18], a case that perfectly matches the issue being researched, so named because of a fact pattern identical to the one being researched, right down to the color of the horse that the defendant rode off upon.

Why are students so focused on case law? It traces to the first Latin phrase they learn in law school, *stare decisis*, succinctly defined by Black's Law Dictionary thusly:

---

[17] Available at: <http://volokh.com/files/howtoreadv2.pdf>.

[18] Bryan A. Garner, A DICTIONARY OF MODERN LEGAL USAGE (2nd ed.) (New York: Oxford University Press, 1995), (a law library must-have) offers this definition: "White-horse case; horse case; gray mule case; goose case; spotted pony case; pony case. These are terms meaning 'a reported case with virtually identical facts, the disposition of which should determine the outcome of the existing case.' The terms are now less commonly used in the law school than formerly; but they are useful terms." [hereinafter GARNER]

[Latin "to stand by things decided"] The doctrine of precedent, under which it is necessary for a court to follow earlier judicial decisions when the same points arise again in litigation.

Since the United States is a Common Law country (with the quirky exception of some laws from Louisiana), court cases establish legal principles. A judicial decision that "determines the outcome of a particular case, and also may regulate future conduct of all persons within the jurisdiction of the court."[19] It establishes a precedent.[20]

"The doctrine of *stare decisis*, or adherence to precedent, requires courts to decide cases consistently with their past decisions involving the same or similar facts and legal principles. Lower courts in a particular jurisdiction are bound not only by their own past decisions, but also by the precedents of higher courts in that jurisdiction. Although a court in State A will not regard the judicial precedents from other states as mandatory authority, the court may nevertheless consider them to be persuasive authority, particularly when there is no precedent in State A on the issue raised is the current case."[21]

Because of this doctrine of *stare decisis*, lawyers and law students must be able to locate all the mandatory (the "law") and, in order to argue well, the most persuasive additional precedents that relate to their research assignments and their clients' cases. And for this reason, many lawyers and law students turn to case law databases first to tackle their research.

A major goal of this chapter is to prove that starting legal research by plowing though case law databases, however, is not the road to effective legal research.

## 2.1.4. Law Making Bodies in the United States

In this chapter the term "government" is given an American meaning. Government actors are defined as those individuals - elected or appointed - who

---

[19] West's ENCYCLOPEDIA OF AMERICAN LAW.

[20] The term "precedent" is used differently in Civil Law, where "precedents" are only those court decisions that have been acknowledged to be important by the society and scholars.

[21] LexisNexis, LESSONS IN LEGAL RESEARCH: A MANUAL FOR INSTRUCTORS (2004 ).

have some official role in the legal regulation of American life or commerce. These government actors belong to one of three branches of government:

- The Legislative
- The Executive
- The Judiciary

As discussed above, judges in the United States make "law" by issuing decisions. However, courts are not the only law-making arm in the United States. But what, exactly, is "law?" According to West's Encyclopedia of American Law, "… the word law refers to any rule that if broken subjects a party to criminal punishment or civil liability." In other words, failure to obey the law could result in either going to jail or paying someone else money, often a lot of money.

The United States has three branches of government, as illustrated below, and each branch produces its own body of law, as guided by the United States Constitution.

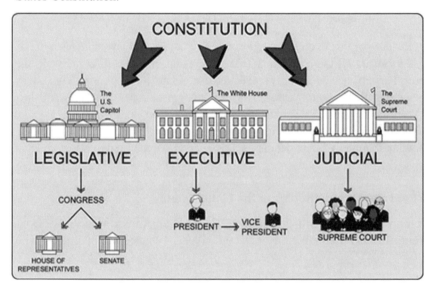

*Table 2: United States Three Branches of Government*

- The Legislative Branch produces statutes.
- The Executive Branch issues orders, regulations and administrative opinions.
- The Judicial Branch writes those millions of judicial decisions (also called opinions or just "cases" – the terms are used interchangeably) which are the focus of law school education and comprise the bulk of

the content in the gigantic computer-assisted legal research databases LexisNexis and Westlaw.

All of these types of law, and how to research them, are discussed in detail below.

### 2.1.5. Tools for Legal Research in the U.S.

Bibliographic resources in the law are broadly divided into two categories:

- Primary sources are those publications – in print or online – that contain the actual text of law, such as statutes, code sections, agency regulations, court decisions, or decisions of administrative law judges. These may be government produced sources or commercial sources, but the contents are the work-product of government actors.
- Secondary sources are those publications – again, either in print or online – that explain the law. The publications are almost always commercially produced and are authored mainly by attorneys or law professors.

Primary:

| Judicial | Legislative | Administrative |
|---|---|---|
| Cases | Constitutions | Regulations |
| Rules of Court | Statutes | Decisions |
| | Ordinances | |
| | (Legislative History) | |

Secondary:
-Treatises                    -Practitioner Aids
-Restatements                 -Law Reviews

*Table 3: Primary and Secondary Sources of Legal Research*

## 2.2 Effective Legal Research

The most effective way to begin almost any legal research project is by first consulting a secondary source. And this is true for both the novice and highly experienced legal researcher. Indeed, for an experienced researcher, some legal questions can be answered solely with a good secondary source – although, as we will learn later – there is always the caveat that all replied upon statutes or cases must be checked for their currency – that is, to determine if the are "still good law." The use of "citators," such as Shepard's, described later in this chapter (section 2.4), are needed to determine all-important currency.

### 2.2.1. Secondary Sources First

Effective United States legal research involves starting with a secondary authority. There are different types of secondary authorities, and any can serve as a launch point. All of these secondary authority research tools are footnote-rich and have numerous reference and connections to other research tools, both primary and secondary. Therefore, it matters little which secondary source one starts with, with just a few scope and coverage caveats as described below.

The important thing to remember is that a secondary source – treatise, legal encyclopedia, legal dictionary, loose-leaf set, law review article – will provide the spark which starts the research engine, in a process that looks like this:

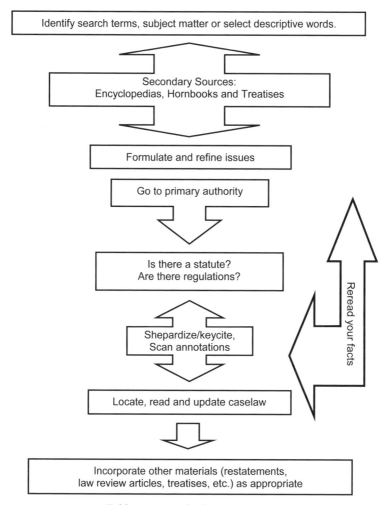

*Table 4: Research Flowchart for U.S.*

## 2.2.1.1. Treatises

The most successful legal research is often started by identifying a good legal treatise and getting background and context there. What is a legal *"treatise?"* They are monographs which are comprehensive guides to discrete areas of law, written by experts in the field. The American Bar Association has produced a very useful book[22] called "Association's List of Recommended Law Books for Libraries."[23] This list of a few hundred major treatises is divided by topic. If, for example, a law student or lawyer wanted to research an issue of copyright law, the list provides citations to three classic works on copyright,

> Nimmer on Copyright
> Copyright principles, law, and practice by Paul Goldstein,
> Latman's The copyright law by William F. Patry.

And any of these would be excellent starting points.

Treatises give an overview to the researcher new to the subject and then an in-depth analysis not found in other secondary sources, such as legal encyclopedias. One small caveat with treatises: The authors may have a certain point of view which needs to be considered.

However, as a starting point, treatises are nonpareil. They will always lead the researcher to the most important cases and statutes in the subject area (at least as of time of publication). These cases and statutes will then give the researcher "hooks" to pull in more law for analysis and synthesis. So in addition to offering background and explanation of the law, treatises are also case-finding and statute-finding tools, with an expert in the field identifying the relevant cases and statutes.

A treatise will cite many cases and discuss some of these cases in far greater detail than others. A case which gets, say, three pages of discussion in a treatise is going to be a much more useful research "hook" than a case which merely gets cited in a "string citation" (a group of cases standing for a

---

[22] The last published edition is the Second as of 1986. Recommended Law Books (2. Ed.) (Ed. James A. McDermott) (Illinois, Chicago: Committee on Business Law Libraries, Section of Corporation, Banking and Business Law, American Bar Association, 1986 – ISBN 978-0897072397).

[23] An (Stanford Library) updated version is available on the book's corresponding website to this book, <www.geocities.com/legalrm>.

similar proposition) or in a footnote. When a treatise gives greater depth of treatment to a particular case, then the researcher should consider that case as one of the most important ones and use that case for subsequent research.

---

**Research Tip #2.1**
Pay attention to the depth of treatment cases receive
in secondary sources.  Cases with greater treatment can be
the most useful research "hooks."

---

### 2.2.1.2. Looseleaf services

The three treatises listed above are all *"looseleaf services."* Looseleaf services are very common and very popular in United States law libraries.

A looseleaf service is a book that is published in big spiral binders, so that pages can be easily added or removed.

There are two categories of loose-leaf services:

- Newsletter type and
- Interfiled type.

The three treatises listed above are all of the interfiled variety.  This means that any pages can be removed as the law changes and new pages interfiled throughout the volumes.

The newsletter type of looseleaf service are frequently weekly, and each week a new issue is added to the binder, but no pages are ever removed.  An example of this type is the very popular BNA[24] United States Law Week.

Major looseleaf sets, such as CCH's[25] Federal Standard Tax Reporter are complete libraries in themselves, and attorneys practicing tax law, for example, can often find an answer to a client's question by consulting this set alone.

Looseleaf sets can be complicated and some of them use unusual numbering sequences. Almost all looseleaf sets have a section explaining how to use the set.  The researcher should carefully read these pages first.

Looseleaf sets are traditionally published in print but more and more of these sets are offered as online databases as well, with the advantage that they

---

[24] Bureau of National Affairs.
[25] Commerce Clearing House.

are kept current online and no one has to remove or add pages.

Looseleaf sets on various topics can be found by consulting Legal Loose-leafs in Print, by Arlene L. Eis and published by InfoSources Publishing Company. One can also search the websites or print catalogs from some of the major looseleaf publishers, such as Thomson West, BNA, LexisNexis, and Matthew Bender, among others.

### 2.2.1.3. Hornbooks

"*Hornbook*"[26] is a term used to describe one-volume treatises on specific subjects of law. They may or may not be published by the West Publishing Company (now a part of Thomson-West) as part of their Hornbook Series®.[27] Readings from popular hornbooks, such as Prosser on Torts, are often made assigned reading by American law school professors. Hornbooks are useful to read when researching a new area of law or when time is limited. Even if time is not limited, a hornbook remains an excellent research starting point.

### 2.2.1.4. Legal Encyclopedias

A legal encyclopedia looks like any other big multi-volume encyclopedia. It covers many topics – some in more depth than others – and it is well indexed. The difference between a legal encyclopedia and, say, Encyclopedia Brit-

---

[26] "The Hornbook. Dr. Johnson described the hornbook as "the first book of children, covered with horn to keep it unsoiled." Pardon's New General English Dictionary (1758) defined it as "A leaf of written paper pasted on a board, and covered with horn, for children to learn their letters by, and to prevent their being torn and daubed." It was used throughout Europe and America between the late 1400s and the middle 1700s. Shaped like an old-fashioned butter paddle, the first hornbooks were made of wood. The paper lesson the child was to learn was fastened to the wooden paddle and covered with a piece of horn. ...As the art of printing advanced, the hornbook was supplanted by the primer in the book form we know today. Subsequently, West Publishing Company developed its "Hornbook Series," a series of scholarly and well-respected one volume treatises on particular areas of law. Today they are widely used by law students, lawyers and judges." Prefatory page to Dan D. Dobbs, LAW OF REMEDIES: DAMAGES, EQUITY, RESTITUTION (2nd ed.) (West Group Hornbook Series®, 1993).

[27] A complete list of the West Hornbook series at: <www.thomson.com/content/legal/brand_overviews/wg_hornbook>.

tanica (other than the legal focus to the subject matter), is that legal encyclo-pedias are footnote-abundant. And this is a very common characteristic with all legal secondary sources - the text explains the law and the footnotes are rich with citations to statutes, cases and, sometimes, regulations. It is not unusual to see a page of a legal encyclopedia with just a few lines of text, those few lines of text citing dozens and dozens of primary authorities. Those footnotes contain a wealth of legal research leads and pointers to pri-mary sources.

In the United States the two most common legal encyclopedias with na-tional coverage are *American Jurisprudence*, 2d edition (AmJur) and *Corpus Juris Secundum* (CJS). One or both of these will be found in every American law library in print and both now being published by the West Publishing Company are available in Westlaw. AmJur is also available in West's com-petitor, LexisNexis, although that could very well change in the near future.

Both AmJur and CJS provide an analysis of both state and federal law. However, if a researcher is dealing with an issue purely of state law, then a state-specific encyclopedia – if there is one – could be a better tool to use. California is an especially important law-producing state and there are two legal encyclopedias for the state. First there is California Jurisprudence, pub-lished by Thomson West and then there is the unique treatise Witkin's Sum-mary of California Law, also now published by Thomson West. Witkin's Summary of California is highly regarded by judges in California and anyone researching issues of California law would be well advised to begin their research with Witkin's.

### 2.2.1.5. Law Review Articles

When American law students think about secondary sources, they are often first drawn to law review articles. Perhaps the reason for this is that law re-view articles are usually written by their law school professors.

Every law school in the United States produces law reviews.[28] At Stanford Law School there are several being published, including: Stanford Environ-mental Law Journal, Stanford Journal of Civil Rights and Civil Liberties, Stanford Journal of International Law, Stanford Journal of Law, Business &

---

[28] Differently in Europe, see Chapter 3, section 3.1.5.

Finance, Stanford Law & Policy Review, Stanford Technology Law Review, and the major one, the Stanford Law Review. Tomorrow a new one could easily be born.

Within a typical law review, content is divided into:

- articles
- comments
- notes

Comments and notes are usually written by law students and are shorter in length. The articles are usually written by law professors – although practitioners, judges and others also write law review articles – and are well-researched, rigorously cite-checked and can be excellent places to begin research. Some attorneys always begin their research with law review articles.

Unlike legal encyclopedias, which seek to cover all of Anglo-American jurisprudence, law review content is selective and there is not a lot of duplicate efforts (indeed, editors of law reviews seek unique content). So if there is an article related to your topic, you are off to a good start; if there is nothing, then you will have to turn your attention to a different secondary source.

When reading law review articles, keep in mind that the authors have a definite point of view as to what the law should be and make strong policy arguments to advance their point-of-view. Nonetheless, the footnotes can contain truly a wealth of valuable resources and reference librarians and other skilled researches "mine" these footnotes heavily.

Law professors have a habit of sometimes giving their law review articles very clever titles which do not obviously lead the researcher to the subject.[29] Therefore, using an index is especially important when trying to track down law review articles on a particular topic. The careful researcher will consult an index to law reviews (and other periodicals) rather than searching the full text content of these journals in the LexisNexis and Westlaw databases.

The major index which has been around the longest, and has the most historical coverage, is Wilson's Index to Legal Periodicals and Books (available in print and online in WilsonWeb[30]). It is a good index, but not completely

---

[29] For example, a law review article entitled "A Toxic Nightmare on Elm Street," is about a real estate broker's liability for misrepresentation.
[30] <www.wilsonweb.com>.

comprehensive; lesser works – articles less than 5 pages in length, for example – are not indexed.

For current research, we usually steer researchers to a more comprehensive index, one now produced by the Gale division of Thomson Publishing (although it started with the Information Access Corporation with a hard push from law librarians and the American Association of Law Libraries (AALL), notably by Professor J. Myron Jacobstein[31]). This index, unfortunately, goes by different names. In print it is called the Current Law Index. Online it can be called either LegalTrac or the Legal Resource Index. Whatever it is called, it is arguably the best tool for finding contemporary law review articles.

There is also the Index to Foreign Legal Periodicals, which is arranged much like the Index to Legal Periodicals, but surveys foreign (that is, non US, Canadian, English, Irish, Australian and New Zealand journals – all of which are included in both the Legal Resource Index (a/k/a LegalTrac, a/k/a Current Law Index) and Index to Legal Periodicals and Books.

### 2.2.1.6. HeinOnline

An extremely popular database in the United States is HeinOnline. This database contains, among other things, the full text of many, many law reviews – going all the way back to their beginnings, although some recent journal content has a "rolling wall" and is unavailable for a short period of time (one or two years, for instance). The law librarians at Stanford Law School like HeinOnline so much, this is how it is described on their online resources page:

---

[31] "As Association of American Law Libraries president in 1978-79, Mike [Jacobstein] was the right man at the right place at the right time. He personally pushed through AALL's support of a new index of legal periodicals, a move that eventually led to an agreement with Information Access Corporation and the creation of Current Law Index and its Read Only Memory-Computer Original Microform (COM) counterpart, Legal Resources Index, the forerunner of today's LegalTrac. Although this was a controversial move at the time, it was an important first step away from the binding hold of tradition. The days of ossified indexes and limited coverage of materials are hard to remember, but there is a reason for that." Robert C. Berring, Mike Jacobstein, *Truly a Giant*, 97 LAW LIBRARY JOURNAL 633 (2005). This product was a milestone in American legal research.

Need law journals from days of old,
HeinOnline will yield pure gold

Need the Federal Register from way, way back,
HeinOnline is the right line of attack

Need PDF versions of all things black and white,
HeinOnline is the place to go, day or night

Need older treatises, often covered in dust,
HeinOnline's legal classics are a dust-free must

Need US treaties, old and new,
HeinOnline has all the treaties for you

Need material on the Supreme Court,
HeinOnline's Supreme Court library won't let you fall short

Need the single best source of modern legal history,
HeinOnline will suit your needs perfectly!

To see just how much material is available on HeinOnline please see their Overview of Collections at: <www.heinonline.org/home/about/Overview.html>.

### 2.2.1.7. Legal Scholarship Network

While HeinOnline beautifully presents the past there is another resource for seeing the future: The Legal Scholarship Network of the Social Science Resource Center (<www.ssrn.com>)[32] is where many law professors post copies of their working paper drafts of articles that have been accepted for publication in forthcoming law journals. The website is an excellent place to see what is coming down the legal scholarship pike and to read the very latest legal thinking.  Like HeinOnline, this is a subscription service and requires the payment of an annual license subscription fee.

---

[32] SSRN - Social Science Research Network.

## 2.2.1.8. Blogs

While on the subject of law professor publishing, a new avenue for keeping up with current legal thinking is with blogs or, as law blogs are often called, *blawgs*. This area is growing so quickly that any list of blogs would be out of date as soon as it is published. But a good starting point is the Law Professors Blog at:

<www.lawprofessorblogs.com>.

One of the blogs there that American law librarians read upon a daily basis is the Law Library Blog at:

<http://lawprofessors.typepad.com/law_librarian_blog>.

New on the Blawg frontier is also the Legal Scholarship Blog:

<http://legalscholarshipblog.com>

This blog is a collaborative service from faculty and staff at the University of Pittsburgh School of Law and the Gallagher Law Library at the University of Washington School of Law. The blog features law-related calls for papers, conferences, and workshops - with links to relevant websites and papers as well as an event calendar - along with scholarly resources for Research Deans and current and prospective law professors.

Throughout this book we will call your attention to other particularly useful blogs as well.

## 2.2.1.9. American Law Reports (ALR)

American Law Reports (ALR) is a series, published by Thomson West, which can also be a highly useful starting point for research. American Law Reports does two things: It republishes selected decisions and it publishes "annotations" about those decisions or other legal developments. It is the annotations for which this set has value.

The American Law Reports annotations do not cover the gamut of legal subjects. Like law reviews, the coverage is selective. If, however, a topic you are researching is covered, then you are in tremendous luck. American Law Reports seeks to collect and analyze all of the relevant cases on that particular topic. Although called an "annotation" it is really much more like a detailed, comprehensive-in-scope law review article, but far more objective and without an scholar's particular point of view. ALR annotations offer "blackletter"[33] law principles and a collection of the cases – all of the cases – on a particular topic. ALR annotations are kept current with *"pocket parts"* (paper inserts in the back of each volume) supplementation, and there is even a toll-free phone number that researchers can call to get these very latest cases on the topic.

American Law Reports are published in print and are available electronically in LexisNexis and Westlaw and the annotations are automatically kept current there.

American Law Reports have a detailed index and a *"digest"*[34] for finding annotations. This "digest" now uses the West Key Number system taxonomy, which is discussed in detail below.

While most of the American Law Reports annotations deal with important cases, the set also addresses important statutory developments. For example, in 2007 President George W. Bush signed into law changes that Congress passed (at the president's urging) to the Foreign Intelligence Surveillance Act of 1978. Since this is so timely and so important, the editors at the American Law Reports wrote an annotation: "Validity, Construction and Application of Foreign Intelligence Surveillance Act of 1978 (50 U.S.C.A. sec. 1801 et seq.) Authorizing Electronic Surveillance of Foreign Powers and Their Agents."[35]

### 2.2.1.10. Restatements of the Law

Restatements of the Law, published by the American Law Institute, are officially "secondary sources" yet they are so highly-regarded and so frequently-cited that they come close to being "primary sources." They are not techni-

---

[33] "Blackletter" is a term "applied to legal principles that are fundamental and well settled." See GARNER *supra* note 18.

[34] A digest is an essential case-finding tool. It is a multivolume index to the law consisting of major topic headings, thousands of subheadings, and headnotes (short summaries of legal propositions stated in published court cases).

[35] 190 A.L.R. Fed. 385 (2007).

cally primary sources because they are not produced by law-makers, at least not writing in their official capacities. The authors of the restatements are panels of highly distinguished law professors, judges and practitioners.

Restatements of the Law are "blackletter" principles of law. The authors have made an effort to "restate" what they law is for the different areas studied. Restatements of the Law have been prepared for the following subjects:

- Agency
- Conflict of Laws
- Contracts
- Employment Law
- Foreign Relations Law of the United States
- Judgments
- The Law Governing Lawyers
- Property
- Restitution and Unjust Enrichment
- Security
- Suretyship and Guaranty
- Torts
- Trusts
- Unfair Competition

A complete catalog of American Law Institute publications can be found at:

<www.ali.org>

All topics with the exception of Restitution and Security have been published in a second or third edition. The restatements contain detailed Reporter's Notes citing statutory and case authority.

Restatements are not ideal as a research starting point but once applicable restatement sections are determined from other sources they can make the law easier to understand and provide numerous citations for continuing the research.

The restatements, even if a little difficult to begin research with, are extremely important and judges rely upon them heavily. According to a column in the National Law Journal,[36]

> "We are told that lawyers and judges have no time to read because of their heavy workload. But they have time to read and digest the Restatements of the Law and the lengthy comments that are appended to them as well as the voluminous Reporters' Notes. ... this past year alone there were more than 3,000 citations to Restatements."

Restatements tell you what the law is perhaps better than any other secondary source.

### 2.2.1.11. Legal Dictionaries

Last, but not least, are legal dictionaries. There are many different legal dictionaries, but the two main ones are Black's Law Dictionary (available in Westlaw) and Ballentine's Law Dictionary (available in LexisNexis). Above we gave the Black's definition for *stare decisis*. To show how dictionaries can be helpful in research, here is Ballentine's definition of negligence.[37]

> TERM: negligence.

> TEXT: 1. A word of broad significance which may not readily be defined with accuracy. *Jamison v Encarnacion*, 281 US 635, 74 L Ed 1082, 50 S Ct 440. The lack of due diligence or care. A wrong characterized by the absence of a positive intent to inflict injury but from which injury nevertheless results. *Haser v Maryland Casualty Co.* 78 ND 893, 53 NW2d 508, 33 ALR 1018. In the legal sense, a violation of the duty to use care. *Fort Smith Gas Co. v Cloud* (CA8 Ark) 75 F2d 413, 97 ALR 833. The failure to perform an established duty which proximately causes injury to the plaintiff. *Northern Indiana Transit v Burk*, 228 Ind 162, 89 NE2d 905, 17 ALR2d 572. The failure to exercise the degree of care demanded by the circumstances; the want of that care which the law prescribes under the particular circumstances existing at the time of the act or omission which is involved. The omission to do something which a reasonable man, guided by those considerations which ordinarily regulate human affairs, would do, or doing something which a prudent and

---

[36] Aaron D. Twerski, *Legal Scholarship: It should be relevant again*, THE NATIONAL LAW JOURNAL, September 3, 2007, p. 22.

[37] Copyright (c) 1969 Ballentine's Law Dictionary (LexisNexis Law Publishing, a division of Reed Elsevier, plc.).

reasonable man would not do. 38 Am J1st Negl § 2. More particularly, the failure of one owing a duty to another to do what a reasonable and prudent person would ordinarily have done under the circumstances, or doing what such person would not have done, which omission or commission is the proximate cause of injury to the other.

2. A negligent act is one from which an ordinarily prudent person would foresee such an appreciable risk of harm to others as to cause him not to do the act, or to do it in a more careful manner.

3. What constitutes "operation" or "negligence in operation" within statute making owner of motor vehicle liable for negligence in its operation.

AUTHORITY:

1. 38 Am J1st Negl § 2.

2. *Haralson v Jones Truck Lines*, 223 Ark 813, 270 SW2d 892, 48 ALR2d 248.

3. Anno: 13 ALR2d 378.

Note that this one dictionary definition provides references to a legal encyclopedia (American Jurisprudence), numerous "hook" cases, and an American Law Reports annotation. With these key references, the researcher can easily expand research about the tort of negligence.

Any of the above secondary sources will provide the researcher with citations to primary sources, including the United States Constitution, federal and or state statutes, administrative rules and decisions, and cases, often numerous cases.

Many treatises and looseleaf services are available online in LexisNexis, Westlaw or other computer-assisted legal research databases. Westlaw has a box at the upper-right hand side of the search welcome screen entitled "Secondary Sources" with links to Black's Law Dictionary, American Jurisprudence, American Law Reports, and much more. In LexisNexis, the "Research System" screen includes a section "Secondary Legal" which includes links to Matthew Bender publications, restatements, BNA publications, and much more. An advantage to using a secondary source online in LexisNexis or Westlaw is that most of the cited sources will have links to the full text of those sources.

## 2.2.2. The Constitution of the United States of America – the "supreme law of the land"

Before we move along to the next step in the legal research process – seeking statutes, we must say a word about the United States Constitution. Article VI of the United States Constitution presents its legal importance:

> "Article VI
>
> Section 1, Clause 2, Supreme law.
>
> This Constitution, and the Laws of the United States which shall be made in Pursuance thereof; and all Treaties made, or which shall be made, under the Authority of the United States, shall be the supreme Law of the Land; and the Judges in every State shall be bound thereby . . . "

The annotated text of the Constitution is found in the different compilations of the United States Code, discussed below. In addition, the United States Library of Congress has prepared a very useful massive volume The Constitution of the United States of America which includes text, commentary, historical analysis and summaries of important case law.

In addition to the many thousands of cases that have interpreted the United States Constitution, researchers also look to what the framers of the Constitution intended, "since its words so seldom resolve a legal issue. ... The Philadelphia Constitutional Convention in 1787 did not create an official record of its proceedings, but James Madison and other delegates kept extensive notes. Debates of state conventions, which ratified the Constitution, are also available. Finally, The Federalist, with essays by James Madison, John Jay, and Alexander Hamilton supporting the Constitution's adoption, is considered an essential source of contemporaneous opinion."[38]

Each state in the United States has its own constitution, and these are most easily found published in that state's annotated code.

---

[38] See David S. Clark and Tugrul Ansay, INTRODUCTION TO THE LAW OF THE UNITED STATES 39 (2nd ed.) (The Hague/New York: Kluwer, 2002) (Chapter 3: The Sources of Law) [hereinafter CLARK]. THE FEDERALISTS PAPERS (ed. By Isaac Kramnick) (Harmondsworth, Middlesex, England: Penguin, 1987).

### 2.2.3. Statutes

Effective legal research begins with a reading of secondary sources. When reading these secondary sources, the researcher should always be on the look-out for statutory references. Aside from the fact that statutes are controlling, they are also perfect research "hooks" for pulling in more information, including the always sought-after cases. The researcher in the United States can often pick and choose from case law. But if there is a statute on point, it is controlling and must be read and cited. It is also the "hook" on which all the relevant cases and additional secondary authority can easily be located. Legal research systems in the United States will annotate statutes with case citations, helping the researcher to find case law.

The researcher's threshold question when looking for primary sources is:
- Is there a statute?
- So what is a statute?
- How does it differ from a code?

It is critically important to understand the distinction between statutes and codes and the process of codification in the United States. It should be emphasized that the question "is there a statute" can often be answered by a secondary source, such as a treatise, complete with a full citation. Secondary sources really can save the careful researcher a lot of precious research time. But finding the key statutes is essential, as legislation, when it applies, is controlling. An applicable statute cannot be overlooked.

Before considering the statutes versus code question, a quick review of how a bill becomes law is in order – that is, how the legislative branch of government works.

The United States Congress is bicameral, consisting of two houses:
- The Senate, and
- The House of Representatives.

Proposed legislation is introduced as a 'bill." A bill can be introduced in either house of Congress. The bill is first assigned to a committee and hearings can be held. The committee votes on the bill and then the floor of the House or Senate, depending upon where the bill was introduced, also votes. If the bill passes the committee vote and then the floor vote, its name is changed to "act" (but it still is not yet law) and it is sent over to the other house where the process is repeated. If the act passes votes in committee and on the floor there, then it goes to the president for his (or, perhaps soon, her) signature. It is now a law.

Once the bill becomes law, it is assigned a law number, called Public Law number. This number consists of the number of the Congress, e.g., 110, followed by a number assigned to laws as they are created, one after another.

For example, Public Law 109-1, abbreviated P.L. 109-1, "To accelerate the income tax benefits for charitable cash contributions for the relief of victims of the Indian Ocean tsunami," was the first law passed by the 109th Congress. These public laws are also known as session laws, since a bill must be passed within one session of Congress. If a bill fails to become law in a particular session of Congress, it cannot be tided over to the next session. The whole process must begin anew.

These laws are first published as "slip laws" – literally on slips of paper (although one law can be hundreds of pages long) and then they are published, one after another, in a set of books called the Statutes at Large.

All of this activity, going as far back as the 93rd Congress as of this writing, is also documented online at a wonderfully rich and free government website called *Thomas* (named after Thomas Jefferson), available at <Thomas.loc.gov>. Anyone interested in lawmaking at the national level in the United States should explore this site very carefully.

Legislative law-making in the United States is an active, organic process. Laws are constantly being amended, or repealed. Therefore, for current research purposes, a book which contains a static representation of the law, such as the Statutes at Large, is of little value.

Statutory research is most effectively conducted in published codes. A code is best defined as a subject arrangement of public laws. But it is more than that too: In addition to arranging the laws by subject, the Law Revision Counsel's office in Congress organizes, edits slightly and adds numerous enhancements to facilitate research. From its website: "The Office of the Law Revision Counsel prepares and publishes the United States Code, which is a consolidation and codification by subject matter of the general and permanent laws of the United States." (<http://uscode.house.gov>).

The United States Code, as officially published by the government, can be accessed from the Government Printing Office (GPO) Access website. This is a perfect starting point for locating laws from any branch of government in the United States. GPO is the office charged with publishing law from Congress and regulations from the Executive Branch administrative agencies. The website can be accessed at <www.gpoaccess.gov>.

The government published official version of the United States Code has severe limitations, however. Its chief limitation is the slowness that it is published and revised. As mentioned above, laws are constantly being amended and attorneys in the United States need to know what the law looks like today. A question United States attorneys constantly ask about statutes (and cases) is: "Is it still good law?"

To answer that question best, research needs to be accomplished in one of the annotated codes that are commercially published. There are two main ones:

- United States Code Annotated, published by Thomson West, and
- United States Code Service, published by LexisNexis.

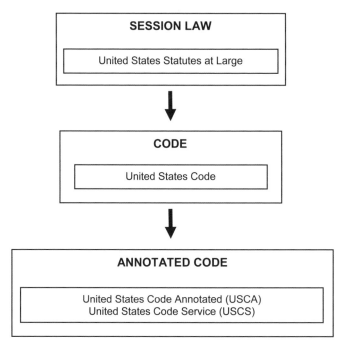

*Table 5: From Session Law to Code to Annotated Code*

Both of these annotated codes do the same thing: They publish the United States Code and keep it current, with monthly updates and cumulative "*pocket parts*" (paper inserts in the back of each volume). This is very important as an attorney's primary concern is always with currency. This is such an important consideration, that, in addition to consulting a current annotated code, attorneys will always "*Shepardize*" important code sections. Shepardizing is explained in detail below, but what it involves is using specialized research citator tools – such as Shepard's Citations or *KeyCite*® – for citation verification.

These commercial annotated editions of the United States Code are expensive but they are also essential research tools not just for their currency, but for the "annotations" that they contain. For any code section, if there are cases which have interpreted, construed, ruled on the Constitutionality, or even just cited in any way the code section, then the case is briefly described and given a full citation within an annotation which follows the code section. For some code sections there are hundreds, even thousands, of case annotations. The annotations present the cases in an organized arrangement by topic and each case is given a short summary of its legal holding.

The annotated codes are extremely useful for these annotations, as attorneys and law students can quickly scan these case annotations to locate cases for further research. Each annotation will include a case citation with which the case can be retrieved, either from a book or from an online database such as LexisNexis or Westlaw.

So how does a researcher find a code section in one of these codes? An excellent starting point – for this and most research – is with the index volumes. Carefully produced indexes are found in both USCS and USCA.

It also helps if you know which title of the United States Code is applicable to your research. The United States Code is divided into 50 titles, with the following subject classifications:[39]

| Title Number | Title name |
|---|---|
| TITLE 1 | General provisions |
| TITLE 2 | The congress |
| TITLE 3 | The president |
| TITLE 4 | Flag and seal, seat of government, and the states |
| TITLE 5 | Government organization and employees |
| TITLE 5A | Government organization and employees (appendix) |
| TITLE 6 | Surety bonds [repealed] |
| TITLE 7 | Agriculture |
| TITLE 8 | Aliens and nationality |
| TITLE 9 | Arbitration |
| TITLE 10 | Armed forces |
| TITLE 10A | Armed forces (appendix) |
| TITLE 11 | Bankruptcy |
| TITLE 11A | Bankruptcy (appendix) |
| TITLE 12 | Banks and banking |
| TITLE 13 | Census |
| TITLE 14 | Coast guard |
| TITLE 15 | Commerce and trade |
| TITLE 16 | Conservation |

---

[39] Source: GPO Access, <www.gpoaccess.gov>.

| TITLE 17 | Copyrights |
|---|---|
| TITLE 18 | Crimes and criminal procedure |
| TITLE 18A | Crimes and criminal procedure (appendix) |
| TITLE 19 | Customs duties |
| TITLE 20 | Education |
| TITLE 21 | Food and drugs |
| TITLE 22 | Foreign relations and intercourse |
| TITLE 23 | Highways |
| TITLE 24 | Hospitals and asylums |
| TITLE 25 | Indians |
| TITLE 26 | Internal revenue code |
| TITLE 26A | Internal revenue code (appendix) |
| TITLE 27 | Intoxicating liquors |
| TITLE 28 | Judiciary and judicial procedure |
| TITLE 28A | Judiciary and judicial procedure (appendix) |
| TITLE 29 | Labor |
| TITLE 30 | Mineral lands and mining |
| TITLE 31 | Money and finance |
| TITLE 32 | National guard |
| TITLE 33 | Navigation and navigable waters |
| TITLE 34 | Navy [repealed] |
| TITLE 35 | Patents |
| TITLE 36 | Patriotic and national observances, ceremonies, and organizations |
| TITLE 37 | Pay and allowances of the uniformed services |
| TITLE 38 | Veterans' benefits |
| TITLE 38A | Veterans' benefits (appendix) |
| TITLE 39 | Postal service |
| TITLE 40 | Public buildings, property, and works |
| TITLE 40A | Public buildings, property, and works (appendix) |
| TITLE 41 | Public contracts |
| TITLE 42 | The public health and welfare |
| TITLE 43 | Public lands |
| TITLE 44 | Public printing and documents |
| TITLE 45 | Railroads |
| TITLE 46 | Shipping |
| TITLE 46A | Shipping (appendix) |
| TITLE 47 | Telegraphs, telephones, and radiotelegraphs |
| TITLE 48 | Territories and insular possessions |
| TITLE 49 | Transportation |
| TITLE 50 | War and national defense |
| TITLE 50A | War and national defense (appendix) |

*Table 6: United States Code, 2000 Edition*

If a lawyer or law student was researching, say, railroads, he or she would find all of the laws on railroads codified in title 45 of the United States Code. This information can be helpful for, in addition to the excellent multi-volume main index to the set, each title of the United States Code also has its own separate index, which is more detailed than the general index. Armed with the knowledge that title 45 contains all of the federal railroad statutes, the

researcher could then use the index to title 45 for more precise index searching.

---

**Research Tip #2.2**
If you know the United States Code title for your research area,
use the index that accompanies that title, rather than the
general index.

---

All of the code editions include useful tables for research, with the two most
useful tables being these:

Acts Cited by Popular Name (e.g., "Patriot Act")

The researcher will frequently be asked to retrieve a statute by its so-
called popular name, such as The Patriot Act. But the actual name of this
legislation is the Uniting and Strengthening America by Providing Appropriate Tools Required to Intercept and Obstruct Terrorism Act of 2001. The
Acts Cited by Popular Name table will steer the researcher to the correct
name of the statute and also give its citation, where the researcher can find it
in the United States Code.

In addition to the Popular Name Table found in any addition of the United
States Code there is another very useful publication called Shepard's Acts
and Cases by Popular Names. This set, published by LexisNexis, provides
citations to both federal and state legislation, indexed under popular names.
It also lists many cases which have come to be known by a popular name,
such as "Miranda."

Statutes at Large table, showing where the Acts of Congress are found in the
Code.

Secondary sources will often cite to a Public Law as published in the Statutes at Large, particularly when citing to new legislation, and the researcher
will need to convert that citation to a United States Code cite in order to perform effective and current research and find the text of the statute as codified.
The Statutes at Large Table will enable the researcher to pin point exactly
where the statutory provides became codified. One statute could have its
sections codified in a number of different titles of the United States Code, so
this is a very useful locating tool. The United States Congress has made a
copy of this table available online at:

<http://uscode.house.gov/classification/table3.pdf>

In addition to titles and code sections, the United States Code organizes its content into "chapters." It is always very important for the careful researcher to review all of the code sections found with a particular chapter of the title he or she is researchers.

Readers may be familiar with the phrase "Chapter 11 bankruptcy." This is a particular type of bankruptcy proceeding available to debtors in the United States. It is called a "Chapter 11" bankruptcy because all of the legal requirements for a particular type of financial reorganization are grouped together in Chapter 11 of the title of the Untied States Code dealing with bankruptcy, (which also happens to be Title 11). When researchers cite to United States Code sections, however, they do not cite to the chapter numbers, only title and section. But researchers should not limit their statute analysis to code sections in isolation – the entire chapter in which the cited code section is found could also be applicable to the research.

### 2.2.3.1. Legal citation

And now a word here about legal citation. American lawyers and judges are obsessed with correct legal citation. It begins in law school where many American law students struggle with (and learn to despise) different citation manuals.

Used at Stanford Law School, and widely used elsewhere, is *The Bluebook*: A Uniform System of Citation, 18th edition.[40] This is commonly called just "the bluebook" and checking citations for style is called "*bluebooking.*" There are few tasks dreaded by law students more than "bluebooking."

There are other citation manuals, such as ALWD Citation Manual: A Professional System of Citation, 2d Edition, written by the Association of Legal Writing Directors (ALWD) and published by Aspen Publishers.

For a United States Code section, the citation is fairly straightforward and the Bluebook gives these examples:

> Citation of an entire statute, the Comprehensive Environmental Response, Compensation, and Liability Act, as codified in the United States Code:

---

[40] The Bluebook is compiled by the editors of the Columbia Law Review, the Harvard Law Review, the University of Pennsylvania Law Review, and the Yale Law Journal.

> Comprehensive Environmental Response, Compensation, and Liability Act, 42 U.S.C. §§ 9601-9675 (2000).

First is given the official name of the act. 42 is the United States Code title number. §[41] is a symbol meaning "section sign" and when paired, §§, it becomes plural, for sections. 9601-9675 is the span of code sections that contain the full statute. And 2000 is the date of the code.

The citation for an individual provision of the United States Code is set forth thusly:

> 28 U.S.C. § 1291 (2000).

It should be noted that the Bluebook requires citation to the official United States Code. This is a bit of a fiction in the United States. Lawyers and law students do not really use the official United States Code – it is published far too slowly for current legal research. Instead, lawyers and law students use one of the two commercial code publications, United States Code Annotated or United States Code Service. These sets, in addition to presenting their voluminous case citations, keep the code current. There are *"pocket parts"* (paper inserts in the back of each volume) and these "pocket parts" are supplemented by monthly updates. So lawyers use the unofficial but cite to the official. Everyone does it, at least when they are adhering to Bluebook rules.

But as the Bluebook itself notes, "[m]any state and federal courts promulgate local citation rules, which take precedence over Bluebook rules in documents submitted to those courts. ... When preparing court documents, always check the most recent version of the court's local citation rules."[42]

## 2.2.3.2. State legislation

The state law legislative process is very similar to the federal law-making process. In California, for example, the process looks like this:

---

[41] This symbol is used differently in Europe, see chapter 3.

[42] THE BLUEBOOK: A UNIFORM SYSTEM OF CITATION Preface, p. V (18th ed.) (Cambridge,, Massachusetts: Harvard Law Review Assn., 2005).

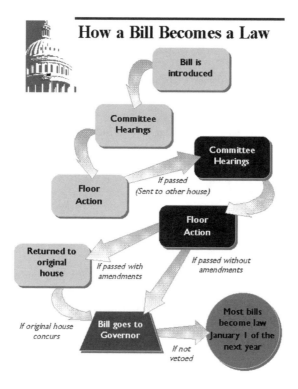

*Table 7: How a Bill Becomes Law in California*

The two houses of the bicameral state legislature are:
- the California Senate and
- the California Assembly.

The states publish the passed laws chronologically as "session laws" in a volume called Statutes and Amendments to the Codes and these session laws are later codified and published in annotated codes (also called compiled codes or revised codes).

Again, successful research is done with the codes and not with the earlier session laws and the best entry point is usually the code index. Each state code will also include tables that refer researchers from the session law citation to the code citation.

Unlike the United States Code, which is one single code divided into fifty titles, in California there are 28 separate and distinct codes that all have their own names and these names are an important part of the citation. For example, California Business and Professions Code, § 6060 sets forth the requirements for being a lawyer in California.

West's Ann.Cal.Bus. & Prof.Code § 6060

West's Annotated California Codes
Business and Professions Code
Division 3. Professions and Vocations Generally
Chapter 4. Attorneys
Article 4. Admission to the Practice of Law
§ 6060. Qualifications; examination

To be certified to the Supreme Court for admission and a license to practice law, a person who has not been admitted to practice law in a sister state, United States jurisdiction, possession, territory, or dependency or in a foreign country shall:

(a) Be of the age of at least 18 years.

(b) Be of good moral character.

(c) Before beginning the study of law, have done either of the following:

(1) Completed at least two years of college work, which college work shall be not less than one-half of the collegiate work acceptable for a bachelor's degree granted upon the basis of a four-year period of study by a college or university approved by the examining committee.

(2) Have attained in apparent intellectual ability the equivalent of at least two years of college work by taking any examinations in subject matters and achieving the scores thereon as are prescribed by the examining committee.

(d) Have registered with the examining committee as a law student within 90 days after beginning the study of law. The examining committee, upon good cause being shown, may permit a later registration.

(e) Have done any of the following:

(1) Had conferred upon him or her a juris doctor (J.D.) degree or a bachelor of laws (LL.B.) degree by a law school accredited by the examining committee or approved by the American Bar Association.

(2) Studied law diligently and in good faith for at least four years in any of the following manners:

(A) In a law school that is authorized or approved to confer professional degrees and requires classroom attendance of its students for a minimum of 270 hours a year.

A person who has received his or her legal education in a foreign state or country wherein the Common Law of England does not constitute the basis of jurisprudence shall demonstrate to the satisfaction of the examining committee that his or her education, experience, and qualifications qualify him or her to take the examination.

(B) In a law office in this state and under the personal supervision of a member of the State Bar of California who is, and for at least the last five years continuously has been, engaged in the active practice of law. It is the duty of the supervising attorney to render any periodic reports to the examining committee as the committee may require.

(C) In the chambers and under the personal supervision of a judge of a court of record of this state. It is the duty of the supervising judge to render any periodic reports to the examining committee as the committee may require.

(D) By instruction in law from a correspondence law school authorized or approved to confer professional degrees by this state, which requires 864 hours of preparation and study per year for four years.

(E) By any combination of the methods referred to in this paragraph (2) .

(f) Have passed any examination in professional responsibility or legal ethics as the examining committee may prescribe.

(g) Have passed the general bar examination given by the examining committee.

(h)(1) Have passed a law students' examination administered by the examining committee after completion of his or her first year of law study. Those who pass the examination within its first three administrations upon becoming eligible to take the examination shall receive credit for all law studies completed to the time the examination is passed. Those who do not pass the examination within its first three administrations upon becoming eligible to take the examination, but who subsequently pass the examination, shall receive credit for one year of legal study only.

(2) This requirement does not apply to a student who has satisfactorily completed his or her first year of law study at a law school accredited by the examining committee and who has completed at least two years of college work prior to matriculating in the accredited law school, nor shall this requirement apply to an applicant who has passed the bar examination of a sister state or of a country in which the Common Law of England constitutes the basis of jurisprudence.

The law students' examination shall be administered twice a year at reasonable intervals.

CREDIT(S)

(Added by Stats.1939, c. 34, p. 353, § 1. Amended by Stats.1953, c. 1090, p. 2578, § 1; Stats.1959, c. 1084, p. 3148, § 1; Stats.1970, c. 251, p. 513, § 1; Stats.1971, c. 1748, p. 3740, § 14; Stats.1972, c. 1285, p. 2559, § 4.3; Stats.1973, c. 1052, § 1; Stats.1974, c. 316, p. 631, § 1, eff. May 31, 1974; Stats.1987, c. 239, § 1.) ; Stats.1990, c. 707 (A.B.3946), § 1; Stats.1996, c. 168 (S.B.1950), § 1; Stats.1996, c. 866 (S.B.1321), § 3; Stats.2001, c. 46 (S.B.817), § 1; Stats.2002, c. 664 (A.B.3034), § 12.)

Note how following the code section is a section called "Credit(s)." All codes – state and federal – follow this practice of presenting the legislative history in citation form immediately following each code section. With this information the researcher can determine when the legislation was first created and obtain citations to all subsequent amendments.

The codes of California are found in two publications: West's Annotated California Codes and Deering's California Codes Annotated.

The codes are also found in all of the various computer-assisted legal research databases, including the two giants in the market, LexisNexis and Westlaw.

And, of course, more and more legislative information is being made available on the Web by the states. In California, bills, bill status information, codes and more are available at http://www.leginfo.ca.gov/

LexisNexis and Westlaw are heavily used by United States attorneys and these services offer many "bells and whistles" for researching statutory law not available on official (and free) websites. LexisNexis and Westlaw have current and past editions of state and federal codes.

Searching LexisNexis and Westlaw databases can be done in a number of ways. Documents, especially code sections, can easily be called up by citation, using a very powerful FIND feature.

Documents can also be located using one of two search strategies for searching full text material:

- Combining Terms and Connectors or using
- Natural Language.

Due to the brevity of many code sections and also the non-intuitive language used by legislators, full text searching for code sections can be frustrating and non productive.

Most American law students start their LexisNexis and Westlaw searching using Natural Language. They drill down to a search window, select "Natural Language" and then type in whatever comes to mind. With Natural Language, there is always a search result, as the computer will run its sophisticated algorithms and provide the best matched documents. Natural Language searching is least effective with statutory searches (and most effective with case searches).

More precise searching can be done using Terms & Connectors (more on this with case law, below).

Each document is divided into parts – LexisNexis calls these parts "segments" and Westlaw calls them "fields." Search precision can be gained by applying Terms & Connectors searching to just segments or fields.

Both LexisNexis and Westlaw offer many special features for doing statutory research online. For example, LexisNexis offers this succinct summary of its various statutory searching capabilities:

> Researching statutes can be challenging. LexisNexis provides several tools to make the process quick and easy. Below are some of the more common statutory research tasks and how to perform them on LexisNexis.

Get a Statute by Citation
- Sign-on with your ID & Password at <www.LexisNexis.com/lawschool>.
- Click the Research System tab at the top of the page.
- Click the Get a Document tab at the top of the page.
- Type 18 U.S.C. 3109 in the Get by Citation form and click the red Get button.

Use the blue Citation Formats link when you are unsure of the proper format to retrieve a citation.

Get a Statute by Popular Name
- Click the Search tab at the top of the page.
- Click Federal Legal – U.S. > United States Code Service (USCS) Materials > USCS Popular Names Table.
- Type Cyber Security Enhancement Act of 2002 as a terms & connectors search.
- Bullet Table of Contents and click the red Search button.

Retrieve the Public Law, P.L. 107-296, to see the Act as enacted and where it is codified within the United States Code.

Search Statutes through Table of Contents Headings
- Click the Search tab at the top of the page.
- Click States Legal – U.S. > Ohio > Statutes & Regulations > OH – Page's Ohio Revised Code Annotated.
- Type Burglary as a terms & connectors search.
- Bullet Table of Contents and click the red Search button

If you want to search a specific title of a code then scroll down and check the box next to the desired title before clicking the search button.

Use the Practitioner's Toolbox
- Retrieve 18 U.S.C. 3109 through the Get a Document tab.
- The Practitioner's Toolbox is located to the right of the statute's heading.
1. History – provides a link to the statute's direct history.
2. Interpretive Notes & Decisions – provides a link to a topical Table of Contents for the cases citing the statute (also called annotations).
3. History; Ancillary Laws and Directives – provides a link to the statute's indirect history.
4. Related Statutes & Rules – provides links to related statutes & rules.
5. Research Guide – provides links to related secondary sources.
Use the Practitioner's Toolbox to quickly and easy locate related cases, statutes & secondary sources.

Find Statutory Interpretation through Annotations
- Retrieve 18 U.S.C. 3109 through the Get a Document tab.
- Click Interpretive Notes & Decisions in the Practitioner's Toolbox.
- Click the green down arrow for Warrantless Searches.
You can also use the FOCUS Terms bar at the top to search through the Annotations for a specific issue.

Browse through Statutes
- Retrieve Cal Bus & Prof Code 23007 through the Get a Document tab.
- Click the Bluebook Browse link at the top middle of the page.
- Click the Next Arrow to view the next section of the California code.
- Click the Previous Arrow to view the preceding section of the California code.
Through Book Browse you can browse through an entire code if necessary.

Shepardizing Statutes
- Click the Shepard's tab at the top of the page.
- Type 18 U.S.C. 2234 in the Enter Citation to be Checked form and click the red Check button.
- Select the link for Exact Match from the report list.
If you need the Citing References for a specific subsection select the appropriate report from the report list. If no report exists for your subsection then there are no references.

Printing Statutes Only
- Retrieve 42 U.S.C. 2000e through the Get a Document tab.
- Click the blue Print link at the top right of the statute.

- Click Custom in the drop-down menu under Document View.
- Click the Clear All button and select the Text segment.
- Click the OK button then the red Print button.

Using the Text segment reduces the number of pages printed from over 200 to 3 by printing only the text of the statute without editorial enhancements.

*Table 8: Researching Statutes on LexisNexis[43]*

Despite all of the electronic features offered by LexisNexis (described above) and Westlaw (which offers similar functions), using a code in print still offers the researcher, particularly a researcher new to United States law, some distinct advantages. The major advantage is the ease in seeing the statutory language in context – the reader can simply flip pages back and forth to read the other code sections within the same chapter and quickly grasp the organization of the laws. While this process can also be done online in LexisNexis or Westlaw, it requires some skill, and since these databases are very expensive, it can also be cost-effective for the lawyer in the United States to simply pick up a volume of the code.

## 2.2.3.3. Legislative Histories

In addition to a careful reading of the statute (as found in its code section(s)), and perusing the various subsequent cases that have construed or interpreted the statute, researchers in the United States also on occasion try to glean "legislative intent" by looking backward and reading the legislative history of a statute. As noted below, legislation can be ambiguous, even intentionally so; the documents in the legislative history are often used to try and understand a more precise meaning of the statute.

There is a long-running debate on the use of legislative histories in the United States. Some judges use them; others will not.[44]

---

[43] Source: LexisNexis Total Practice Solutions.

[44] See Charles Rothfeld, *Read Congress's Words, Not its Mind, Judges Say*" NEW YORK TIMES, April 14, 1989, p. B5 and James J. Brudney, *Liberal Justices' Reliance on Legislative History: Principle, Strategy, and the Scalia Effect*, OHIO STATE PUBLIC LAW WORKING PAPER NO. 95, Center for Interdisciplinary Law and Policy Studies Working Paper Series No. 64. Professor Brudney's article "conducts an in-depth examination

As a bill winds its way through Congress, a paper trail is created. And this paper trail can help shed light on the meaning and interpretation of the statutory language. As part of the legislative compromise, often statutory language ends up being vague, and cases and legislative history documents are used to try and make the precise meaning of the statute more clear.

To compile a legislative history is to gather all of the following documents:

- The bills (as introduced and as amended)
- Committee reports
- House or Senate Documents
- Debates text
- Hearings transcripts (sometimes)

Of all of these documents, the committee reports are considered the most important part of the legislative history.

Each bill is assigned to a committee, where it either "dies" or advances. If the committee recommends passage, a committee report is usually issued.

From committee, the bill goes to the full body (House or Senate) where the bill may be debated. Debates are published in the Congressional Record. If the bill passes the first body it is then introduced in the other; at this point it becomes an "act." The act is assigned to committee and the process is repeated. At this point there are generally two reports: A House Report and a Senate Report.

In the House and Senate versions of the legislation are at variance, the law will be heard by a conference committee, composed of both senators and representatives. Here the committee will try and hammer out an agreed upon final version of the legislation. This conference committee will issue a report, usually called a House Report (even though the committee consists of both House and Senate members). A very useful print source for the text of these reports can be United States Code Congressional and Administrative News (USCCAN), published by Thomson West, which will publish at least

---

of Supreme Court Justices' reliance on legislative history during the Burger, Rehnquist, and early Roberts eras."

important excerpts from at least one committee report for each public law. It can be an excellent starting point and, with a limited research budget, it may be all that is needed to answer a statutory question.

The president may publish a message when signing the bill into law. These signing statements are published. If the law started as a House bill, this message is published as a House document; if originally a Senate bill, the message is published as a Senate Document.

The issuance of signing statements has created recent controversy in the United States.[45] The United States General Accountability Office, the government's oversight agency, did a study of presidential signing statements and drew this conclusion:[46]

"Federal courts infrequently cite or refer to presidential signing statements in their published opinions, and these signing statements appear to have little impact on judicial decision-making. When they do cite signing statements, it is for a variety of reasons. The most common use of a signing statement is to supplement discussion of legislative history such as committee reports. ... The federal courts have only in rare instances treated presidential signing statements as an authoritative source of statutory or constitutional interpretation."

All of the above documents, for more recent legislation at least, are available online in *Thomas* (<Thomas.loc.gov>). Earlier documents are found in a variety of locations depending upon the date of the legislation. Where to look for certain documents depends upon the date of the legislation. And since compiling a legislative history can be a very time-consuming process, it is always a good first step to see if someone has already done the work. Various publications, such as Sources of Compiled Legislative Histories, will identify where compilations may already exist. The following chart is a good guide to anyone attempting to compile a legislative history:

---

[45] See Dahlia Lithwick, *Sign Here – Presidential Signing Statements Are More Than Just Executive Branch lunacy*, SLATE, posted Jan. 30, 2006.

[46] United States Government Accountability Office, Presidential Signing Statements Accompanying the Fiscal Year 2006 Appropriations Acts, June 18, 2007.

Has someone already compiled a legislative history?

*Nancy Johnson's Sources of Compiled Legislative Histories
*USCCAN might be enough
*Committee Print
*Try the library catalog

## GET BASIC INFORMATION ABOUT THE LAW:

U.S. Code, U.S.C.A., U.S.C.S.:
**Use to find the Public Law
Number & Date of Enactment**
*Popular Name Tables*

≤1956: Chapter Number
≥1957: Public Law
Number

To find
the Bill #
use the
*Statutes
at Large*

When was the Statute enacted?

**Pre 1941**:
*LexisNexis Congressional Indexes* (from 1789 to 1969)

and

*Congressional Record* and *Congressional Globe* "History of Bills and Resolutions"

**1941 to 1969**:
*USCCAN* to locate excerpts from reports, hearings and dates of consideration in the Cong. Record

*LexisNexis Congressional Indexes* (from 1789 to 1969)

**After 1963**:
Use the *Statutes at Large* "Guide to Legislative History of Bills Enacted in Public Law" (1963-1974)

**After 1969**:
Use the *CIS Index* to locate citations to House/Senate hearings, reports and the Congressional Record

**1969-1974**:
Use the *Statutes at Large* "Guide to Legislative History of Bills Enacted in Public Law" (1963-1974)

**After 1972**:
Westlaw's Statutes-Plus contains HR/Senate Reports

**After 1984**:
CIS has annual legislative history volumes

THOMAS (Thomas.loc.gov) continues to grow

*Table 9: How to Compile a Federal Legislative History*

Compiled legislative histories usually omit hearing transcripts. This is because hearing transcripts are not considered part of the legislative history. The reason for this is that the hearings are the publication of the comments made by people who have been invited to Washington to provide testimony to Congress, in an effort to educate the law-makers. In other words, these are not the words of the law-makers themselves, but the words of various experts; as such this testimony cannot be used to determine legislative intent. Nonetheless, hearings can contain extremely useful information and should not be overlooked when doing exhaustive research on a topic.

---

**Research Tip #2.3**
Want a quick understanding of what a statute is all about?
Use USCCAN![47]
Find the statute in USCCAN and locate the report(s)
printed or excerpted there. Often this "thumbnail" sketch helps a lot and it is quick and easy.

---

## 2.2.4. Regulations and administrative law decisions.

If the researcher's first question is: Is there a statute? His or her very next question should be: Are there regulations?

Regulations are laws issued by administrative agencies, which are part of the United States Executive Branch of government. Agencies issue regula-

---

[47] USCCAN - United States Code Congressional and Administrative News - is a West Group publication that collects selected Congressional and administrative mate-rials for publication in a single resource. USCCAN is published in monthly pamphlets that contain a cumulative subject index and cumulative Table of Laws Enacted in addition to the selected documents. Among other documents, USCCAN. publishes the full text of new federal laws, selected committee reports from the House and Senate, signing statements, presidential proclamations, executive orders, reorganization plans, President's messages, Federal Regulations, proposed constitutional amendments, Federal court rules, and sentencing guide-lines all arranged in chronological order. When published in bound volumes, the legislative history documents are placed in separate volumes apart from the rest of the materials published by USCCAN.

tions pursuant to Congressional authority. For every agency regulation there is a source statute. It is important to remember that administrative rule-making is delegated authority, delegated to the Executive Branch.

Administrative agencies can write highly detailed regulations on subjects which far exceed the competence of Congress. For example, in 1973 Congress passed the Endangered Species Act, with the laudable intent of preserving endangered species in the United States.

On September 11, 2007, the Fish and Wildlife Service, an administrative agency, charged with authority pursuant to the Endangered Species Act, issued a ruling on the copepod Acanthocyclops columbiensis's status as an endangered species.[48] Congress just does not possess the expertise to make such fine rulings on different amphipods.

The reach and effect of administrative rules should not be underestimated and, indeed, regulations may adversely affect clients more than any other source of law.

We were putting the finishing touches on this book during the waning months of the administration of President George W. Bush, and as a New York Times[49] article pointed out, "With Congress in Democratic hands and his political capital all but spent by the Iraq war, Mr. Bush has scant hope of pushing significant domestic legislation through Congress. But he still controls the executive branch and can accomplish much through regulation and executive edict."

Indeed, as the authors of this book were making our final edits, "President Bush and his cabinet and staff [were] busily writing far-reaching rules to keep his priorities on the environment, public lands, homeland security, [and] health in safety in place ..."

Of course, the next president might very well undo all of this last-minute law making, as "[o]ne of Mr. Bush's first official acts as president was to

---

[48] 72 Fed. Reg. 51766.

[49] John M. Broder, *A Legacy Bush Can Control*, THE NEW YORK TIMES, Week in Review, Sunday, September 9, 2007, p. 1. The history of regulation in the United States is truly fascinating and one of the best expositions on this history is found in the CONGRESSIONAL QUARTERLY'S FEDERAL REGULATORY DIRECTORY (Washington D.C.: Congressional Quarterly Inc., 1979/80). The first chapter, "Federal Regulation: An Introduction," gives a readable and interesting history of regulation in the United States.

withdraw the Clinton regulations that had not yet been published in the Federal Register and delay the effective date of those that had."

Ostensibly, the reason why agencies issue regulations is that these deal with areas of law that are far too detailed and technical for Congress to address. Agencies have the subject expertise to flesh out the legal requirements for the broad areas that Congress wants regulated, the minutiae of particulate matter concentrations, for example.

Agency activities are well-documented in a very important publication called the Federal Register. The Federal Register serves two chief functions:

- It provides announcements of proposed regulations, including contact information where public comments can be made and
- It publishes the final regulation. This is the first place of publication.

The Federal Register is a very important tool and many lawyers in the United States routinely read it looking for proposed regulations in areas that could affect their clients.

When a proposed regulation is first published in the Federal Register a government official's name and contact information are always provided. This contact person, for a period of time anyway, knows more about the proposed regulation than probably any other individual on the planet. Researchers needing more information would be wise to try and contact this official.

The United States Government Printing Office (GPO) does an excellent job of publishing the Federal Register online and it even enables anyone to sign up for automated delivery and updates. It is listed on the GPO Access page under Executive Resources at: http://<www.gpoaccess.gov/index.html>. Anyone interested in researching United States law should peruse this website with great care.

The Federal Register, much like the Statutes at Large, publishes laws one after another, with no subject arrangement. This makes it a good tool for current awareness, but not a good tool for subject matter research.

Like the statutes from Congress, the regulations from Executive Branch agencies are also codified – that is, placed in a subject arrangements. The code for federal regulations is called the Code of Federal Regulations, abbreviated as CFR.

Just like the United States Code, the Code of Federal Regulations is divided into 50 titles. Some, but not all, of the subjects of these titles overlap with the subjects of the United States Code titles. Here is a chart which compares the two codes:

|  | USC | CFR |
|---|---|---|
| Title 1 | General provisions | General provisions |
| Title 2 | The Congress | [reserved] |

| Title 3 | The President | The President |
|---|---|---|
| Title 4 | Flag and seal, seat of government, and the states | Accounts |
| Title 5 | Government organization and employees | Administrative personnel |
| Title 6 | Domestic security | Homeland security |
| Title 7 | Agriculture | Agriculture |
| Title 8 | Aliens and nationality | Aliens and nationality |
| Title 9 | Arbitration | Animals and animal production |
| Title 10 | Armed forces | Energy |
| Title 11 | Bankruptcy | Federal elections |
| Title 12 | Banks and banking | Banks and banking |
| Title 13 | Census | Business credit and assistance |
| Title 14 | Coast guard | Aeronautics and space |
| Title 15 | Commence and trade | Commerce and foreign trade |
| Title 16 | Conservation | Commercial practices |
| Title 17 | Copyrights | Commodity and securities exchanges |
| Title 18 | Crimes and criminal procedure | Conservation of power and water resources |
| Title 19 | Customs duties | Customs duties |
| Title 20 | Education | Employees' benefits |
| Title 21 | Food and drugs | Food and drugs |
| Title 22 | Foreign relations and intercourse | Foreign relations |
| Title 23 | Highways | Highways |
| Title 24 | Hospitals and asylums | Housing and urban development |
| Title 25 | Indians | Indians |
| Title 26 | Internal revenue code | Internal revenue |
| Title 27 | Intoxicating liquors | Alcohol, tobacco products and firearms |
| Title 28 | Judiciary and judicial procedure | Judicial administration |
| Title 29 | Labor | Labor |
| Title 30 | Mineral lands and mining | Mineral resources |
| Title 31 | Money and finance | Money and finance: Treasury |
| Title 32 | National guard | National defense |
| Title 33 | Navigation and navigable waters | Navigation and navigable waters |
| Title 34 | Navy [repealed] | Education |
| Title 35 | Patents | Panama canal |
| Title 36 | Patriotic and national observances, ceremonies, and organizations | Parks, forests, and public property |
| Title 37 | Pay and allowances of the uniform services | Patents, trademarks, and copyright |
| Title 38 | Veterans' benefits | Pensions, bonuses and veterans' relief |
| Title 39 | Postal service | Postal service |
| Title 40 | Public buildings, property, and works | Protection of environment |
| Title 41 | Public contracts | Public contracts and property management |
| Title 42 | The public health and welfare | Public health |

| Title 43 | Public lands | Public lands: Interior |
|----------|--------------|------------------------|
| Title 44 | Public printing and documents | Emergency management and assistance |
| Title 45 | Railroads | Public welfare |
| Title 46 | Shipping | Shipping |
| Title 47 | Telegraphs, telephones, and radiotelegraphs | Telecommunication |
| Title 48 | Territories and insular possessions | Federal acquisition regulations system |
| Title 49 | Transportation | Transportation |
| Title 50 | War and national defense | Wildlife and fisheries |

*Table 10: Titles of USC and CFR Compared*

Each title of the CFR is divided into chapters – just like the United States Code. The chapters combine regulations on the same subjects. The chapter numbers are designated with Roman numerals. The use of chapters is a useful organizational tool which should not be overlooked.

The chapters are further divided into parts. The parts are finally divided into sections. When you cite to a CFR regulation you do not cite to the part number, although it is "part" of the citation!

> For example, the regulation found here:
>
> Title 6--homeland security
> Chapter I--department of homeland security, office of the secretary
> Part 25_regulations to support anti-terrorism by fostering effective
> Sec. 25.4 Designation of qualified anti-terrorism technologies.
>
> Is cited thusly:  6 CFR § 25.4

The regulations in the Code of Federal Regulations are organized by part and subpart and together these are cited as a section.

### 2.2.4.1. How to find regulations

Since regulations are issued pursuant to Congressional authority, for every regulation there is an authorizing statute. All of the indexes to the CFR include a Parallel Table of Authorities where the researcher with a United States Code section citation can see if there are regulations listed for that code section. The Parallel Table of Authorities is also online at <http://www.access.gpo.gov/nara/cfr/cfr-table-search.html> in both text and PDF versions.

The official CFR also includes an index volume. The government-produced index, however, is weak and not nearly detailed enough for complete legal research. Several commercial enterprises have produced much more detailed indexes to the Federal Register and Code of Federal Regulations, such as the highly-detailed and excellent indexes published by Congressional Information Service, Inc. (CIS).

The Federal Register and the CFR are published by the United State Government Printing Office (GPO). In addition to the print volumes, available at most law school libraries in the United States as part of their Government Depository status, electronic versions going back to 1996 are available on the GPO Access website (<www.access.gpo.gov>). Here the researcher will find browse, text search and citation search features for all issues of the CFR that are online.

The full text of the CFR is online at the GPO Access website and in all of the various computer-assisted legal research databases, including LexisNexis and Westlaw.

Lawyers and law students will also "*Shepardize*" CFR cites for history and citing references.

---

**Research Tip #2.4**
Never look at a code section in isolation. Always read
the sections immediately preceding and following and
it's best to look at all of the sections in the same chapter.

---

Just like researching the United States Code, or the state codes, the research does not stop once the relevant sections are identified. The researcher always has to ask: Is this still good law? - Are there cases?

Updating the CFR in print is a cumbersome process. A research tool called List of Sections Affected, or LSA, needs to be consulted.

The CFR volumes are printed upon an annual basis, with the following schedule:

| CFR Tables | Dates of Annual Revision |
|---|---|
| Titles 1-16 | January 1 |
| Titles 17-27 | April 1 |
| Titles 28-41 | July 1 |
| Titles 42-50 | October 1 |

*Table 11: Dates of Annual Revision of CFR Titles*

The List of CFR Sections Affected lists proposed, new, and amended Federal regulations that have been published in the Federal Register since the most recent revision date of a Code of Federal Regulations (CFR) title. It is published by the Office of the Federal Register, National Archives and Records

Administration.

Each LSA issue is cumulative and contains the CFR part and section numbers, a description of its status (e.g., amended, confirmed, revised), and the Federal Register page number where the change(s) may be found. The LSA is issued monthly and four of these monthly pamphlets also serve as annual cumulations for the CFR. On GPO Access, the LSA also contains three supplemental services: the List of CFR Parts Affected Today, Current List of CFR Parts Affected, and Last Month's List of CFR Parts Affected.

- List of CFR Parts Affected Today: Lists the CFR parts affected by change(s) appearing in most current issue Federal Register. The Federal Register is published Monday through Friday, except Federal holidays.
- Current List of CFR Parts Affected: Lists the CFR parts affected by change(s) since the last monthly issue of the LSA.
- Last Month's List of CFR Parts Affected: Lists only the CFR parts affected by change(s) during the last month.

Whether done in paper on online at the GPO Access site, to bring CFR sections up-to-date, the researcher must consult both the LSA pamphlets, starting with the annual cumulation and also the most recent issues of the Federal Register. The Federal Register volumes will pick up where the LSA pamphlets leave off. Each issue of the Federal Register has a cumulative LSA table so, at most, the researcher will only need to consult two issues of the Federal Register – the one which covers the month after the most recently monthly pamphlet and the most recent one available. All of the LSA tables – in the pamphlets or in the Federal Register – make reference to Federal Register pages on which the regulation under investigation has been affected. So the researcher will have to find those pages of the Federal Register – either in print or online – to determine the current status of the regulation.

Fortunately, all this manual updating is no longer needed due to a great new government database called the Electronic Code of Federal Regulations (eCFR). The eCFR provides the full text of the entire CFR and it is completely up to date, within one day!  No further updating is needed. It is available at:  <http://ecfr.gpoaccess.gov> and it is one of the best things the United States government has done for law librarians and legal researchers.

Both LexisNexis and Westlaw keep their versions of the Code of Federal Regulations current. These databases cost money,[50] but attorneys' time costs money too – often lots of it – and it is more cost-effective to use a CALR database to retrieve a current CFR section than it is to update the material manually.

Regulatory research can be confusing, with all of the extremely technical language being used. The government-produced print index is weak and the parallel table of authorities has omissions. If a first check of the index and table reveal no regulations, it is not a safe assumption that there are none. It is better to check the annotated United States Code for CFR references, but even here the system is not perfect. Westlaw has devoted substantial resources to improving this situation and they now offer what is arguably the best index to the CFR with their Regulations Plus (RegsPlus) index. On top of that, Westlaw has now annotated the CFR, so that case law citations can also easily be found. With eCFR and RegsPlus, what was once difficult research has been made easy and complete.

---

[50] As of March 2006, for example, under per-minute charges, it costs $ 7.16 per minute to search the CFR database in Westlaw. Westlaw® Plan 1 Pricing Guide, on file with the authors.

Index
Linking
Agency Tracking

Proposed Regulations
KeyCite
Federal Register

Annotations
Historical FR
Agency Content
Versioning

*Table 12: Enhanced Regulatory Searching on Westlaw[51]*

## 2.2.4.2. Executive Orders

The President of the United States, as head of the Executive Branch, issues Executive Orders. These have the force of law – often a very powerful source of law. It was an Executive Order, for example, which interned Japanese-Americans to relocation camps during World War II.[52] Presidential Executive Orders are published in Title 3 of the Code of Federal Regulations, as well as being available in a variety of other locations including the Weekly Compilation of Presidential Documents, Public Papers of the Presidents, and our fa-

---

[51] Source: Dan Henry, Esq. , Thomson West Account Representative.

[52] Executive Order 9066 was a presidential executive order issued during World War II by U.S. President Franklin D. Roosevelt on February 19, 1942, using his authority as Commander-in-Chief to exercise war powers to send ethnic groups to internment camps. 7 Fed. Reg. 1407 (Feb. 25, 1942).

vorite source, HeinOnline.

### 2.2.4.3. Regulations.gov

Participatory government took a gigantic electronic step forward when the United States created this relatively new website. Regulations.gov is a site where the public can find, view and post comments on proposed regulations and other administrative agency actions. The technology easily enables thousands, if not millions, of people to comment upon proposed rules; a question remains if the technology enables a thoughtful electronic processing of those comments. Regulations.gov allows anyone to participate in the rule-making process and to view all of the comments made by others.

### 2.2.4.4. Agency decisions

Agencies do more than write regulations. Agencies also possess a quasi-judicial function. Administrative Law Judges (ALJs) hold hearings and settle disputes. As part of this judicial function, ALJs will issue decisions. As Armstrong and Knott point out, "Publication of administrative decisions is irregular at best."[53]

Unlike the decisions from the courts of the Judicial Branch, agency decisions do not follow the same rules of stare decisis. So, while certainly of great importance to the parties of the dispute, the decisions are not binding on others and do not create precedent.

But since it is more likely than not that an agency will follow its own rulings, these decisions are nonetheless important to lawyers representing clients in similar matters.

Some agencies, like the Federal Communications Commission, issue care-

---

[53] J.D.S. Armstrong and Christopher A. Knott, WHERE THE LAW IS: AN INTRODUCTION TO ADVANCED LEGAL RESEARCH 174 (2nd ed.) (St. Paul: Thomson West, 2006). "Generally speaking, there are three different ways that agency decisions are made available to researchers; on the agency's website, in official publications of the agency, or in commercial publications. It is increasingly common for agencies to make hearing decisions available on their websites. You should know, however, that often these decisions are reproduced with no indexes or finding aids, and are usually arranged by date or party name. There is rarely any kind of subject access to the decisions. A few agencies publish their decisions in official reporters …"

fully bound published complications of their decisions; others do not.

The best sources for the text of administrative law decisions are the agency websites themselves and also the pricey LexisNexis and Westlaw databases.

Looseleaf services, discussed above, sometimes will include selected administrative agency decisions. A very useful table which indicates what looseleaf services have this information is: "Sources of Federal Regulatory Agency Rules, Regulations and Adjudications," found in Appendix D to Morris L. Cohen, Robert C. Berring and Kent C. Olson, How to Find the Law.[54]

### 2.2.4.5. State administrative law resources

Each state in the United States also has three branches of government: Legislative, Judicial and Executive. The Executive branch for the states all issue regulations, much the same way as the federal Executive branch does.

Most states have some version of a notice publication similar to the Federal Register, although it will be called by different names. In California, it is called the Notice Register. Since states generate far few regulations than the many federal agencies, no state issues its register upon a daily basis. A few states do not publish a register at all.

But all states codify their regulations and some sort of code is available. In California it is the California Code of Regulations.

For more on state regulations, a good resource is William H. Manz, Guide to State Legislative and Administrative Materials.[55]

### 2.2.4.6. Online sources of administrative law

Since law students Online sources of administrative law in the United States

---

[54] Morris L. Cohen, Robert C. Berring and Kent C. Olson, HOW TO FIND THE LAW (9th ed.) (St. Paul, Minnesota: Thomson West publishing as part of its Hornbook Series, 1989).

[55] William H. Manz, GUIDE TO STATE LEGISLATIVE AND ADMINISTRATIVE MATERIALS (2002 ed.) (Buffalo, New York: William S. Hein, 2002).

do 90% or more of their research online[56] the charts below is offered as guidance to locating the following administrative materials online:
- Federal Register
- Code of Federal Regulations (CFR)
- Administrative Agencies
- Administrative Decisions
- California Administrative Law

| Federal Register | Code of Federal Regulations |
|---|---|
| Federal Register (Print)<br><br>There is also an index to the Federal Register, published by CIS. Also, historical indexes to the Federal Register are available on HeinOnline from 1936-1995. | Code of Federal Regulations (print)<br><br>There is also an index to the CFR in USCS. |
| LexisNexis Congressional<br>1989-<br>Search by keyword, FR citation. | LexisNexis Congressional<br>Search by keyword, CFR citation, statutory authority. |
| GPO Access<br>1995- | GPO Access<br>1997- (some titles 1996-)<br><br>eCFR (National Archives and Records Administration)<br>A beta version of the CFR that incorporates changes in rules and regulations to present a currently updated CFR. |
| LexisNexis<br>1980-<br><br>Westlaw<br>1980-<br><br>HeinOnline<br>1936-1998 | LexisNexis<br>Historical version back to 1981.<br><br>Westlaw<br>Historical version back to 1984. |

*Table 13: Sources for the Federal Register and the Code of Federal Regulations*

[56] Erika V. Wayne & J. Paul Lomio, BOOK LOVERS BEWARE: A SURVEY OF ONLINE RESEARCH HABITS OF STANFORD LAW STUDENTS 6-7 (Robert Crown Law Library Legal Research Paper Series, Research Paper No. 2) (2005) <http://www.law.stanford.edu/publications/projects/papers/OnlineResearchSurveys.v211.pdf>.

| Administrative Agencies | Administrative Decisions |
|---|---|
| The United States Government manual | Finding the Law[57] |
| The United States Government manual at the GPO | Appendix C - Sources of Federal Regulatory Agency Rules, Regulations and Adjudications |
| Federal regulatory directory | Federal Administrative Decisions and Other Actions (University of Virginia) Extensive list of agencies and links to administrative decisions if available on the Internet. |
| United States Federal Government Agencies Directory (Louisiana State University) Federal Web Locator (Center for Information Law and Policy)<br><br>Both web sites have complete listings for executive agencies. | |
| LexisNexis Federal Legal - U.S. : Administrative Agency Materials : Individual Agencies<br><br>Westlaw Other Administrative & Executive Materials | LexisNexis Federal Agency Decision File and Federal Legal - U.S. : Administrative Agency Materials : Individual Agencies<br><br>Westlaw Other Administrative & Executive Materials |

*Table 14: Sources for Administrative rules and decisions*

| California Code of Regulations and Notice Register |
|---|
| California Code of Regulations This California Code of Regulations (CCR) Website contains the text of the regulations that have been formally adopted by state agencies, reviewed and approved by the Office of Administrative Law, and filed with the Secretary of State.<br><br>California Regulatory Notice Register Full text of the Notice Register starting July 2000 and table of contents only from January 1998. California State Agencies |

*Table 15 California Code of Regulation and Notice Register*

---

[57] Robert C. Berring, FINDING THE LAW (11th ed.) (St. Paul, MN: West Publishing, 1999).

## 2.2.5. Case Law Research

Last, but certainly not least, we come to the law produced by the Judicial Branch of government.

Some might argue that judges do not make law. In fact, on the home page of the Administrative Office of the United States Court's Understanding the Federal Courts, it states:

> "Through fair and impartial judgments, the federal courts interpret and apply the law to resolve disputes. The courts do not make the laws. That is the responsibility of Congress. Nor do the courts have the power to enforce the laws. That is the role of the President and the many executive branch departments and agencies."[58]

In this regard, it can be suggested that courts "explain" the law, as they apply it to facts under their review. Explaining the law is how we defined secondary sources, above. However, no one in the legal research world would suggest that compilation of judicial opinions are secondary sources.

Legal research properly begins with an examination of true secondary sources, and then a careful review of all controlling statutes and regulations. This is the best way to begin legal research. But legal research always includes case analysis, and generally this is where the research process slows and then stops.

One reason why legal research bogs down in the case law realm is the sheer vastness of the body of law involved. Whereas one could, conceivably, read from cover to cover the entire United States Code (although arguably would not be the same person afterwards), there are millions and millions of cases out in the case law universe, and that is counting only the published cases. By the year, 2000 there were an estimated 5.2 million published judicial decisions "with about 100,000 cases added annually."[59]

LexisNexis and Westlaw became the gigantic economic forces (annual sales in excess of 1 billion dollars) that they are because of their case law resources. They have branched out to include everything a lawyer needs in his or her practice, but the case law core remains their raison d'être

---

[58] <www.uscourts.gov/understand03/content_1_0.html>.
[59] CLARK *supra* note 36, at 38.

In the United States there are two parallel court systems: federal and state. The chart below summarizes the differences:

| Comparing Federal and State Court Systems | |
|---|---|
| The U.S. Constitution is the supreme law of the land in the United States. It creates a federal system of government in which power is shared between the federal government and the state governments. Due to federalism, both the federal government and each of the state governments have their own court systems. | |
| **The Federal Court System** | **The State Court System** |
| STRUCTURE | |
| Article III of the Constitution invests the judicial power of the United States in the federal court system. Article III, Section 1 specifically creates the U.S. Supreme Court and gives Congress the authority to create the lower federal courts. | The Constitution and laws of each state establish the state courts. A court of last resort, often known as a Supreme Court, is usually the highest court. Some states also have an intermediate Court of Appeals. Below these appeals courts are the state trial courts. Some are referred to as Circuit or District Courts. |
| Congress has used this power to establish the 13 U.S. Courts of Appeals, the 94 U.S. District Courts, the U.S. Court of Claims, and the U.S. Court of International Trade. U.S. Bankruptcy Courts handle bankruptcy cases. Magistrate Judges handle some District Court matters. | States also usually have courts that handle specific legal matters, e.g., probate court (wills and estates); juvenile court; family court; etc. |
| Parties dissatisfied with a decision of a U.S. District Court, the U.S. Court of Claims, and/or the U.S. Court of International Trade may appeal to a U.S. Court of Appeals. | Parties dissatisfied with the decision of the trial court may take their case to the intermediate Court of Appeals. |
| A party may ask the U.S. Supreme Court to review a decision of the U.S. Court of Appeals, but the Supreme Court usually is under no obligation to do so. The U.S. Supreme Court is the final arbiter of federal constitutional questions. | Parties have the option to ask the highest state court to hear the case. |
| | Only certain cases are eligible for review by the U.S. Supreme Court. |
| SELECTION OF JUDGES | |
| Article III, Section 1 of the Constitution states that federal judges are to be nominated by the President and confirmed by the Senate.<br><br>They hold office during good behavior, | State court judges are selected in a variety of ways, including<br>• election,<br>• appointment for a given number of years,<br>• appointment for life, and combinations |

| | |
|---|---|
| typically, for life. Through Congressional impeachment proceedings, federal judges may be removed from office for misbehavior. | of these methods, e.g., appointment followed by election. |
| **TYPES OF CASES HEARD** | |
| • Cases that deal with the constitutionality of a law;<br>• Cases involving the laws and treaties of the U.S.;<br>• Ambassadors and public ministers;<br>• Disputes between two or more states;<br>• Admiralty law, and<br>• Bankruptcy. | • Most criminal cases, probate (involving wills and estates),<br>• Most contract cases, tort cases (personal injuries), family law (marriages, divorces, adoptions), etc.<br><br>State courts are the final arbiters of state laws and constitutions. Their interpretation of federal law or the U.S. Constitution may be appealed to the U.S. Supreme Court. The Supreme Court may choose to hear or not to hear such cases. |
| **ARTICLE I COURTS** | |
| Congress has created several Article I or legislative courts that do not have full judicial power. Judicial power is the authority to be the final decider in all questions of Constitutional law, all questions of federal law and to hear claims at the core of habeas corpus issues.<br><br>• Article I courts are U.S. Court of Veterans' Appeals, the U.S. Court of Military Appeals, and the U.S. Tax Court | |

*Table 16: Comparing Federal and State Court Systems[60]*

The federal system includes the following courts:

---

[60] Source: <www.uscourts.gov/outreach/resources/comparefedstate.html>.

**THE UNITED STATES FEDERAL COURTS**

| SUPREME COURT | UNITED STATES SUPREME COURT |
|---|---|
| APPELLATE COURTS | **U.S. Courts of Appeals**<br>12 Regional Circuit Courts of Appeals<br>1 U.S. Court of Appeals for the Federal Circuit |
| TRIAL COURTS | **U.S. District Courts**<br>94 judicial districts<br>U.S. Bankruptcy Courts<br>**U.S. Court of International Trade**<br>**U.S. Court of Federal Claims** |
| FEDERAL COURTS AND OTHER ENTITIES OUTSIDE THE JUDICIAL BRANCH | Military Courts (trial and appellate)<br>Court of Veterans Appeals<br>U.S. Tax Court<br>Federal administrative agencies and boards |

*Table 17: The United States Federal Courts*[61]

The United States District Court is the trial level court for federal cases. In addition to settling disputes this court also has a role in interpreting federal

---

[61] Source: Understanding Federal Courts, Administrative Office of the Courts, <http://www.uscourts.gov/understand03/media/UFC03.pdf>.

67

statutes. Federal District Court Judge D. Brock Hornby writes about "the business of the U.S. District Courts" and makes this observation about the court's "increased demands for law exposition":[62]

> Congressional lawmaking carries a particular implication for federal courts' work. When Congress drafts a statute, it cannot possibly foresee all the disputes it will encompass or engender. As a result, statutory language often turns out ambiguous for particular circumstances. Sometimes, to submerge disagreement so as to get the law enacted, Congress intentionally chooses ambiguous language. Either way, users ask federal courts to expound upon what the new law means and the circumstances to which it applies. America's laws continue to multiple (about 1,900 pages of new statutes per session in the 1950s, 6,750 pages per session in the 1990s; about 14,477 new Federal Register pages in 1960, 80,322 in 2002) and, with them, insatiable demand for authoritative interpretation. The demand comes from individual users. It comes also from user segments, such as American business (e.g., trade association lawsuits), consumers, and the public (e.g., environmental groups). Alternative dispute resolution (mediation and arbitration) does not provide the authoritative interpretation; only courts do.

The 94 U.S. judicial districts are organized into 12 regional circuits, each of which has a United States court of appeals (see further Appendix 3). A court of appeals hears appeals from the district courts located within its circuit, as well as appeals from decisions of federal administrative agencies.

In addition, the Court of Appeals for the Federal Circuit has nationwide jurisdiction to hear appeals in specialized cases, such as those involving patent laws and cases decided by the Court of International Trade and the Court of Federal Claims.

### 2.2.5.1. State court system

The state court model runs parallel to the federal system, with litigation start-

---

[62] D. Brock Hornby, *The Business of the U.S. District Courts*, 10 GREEN BAG 2d 453, 457 (Summer 2007) citing statistics from Barnes, *Adversarial Legalism, the Rise of Judicial Policymaking, and the Separation of Powers Doctrine, in* MAKING POLICY, MAKING LAW: AN INTERBRANCH PERSPECTIVE 35 (Miller & Barnes, eds.)(Washington, D.C.: Georgetown University Press, 2004) and Marc Galanter, *The Vanishing Trial*, 10 DISP. RESOL. MAG. 3 (Summer 2004).

ing in trial courts and a first appeal following by an appeal to the state's highest court, usually, but not always, called the state Supreme Court.

A state court structure, using California[63] as a model, looks like this:

| COURT OF LAST RESORT |
| --- |
| **California Supreme Court** |
| <ul><li>Chief Justice and 6 Associate Justices</li><li>Justices appointed by Governor and confirmed by voters statewide for 12-year terms</li><li>Required by the Constitution to review all death penalty judgments</li><li>Has authority to review decisions of CA courts of appeal (reviewed 8,917 filings in 2001-2002 issued 101 opinions)</li><li>Appellate court with final authority on matters regarding the California Constitution and state law</li></ul> |
| INTERMEDIATE APPELLATE COURT |
| **California Courts of Appeal** |
| <ul><li>105 justices in 6 appellate districts, 9 court sites and 19 divisions</li><li>Justices appointed by Governor and confirmed by voters statewide for 12-year terms</li><li>25,465 cases filed in 2001-2002</li><li>Have appellate jurisdiction over cases that superior courts hear and in other areas decided by statute</li><li>Establish precedent for superior courts to follow, correct errors</li></ul> |
| COURTS OF GENERAL JURISDICTION |
| **California Superior Courts** |
| <ul><li>1,498 authorized judges in 58 counties</li><li>Judges are elected by voters in their counties to serve 6- year terms</li><li>Over 8 million cases filed in 2001-2002</li><li>Decide cases by applying the law to the facts in individual cases</li><li>Trial courts with original jurisdiction in criminal, civil, family, probate, mental health, small claims, juvenile and traffic matters</li></ul> |

*Table 18: California Court Structure*

It should be pointed out that once a case is filed in a court, it can move up and

---

[63] The California Judicial System is the largest court system in the United States, with 2,000 judicial officers and 19,000 employees, serving 34 million people. Source: Administrative Office of the Courts, CA Judicial Branch Fact Sheet, Jan 2004.

down the court system in almost elevator-like fashion, unlike the flow of litigation in European courts. Sometimes the litigation moves in a one-direction linear fashion: Complaint filed, answer filed, hearing held, decision reached. End of the story. But more often than not, the litigation rides through the court system as if on an elevator. There can be interlocutory appeals (appeals heard by an appellate court before the initial litigation is concluded); motions are constantly filed and there are often mini-hearings on those motions; and even once a judgment is reached it often is not the end of the story. That judgment may get appealed to a higher court, and that higher court may then remand the matter back to the trial court for reconsideration. Up, down,

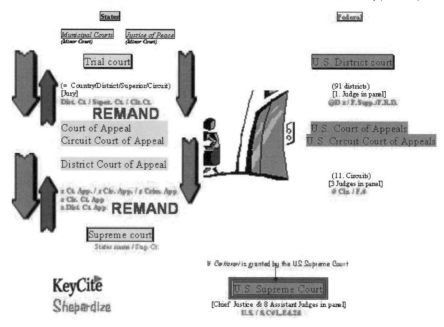

*Table 19: "Elevator"/Remand-system in US Courts*[64]

---

[64] Source: Course material for non-Americans "Finding Law in the U.S." by Henrik Spang-Hanssen.

An illustrating example is a long row of court decisions concerning the federal Child Online Protection Act (COPA):[65]

American Civil Liberties Union v. Reno, 1998 WL 813423 (U.S. District Court for E.D.Pa. Nov 23, 1998) (NO. CIV. A. 98-5591)
*Temporarily Restraining Order issued*
American Civil Liberties Union v. Reno, 31 F.Supp.2d 473 (U.S. District Court for E.D.Pa. Feb 01, 1999)
*Affirmed by*
American Civil Liberties Union v. Reno, 217 F.3d 162 (U.S. Courts of Appeals for 3rd Circuit (Pa.) Jun 22, 2000)
*Vacated by*
Ashcroft v. American Civil Liberties Union, 535 U.S. 564, 122 S.Ct. 1700 (U.S. Supreme Court, May 13, 2002)
*On Remand to*
American Civil Liberties Union v. Ashcroft, 322 F.3d 240 (U.S. Court of Appeals for 3rd Circuit (Pa.) Mar 06, 2003)
*Affirmed and Remanded by*
Ashcroft v. American Civil Liberties Union, 542 U.S. 656, 124 S.Ct. 2783 (U.S. Supreme Court,, Jun 29, 2004)
*On Remand to*
American Civil Liberties Union v. Gonzales, 478 F.Supp.2d 775 (U.S. District Court for E.D.Pa. Mar 22, 2007)

Most appeals are taken as a matter of right. However, most appeals to the United States Supreme Court are at the Supreme Court's discretion, and this application process is commenced in most instances by filing a petition for certiorari, or "cert. petition." If the Court agrees to hear the appeal, then cert. is granted; if they decline, then it is denied. Of course, the U.S. Supreme Court receives many more applications than it can possibly handle, so the justices pick and choose wisely as to which ones need to be decided, and these are generally the most pressing legal issues of the day. And the elevator stops at the Supreme Court. Once it issues its decision, that's the end of the process for those litigants. A common saying is that "the Supreme Court is not final because it is infallible but it is infallible because it is final."[66]

---

[65] Codified as 47 U.S.C. § 231 (1998).

[66] *Brown v. Allen*, 344 U.S. 443, 540 (1953) (Jackson, J., concurring).

## *2.2.5.2. Publication of judicial decisions*

### 2.2.5.2.1. Published and unpublished

Judges write opinions. These are also called decisions, or orders or rulings. They are also called cases. All these terms refer to the same thing: a writing of the court. These opinions can be published or unpublished – that is up to the judge – he or she decides whether or not a particular decision should be published. There used to be a huge distinction between published and unpublished decisions, with unpublished opinions having no precendential value. This distinction is rapidly eroding and legal researchers seek out both published and unpublished opinions as various courts lift the injunction against citing unpublished decisions.

> "After years of extensive debate, reams of commentary and vigorous opposition from several circuit judges and many attorneys, the Committee on Rules of Practice and Procedure and the U. Supreme Court have answered 'yes' to the question of whether unpublished federal opinions are citable. Rule 32.1 of the Federal Rules of Appellate Procedure, effective Dec. 1 [2006], lifts restrictions on citing unpublished federal opinions . . . ."[67]

The increased drive to cite unpublished decisions has become controversial, and a working paper posted to the Legal Scholarship Network offers this analysis in its abstract:[68]

> This Article advances a relatively simple thesis - unpublished opinions should be non-precedential, at least until these opinions can be readily researched by all attorneys. Unfortunately, based upon the questionable assumption that technological advances have made unpublished opinions readily available, some jurisdictions have recently given unpublished opinions full precedential value and this trend appears to be the next frontier in the crusade over unpublished opinions. In truth, although unpublished opinions are increasingly available, many unpublished opinions are not as readily available as published opinions. By affording precedential value to these difficult to research unpub-

---

[67] Paul D. Fogel and David J. de Jesus, *Unpublished Opinions*, Forum Column, DAILY JOURNAL, December 20, 2006.

[68] Andrew T. Solomon, *Making Unpublished Opinions Precedential: A Recipe for Ethical Problems & Legal Malpractice?*, 26 MISS. C. L. REV. 185 (2007).

lished opinions, jurisdictions will possibly create ethical and legal malpractice problems for attorneys.

This Article does not attempt to comprehensively report on which unpublished opinions, on both the state and federal levels, are readily available. Instead, it focuses upon the availability of Fifth Circuit unpublished opinions and shows an example of a jurisdiction which has made some of its unpublished opinions precedential, even though those opinions are difficult, and sometimes virtually impossible, to research. The Article ultimately makes two recommendations: (1) the Fifth Circuit should change its rule regarding the precedential value afforded to unpublished opinions, and (2) other jurisdictions should avoid the Fifth Circuit's mistake and only consider making unpublished opinions precedential when those opinions are readily available and can be comprehensively researched. By adopting these recommendations, courts will minimize the risk that attorneys will face ethical and legal malpractice problems for failing to use binding unpublished opinions in their client representation.[69]

[69] *Rules for Unpublished Opinions Violate Due Process, Suit Says*, by Linda Rapattoni, Daily Journal Staff Writer, October 5, 2007: An Orange County law firm sued the California Supreme Court and an appellate division Thursday, contending rules barring lawyers from citing unpublished opinions violate due process and equal protection rights. The suit appears to be the first to challenge the rules in federal court. Bisnar Chase of Newport Beach filed the complaint in U.S. District Court in San Francisco in Hild v. California (Supreme Court, C075107JCS). The Hild suit alleges the appellate court violated the new guidelines the state Supreme Court adopted when it filed its June 25, 2007, opinion. In Joshua Hild, vs. Southern California Edison Co., a three-justice panel of the 2nd District Court of Appeal rejected the verdict in an unpublished opinion. A petition for review is pending before the California Supreme Court. Courts don't do it regularly, but the California Supreme Court has reviewed unpublished opinions on a number of occasions. California Constitution, Article VI, Section 14 states it's up to the courts to decide which opinions they publish. "The Legislature shall provide for the prompt publication of such opinions of the Supreme Court and the courts of appeal as the Supreme Court deems appropriate," it says. The U.S. Supreme Court last year adopted Rule 32.1 allowing citation of unpublished opinions, which the 9th U.S. Circuit Court of Appeal, whose jurisdiction includes California, had opposed. California's system is much larger than the federal system and has a constitutional requirement to give a longer reason for each opinion than the one to two paragraphs typical in federal opinions. - - From a Civil Law point

## 2.2.5.2.2. Official and unofficial

An "official" report is one that is published by the government itself or published by a commercial publisher under contract with the government. All other reports are "unofficial." When a court releases its decision, the text of opinion itself will be exactly the same whether published officially or unofficially. What might differ between unofficial and official versions are editorial enhancements. This official/unofficial distinction is a minor one, important only for some citation rules. Generally speaking, an official citation must be given before an unofficial citation. But these citation conventions are rapidly changing, especially with the very heavy reliance upon online versions of court decisions.

## 2.2.5.2.3. Trial and appellate courts

Cases start with a trial court. In the federal system, this is the United States District Court. Many of the decisions of the United States District Court are published. In the state system, a case also begins with a trial court. Often this is called a "superior court" but state trial courts go by other names as well. In New York, for example, the trial court is given the very confusing designation of "supreme court." State trial court decisions are seldom published.

## 2.2.5.2.4. Reporters

Judicial opinions are published in sets called "reporters." Therefore, a published opinion is also called a reported opinion.

Usually state court trial opinions are not published. There are several reasons for this. One reason is that decisions are often reached without a written opinion. And even if the trial court judge does write an opinion, it is recognized that it is binding only upon the parties to the litigation – there is not a

---

of view, it would held that any decision (written or unwitten - as long there exist proof of the courts decision) of any court in a democratic and civilized country can be used in a later case. Only in non-democratic countries can you be forbidden to refer to a previous court decision. Another aspect is of cause (from a Civil Law point of view) is whether the case can be said to be "precedence", thus requiring a (civil law) court to build its decision on the previous case.

wider precedent setting value to the trial court ruling. There are exceptions, and some very notable trial court decisions have been published; but this is rare.

Decisions of the federal trial court, the United States District Court, are different. These are considered more important and are often published.

### 2.2.5.2.5. Publication of Federal Court Decisions – U.S. Supreme Court

Everything the United States Supreme Court does is published – every decision, every order, every ruling. The first reports of the U.S. Supreme Court followed the early English method, called nominative reports. Commercial reporters would write down the decisions spoken from the bench. These early decisions were cited by the name of the reporter. This practice of citing to named reporters ceased is most jurisdictions by the middle of the 19th century.

By tradition, the first ninety volumes of U.S. Supreme Court decisions are cited by including the name of the commercial reporter. For example, 2 U.S. (2 Dallas) 3 (1791).

Decisions of the U.S. Supreme Court are published officially in the United States Reports and unofficially in Supreme Court Reports, Supreme Court Reporter, Lawyers' Edition, BNA[70] U.S. Law Week, and CCH's[71] United States Supreme Court Bulletin and in many online databases, including the Supreme Court's own website, LexisNexis, Westlaw, and the many new alternatives to LexisNexis and Westlaw that are cropping up such as Bloomberg Legal, FastCase, LoisLaw, Justia, Versuslaw and Wikilaw.[72]

Any discussion of the U.S. Supreme Court must include a reference to a resource-rich blog, SCOTUSblog.com (SCOTUS is an acronym for Supreme Court of the United States). The blog one of the very most important and popular law blogs in the United States.

This blog reports on the activities of the United States Supreme Court and

---

[70] Bureau of National Affairs.

[71] Commerce Clearing House.

[72] <http://about.bloomberg.com/about/professional/blaw.html>, <www.fastcase.com>, <www.loislaw.com>, <www.versuslaw.com>, <www.justia.com>, and <www.wikilaw.com>.

includes detailed analysis and discussion of each term of the Court. Previews and summaries of arguments are posted. In addition, somehow – and we do not know how they do this – there are times when the SCOTUSblog site will include the text of the latest Supreme Court decisions before they are even posted on the official Supreme Court website at <http://www.supremecourtus.gov>.

Anyone interested in understanding United States law would be wise to read SCOTUSblog.com upon a daily basis, at least when the Supreme Court is in session (from the first Monday in October to its summer adjournment).

American Law Reports also follows the Supreme Court very closely and a recent annotation is this one: "2006-2007 United States Supreme Court Review," 21 A.L.R. Fed. 2d 559 or 26 A.L.R. 6th 659 (2007).

### 2.2.5.2.6. Lower Federal Court Reporting

The decisions of the United States Court of Appeals are published in print only by the West Publishing Company in its Federal Reporter. There is no official reporter. Decisions from the United States District Court are published in print by the West Publishing Company in its Federal Supplement and Federal Rules Decisions. There is no official reporter.

Very early United States federal cases were published in Federal Cases. This is a set organized by West and placed cases in alphabetical order. The more significant cases during the period 1789 to 1880 were published in Federal Cases. Cases in this set are numbered consecutively and, by tradition, that number is used as part of the case citation.

Between 1880 and 1932 all federal cases were published in the Federal Reporter. In 1932, the trial court decisions were pulled out from the Federal Reporter and published instead in the Federal Supplement.

Federal Rules Decisions contains decisions of the United States District Courts that involve criminal or civil rules. This set only contains District Court decisions, even if a Court of Appeals considers a federal rule upon appeal (the appellate decision, if published, is published in the Federal Reporter). There is no overlap between the Federal Rules Decisions and Federal Supplement – a published case is either in one or the other.

In 2001, the West Publishing Company, in our opinion, got a little carried away and began to publish unpublished decisions. This set is called the Federal Appendix and it contains opinions issued by the U.S. Courts of Appeals that are not published in the Federal Reporter. Opinions are included from all circuits except for the 5th and 11th, which do not provide their "unpublished" opinions to any publisher.

The United States Court of Appeals, as indicated, are divided by circuits as seen in this map (see also Appendix 3):

*Table 20: Geographic Boundaries of U.S. Courts of Appeals & U.S. District Courts[73]*

## 2.2.5.2.7. Publication of State Court Decisions

With fifty states plus the District of Columbia, there is a wide variety in how state judicial opinions are published. The West Publishing Company has tried to make some sense of it all with their National Reporter System.

The West Publishing Company has divided the states into seven regions.

Reported appellate decisions from the states that fall within these regions are then published in:

- Atlantic Reporter,
- North Eastern Reporter,

---

[73] Source: Administrative Office of the U.S. Courts, <www.uscourts.gov>.

- North Western Reporter,
- Pacific Reporter,
- Southern Reporter,
- South Eastern Reporter, and
- South Western Reporter.

In states like California, with its separate official reports, the West reporters are unofficial. In some other states, the West Publishing Company is under contract to publish the decision, so they are official. Some states use other publishers or their own printing office. In some states with no official reports and no contract with West, the West reporters remain unofficial but are the only source for a print citation. All of this is rapidly changing in the online world and the next edition of this book will most likely see a radically different landscape of court reporting and citation.

Early state cases, like early federal cases, are sometimes cited by a nominative reporter. The first edition of Price and Bitner[74] has a detailed appendix will all nominative reporters identified.

Of course, no United States law student and increasingly few attorneys use actual books for their case law research. Few in the United States will ever pick up a bound reporter of decisions. Instead, most lawyers and law students reply upon online databases for their case law research. Nonetheless, the citation fiction requires that cases be cited by their print versions.

For example, a student or lawyer wishing to cite the very famous *Miranda decision*[75] – regardless of where he or she finds it – cites it thusly:

> The name or title of the case is *Miranda v. Arizona.* It is reported (published) in volume 384 of United States Reports (the official and therefore preferred citation) beginning at page 436. The case was decided in 1966.

> The case citation could also look like this:

> 384 U.S. 436, 10 Ohio Misc. 9, 86 S.Ct. 1602, 10 A.L.R.3d 974, 16 L.Ed.2d 694, 36 O.O.2d 237, 39 O.O.2d 63 (1966).

---

[74] Miles O. Price and Harry Bitner, EFFECTIVE LEGAL RESEARCH: A PRACTICAL MANUAL OF LAW BOOKS AND THEIR USE (New York: Prentice Hall, 1953).

[75] *Miranda v. Arizona*, 384 U.S. 436 (1966).

Since the case is extra important it is published in a lot of different places. This multiple publication effect can aid a researcher who is plowing through the LexisNexis or Westlaw database combing through lots and lots of cases. Cases with more citations than others can be bigger, more important cases. A cite to ALR means that the case is published in American Law Reports and therefore the subject of a detailed, lengthy annotation there. This can be research pay dirt.

---

**Research Tip #2.5**
Pay attention to the number of places a case is reported.
Cases with lots of different reports are extra important.
Cases with ALR citations can especially lead to fruitful sources.

---

## 2.2.5.2.8. Indexing Case Law

John West, the traveling salesman who, with his brother Horatio, founded the West Publishing Company in 1876, was a genius. He had no law training, but he saw the need for lawyers to be able to locate needed court decisions. His company has taken on, and succeeded, to create a taxonomy for law. A gigantic super index called the West Digest System. It is a marvel. And for the European lawyers reading this, you might be interested to know that the man currently in charge of the West Digest System, Dr. Dan Dabney, has his office in Switzerland.[76]

Dan Dabney recently spoke at the American Association of Law Libraries annual convention during a program entitled "Indexes, Taxonomies, and the Google Generation." Law librarian Bill Ketchum reported on the talk for a library journal and made this comment about Dr. Dabney's presentation:[77]

> Taxonomies
> "We call a system of classification, especially a hierarchical one, a 'taxonomy.' ... West's Key Number System is a taxonomy of legal concepts. A sys-

---

[76] Dan Dabney, Senior Director, Thomson Global Services, Landis-Gyr-Strasse 3, CH-6300 Zug, Switzerland, Phone: +41 (0)41 709 04 49, Email: daniel.dabney@thomson.com.

[77] Ketchum, Bill, *Indexes, Taxonomies, and the Google Generation*, SCALL NEWSLETTER, September 2005.

tem thus organized with entries and sub-entries to show the contexts in which a term is used (and that it may occur in more than one context) can be extremely useful to a researcher. Dan Dabney pointed out that in law we often want not only the answer to the question, but also the limits of that answer, such as when and how rule applies or does not apply. In text searching you do not see these 'boundaries.' You don't have a good map of the information space …"

Traditionally – and, again, all of this is changing rapidly in the online world – when a judge wrote an opinion that he or she wanted published, it was sent to the publisher, more often than not, the West Publishing Company. There a team of editors would review the opinion for grammar, punctuation and other minor-league editing tasks, and conferring with the judge on any possible needed changes.

After that first editorial task was completed, the opinion went to the big league editors, the editors charged with assigning "key numbers" to the opinion. These editors had to work their way up the chain at West – they all had to serve time as minor league editors and, in addition, they all had to possess law degrees and be a member of a state bar. West would not allow just anyone to index court opinions.[78]

The key numbers are part of the West American Digest System. The key number system is a patented system. West has taken law as a subject and divided it into over 400 subject areas, called topics. These subjects are then further divided into subtopics, which are subdivided into what are called "Key Numbers." "There are over 100,000 individual Key Numbers used in the arrangement."[79] The topic and subtopic together comprise the key number.

Key number editors assign a key number for every point of law found in an opinion. There can be anywhere between one and dozens of key numbers for any one opinion.

The editors then write a little paragraph summarizing the point of law rep-

---

[78] For a glimpse into the famous West Publishing Company, a company that has affected legal research more than any other, see Jill Abramson, John Kennedy and Ellen Joan Pollock, *Inside the West Empire*, THE AMERICAN LAWYER (October 1983), p. 90.

[79] West's ANALYSIS OF AMERICAN LAW: GUIDE TO THE AMERICAN DIGEST SYSTEM (2007 ed.) (St. Paul: Thomson West, 2007).

resented by the key number. These paragraphs, along with the key numbers, are superimposed upon each opinion. The key number with its paragraph of text is called a headnote. Headnotes are numbered and the corresponding paragraphs in the judges' opinions are linked by the same number placed in brackets (the brackets indicate that this numbering is done by someone other than the judge who wrote the opinion). If a researcher wanted to read only that part of the opinion that corresponded to a certain headnote, he or she could then look for the headnote's bracketed number in the opinion. For a lawyer, for whom time is literally money, this helps speed the research process.

Digest volumes are then created by rearranging all of the headnotes into a topic and subtopic arrangement. Since cases are published chronologically, it is only by copying and then rearranging the headnotes into a topical scheme that case law research – before the computer anyway – can be accomplished.

Digests are the print index to case law. They are terrific tools for finding cases.

There are three ways to use a Digest:

- First, if you know nothing, just start in the Descriptive Word Index. Look up the words that come to mind until you find a reference to a Digest Topic and then turn to the table of contents for that topic.
- Second, if you know the Topic, but don't have a specific headnote, you can turn to the Outline of Law that is presented at the beginning of the topical area. For example, Negligence as a topic leads to these general subtopics (k stands for key numbers):

272 NEGLIGENCE
I. In general, k200-k205
Ii. Necessity and existence of duty, k210-k222
Iii. Standard of care, k230-k239
Iv. Breach of duty, k250-k259
V. Heightened degrees of negligence, k272-k276
Vi. Vulnerable and endangered persons; rescues, k281-k285
Vii. Sudden emergency doctrine, k291-k295
Viii. Dangerous situations and strict liability, k301-k307
Ix. Trades, special skills and professions, k321-k323
X. Sports, games and recreation, k331-k333
Xi. Fires, k341-k344
Xii. Negligent entrustment, k351-k355
Xiii. Proximate cause, k370-k454
Xiv. Necessity and existence of injury, k460-k463
Xv. Persons liable, k480-k484
Xvi. Defenses and mitigating circumstances, k500-k575
Xvii. Premises liability, k1000-k1320

Xviii. Actions, k1500-k1750
Xix. Criminal negligence, k1800-k1809

- Third, if you have a headnote, you can turn directly to that part of the digest and locate all of the cases – state and federal -- that contain the headnote topic and subtopic – that is, all the cases that address the same points of law. This pin-point approach works whenever you have a relevant case in hand, such as a case found from reading secondary sources.

Publishers other than West also publish court decisions and produce their own digests to the reporters. However, the West system is the granddaddy of them all and the one used the most widely.

Think of the digest as the index to case law. In other words, the digest is used to find cases.

It should be noted that when a case is reported by more than one publisher, the headnotes are the intellectual property of the publisher, and not written by the court. Therefore, there will be differences. Even though both publishers are working with the same published decision, they will index the opinion differently. In the California case of *Northwestern Mutual Insurance v. Farmers' Insurance*,[80] for example, the version in the official reporter contains sixteen headnotes while the version in the unofficial West reporter contains twenty-one headnotes, with some different topics chosen.

The American Digest System is the most comprehensive digest of American cases. The set is enormous both in coverage and size. It is divided into several units, each covered all of the reported case decisions – state and federal – for a specific time span.

The Century Digest covers the period up to 1896. The "key number" arrangement used in this first digest is slightly different than that in subsequent units. A cross reference table can be found in volume 21 of the First Decennial digest (and a very common characteristic of law books is that whenever there is a major revision, there is usually a table that will lead the researcher from the old system to the new one).

Digests topics slowly evolve over time and sometimes reflect the mores of

---

[80] *Northwestern Mutual Insurance Co. v. Farmers' Insurance Group*, 76 Cal. App.3d 1031, 143 Cal. Rptr. 415 (1978).

the times. For example, the original topic "bastards" become "illegitimate children" and later became "children out-of-wedlock."

The Decennial Digests cover ten-year chunks of time. These are followed by the General Digest, which picks up where the latest decennial leaves off.

There is also the Federal Digest, covering all federal cases; and two digests for the Untied States Supreme Court:

- United States Supreme Court Digest and
- United States Supreme Court Digest: Lawyer's Edition.

For the regional reporter system, there are the following digests:

- Atlantic Digest,
- North Western Digest,
- Pacific Digest,
- South Eastern Digest,
- Southern Digest.

There are no regional digests for the South Western or North Eastern reporters.

There are state digests for nearly every state and for big states, like New York and California, there are more than one digest available. In addition to indexing state court decisions, the state digests will include federal court cases which arose in those states.

Of course, the preferred research tool is the computer, and users can create customized digests in both Westlaw and LexisNexis.

To create a customized digest in Westlaw, first click on "Site Map" at the top of any Westlaw screen. Then click on "Key Number Digest (Custom Digest)."

Westlaw has harnessed the power of the computer to take its digest system one step further with push-button ease for the law student or attorney unfamiliar with the key number system. Weslaw's new KeySearch feature will guide the researcher through the process of finding applicable topic and key numbers. The KeySearch system begins with the researcher clicking on very general legal areas and then guides the researcher to narrower and narrower topics until a precisions-based research screen is presented.

While Westlaw got the big head start on LexisNexis in the case indexing arena, and the complete West Digest System is fully integrated in the massive Westlaw database, LexisNexis too provides case indexing tools and in recently years has devoted substantial efforts to increase its case indexing research tools.

LexisNexis also now writes headnotes for its decisions. Unlike Westlaw, however, the LexisNexis headnotes are taken straight from the text of the opinion, verbatim.

In LexisNexis to find cases by topic or headnote click the Search tab at the top of the Research System. Click by topic or Headnote in the red bar under the Search Topic. One can then explore the topic using two approaches.

- Option 1: Find a Headnote Topic through a terms search (e.g., type negligence and click the red Find button to retriever all the topics related to negligence).
- Option 2: Explore Legal Topics. Find a Headnote Topic by drilling-down through all of the Search Advisor categories. Once one have selected a Headnote Topic one will find related case law and secondary sources through the search form for that topic. One can then search cases and secondary sources covering the Topic with terms or retrieve all the cases with ones Headnote topic.

LexisNexis also enables the researcher to easily find more cases once he or she has found something that looks useful. In reading a case online in LexisNexis, if the researcher locates a headnote that is on point, all he or she has to do is click on the blue "More Like This Headnote" link at the end of the headnote quote. The researcher can then define what jurisdictions he or she is interested in and then hit the red Search button and the database will cull all similar cases from that jurisdiction.

## 2.3. Boolean Searching and Natural Language Full Text Searching

LexisNexis and Westlaw offer much, much more than "just" topical searching. The databases, as discussed above, can be searched using Terms & Connectors or Natural Language.

Terms & Connectors searching gives the researcher the ability to construct highly detailed, highly specific searches, leading to very focused results.

For example, a Westlaw Terms & Connector search, using field limitations, might look something like this:

> Sy ((employ! /s will) or ("wrongful term!) or (unjust pre/2 dismiss!)) and date(after 2000)

> This search would limit itself to the synopsis field where the editors have written a paragraph summarizing what the case is about. It would use the Boolean "or" to retrieve cases with certain words and phrases appearing in certain word order as typed in by the researcher.

> Another example on narrowing a search:

(AU(Lomio) & ((Cyberspace Internet) /s "Domain name")) & DA(AFT 12/31/1999) % Child-pornography

This search will deselect any document containing the word child pornography (or spelled child pornography or child-pornography) and only search for documents after 31 December 1999, which has Lomio as author and contain a sentence with the phrase domain name and either the word cyberspace or internet.

Searching the synopsis field or the Key Numbers can give the skilled researcher great precision in his or her results. However, it is very important to stress the words in the synopsis and the words in the Key Numbers are not the words of the judge. Synopsis fields and Key Numbers, while excellent tools for gaining search precision, should never be cited as legal authority – only the words of the judge count as precedent.

Successful Terms & Connectors searching, using the powerful Boolean search engine, requires practice and it is only by trial and error that law students become accomplished in such searching. Fortunately, law schools pay flat fees for LexisNexis and Westlaw access, enabling their students to gain proficiency through heavy use. It is really the only way to learn. If you are about to attend a United States law school, there will be abundant opportunities to receive training on both the LexisNexis and Westlaw system. To quote famous law librarian Bob Berring: "Take the training!"[81]

LexisNexis and Westlaw are incredibly powerful research tools and a complete explanation of all of their features is far beyond the scope of this book. But listed below is a chart showing just some of the tools available to construct searches for precision. But, again, to echo the words of Professor Berring: ""Take the training!"

Westlaw and LexisNexis use nearly the same Boolean connectors (but be

---

[81] "The most important message we can give you is: TAKE THE TRAINING. ... Westlaw and LexisNexis are both designed with very snazzy front ends that make them easy to use intuitively. Let's face it, a chimp could use these systems and get results. Do not limit yourself like that. Take the systems seriously. ... Each of these systems has incredible power if you know how to use it. ... Westlaw and LexisNexis are full-blown universes of information. There is always more than you think." Robert C. Berring and Elizabeth A. Edinger, LEGAL RESEARCH SURVIVAL MANUAL (St. Paul, Minnesota: West Group, 2000).

aware that a space in Westlaw means the Boolean OR, and phrases must be carefully placed within quotation marks):

| Connector etc. | Type | Retrieves documents | Example |
|---|---|---|---|
| AND | & AND | Both terms | Narcotics & warrant |
| OR | [a space] OR | Either term or both terms | Car automobile |
| Grammatical connector | /p | Terms in the same paragraph | Hearsay /p utterance |
| Grammatical connector | /s | Terms in the same sentence | Design /s defect |
| Grammatical connector | +s | First term preceding the second in the same sentence | Attorney +s fee |
| Numerical connector | /n | Terms within n terms of each other (where n is a number from 1 to 255) | Personal /3 jurisdiction |
| Numerical connector | +n | The first tem preceding the second by n terms (where n is a number from 1 to 255) | 42 +7 1942 |
| Phrase | " " | Terms appearing in the same order as in the quotation marks | "attractive nuisance" |
| Exclude | % but not | Search terms following the percent symbol is deselected | NOT California |
| Round bracket/ parentheses | ( ) | Parentheses work in the same way that they do in algebra. Thus, the items in the parenthesis are searched first before the items outside of the parenthesis. | "California law" ("European law") |
| One joker character in a word | * | To search with one viable character. E.g. to retrieve grew and grow | Gr*w |
| Two joker characters in a word | ** | To search a word with two viable characters. E.g. jury, juror (but not jurisdiction) | Jur** |

| Compound words | - | A search on a compound word to retrieve all varia-tions (whistleblows, whistle-blow, whis-tle blow | Whistle-blow |
|---|---|---|---|
| Root Expander/ variant endings | ! | To retrieve words with variant endings (contributed, con-tributor, contribu-tory) | Contribut! |
| Author | AU( ) | Search only a particular author | AU(Lomio) |
| Court | CO( ) | Search only a particular court | CO(Ohio) |
| Date | DA(mm/dd/year) | To search for documents of a specific date | DA(12/31/2000) |
| After a date | DA(AFT mm/dd/year) | To search for documents after a given date | DA(AF 12/31/1999) |
| Before a date | DA(BEF mm/dd/year) | To search for documents before a given date | DA(BEF 12/31/2000) |
| In-between dates | DA(AFT mm/dd/year and BEF mm/dd/year) | To search for document between to given dates | DA(AFT 12/31/2000 and BEF 12/31/2001) |

*Table 21: Terms and Connectors Search Capabilities in LexisNexis & Westlaw*

LexisNexis and Westlaw each have toll-free numbers (in the United States these are the so-called 800 numbers) and each now offers their customer service via online chat features. Both companies maintain stables of research attorneys standing by 24-hours a day, 7 days a week, waiting to take your research call or respond to your online chat. Use them as they can try a vari-ety of searches – on their dime – and then walk you through a productive search. Law firm librarians call this research technique "fishing for free."

---

**Research Tip #2.6**
Fish for Free!
Use the LEXISNEXIS and WESTLAW toll free phone numbers or
their Instant Message services
to get the research attorneys to run searches for you and
to help devise a successful research strategy.

---

If you do not have access to LexisNexis and Westlaw training sessions but have an account, there are numerous tutorials on each vendor's website,[82] and each company produces tons of literature showing how to use their products. Find out who your LexisNexis and Westlaw representative are and ask for their help.

### 2.3.1. LexisNexis and Westlaw are not the only online games in town

Courts are increasingly publishing their decisions on their own websites. For links to federal court websites see <www.uscourts.gov/courtlinks>.

And if you are a European lawyer or law student who would like to get a free taste of American decisional law jurisprudence, a brilliant student from the Stanford Advanced Legal Research class makes this suggestion:[83]

> "… [C]ertain judges' opinions have more precedential value, or clearer statements of the law, than others. The classic example here is Judge Posner [a judge on the Seventh Circuit Court of Appeals in Chicago since 1981] who writes clearly and is well-respected throughout the entire judicial system. A case-on-point from him might be more persuasive than one by another jurist. If you are looking … for a well-established point of law, consider searching Project Posner, which is a database of all of Judge Posner's opinions. Posner's writing is clear and persuasive and he has been a judge for a long time, so he has considered many different issues. Project Posner is at <www.projectposner.org>"

---

[82]      <www.lawschool.Westlaw.com>                    and <www.LexisNexis.com/lawschool/learning/tutorials>.

[83] Thomas Nosewicz, Case Research Pathfinder, available on the Stanford Law School Advanced Legal Research wiki, <sliki.jot.com> (Anyone who requests free access may be invited).

Various aggregator databases are pulling the cases from court websites and creating easily searchable databases of judicial opinions. One of our favorites is Justia.com. This resource is rapidly developing as a leading source for free docket information (federal court filing records), in addition to court decisions, regulations and law blogs.

Justia's mission is to make legal information and resources free and easy to find online, and law librarians applaud such efforts. Legal research has become big business in the United States and we librarians take some blame for ceding so much of the legal landscape to commercial enterprises.

Justia aggregates government cases, codes and regulations, as well as community generated content such as blogs, and provides them in easy to use databases that are freely accessible to all.

Individual Justia projects include the following:

- US Federal District Court Opinions and Orders - database and the full text of district courts' opinions and orders since 2004. Researchers can do a full text search of the opinions, or browse decisions by state, court, type of lawsuit and judge. Researchers can also subscribe to RSS feeds of new cases in particular categories, courts or judges. The database is updated daily.
- US Supreme Cases - database of all US Supreme Court Decisions since the 1790s with links to secondary sources including legal blogs and online databases such as Google Book Search. For cases recent cases there is access to mp3 audio of most Supreme Court oral arguments from Oyez.org.
- US Federal Case Filings - database provides US District Courts' civil case filings. Researchers can Search new cases by state, court, lawsuit type (eg patent law) or party name. Researchers can also subscribe to RSS feeds of search results to receive updates of new cases. Includes opinions and orders where available.
- US Regulation Tracker - database of the federal register, allowing you to track new regulations of specific federal agencies and subscribe to RSS feeds for daily updates.
- Blawg Search - searchable database of blog posts of over two thousand law blogs published by law professors, lawyers, judges, legal researchers and librarians or search legal podcasts or browse the law blog directory. Updated multiple times a day.

For some federal district court cases Justia is now downloading all of the Electronic Court Filing (ECF) filings by the parties (a pre-alpha version can be viewed at http://news.justia.com or http://news.justia.com/cases/).

Mary Minow, a lawyer and librarian who maintains the LibraryLaw Blog, has been focusing on cases involving libraries (<http://news.justia.com/cases/library>), and Justia includes all of the Google cases (<http://news.justia.com/cases/google>).

## 2.4. Shepardizing

"Shepardizing" is such an important step in the American law research process that it deserves its own section in the book.

> "Shepardizing" traces back to a set of books started by Frank Shepard in 1873. Mr. Shepard's books became known as Shepard's citators. Not many people live to see their last name turned into a verb but because of Frank Shepard, untold numbers of law students and young lawyers have to told to "Shepardize their cases."

Shepard's Citations is a citator, one of two such tools. The other one is called KeyCite.

What a citator does – both Shepard's and KeyCite – is basically two things:

- One, it tells you the particular history of the case being checked. It answers that critically important question, "is this case still good law."
- Two, it gives you a list, with treatment analysis, of all the subsequent cases which have cited your case.

Citators serve another, lesser, function in listing other research resources, such as secondary sources that cited your case, but usually researchers have found those sources before they turn to their Shepardizing (here we are using Shepardizing in a generic sense, to mean citation analysis accomplished with either Shepard's or KeyCite) task.

LexisNexis and Westlaw both use colorful icons to help the researcher see what treatment their cases have received.

Some opinions are stronger precedents than others. It is not just that judges cite earlier opinions, but the way that they cite these earlier opinions can say a lot about what the later judges think about the earlier opinions.

Sometimes the later judge will like the earlier opinion a lot and wants to add to its importance, to strengthen it. The way he or she does this is by following the case, and Shepard's will make a note – using the letter "f" for followed – in its print volumes.

Sometimes the later judge will not like the earlier opinion at all but does not want to overrule the earlier decision. So the later judge might distinguish his or her case from the earlier one, as a "polite" way of eroding or weakening the earlier court's holding; this is noted by Shepard's with the letter "d" in the print volumes. Or the later judge might not be so polite and expressly criticize the earlier opinion, again without actually striking it down. Or the later judge might like the holding from the earlier court but see a need to explain it better. All of these subsequent actions and others – criticized, distinguished, explained, followed, harmonized, limited, overruled, reversed, questioned – are duly noted by Shepard's.

There is a table of abbreviations in the front of every Shepard's volume which spells out all of the abbreviations used in the set. And this is a very common characteristic with law books: They will often rely heavily upon abbreviations and present the user with a table of abbreviations, usually in the front of the book.

Detailed instructions are found in the front of the print volumes of any Shepard's set. Listed below as Table 22 are the instructions found in the front of Shepard's California Reports.

> The following example shows how citations appear in Shepard's California Citations, Case Edition, as well as how various notations are used to reflect Shepard's legal analysis. These examples should be studied in conjunction with the Preface (pages viii through xi) and the Citing Sources information (pages vi and vii).

> To Shepardize® a decision in Shepard's California Citations, Case Edition, use the Table of Contents (page v) to find the division that corresponds to the reporter in which the decision or ruling was published; then, refer to the volume and page (or paragraph) number of the decision or ruling to find citations to that authority. To create all such citations, be sure to consult all bound volumes and the current soft-covered supplements to Shepard's California Citations, Case Edition.

> The citations in the examples are provided solely for illustrative purposes and should not be relied upon for research.

> The illustration on next page shows that the *Alvarez* case was reported in Volume 14 of the California Reports, Fourths Series at page 968. The case name, together with its date and parallel citations, gives you the information necessary to cite Alvarez correctly in ones brief or memorandum of points and authorities. By looking at all citing references to *Alvarez* one can:

> ▪ find out how *Alvarez* has been treated over time
> ▪ find cases which have discussed the same points of law as Alvarez
> ▪ Discover the strength and weaknesses of ones position and that of ones opposing counsel.

Following the history of the case, one will find citations preceded by editorial, or treatment letters. These letters indicate how subsequent cases have treated or interpreted *Alvarez*. In this example you can see that *Alvarez* was followed by the court in 56CA4th1249, with references to headnote 3. *Alvarez* was cited in the dissenting opinion of 18C4th690. It was also cited in the opinion found at 56CA4th1103. However, the "#" preceding this citation indicates that one should further research this citation before citing it as legal authority.

# ILLUSTRATION

## CITED CASE

### California Reports Fourth Series

| | |
|---|---|
| **Vol. 14** | Volume number in easy-to-find box |
| **–968–** | Page number in large bold print |
| California v | |
| Superior Court | |
| of Los Angeles | |
| County | Case name and date |
| (Alvarez) | |
| 1997 | |
| (60CaR2d93) | |
| (928P2d1171) | Cross references |
| De 03-12-1997 | Review Denied |
| #s 43CA4th616 | History showing Questionable precedent |
| #s 47CA4th1819 | |

### CITING CASES

| | |
|---|---|
| 17C4th162 | |
| j  18C4th690 | Citation from dissenting opinion |
| 56CA4th402 | |
| #  56CA4th1103 | Questionable precedent |
| f  56CA4th$^3$1249 | Citation showing significant treatment and head-note analysis |
| 57CA4th73 | |
| 57CA4th$^1$76 | Citing case showing headnote analysis |
| f  57CA4th626 | Citation showing significant treatment |
| 58CA4th$^1$251 | |
| 59CA4th$^6$838 | |
| #  60CA4th1411 | |
| 7CalL(7)30 | Citation from law review |

*Table 22: How to Use Shepard's California Citations*

Few American lawyers or law students use Shepard's in print anymore, however. The Shepardizing process is so important and the lawyer's time so expensive, that it is usually cost-effective to Shepardize online. Using Shepard's in print requires consulting multiple volumes and there is always a time delay. Online offers ease and currency, and researchers do not have to know what the treatment abbreviations stand for – it is all explained in full online.

In their online systems, both LexisNexis and Westlaw use color-coded icons to alert the researcher to the nature of the subsequent treatment.

---

The final step in doing legal research is updating the law. However, in practice one will often find it best to update as one proceeds through the phases of finding the law and reading the law. The legal research must include careful attention to updating the legal authorities that govern the problem. This include the use of:
- Citators (Shepard's and/or KeyCite)
- Pocket parts and supplements
- Looseleaf reporter services
- - Computerized searches

### Shepardizing/KeyCiting (cases, statutes and regulations)

Makes it possible for legal researchers to ascertain a known authority's history and current status.
To "Shepardize" means to determine the subsequent history of a case, that is, has a case been overruled, modified, followed, criticized, distinguished, etc. In the early 1870's Frank Shepard, devised a method for extracting this information and indexing it. Today, the system is owned by LexisNexis. KeyCite© is Westlaw's equivalent to determine whether a case, statute or regulation is good law and to retrieve citing references.

The two companies' citator-systems are described below.

Citators do not inform whether a court decision has been appealed or a statute made the subject of a proposed amendment, as the deciding factor for the sytems is whether a court has changed a previous opinion or a legislature has passed a bill changing a previous statute. Thus, the systems do not indicate whether a change might be *in process*.

If a scholar has access to Westcheck or LexisNexis' CheckCite,[84] these features should be used to check citations in a dissertation before delivering the final version of the paper.

---

[84] These are features offered by Westlaw and LexisNexis to check citations in a Word document, and the check will generate a report send from Westlaw/LexisNexis on incorrect or incomplete citations. CheckCite (1) collects the citation from a document,

## Signals in LexisNexis (Flag and Citation)

In Shepard's pay special attention to the following indications:

For CASE LAW:

Red hexagon (traffic "stop" sign) – warns that the case has been negatively affected by later action. Check its citations carefully for strong negative history or treatment.
- O – overruled – the citing case expressly overrules or disapproves all or part of the case being Shepardized.
- Q – Questioned – the citing opinion questions the continuing validity or precedential value of the case being Shepardized because of intervening circumstances, including judicial or legislative overruling.

Yellow triangle – warns that the case may have lost some of its value as precedent. Check its citations for potentially cautionary history or treatment.
- C – criticized – the citing opinion disagrees with the reasoning/result of the case being Shepardized, although the citing court may not have authority to materially affect its precedential value.
- D – distinguished – the citing case differs from the case being Shepardized, either involving dissimilar facts or requiring a different application of law
- L – limited – the citing opinion restricts the application of the case being Shepardized, finding that its reasoning applies only in specific, limited circumstances.

Blue circle - indicates that either citing references with analysis or citation information is available.
- E – explained – the citing opinion interprets or clarifies the case being Shepardized in a significant way.
- F – followed – the citing opinion relies on the case being Shepardized as controlling or persuasive authority.

History
- R – Same case reversed on appeal.

Treatment of case
- C –Soundness of decision or reasoning in cited case criticized for reason given.
- D- Case at bar different either in law or fact from case cited for reason given.
- E – Statement of import of decision in cited Case. Not merely a restatement of the facts.
- H – Apparent inconsistency explained and shown not to exist.

(2) verifies citations through the Shepard's Citations Service, (3) generates a summary report that tags problem cites for immediate attention, (4) checks quotations that occurred in the document – character for character – and reporting even punctuation differences.

- O – Ruling in cited case expressly overruled.
- Q – Soundness of decision or reasoning in cited case questioned.

For STATUTES:

- C – constitutional – the citing case upholds the constitutionality of the statute, rule or regulation being Shepardized.
- F – followed – the citing opinion expressly relies on the statute, rule or regulation being Shepardizing as controlling authority.
- Rt – retrospective – the citing opinion discusses retrospective or prospective application of the statute, rule or regulation being Shepardized.
- U  - unconstitutional – the citing case declares unconstitutional the statute, rule or regulation being Shepardized.
- V  - void/invalid – the citing case declares void or invalid the statute, rule or regulation being Shepardized because it conflicts with an authority that takes priority.
- Va – valid – the citing case upholds the validity of the statute, rule or regulation being Shepardized.

## Signals in Westlaw (Flag and Citation)

KeyCite uses the following signals for CASES:

Red flag – warns that a case is no longer good law for at least one of the points it contains.

Yellow flag – warns that the case has some negative history, but has not been reversed or overruled.

Blue H - indicates that the case has some history.
- Direct History – traces the same case through the appellate process and includes both prior and subsequent history. Note, it does not contain information on whether a previous decision is under re-consideration/has been appealed.
- Negative Indirect History – lists cases outside the direct appellate line that may have a negative impact on the precedential value of the case in question.
- Related References – lists cases that involve the same parties and facts as the case in question, whether or not the legal issues are the same.

Green C – indicates that the case has citing references but no direct or negative indirect history. The number of stars tells the depth the case has been examined by other cases).
- **** Examined - extended discussion of the cited case, usually more than a printed page of text.
- *** Discussed - substantial discussion of the cited case, usually more than a paragraph but less than a printed page.
- ** Cited - some discussion of the cited case, usually less than a paragraph.
- Mentioned - brief reference to the sited case, usually in a string citation.

KeyCite uses the following signals for STATUTES:

Red flag –indicates that a section of a statute has been amended or repealed by a recent session law.

Yellow flag –indicates that pending legislation is available for a section (sections merely "referenced," that is, mentioned, in pending legislation are not marked with a yellow flag) or that the section was limited on constitutional or preemption grounds or its validity was

otherwise placed in the following categories:
- Updating Documents – lists citation to recent session laws that have amended or re-pealed the section.
- Pending Legislation – lists citations to pending bills that reference a federal statute.
- Credits – lists in chronological order citations to session laws that have enacted, amended ore renumbered the section.
- Historical and Statutory Notes – describe the legislative changes affecting the sec-tion.

Green C – gives a list of documents that cite the statute. The documents are listed in the following order:
- Pending legislation
- Cases from United States Code Annotated and state statute notes of decisions
- Additional cases on Westlaw that do not appear in notes of decisions
- Administrative materials
- Secondary sources

*Table 23: Updating the Law*

LexisNexis and Westlaw have added impressive additional features to basic Shepardizing, and both Shepard's in LexisNexis and KeyCite in Westlaw can be used to find additional authority. Lawyers in the Untied States are always looking for legal authority to buttress their arguments. Both Shepard's online and KeyCite offer "depth of treatment" and analysis features that enable the researcher to cull through thousands of citing decisions and find the ones that best fit the arguments being made.

In LexisNexis the "FOCUS – Restrict By" link enables the researcher to add custom restrictions, such as jurisdiction or depth of treatment, add head-notes or additional terms, and limit the research in a variety of manners.

In Westlaw, the researcher can similarly manipulate the KeyCite results by clicking on the "Limit KeyCite History Display" arrow at the bottom of the screen.

But neither Shepard's nor KeyCite is self-starting. One must bring a cita-tion to the citator to begin the Shepardizing process and find subsequent ma-terials.

We have discussed using Shepard's and/or KeyCite to check whether or not found cases are "still good law." But citators are used for all of the laws discussed in this chapter. The careful researcher will always run their statute and regulation citations through citators. Statutes and regulations, in addition to cases, can – and should – be "Shepardized."

Shepardizing a statute can produce a longer case list than the cases found in the annotated code. The code editors will be selective in deciding what cases to include within the case annotations, whereas the citators pull them all in – if a case cites a code section, regardless of how or why, Shepard's and KeyCite will list the case citation. If the research aim is to leave no stone unturned – and often in United States legal research it is – then the diligent researcher will check all of his or her important statutes and regulations for case citations using Shepard's and/or KeyCite. It is the practice in some American law firms that important primary sources be checked for current validity in both Shepard's and KeyCite.

## 2.5. When to Stop Researching

In all of the legal research classes at Stanford, students frequently ask the question: How do I know when to stop researching? There is no easy answer to this question as research, in theory, could be never-ending – one case always leads to another.

Sometimes it becomes a practical matter. The attorney may allot a research budget, and the researcher simply stops when this budget is used up – usually measured in time increments. For example, an attorney may say to the researcher, "do not spend more than 5 hours on this assignment." So the researcher stops when the five hours have elapsed. It can be as simple as that. When given a small research budget – such as five hours – it is important to check for valuable resources, such as American Law Reports annotations, since these are comprehensive for the subjects addressed. The researcher should not waste his time – and his client's money – by beginning the research trolling through expensive case law databases.[85] He or she should turn to a secondary source first.

If the researcher is not constrained by a research budget, then the process of "looping" will begin to give the researcher some confidence to stop researching. He or she will keep coming upon the same leading cases, the same statutory language, the same cited regulations. Once the researcher sees the same key references over and over again, and gets the sense that these are the controlling laws, the time may have come to stop.

Of course, tomorrow a new case could come along and completely change

---

[85] LexisNexis and Westlaw can be frightfully expensive. For example, as of March 2006, using Westlaw's Per Minute Charges plan one minute in the ALLCASES database cost $ 16.63. If the Westlaw contract was for Transactional Charges instead, each pressing of "Enter" would have racked up a charge of $ 159.00. Careless searching can results in thousands of dollars of charges.

an earlier and replied-upon holding. For this reason both LexisNexis and Westlaw allow the diligent researcher to set up automated Shepard's and KeyCite searches with the latest developments sent directly to the researcher's e-mail address or hand held device, such as a Palm or Blackberry. The attorney could be walking up the courthouse steps to try a case when his hand-held will light up with an important new precedent to consider.

## 2.6. Hybrid Legal Research is Most Effective

This chapter discussed both books (for example, treatises and print codes) and online databases (for example, LexisNexis and Westlaw). The most effective research adopts a strategy of using both books and the computer. Knowing when to use books, rather than an immediate online search, is a bit of an art, rather than a science. But generally speaking, treatises are easier to use in print, especially when using a particular title for the first time, than they are online (if they are online), and this is largely due to the fact that they have detailed indexes.

Codes are also more useful when used in print, since it is so much easier to see the code sections in their organizational context.

However, earlier in this chapter it was pointed out that it is nearly impossible for any scholar to do proper research on United States legal material without the use of computer-assisted legal research (CALR) databases, such as the ubiquitous LexisNexis and Westlaw research systems. This remains very much the case as law students, lawyers and judges all turn to these databases for the bulk of their research needs. As one law firm librarian points out, "These are tools that lawyers need every day to get their job done."[86]

According to a survey of the 200 largest law firms in the United States, conducted by Law Firm Inc., law firm libraries spent an average of US$ 1,234,631 for LexisNexis searching in 2006, up from US$ 999,825 and an average of US$ 1,681,399 for Westlaw searching, up from US$ 1,494,588.[87]

---

[86] Comment by Trish Webster, library manager for the Detroit, Michigan law firm of Honigman Miller Schwartz and Cohn, reported in Alan Cohen, *Sleuth in the Stacks*, CALIFORNIA LEGAL PRO (Fall 2007), p. 4, 5.

[87] *Idem* at 5.

No legal research text – not this one or any other – can adequately teach how to use LexisNexis or Westlaw. These databases contain vast amounts of legal materials and offer search engines more sophisticated than anything out there. No amount of Google searching can yield legal materials with the depth and precision offered by LexisNexis or Westlaw. Both LexisNexis and Westlaw enable conceptual searching. Both LexisNexis and Westlaw developed powerful search engines over twenty-five years ago, well before the World Wide Web, and each company has devoted millions of dollars since to continually improve the searching capabilities.

LexisNexis and Westlaw maintain heavy marketing presences at American law schools. Law school representatives, all with law degrees, teach a variety of free classes on online legal research, both in group settings and individual sessions. The best way – the only way, really – to learn how to use LexisNexis and Westlaw successfully is to take advantage of this hands-on training. European law students or lawyers who visit law schools in the United States should seek out the librarian and make enquiries about LexisNexis and Westlaw training opportunities. It is an opportunity not to be missed.

---

**Research Tip #2.7**
Seek Out Opportunities to
get hands-on training
with LexisNexis & Westlaw.

---

## 2.7. Conclusion

The government of the United States can be thought of as a three-ring circus: the Executive, Legislative, and Judicial branches are the three rings of government. And like at the circus, there is a show going on all of the time in all three rings.

These three rings extend to both the state level as well. So, in a sense, there are at least fifty-one circus shows going on all of the time in the United States.

But unlike fifty-one separate circuses, there is constant interaction between the different branches of government in the law-making and review Big Tent.

For example, on September 12, 2007, a federal judge (Federal Judicial Branch) in the state of Vermont ruled that the states (via their Executive Branch agencies) have the legal right to regulate greenhouse gas emissions from automobiles.[88] The decision was a review of regulations written by California and then adopted verbatim by eleven other states (state laws are often models for other states). The 244 page written opinion is called *Green Mountain Chrysler-Plymouth-Dodge et al v. Crombie et al.* There are actually multiple plaintiffs and defendants involved with this litigation and one of the plaintiffs, who lost the case, The Alliance of Automobile Manufacturers, reported that it is "considering the options, including an appeal."[89] The deadline for such an action was November 13, 2007, which was after this book went to press. Researchers who want to know what has happened need to just call up the case in LexisNexis or Westlaw and click on the "Shepardize" or KeyCite button.

---

[88] *Green Mountain Chrysler Plymouth Dodge Jeep v. Crombie*, --- F. Supp. ---, 2007 WL 2669444 (D.Vt, September 12, 2007)(No. 2:05-CV-302, 2:05-CV-304).

[89] Healey, James R., *Judge Says States Can Regulate Emissions*, USA TODAY (September 13, 2007), p. 1B.

CHAPTER 3

# Methods in Europe - A Civil Law Method

## 3.1. Civil Law Basics for Americans

This chapter and the following can from the perspective of an American reader be taken as an example of how a lecturebook/textbook is written per currently prevailing European culture.

Furthermore, this chapter has - because of pagelimitations (printingcosts) - to be somewhat general in style and content, as the only other alterative would be to provide a chapter for each of the 47 countries in Continental Europe.

The chapter provides necessary basic skills to enable the study of the law of a civil law country – that is, in its own environment.

Keep in mind the information on differences given in Chapter One.

Also, see Addendum in the back of the book on the necessary requirements for being able to study a foreign country's law.

For a person who is brought up with and taught Common Law, studying the law of a Civil Law country is somewhat like coming to a whole new world.

---

**Research Tip #3.1**

An American lawyer studying the law of a country on the European continent has to disregard nearly everything he or she has been taught on Common Law and focus on trying to feel at home on a completely different planet.

---

It is not wholly fallacious to explain law in Civil Law countries by saying that the legislator enacts a statute, scholars discover its meaning, and judges, assisted by their conclusions, give the statute a precise application through their decisions. A Civil Law lawyer ("jurist") will consult works of scholars if these faithfully describe the rule in a statute, and decisions of judges, because these are instances in which this rule has been enforced.[1] However, it is very important to notice that courts in continental Europe do not (really – see on exceptions, further in section 3.3.3.2 and 3.3.4.2.) "make" law.[2]

Civil Law is today the dominant legal tradition in most of Europe,[3] all of Central and South America, many parts of Asia and Africa, and even a few enclaves in the Common Law world (that is, the American State of Louisiana and Territory of Puerto Rico, the Canadian Province of Quebec, and Scotland[4]).

---

**Research Tip #3.2**

English words and terms are often used with different meanings in continental Europe as opposed to in the U.S.[5]

---

The following subsections (3.1.1. – 3.1.9.) will try to give the American lawyer an idea of the mindset of a European continental lawyer and a little about the basic legal learning of such an individual.

---

[1] Rodolfo Sacco, *Legal Formants, A Dynamic Approach to Comparative Law* (Installment I of II), 39 AM. J. COMP. L. 1, 21-22, 24 (1991) [hereinafter SACCO I].

[2] However, even in America, at least one famous U.S. Supreme Court Justice, Felix Frankfurter has claimed that in reality the U.S. Supreme Court no longer makes Common Law, as virtually all cases since 1947 have rested on statutory grounds. Felix Frankfurter, *Some Reflections on Reading of Statutes*, 47 COLUM. L. REV. 527 (May 1947).

[3] Except England, Wales & Northern Ireland (which have a form of Common Law distinctive from U.S. Common Law), but including Ireland and Scotland

[4] Scottish law is a hybrid of Civil (Romanistic Legal Family) Law and Common Law elements.

[5] A project for a Dictionary with Civil Law Glossary and Common Law Glossary can be found at <http://civillawdictionary.pbwiki.com>. Also, the Internet Public Library has posted translation-dictionaries that, given a word in one language, will show the identical or related word in another language. See <http://www.ipl.org/div/subject/browse/ref28.80.00>.

The rest of the chapter seeks to explain how a Civil Law[6] lawyer does legal research and to go over the methods he or she uses.[7]

---

**Research Tip #3.3**
Beware that legal research approaches in Civil Law vary by country and by topic, and no single procedure will work for all purposes.

---

### 3.1.1. Introduction

An American doing research on the law of a Civil Law country must be aware of the major differences between the Civil and Common Law systems, and the effect of these differences on how legal problems are viewed and how research is conducted. See Table 1: Comparison between Common Law and Civil Law thinking, above in Chapter 1.

Any sophisticated comparative[8] lawyer in both the Civil Law and Common Law systems has long ago abandoned discussions of relative superiority or inferiority of the two.[9]

A rule of law may be worked out either by developing the consequences that it involves (American scholars' preference), or by developing the wider principles that it presupposes (the Civil Law scholars' preference).[10]

The American scholar will be astonished by the lack of footnotes/endnotes

---

[6] The term "civil law" refers to the Roman law based tradition of continental Europe, from where it has spread to all parts of the globe. Herbert Hausmaninger, THE AUSTRIAN LEGAL SYSTEM 299 (Vienna: Manzsche Verlags- und Universitätsbuchhandlung) [hereinafter HAUSMANINGER].

[7] "Legal method" is the line of action the courts and any other, who have to decide a legal question must use. Jens Evald, RETSKILDERNE OG DEN JURIDISKE METODE 129 [Source of Law and the Legal Method] (2nd. ed.) (Copenhagen: DJØF Publishing, 2000).

[8] Modern comparative law is a critical method of legal science ... a discipline where a detailed method cannot be laid down in advance, K. Zweigert & H.Kötz, INTRODUCTION TO COMPARATIVE LAW 33, 251 (3rd ed.)(Tony Weir trans., Clarendon Press, Oxford 1998) [hereinafter ZWEIGERT]. See further below Chapter 7.

[9] John Henry Merryman, THE CIVIL LAW TRADITION: AN INTRODUCTION TO THE LEGAL SYSTEMS OF WESTERN EUROPE AND LATIN AMERICA 3 (2nd ed.) (Stanford, California: Stanford University Press, 1985) [hereinafter MERRYMAN].

[10] MERRYMAN *supra* note 9 at 67 quoting German legal scientist Rudolph Sohm.

and citations (and lack of exact page or "pinpoint cite" references)[11] in European scholars' work on the scholarship of others and on court decisions. In Europe, many regard large amounts of footnotes as a plague. As a result, there will often only be a bibliography in the back of the continental European book or article, without page references – and there will hardly ever be a case list. As for court decisions, references will only be made in footnotes, without specific-page citations (and frequently lacking mention of the names of the parties – with only the case reporter, year and first page given).

To the lawyer from a Common Law country, Civil Law is quite strange. It has different legal institutions, procedures, and traditions, and has little interest in precedents and types of cases. The continental lawyer thinks systematically, or in the abstract, and finds – as an absolute necessity, in any functioning legal system – need for a civil act or code, a commercial act or code, a act or code of civil procedure, and an integrated structure of legal concepts rationally ordered.

Thorough research on a foreign[12] law issue can only be undertaken in the language of the jurisdiction. In researching the law of Civil Law countries, lawyers limited to English-language[13] material will be seriously handicapped.[14] However, the increasing availability of "secondary" sources in

---

[11] In the U.S., "the scholarly backbone of any law review article are the footnotes." Dana Neacşu, *Google, Legal Citations, and Electronic Fickleness: Legal Scholarship in the Digital Environment* at 1 (Social Science Research Network, June 2007). Available at SSRN: <http://ssrn.com/abstract=991190>.

[12] "Foreign law" here means the domestic law of another national jurisdiction.

[13] It is extremely costly to make authorized translations. The European Commission's Directorate-General for Translation (DGT) is the largest translation service in the world. Located in Brussels and Luxembourg, it has a permanent staff of some 1 750 linguists and 600 support staff. The DGT works only for the Directorates-General and Services of the Commission as each EU institution has its own translation service. See Translation tools and workflow <http://ec.europa.eu/dgs/translation/bookshelf/tools_and_workflow_en.pdf>. See also E.U. Directorate General for Interpretation (DG Interpretation (formerly known as SCIC) <http://scic.cec.eu.int/europa/jcms/j_8/home>.

[14] American law students are frequently, surprised by the lack of foreign primary sources published in English. They need to learn that English is for most of the world not the first language – and thus not the official language used for publication. Thus, American students have – as students of the rest of the world – to learn foreign languages.

English, as well as sometimes unofficial translations of parts from information from the country or countries in question, allows quite effective preliminary study of many foreign legal issues. Such study may help the American lawyer to determine the general nature of a problem, and can facilitate communication with any foreign law specialist who may be called upon to assist. Nevertheless, any serious legal problem involving another jurisdiction will require consultation with a lawyer trained (and licensed) in that jurisdiction. This in turn implies that in training future lawyers, each law school (whether in the United States or Europe) should strive to include in its faculty diverse scholars brought up in different legal systems from that of the country of the law school.[15]

During the 17th and 18th centuries, so-called "enlightened periods" in Europe, many continental countries undertook comprehensive and systematic reorganizations of their laws. The resulting legal codifications were "drafted primarily not by legal elites, such as academic scholars or judges, but by philosophically and politically educated representatives of the administration."[16]

Today in Europe – and in the E.U. – nearly all suggestions for amendments of existing legislation or creation of new acts are drafted by government administrators, not by commissions of scholars and other legal experts. However, the latter often will provide white papers[17] with recommendations, but even here usually only after having been appointed by a minister of the

---

[15] It is not just the law courses that are changing. It is also the faculty, *ABA Journal*, July 2007, page 64.

[16] Ralf Michaels & Nils Jansen, *Private Law and the State: Comparative Perceptions and Historical Observations*, in Rabels Zeitschrift Für Ausländisches Und Internationales Privatrecht, vol. 71, no. 2, 2007 p. 32. [hereinafter MICHAELS-I] However, only to the extent that the particular country belongs to the Germanic Legal Family (see discussion in Chapter 6 below) will Roman law have played an important role, otherwise *idem* at 33. In contrast to European codifications, the American Restatements were initiated as a non-state, professional enterprise and have remained as such.

[17] A white paper is used in many countries and is an official report setting out government policy on an issue to be voted on by the country's parliament. Compare this with "green paper," which is also an "official," heavily researched report on a topic, or a government document that proposes and invites discussion on approaches to a problem (and may lead to issuance of a white paper).

particular portfolio and having been given a task-list. Overall, most legislative bills in Europe nowadays come from government proposals, although they can still also come from members of parliament and parliamentary committees.

In continental Europe, law and its enforcement are strictly separated. Accordingly, European lawyers can focus on the law regardless of its enforcement. In contrast, in the Common Law tradition, the conflation of the law of rights and the law of remedies adds enforcement as a necessary element.[18]

Americans talk about government (separate from society), whereas Europeans talk about "the state." In Europe, the debate does not deal with a distinction between public and private spheres and its impact on law, but with the distinction between private and public law.[19]

---

**Research Tip #3.4**

A characteristic of Civil Law is that (a) public law and (b) private law are treated as inherently different and clearly distinguishable.[20] Furthermore, the term "private law" has a different meaning in European and in American law[21] in general, and the place of private law within each differs.

---

Thus, The Anglo-American lawyer should be aware of the continental European division between private law in the narrow sense and commercial law, which the Romanistic and Germanic legal families (except Switzerland and Italy) still recognize by having different codes.[22] The areas in European

---

[18] Ralf Michaels & Nils Jansen, *Private Law Beyond the State? Europeanization, Globalization, Privatization*, 54 AM. J. COMP. L. 843, 853 (Fall 2006) [hereinafter MICHAELS-II].

[19] In the United States, the public/private distinction is an illusion, *idem* 853, 857, 858. In Europe, private law is that part of a legal system that deals with the relationships between natural and artificial persons (that is, individuals, business entities, non-profit organizations). It is to be distinguished from public law, which deals with relationships between natural and artificial persons and the state as the other party.

[20] MERRYMAN *supra* note 9 at 63.

[21] In the U.S.: The body of law that concerns individual people and their property and relationships. See BLACK'S LAW DICTIONARY (8th ed.) (St. Paul: West. 2004).

[22] Grossly simplified, in Germany, the core of the law is private and the rest is contingent politics; in the U.S., the core of the law is public (regulatory) law and the rest is con-

private law are:

- Civil law[23]
- The law of obligations, including Contract law
- Tort law
- Property law
- Family law family-related issues and domestic relations including, but not limited to marriage, civil unions, divorce, spousal abuse, child custody and visitation, property, alimony, and child support awards, as well as child abuse issues, and adoption.
- Succession law
- Labor law
- Commercial law
- Corporations law
- Competition law[24] (including U.S. antitrust law)

Public law in Civil Law has two components: constitutional law (the law by which the governmental structure is made up) and administrative law (the law governing the public administration and its relations with private individuals).

In private relations, public and private parties are equal. In public legal relations, the state is a party and superior to the private individual.

The Civil Law legal technique is directed primarily to interpreting statutory texts or analyzing concrete problems so as to "fit them into the system" conceptually.[25] Instead of searching for precedents in factually similar judicial decisions, a Civil Law lawyer looks first to the abstract provisions of the code for a logical and appropriate legal principle. Among the very helpful sources are extensive article-by-article commentaries on each phrase, paragraph or article of an act or code. These are mostly written by the civil servants of the government ministry that introduced the bill, a judge with spe-

---

tingent private ordering, MICHAELS-II *supra* note 18, at 843, 852, 847-851 and footnote 9.

[23] The area of law in Civil Law countries governing relations between private individuals.

[24] In Europe, competition law covers both what in the U.S. is called antitrust law and also the law on pricing and profits (from a pure social and public economic perspective). Competition law covers issues of monopoly and trade practices generally as well.

[25] ZWEIGERT *supra* note 8 at 181.

cialty in the code in question, or another highly regarded specialists.

Secondary sources – in the Civil Law sense - are the government minister's or secretary's commentaries to the bill when introduced in parliament and officially issued expert white papers upon which the bill was drafted.[26]

The next group in the hierarchy of "*law-foundation-source*" are court decisions, which determine whether the given facts allow the use of an article of a code or act and what result the use of the statute implies – thus determining the decision of the court. However, court decisions in Civil Law countries usually do not have any impact or lawmaking validity (no *stare decisis* effect).

In those countries having a Parliamentary Ombudsman,[27] statements from that independent official are of particular relevance in the area of administrative law.

In addition to the formal sources of the Civil Law, there is an overlay of concepts and principles - primarily derived from legal scholarship.

Although scholarly articles can provide the researcher some valuable input, they have far from the degree of impact on legislation and court decisions that articles in American law reviews from experts can have in the U.S. (as references in court decisions or as incentives for a legislative bills, etc.). This is so even though in Europe professors, judges and practitioners – not students – are the editors of law reviews/journals, of which there usually exist only one or two for the whole country.

It is a fundamental mistake to claim, as some American hornbooks on legal research do, that once one has identified the primary and secondary sources of European law that might be relevant the research proceeds much

---

[26] One commentator has asserted that the European teacher-scholar is the real protagonist of the Civil Law tradition, and that the Civil Law is a law of professors. MERRYMAN *supra* note 9 at 68 and footnote 46 below. However, drafts to bills are made by civil servants working in the ministry departments and the European Unions' Commission.

[27] An ombudsman (sometimes named "Parliamentary Commissioner") is an official (usually appointed by the government or by parliament), who is charged with representing the interests of the public by investigating and addressing complaints reported by individual citizens. Ombudsman exist in: Australia, Bulgaria, Croatia, Czech Republic, Cyprus, Denmark, Estonia, European Union, France, Finland, Greece, Iceland, India, Ireland, Israel, Italy, Macedonia, Netherlands, New Zealand, Norway, Philippines, Poland, Portugal, Sweden..

as it would for a problem of U.S. law.[28] This is because the distinction in the U.S. of "primary" and "secondary" sources is differently from the use in Civil Law (where a distinction rather follows by the terms "*hard*" and "*soft*" law, see further Chapter 3, sections 3.1.1.1. & 3.3. below). Case law has extreme little impact in Europe.

An American legal researcher should be extremely cautious about using what would typically be his or her normal method of relying primarily on what is stated on a statute's face, as Civil Law lawyers are brought up in a system where statutes have been enacted based on abstract thinking and thus require considering whether interpretations should be made.

Using and interpreting Civil Law codes may necessitate understanding their underlying philosophies. For instance, the Code Civile of France is based on revolutionary thinking and a desire for wholesale change from the past, whereas the German Code is based on a historical study of the past and a desire to codify previous "law."

The Civil Law legal scholar is more interested in developing and elaborating a theoretical "scientific" structure than he is in solving concrete problems. The work of "legal science" is carried on according to the methods of traditional formal logic. Intuition and the subconscious, despite their powerful influence on human affairs, are excluded from this process ("logically formal rationalism"[29]). Thus, insight, history,[30] and theories of the social sciences,

---

[28] J.D.S. Armstrong & Christopher A. Knott, WHERE THE LAW IS: AN INTRODUCTION TO ADVANCED LEGAL RESEARCH 211 (2nd ed.) (St. Paul: West, 2006).

[29] Max Weber, WIRTSCHAFT UND GESELLSCHAFT; GRUNDRISS DER VERSTEHENDEN SOZIOLOGIE. MIT EINEM ANHANG; DIE RATIONALEN UND SOZIOLOGISCHEN GRUNDLAGEN DER MUSIK (4 ed. ew hrsg. Aufl., besorgt von Johannes Winckelmann, Tübingen 1956); Guenther Roth & Claus Wittich, eds. Max Weber, ECONOMY AND SOCIETY: AN OUTLINE OF INTERPRETIVE SOCIOLOGY, (trans. Ephraim Fischoff [and others], New York: Bedminster Press, 1968). MERRYMAN *supra* note 9 at 64.

[30] A wealth of information about the history of Europe and its institutions since 1945 is available from European NAvigator (ENA) - an educational platform that focuses particularly on the development of a united Europe. ENA is available in English, French, German and Spanish, though some documents are available in other languages at <www.ena.lu>. Using the site is free, although the documents are protected by copyright. ENA is developed by the CVCE (Centre Virtuel de la Connaissance sur l'Europe - Virtual Resource Centre for Knowledge about Europe), a Luxembourg-based public

for example, are excluded as non-legal.[31] However, there is a growing trend away from this point of view.

In Europe today, Civil Law and Common Law show some signs of convergence. In the United Kingdom, statutory law increasingly overrides traditions of judicial law-making, while on the continent, legal theory increasingly acknowledges the fact and necessity of judicial precedent and law-making. Important areas of the law have also been unified under international treaties. British judges faithfully implement European Union law that is based primarily on Civil Law notions. The Court of Justice of the E.U. creatively applies principles from both legal worlds. Yet, despite refreshing input from the Common Law, the dominant legal culture of the European Union and the emerging *ius commune Europaeum*[32] remain very much in the Civil Law tradition.[33]

### 3.1.1.1. Some terms for the American Students/Scholar to keep in mind

This subsection gives only a broad overview of some terms that will be dealt with more in the following sections, but that the American should be "on guard for."

In Civil Law countries, law students do not undertake research "projects." Instead they perform "scientific" studies and research. Only scholars do legal research projects, and only after they have gained funding for specific projects. In Civil Law countries, students study at universities, not at law schools.

Courses on "legal research" in Europe are not about how and where to find "the law" physically or online. Broadly stated, the legal research courses in

---

undertaking that is actively supported by the Ministry of Culture, Higher Education and Research.

[31] MERRYMAN *supra* note 9 at 65.

[32] See Glossary in Appendix 1.

[33] HAUSMANINGER *supra* note 6 at 320.

Europe deal with the theoretical (scientific) question of "what is law (in the European sense)" and how to (correctly) interpret "the law." These are the courses taught by law professors and the issue of where physically to find the law is not taught. Providers such as Westlaw and LexisNexis do not offer courses for students outside the U.S. At many universities, only librarians and law professors have access to online databases; therefore, students are obliged to ask a librarian to find articles for them. Only, at a few universities outside the U.S. do students have access to Westlaw and/or LexisNexis – often with only single account-access for all students.

Thus, legal research in the American sense are left to the librarian by most Civil Law scholars, that is, the finding of books and articles on a special sub-ject. Once these are collected by the law/reference librarian, the law-yer/scholar in Europe will examine them and use the "scientific legal method" skills he/she was taught by the law professor while studying law at a Civil Law university.

The scientific legal method deals in broad terms with
- what is the law on a special issue,
- how the law-material is to be interpreted and
- which few court decisions are classified as precedent (and therefore to be considered important) – in the Civil Law sense — as opposed to all other (normal) court decisions that have no relevance for a Civil Law lawyer and the courts.

The Civil Law lawyer uses the term "sources of law" in two different ways. He/she uses the term as in the U.S. meaning,34 that is, something (such as a

---

[34] In the context of legal research, the term "sources of law" can refer to three different concepts which should be distinguished. (1) sources of law can refer to the origins of legal concepts and ideas; (2) sources of law can refer to governmental institutions that formulate legal rules; (3) sources of law can refer to the published manifestations of the law. The books, computer databases, microforms, optical disks, and other media that contain legal information are all sources of law. J. Myron Jacobstein & Roy M.

constitution, treaty, statute, or custom) that provides authority for legislation and for judicial decisions; a point of origin for law or legal analysis. It is also termed fons juris.35

However, he/she also employs the term in a way that it would be more proper to call "*source of law*" (without the plural "s"). By this is meant that the Civil Law lawyer uses the phrase as a scientific term, where he/she discusses what should be allowed to be a source of law. For example, should "Custom" or "Legal Cultural Tradition" be allowed to be a "source of law"? This is bound to be confusing for American readers. Accordingly, it would seem best to reformulate "source of law" to "*law-foundation-source*,"[36] which term will be used for the reminder of this chapter.

Civil Law is made by parliament, not by the "government," which latter term is used totally differently than in the U.S. The Civil Law term "legislation" refers only to acts by parliament and decrees/rules issued through delegation from such acts.

Only a few presidents in Civil Law countries have power to issue decrees, as under most Constitutions they are actually not part of the "government" (that is, they are not part of what is called the executive branch in the U.S.). The "government" or "cabinet" is not directly elected by the voters but is a group of people that has the support of the Parliament (or at least is not one voted out by a majority of the parliament members) – the "Parliamentarisme" principle.[37]

---

Mersky, FUNDAMENTALS OF LEGAL RESEARCH 1-2 (5th ed.) (Westbury, N.Y. : Foundation Press, 1990).

[35] BLACK'S LAW DICTIONARY (8th ed.) (St. Paul, Minnesota: West, 2004).

[36] The Danish term is "retskilde" and the course is termed "Retskildelære".

[37] On this, see further Appendix A in Addendum in the back of the book.

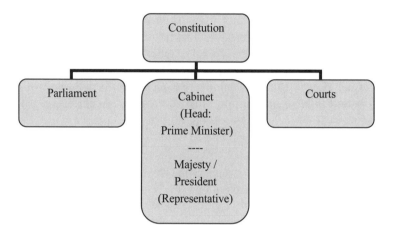

*Table 24: Division of power in most European Countries*

Civil Law lawyers do not talk about branches of law. Instead they talk about the  hierarchy of law based on the learning from the basic "legal research-course" on "*law-foundation-source.*"

Moving beyond the "*law-foundation-source,*" another term of special mean-ing in Europe is the "white paper." It is used in many countries and is an official report setting out government policy on an issue to be voted on by the country's parliament. Compare this with a "green paper," which also is an official report, but one that is usually heavily researched on a specific topic, or else a document that proposes and invites discussion on approaches to a problem (and that may lead in turn to issuance a white paper).

Another point to be emphasized is that Civil Law judges do not fill gaps in "the law" (In the U.S. making law). They are restricted only to filling gaps in a very limited number of areas, that is, to make "close" interpretations of statutory text, or in situations where a statute's text explicitly allows a court to fill in a defined "gap" in the statute or act.

A Civil Law lawyer does not use the term "*still* good law" (author emphasis). The *stare decisis* doctrine is not used. Shepardize (citatior) is a word and something a Civil Law lawyer never had heard about during his/her education. In Civil Law one talks about what is "good law", that is, which Acts are the newest and which are the newest cases that is regarded as having precedence. Thus, the Civil Law lawyer do not need to use the word "still" because he/she only is concerned about the "newest," since newest automatically has recalled for ever what was older ("lex posterior principle").

As for the terms as "section," "paragraph," "subsection" and "statute," these are often used as synonyms in Civil Law.

Finally, in Civil Law there is a distinction between "*hard*" (sometimes termed "binding") and "*soft*"[38] law. This distinction is sometimes characterized as between "primarily" and "secondary" sources of law; these terms will no doubt be confusing for American readers, as they have a totally different meaning under U.S. Common Law, in which case law is a "primarily source."

### 3.1.2. State sovereignty

The Member States of the European Union retain full sovereignty. The E.U. is not a true federation like the United States.[39] However, the European Court of Justice has in some decisions expressed another point of view, see below Chapter 3 section 3.3.4.2.

The E.U. does not have any "Constitution" The so-called "E.U. Constitu-

---

[38] The term "soft law" refers to quasi-legal instruments which do not have any legally binding force, or whose binding force is somewhat "weaker' than the binding force of traditional law. Also, it is associated with international law.

[39] On the so-called "proportionality principle" and "the subsidiary principle," see Chapter 4, section 4.1 below.

tion," which was rejected by some Member States' citizens in referendums, was nothing more than a compilation of previous E.U. treaties with some amendments. Therefore, in terms of public international law, the E.U. Constitution was a treaty between sovereign states.

### 3.1.3. The European Continental Court System

Overall, the European Civil Law counties' court systems consist of a three-tiered framework, in which the judiciary in overall does not make law, and where appeals only go upwards, that is, the U.S. practice of case remands (sent back to the lower court) is not an option.

Appeals courts in Civil Law countries are often allowed to consider the whole case before them *de novo*, finding the facts and accepting new evidence and arguments and pleadings.[40] The reason for allowing this practice during appeals is because a jury system is not used in civil cases in Europe (with extreme exceptions). In other words, in Europe only judges decide civil cases, whether in the first instance or appeal.

Civil Law on the European continent does not entertain the two parallel English court systems of "law" and "equity".[41]

Some states' constitutions in Europe create extra, special court(s), such as an Impeachment Court (to deal with removal of judges or governmental ministers) and/or a Constitutional Court (to deal with interpretation and other significant questions related to the Constitution,[42] including as well as

---

[40] In these instances, new evidence to support the parties' claims and allegations is often submitted by the parties, although entirely new claims and/or allegations require the consent of the other party or the court.

[41] In the United States, this distinction between law and equity remains important in: (a) categorizing and prioritizing rights to property; (b) determining whether the Seventh Amendment's guarantee of a jury trial applies (that is, the determination of a fact that is necessary for the resolution of a "law" claim) or whether the issue can only be decided by a judge (namely, issues of equity); and, (c) the principles that apply to the grant of equitable remedies by the courts. In Common Law legal systems, the law-equity distinction is crucial to understanding almost all important doctrinal areas of law.

[42] Sweden is an interesting case in that it has four Constitutional laws: the Constitution Act, the Act of Succession, the Freedom of the Press Act, and the Freedom of Speech Act,     Legal     order     –     Sweden

whether or not laws that are challenged are in fact constitutional[43]). Some European countries also have a special highest-level appeal court for administrative justice.[44]

Other states' constitutions allow their supreme courts[45] to decide whether statutes made by their parliaments are unconstitutional.[46] Some European supreme courts have the privilege to decide which cases should be allowed/ presented before them (thus allowing a second appeal). Other states have a special organ/committee to deal with questions of permission (or "leave").

As for national courts or tribunals of Member States of the E.U., which may be called upon to decide disputes involving E.U. law, they may, and sometimes must, submit questions to the E.U. Court of Justice for a preliminary ruling. The E.U. Court will then provide an interpretation, or review the legality, of a rule of European Community law. Thus, the E.U. Court of Justice works in conjunction with the national courts. But the latter, no matter the high level they may occupy in their own countries, merely apply E.U. law.

In European Civil Law countries, courts typically only employ a jury in the most serious criminal cases, e.g. in cases involving murder. The criminal bench usually consists of a full-time judge together with several lay citizens.

---

<http://ec.europa.eu/civiljustice/legal_order/legal_order_swe_en.htm>. See unofficial translations into English at <http://www.servat.unibe.ch/law/icl/sw__indx.html>.

[43] See Albania, Austria, Belgium, Bosnia and Herzegovina, Bulgaria, Croatia, Czech Republic, France, Germany, Greece, Hungary, Italy, Latvia, Lithuania, Republic of Macedonia, Poland, Portugal, Romania, Serbia, Slovakia, Slovenia, and Spain.

[44] France: the Conseil d'État; Finland: Korkein Hallinto-oikeus; Polen: Supreme Administrative Court of the Republic of Poland; Sweden: Högsta Förvaltningsdomstolen.

[45] In various European countries, the court of last resort is called the "Courts of Cassation" rather than the "Supreme Court" (and some of these courts do not deal with constitutional questions): Belgium: Hof van Cassatie (in Flemish) / Cour de cassation (in French); France: the Cour de cassation; Greece: the Areios Pagos; Italy: Corte Suprema di Cassazione; Romania: Înalta Curte de Casație și Justiție.

[46] Since the first Danish Constitution of 1849, the Danish Supreme Court has only once – in the so-called "Tvind Case" – declared a statute unconstitutional. See *Selvejende Institution Friskolen i Veddinge Bakker v. Undervisningsministeriet* [The private independent School in Veddinge Hills v. Danish Ministry of Education], UfR 1999.842 H (Danish Supreme Court, 19 February 1999; docket no. I 295/1998)(holding that §7 of Law no. 506 of 12 June 1996 is illegal as regards the appellant).

Juries are almost never used in civil lawsuits.[47]

Judges in Europe are full-time judge civil servants appointed (not elected) for life (until they reach a mandatory retirement age).[48] Normally, they can only be removed by some kind of an impeachment process.

Some European countries do not allow judges to write dissents. In some countries it is not permitted to indicate with panel decisions which judges were in the majority and which were in the dissent.

During litigation, the parties' attorneys correspond with and meet before a judge or judges in successive court sessions. These sessions normally conclude with a final meeting (sometimes over several days), where counsels present their clients' cases for the court, and where the parties, witnesses, and experts are heard during questioning from counsels and from the judge(s). Counsels finish their presentations by oral pleading and rebuttal.

Due to the dogma of "certainty" in any legal system, it is vital to understand the Civil Law judicial tradition, because the function of the judge within that tradition is to interpret and to apply "the law" as it is technically defined in his or her jurisdiction.[49] A judge under the Civil Law generally does not turn to books and articles by legal scholars or to prior judicial decisions for guidance. Separation of powers between the judicial and legislative branches preserves the latter is lawmaking monopoly. However, some European constitutions allow a judge to declare a statute unconstitutional. Even so, court decisions in Europe are in general not (a source of) law. The doctrine of *stare decisis* is not followed in Civil Law legal systems, although in practice judges are influenced to some extent by prior decisions. In general, a Civil Law judge is restricted to interpreting the article of a code without filling in any of a code's gaps.

---

[47] In the southern countries of Europe, in criminal cases, a judge will be used to lead the investigation; in northern Europe, in contrast, a special branch of the police will conduct the investigation and present the case before a court.

[48] Only in certain countries do judges come from a self-recruiting professional elite. MICHAEL-I *supra* note 16, at 35.

[49] MERRYMAN *supra* note 9 at 2. Even in American states, which probably have as much legislation in force as exists in Europe, a judge must follow the principle of legislation being superior to judicial decisions (that is, statutes supersede contrary judicial decisions (constitutional questions aside)). *Idem* at 26.

### 3.1.3.1. Where to find case decisions

In many Civil Law countries, there may be just only one official case reporter, and only a small number of judicial decisions are published. For the legal researcher, even these decisions can be of little value, because numerous European judicial opinions treat solely the legal issue(s) that the courts found necessary to decide the cases upon, and do not deal with all the issues presented. This circumstance is due in no small part to the fact that courts in Civil Law countries do not make law and that the doctrine of *stare decisis* is not observed.

Reporters will only be published in the official language, which is used in the courts.

Almost always, case law can only be found in hard copies published by the official publisher, which may or may not include, a yearly Table of Contents and/or an Index according to the subject matter of the cases. Some publishers make headnotes for each case. In the last couple of years, in some countries, published case decisions have also been made available online on a subscription basis.

American legal researchers ordinarily cannot find European court decisions in English and, in any event, only the state-authorized translator's documents can be relied upon.

Interestingly, for the American scholar, in Civil Law legal citators such as Shepard's and KeyCite – as well as Bluebook signals – are non-existing.

### 3.1.4. Legislation - Codes

Law - acts, codes,[50] and statutes (the terms in continental Europe are used casually and without any particular distinctions) - is made by national parliaments. As for Member States of the European Union, law may also be made by the European Parliament (see Chapter 4). It must be emphasized that no

---

[50] In the United States a code is a complete system of positive law, carefully arranged, edited and officially promulgated; a systematic collection or revision of laws, rules, and regulations (however a Civil Lawyer will soon realize that references to sections or paragraphs might not have been "corrected" as to which section the actual texts is found. For example 8 U.S.C.A. 101 is in fact become 1101).

European country has a "code" like the *United States Code*[51] that compiles and topically arranges all national statutes. Most of the Civil Law countries that have a code only compile statutes related to what in Civil Law is termed "private law." See above section 3.1.1. and below Table 24.

Statutes are divided into acts, ordinances and regulations. Acts are authored by parliament, ordinances/decrees/rules are authored by the government, and regulations are issued by the authorities/agencies.

It is normally stated in an act when it will come into force. However, it is sometimes the case, that entry into force is governed by a separate, so-called promulgation act, or the government is empowered by the act to determine the date of coming into force and this later takes place by means of a separate published decree in the official gazette/journal. In any case, it is a precondition/ requirement in many Civil Law countries that an act from parliament cannot take effect / go into force before the enforcement date has been published in the national gazette.

Again, the Anglo-American lawyers should remember the continental European division between private law in the narrow sense and commercial law, which the Romanistic and Germanic legal families – except Switzerland and Italy – still recognize by having different codes.

Rules governing a single transaction may be placed in widely separated parts of a Civil Law country's different acts or code, which are abstract in terminology / language, whereas the Anglo-American view is that all aspects of a unitary transaction should be dealt with in the same place in the system (usually defined as a "chapter" of the code).[52]

In Civil Law jurisdictions,[53] the codification[54] movement developed out of

---

[51] The Civil Code of the State of Louisiana (the only Civil Law state in the United States), follows the institutions system and is divided into five parts: Preliminary Title; Of Persons; Things and Different Modifications of Ownership; Of Different Modes of Acquiring the Ownership of Things; Conflict of Laws. See WEST'S LOUISIANA STATUTES ANNOTATED, Section 9 (St. Paul: West, 2000).

[52] ZWEIGERT *supra* note 8 at 145.

[53] Even though ancient Rome made compilations like the Corpus Iuris Civilis, much of the ancient Roman era laws were left mostly uncodified. Previously, Denmark had codes such as: The Law of Jutland of 1241 and King Christian V's Danish Code of 1683.

[54] Codification is the process of collecting, arranging, and systematizing and restating the law of a jurisdiction in certain areas, usually by subject.

the philosophy of the Enlightenment and began in earnest in several European countries during the late 18th century. However, it only gained significant momentum with the enactment of the French Napoleonic Code[55] in 1804. The tradition of having a civil code in the European Civil Law countries has been followed in Austria, Germany,[56] Italy, the Netherlands, Portugal, Spain, and Switzerland.[57]

Most Civil Law systems include separate codes or acts of civil procedure and criminal procedure, which should be distinguished from administrative procedure for administrative tribunals or boards of appeal and – where they exist – administrative courts.

In Europe (including the E.U.), it is not common to have an assembled, up-to-date compilation like the U.S. Code. New laws are published in the official journal or gazette in the order they are enacted – similar to the American collection in *Statutes at Large*.[58] To a certain extent, quasi-official, consolidated versions of specific acts will be made available but such versions are not always published in the official journal or gazette; nonetheless,

---

[55] Code Napoléon (originally called the Code Civile des Français, which entered into force on March 21, 1804), today known as *Code Civile*. .

[56] The Bürgerliches Gesetzbuch (or BGB) is the civil code of Germany. Its development began in 1881 and came into force on January 1, 1900. It is structured as follows: General (covering personal rights and legal personality); Obligations (including sales and contracts); Law of Real Rights (covering things and immovable and movable property); Family Law (domestic relations); Law of Inheritance (succession). The civil codes of Portugal and Switzerland are similar to Germany's.

[57] ZWEIGERT *supra* note 8 at 100-109. .

[58] See <http://thomas.loc.gov/> [press "Public Laws" link]. In the United States, acts of Congress are published (1) chronologically in the order in which they become law on an individual basis in official pamphlets called "slip laws;" and (2) are grouped together in official bound book form, also chronologically, as "session laws", that is, the United States *Statutes at Large* (*Stat.*). (3) Because each Congressional act may contain laws on a variety of topics, many acts, or portions thereof are also split up, rearranged and published in a topical, subject matter codification, that is, the United States Code. Generally, only "Public Laws" are codified. Even in code form, however, many statutes by their nature pertain to more than one topic. Further, portions of some Congressional acts, such as the provisions for the effective dates of amendments to codified laws, are themselves not codified at all, Tobias A. Dorsey, *Some Reflections on not Reading Statutes*, 10 GREEN BAG 2d 283, 288 (Spring 2007).

they can often be found in online systems.

Today, European civil servants in ministries ordinarily create the drafts of legislative bills. Expert white papers can influence these bills, but it will most often be a minister who appoints the expert panel that authors a white paper, and so the panel's work is influenced by the government from the very beginning. Thus, European legal scholars do not have real influence on their nations' legislation and, moreover, they are only seldom called upon to appear before a European parliament commission.[59]

As for the structure of an act in Europe, one must beware that in Europe there exists no specific rank-order of the following terms: Title, Chapter, Section, and Paragraph. Furthermore, the terms section, paragraph and (single) statute are sometimes used as synonyms.

---

**Research Tip #3.5**

In Europe, the symbol "§" can be used for a paragraph, section, and even a single statute.[60]

---

The timeline of legislation in Continental Europe has broadly the following pattern:

---

[59] Unlike in the United States, where law professors are frequently called upon to testify before Congress.

[60] In the United States, the symbol "§" is used for to mean "section." In Europe, the phi-symbol ($\pi$) "¶" is never used.

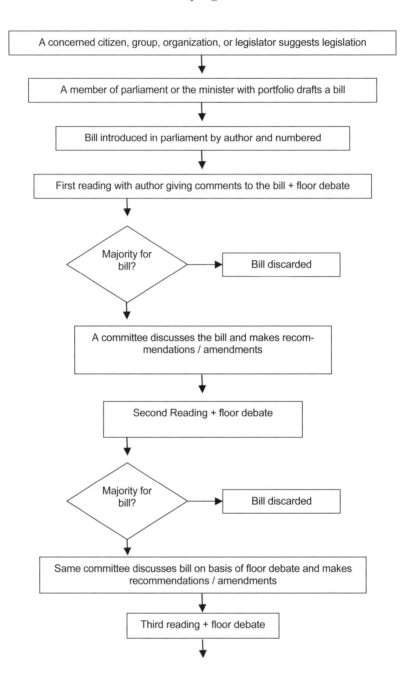

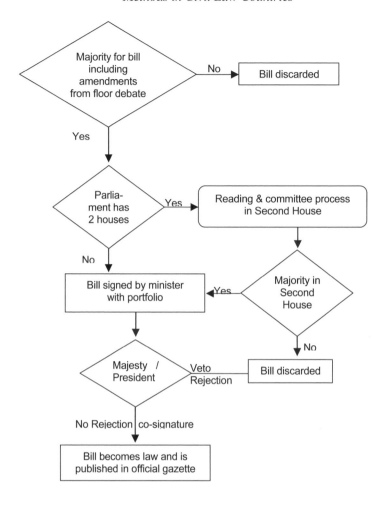

*Table 25: Timeline of legislation in Continental Europe*

### 3.1.4.1. Where to find acts/codes

All acts/codes can be found in printed in the official gazette/journal (in the official language). Many European countries also publish new legislation online (in the official language).

As for legislation in Member States of the European Union <http://curia.europa.eu/en/content/outils/liens/index.htm> is often an easy gateway to find links in English language to a country's online database for newer legislation.

Also, see this books corresponding website at
<www.geocities.com/legalrm>.

### 3.1.5. Law Reviews/Journals in Europe

In all European countries, there are academic law journals or reviews,[61] but
they are not[62] edited or managed by law students as in the U.S.[63] In addition,
they are not related to a single university, but are national or regional publications.[64] A regional or national editorial board consisting of professors, judges,
and other highly qualified experts, scrutinizes each submitted article.[65] Consequently, it is much more difficult to get an article printed in a law jour-
nal/review in Europe than in the U.S.[66] Normally authors of articles in European law journals/reviews are scholars or persons writing dissertations for a
PhD or the higher-ranking European Doctor Juris degree (dr.jur.[67]). It is ex-

---

[61] Some law journal/review title-words in Europe, if translated directly into English, would
be rendered as "Yearbook" or "Weekly Magazine" (e.g., consider "Neue Juristische
Wochenschrift" (NJW)).

[62] This is also due to the fact that continental European-financed and -run universities do
not receive money for law journal/review publication. Also, acting as an editor is not
regarded as an educational task for European law students.

[63] In the U.S., membership on law review staff is highly sought after by law students and
often has a significant impact on their subsequent careers. Most law reviews select
members after their first year of studies, either via a writing competition, or on the basis of grades, or through some combination thereof. Membership is normally divided
into staff (second-year students) and editors (third-year students). Submitted articles
will frequently be revised by the staff and editors (with/without consent from the authors).

[64] See, e.g., Neue Juristische Wochenschrift (NJW), Österreichische Juristen-Zeitung
(ÖJZ), Juristische Blätter (JBl), Ugeskrift for Retsvæsen (UfR), Tidsskrift for Skatteret
(TfS).

[65] The author will have the final say about the content of the article before it is printed.

[66] In the U.S., each of the more than 200 law schools has at least one law review.

[67] This is a degree not found in the U.S., where the term "Juris Doctor" (J.D.) only indicates that the person is a "*candidatus*" from a law school. In Europe, a person having
been examined by the law faculty of a university is called a "*candidatus juris*"
(cand.jur.), which degree is higher than a U.S. J.D. and signifies more a U.S. master
degree (J.D. + LLM).

tremely seldom that articles by law students are published.[68] Thus, some scholars in Europe claim that the quality of articles published in law journals in Europe is much higher than in the U.S. Some even claim American law schools law reviews' student-editorial-boards are nothing but simple paper-printing-producers.[69]

In Europe, because of the high cost of printing (in sometimes "minor" national languages), law review/journal production is most often done by professional firms – and these may be multi-national or international publishers – that also manage distribution. Because of the printing and distribution costs, most European law review articles tend to be much shorter than their American counterparts. In addition, there are several European law journals or reviews that are "cross-border" publications,[70] some on specific topics.[71] European law reviews are also rarely offered in electronic[72] versions (and if so mostly on a subscription basis).[73]

---

[68] However, some universities have begun publishing law students' work through the law faculties' websites. For example, see "Justicia" (edited by professors and published by DJØF Publishing, Denmark). Some European law school students have been allowed to create American-style law reviews on their universities' website, but the universities' academic staff is not involved and the writings that are published are mostly from the students themselves. See, e.g., Heidelberg Student Law Review (HSLR) at <http://www.studzr.de/html/menu_oben/uberuns_en.html> and Hanse Law Review (HLR) at <http://www.hanselawreview.org/cgi-bin/site.pl?user=&site=index>.

[69] U.S. Appeals Court Judge Richard A. Posner has suggested that "law schools 'take back' their law reviews, assigning editorial responsibilities to members of the faculty." Richard A. Posner, *Against the Law Reviews:Welcome to the World Where Inexperienced Editors Make Articles about the Wrong Topics Worse* , 2004 (Dec) Legal Affairs 57. For another view, see Erwin N. Griswold, *The Harvard Law Review – Glimpses of its History as seen by an Aficionado*, Harvard Law Review: Centennial Album 1, 19 (1987) at <http://www.harvardlawreview.org/Centennial.shtml>.

[70] For an example, see Recueil des Cours, the Collected Courses of the Hague Academy of International Law/Académie de Droit International de la Haye (Brill Academic Publishers at <http://www.ppl.nl/bibliographies/all/?bibliography=recueil>).

[71] For an example, see International Journal of Law and Information Technology (published by Oxford University Press, at <http://ijlit.oxfordjournals.org/>).

[72] Some of the newer law reviews in the U.S. are only published online.

[73] One such exception is Electronic Journal of Information, Law and Technology (JILT), edited by professors from several universities in the United Kingdom. See <http://www2.warwick.ac.uk/fac/soc/law/elj/jilt/>).

Accordingly, the American legal scholar must be mindful of often only being able to find European law review articles by going to a library and locating a hard copy in the native language.

### 3.1.6. The Legal Families of Continental Europe.

When studying European continental law – or, rather, Europe excluding England, Wales & Northern Ireland (which have a form of Common Law distinctive from U.S. Common Law[74]), but including Ireland and Scotland[75] – one should be aware of which legal family each country's law being studied belongs to. This is because the legal family type has a great impact on the way the law of that country is to be interpreted. The "continental" European legal families (see further on this subject in Chapter 6) are:[76]

- *The Romanistic Legal Family* (France,[77] the Benelux countries,[78] Italy,[79] Spain,[80] and Portugal[81]) – The *Code Civile*[82] of 1804 is the heart of private law in France and the great model for the codes of private law of the whole Romanistic legal family. It is a felicitous blend of traditional legal institutions from the *droit écrit* of the South

---

[74] The American State of Louisiana is regarded a Civil Law country.

[75] Scotland is often said to use the Civil Law system, but in fact it has a unique system that combines elements of an uncodified Civil Law dating back to the Corpus Juris Civilis with an element of Common Law long predating the Treaty of Union with England in 1707. Scottish Common Law differs in that the use of precedents is subject to the courts seeking to discover the principle that justifies a law, rather than to search for an example as a precedent. In addition, the principles of natural justice and fairness have always formed a source of Scottish law. Other comparable pluralistic (or "mixed") legal systems operate in Quebec, the American State of Louisiana, and South Africa.

[76] ZWEIGERT *supra* note 8 at 64.

[77] Stéphane Cottin & Jérôme Rabenou, *Researching French Law* (May 2005 with update May 2007) at <http://www.llrx.com/features/french.htm>.

[78] Belgium, the Netherlands, and, Luxembourg.

[79] Elio Fameli & Fiorenza Socci, *Guide to Italian Legal Research and Resources on the Web* (translated by Deirdre Exell Pirro) (March 2005 with June 2006 update), at <http://www.nyulawglobal.org/globalex/Italy.htm>.

[80] Olga Cabrero, *Guide to legal research in Spain* (Feb. 2005) at <http://www.llrx.com/features/spain.htm >.

[81] ZWEIGERT *supra* note 8 at 104.

[82] or Code Napoléon [Napoleonic Code] (originally called the Code civil des Français).

– influenced by Roman Law – and the *droit coutumier* of the North – influenced by Germanic-Frankish customary law. The *Code Civile* bears throughout the marks of its heritage of the pre-revolutionary law (*ancien droit*). There was never any serious discussion of a complete reception of Roman law into France – unlike Germany later on. From two royal ordinances in the 17th century, came the basis for a division between private law, in the narrow sense, and commercial law, which the Romanistic and Germanic legal families – except Switzerland and Italy – still recognize by having different codes, much to the surprise of Anglo-American lawyers. In France and Italy, the highest court in civil and criminal matters differs in characteristic respects from the comparable supreme courts of the Anglo-American and German legal families.[83] The (highest[84]) French Court of Cassation goes in for lapidary "whereas" clauses. Legal studies in France are part of a general education.[85]

- *The Germanic Legal Family* (Germany, Austria, Croatia, Switzerland, Greece) – The effects of Roman law were much greater in Germany than in France and enormously greater than in England. Germany consisted of many small principalities until 1871. As there was no common German private law, no common German court system, and no common German fraternity of lawyers, Roman legal ideas and institutions were adopted wholesale in many parts of the country and for many areas of law.[86] The Superior German Court will give reasons that are wide-ranging and loaded with citations like a textbook. Legal studies in Germany, are not part of a general education.[87]

- *The Nordic Legal Family* (Denmark,[88] Finland,[89] Iceland,[90] Nor-

---

[83] ZWEIGERT *supra* note 8 at 74-80 & 120.

[84] It should be pointed out that besides this Supreme Court for judicial cases (civil justice or criminal justice), France has other Supreme Courts, for example the Conseil d'État (for administrative justice), and Conseil Constitutionnel (constitutional challenges).

[85] ZWEIGERT *supra* note 8 at 130-131.

[86] ZWEIGERT *supra* note 8 at 133-135.

[87] ZWEIGERT *supra* note 8 at 130-131.

[88] Rasmus H. Wandall, *Researching Danish Law* (July 2006) [hereinafter WANDALL] at <http://www.nyulawglobal.org/globalex/Denmark.htm>.

way,[91] and Sweden[92])[93] – Nordic Legal Family law has few, if any, of the "stylistic" hallmarks of the Common Law. Roman law has played a smaller role in the legal development of the Nordic countries than in Germany. The Nordic Legal Family's laws belong to the Civil Law, but form a special legal family, alongside the Romanistic and German legal families. The political and cultural ties between these countries have always been very close – partly based on the fact that the countries for some hundred years was unified. In the 17th century, the countries each promulgated comprehensive codes unifying private law, criminal law, and procedural law. In the 19th century, they began modernization of their codes, and amendments were made in separate reforming laws. In addition, unified laws between the countries were added. Nordic Legal Family members have resisted tendency toward conceptualism and the construction of large-scale integrated theoretical systems. All of these countries possess constitutions and neither their royal families/presidents  exercise genuine executive power, which power belongs to the government, which constitutes an separate branch pursuant to the constitutions – along with the Parliament and the courts.

*3.1.6.1. Some basic books for different European countries written in English by natives*

The following is a list of some books written in English by natives giving a

---

[89] *Legal           order           –           Finland           at* <http://ec.europa.eu/civiljustice/legal_order/legal_order_fin_en.htm>.

[90] Rán Tryggvadóttir & Thordis Ingadóttir, *Researching Icelandic Law* (2007) at <http://www.nyulawglobal.org/globalex/iceland.htm>.

[91] Hans Petter Graver, *The Approach to European Law in Norwegian Legal Doctrine,* in Peter Christian Müller-Graff & Erling Selvig, eds., EUROPEAN LAW IN THE GERMAN-NORWEGIAN CONTEXT: ORIGINS AND PERSPECTIVES (Berlin: Berliner Wissenschafts-Verlag GmbH, 2001) & at <http://www.arena.uio.no/publications/wp03_18.pdf> [hereinafter GRAVER].

[92] *Legal           order           –           Sweden* <http://ec.europa.eu/civiljustice/legal_order/legal_order_swe_en.htm>.

[93] Usually, Scandinavia is regarded as Denmark, Norway, and Sweden. The Nordic countries are the Scandinavian ones plus Iceland and Finland.

basic introduction to the particular country's law and structure:

- Austria - Herbert Hausmaninger, The Austrian Legal System (Manzsche Verlags- Und Universitätsbuchhandlung, 2003 – ISBN 3-214-00289-9)
- Belgium - Hubert Bocken & Walter de Bondt, Introduction to Belgian Law (Kluwer Law International, 2000 - ISBN-13: 978-9041114563)
- Denmark – Anne Gleerup, Ulla Rosenkjær, Leif Rørbæk, An introduction to Danish law (2nd Ed.) (Denmark: Drammelstrupgaard, 2008 - ISBN-13: 978-87-988688-3-5)
- England - Gary Slapper, The English Legal System (9 Ed.) (Publisher: Routledge Cavendish, 2008 - ISBN-13: 978-0415459549)
- France - Introduction To French Law (Editors: E. Picard & G Bermann) (Kluwer Law International, 2008 - ISBN 978-9041124661)
- Germany – Introduction to German Law (Editors: Joachim Zekoll & Mathias Reimann) (2nd Ed.) (Kluwer Law International, 2005 - ISBN-13: 978-9041122612)
- Greece – Introduction to Greek Law (Editors: Konstantinos D. Kerameus & Phaedon J. Kozyris) (3rd Ed.) (Kluwer Law International, 2008 - ISBN 978-9041125408)
- Hungary – Introduction To Hungarian Law (Editors: TuRul Ansay & Atilla Harmathy) (Kluwer Law International, 1998 - ISBN 978-9041110664)
- Israel - Introduction To The Law Of Israel (Editors: Amos Shapira & Keren C. Dewitt-Arar) (Kluwer Law International, 1995 - ISBN 978-9065448354)
- Italy - Introduction to Italian law (Ed. Jeffrey S. Lena & Ugo Mattei)(Hague/London/New York: Kluwer Law International 2002 - ISBN: 978-9041117076 )
- Netherlands - Introduction To Dutch Law (Editors: Jeroen M.J. Chorus, Piet-Hein. M. Gerver & Ewoud H. Hondius) (4th Ed.) (Kluwer Law International, 2007 - ISBN 978-9041122698)
- Poland – Introduction to Polish Law (Editors: Stanislaw Frankowski & Adam Bodnar) (Kluwer Law International, 2005 - ISBN 978-9041123312)
- Sweden - Michael Bogdan (Ed.), Swedish Law in the New Millennium (Stockholm: Norstedts Juridik, 2000 - ISBN 91-39-00628-X)
- Switzerland - Introduction To Swiss Law (Editors: Francois Dessemontet & Tugrul Ansay) (3rd Ed.) (Kluwer Law International, 2004 - ISBN 978-9041122605)

- United States of America - William Burnham, Introduction to the Law and Legal System of The United States (West Group, 2006 – ISBN 0-314-25393-9)

### 3.1.7. Legal Science and Legal Philosophy

On the European continent, scholars, when studying law, use the following two principal groupings:[94]

- Legal Philosophy – consisting of different legal theories, which explain legal science, including, for example, natural law[95] and legal realism.[96] Each theory analyzes the legal science to explain, what is "law"; what is a legal norm; what is the relation between law and morality; whether "legal science" is an exact science; and what is required for it to be a science, including the role the "legal method" has.
- Legal Science – consisting of "science" in relation to:
  - o "Source of law" – the science about the content of norms, prioritization, binding effect, and political legitimation.
  - o Legal politics – (a) *de lege ferenda* views;[97] and (b) *de sentendia ferenda* views[98]
  - o Legal history or "history of law" (in the European sense, which is totally different from an American perspective).[99]
  - o Legal sociology – analyzing the law from a sociological perspective to explain the law's impli-

---

[94] Ruth Nielsen & Christian D. Tvarnø, RETSKILDER & RETSTEORIER [Source of Law & Legal Theories] 22-26 (1st ed.) (Copenhagen: Jurist- and Økonomforbundets Forlag [DJØF Publishing], 2005) [hereinafter TVARNØ].

[95] On natural law, see TVARNØ *supra* note 94 at Chapter 7.

[96] U.S. legal realism is similar to the Scandinavian. See TVARNØ *supra* note 94 at 323; Karl Llewellyn, Karl N. Llewellyn, JURISPRUDENCE : REALISM IN THEORY AND PRACTICE (Chicago: University of Chicago Press, 1962); Jerome Frank, LAW AND THE MODERN MIND (New York: Brentano's, 1930).

[97] How the law should be (made by legislator).

[98] How a court should use law and rules in relation to specific circumstances.

[99] MERRYMAN *supra* note 9 at 60.

cations on the society and why rules arose.

o Legal dogmatics – systematization, description, interpretation and analysis of existing law (*de lege lata*) with the aim of solving concrete legal problems.

o Comparative law – comparison of legal systems or legal rules on the basis of a specific - for the concrete question - method of analysis.

## 3.1.8. Citations

In European countries, formal citation systems do not exist.

American scholars have to accept that their normal exhaustive, pinpoint citation system is so culturally alien in Continental Europe that it should not be employed; they have to learn to use the "European" system.[100]

Examples of some commonly used citations can be found in the Guide to Foreign and International Legal Citation (GFILC), which is edited partly with the help of scholars from each country.[101]

Oxford University has also made available a Standard for Citation of Legal Authorities.[102]

However, the particular country's courts and legal scholars might use different ways of make citations.

Especially for court decisions in some European countries there are only made reference to the publisher, year and first page, without any mentioning

---

[100] This does not mean the European system is perfect – far from. It often leaves a possibility for a wrong citation because there are no cross-reference in the citation. For example, a case with only citation of the publisher, year and page – without names of the parties – makes it very possible never to be able the case, if its wrongfully cited.

[101] GFILC was published by the New York University Journal of International Law and Politics in 2006. It is available for free download from <http://www.law.nyu.edu/journals/jilp/gfilc.html >. One would expect that this first edition will be updated and expanded. GFILC is also available in a spiral-bound, paperback form by sending U.S.$20 payable to "Journal of International Law and Politics" to: Circulation Department, Journal of International Law and Politics, 110 West Third Street, New York NY 10012, USA.

[102] Standard for Citation of Legal Authorities (University of Oxford, 2006) at <http://www.competition-law.ox.ac.uk/published/oscola_2006.pdf>.

the parties or the court or date (which lack of sufficient reference sometimes make it hard to find an European case if the year or page is wrongfully cited in a European publication/article)..

## 3.2. Legal Research

### 3.2.1. Introduction

As mentioned above, research approaches in Civil Law vary by country and by topic, and no single procedure will work for all purposes.[103]

---

**Research Tip #3.6**
The first step when beginning research, as regards any foreign law,[104] is to consult a legal research guide about the country being researched.

---

In some countries, this information may be available online, but to date it is seldom that the information will be translated into English.[105]

The following sections are based on the approach for Scandinavia[106] (with two Scandinavian countries, Denmark and Sweden, being members of the E.U.)[107] and where the approaches - even being in the same legal family - is

---

[103] In the U.S., legal research methods are frequently taught by law librarians rather than by lawyers/law professors, who do teach such methods in Europe, as librarians there do not engage in teaching legal subjects. A mixture seems to be the right if the aim is to teach international systems and especially on U.S. law., since if a lawyer does not know where to find material in a law library he is lost.

[104] The domestic law of another country.

[105] Some helpful guides in English can be found at "Globalex" <www.nyulawglobal.org>.

[106] Usually, Scandinavia is regarded as Denmark, Norway, and Sweden. The Nordic countries are the Scandinavian ones plus Iceland and Finland.

[107] In Norway's legal culture, legal doctrine is expected to refer to the sources of law as they appear to the judge. In addition, however, legal doctrine is expected to aspire to the status of a science. The Norwegian trend after, World War II, toward internationalization and, at the same time, harmonization with European community law and human rights law, is a factor that must increasingly be taken into account. GRAVER *supra* note 87.

not always the same.

As for member states of the European Union, some guidance in English can be found at <http://www.ec.europa.eu/civiljustice/legal_order /legal_ order_gen_en.htm>. In addition, in May 2001 the Council of the E.U.[108] decided to establishing the European Judicial Network[109] in civil and commercial matters. This network consists of representatives of the member states' judicial and administrative authorities. It meets several times each year to exchange information and experience and boost cooperation between the member states as regards civil and commercial law. The themes for the network are (similar to menus from its website):

- Legal order
- Organisation of justice
- Legal professions
- Legal aid
- Jurisdiction of the courts
- Bringing a case to court
- Applicable law
- Service of documents
- Taking of evidence and mode of proof
- Interim measures and precautionary measures
- Enforcement of judgements
- Simplified and accelerated procedures
- Divorce
- Parental responsibility
- Maintenance claims

---

[108] 2001/470/EC: Council Decision of 28 May 2001, establishing a European Judicial Network in civil and commercial matters, OJ L 174, 27.6.2001, p. 0025–0031.

[109] REPORT from the Commission to the Council, the European Parliament and the European Economic and Social Committee on the application of Council Decision 2001/470/EC ESTABLISHING A EUROPEAN JUDICIAL NETWORK IN CIVIL AND COMMERCIAL MATTERS, (COM/2006/203 final) and annexes (SEC/2006/579) & Final Report: EVALUATION OF THE FUNCTIONING OF THE EUROPEAN JUDICIAL NETWORK IN CIVIL AND COMMERCIAL MATTERS, submitted by The European Evaluation Consortium (TEEC), all at <http://ec.europa.eu/civiljustice/index_en.htm>.

- Bankruptcy
- Alternative dispute resolutions
- Compensation to crime victims

A European Judicial Atlas in Civil Matters provides access to the following information relevant for judicial cooperation in civil matters (in a chosen language):[110]

- Competent Courts
- Legal Aid
- Serving Documents
- Taking Evidence
- Recognising and Enforcing Judgements
- Compensation to Crime Victims
- Filling in Forms
- Links

---

**Research Tip #3.7**

When starting a survey of a new legal issue, it is helpful to read the first parts of a white paper or comments to a proposed bill, as these often provide a valuable overview of the a specific legal area.

---

**Research Tip #3.8**

When dealing with a rule issued by a governmental body in a Member State of the European Union, one has to look for a legal basis, or "law-foundation-source," for the rule not only in national legislation but also in regulations and decisions of the E.U.

---

Furthermore, one should check whether the rule complies with this legal base or whether it goes beyond the scope of the delegation given to the governmental body.

## 3.2.2. Legal Methodology

Legal methodology does not give an answer as to which statute or legal rule

---

[110] See <http://ec.europa.eu/justice_home/judicialatlascivil/html/index_en.htm>.

should be used in relation to a certain legal problem, but instead states on which basis the answer can be found, that is, the method by which a "law-foundation-source" is analyzed and used when a legal problem is raised.[111] The aim is to make the lawyer capable of obtaining a correct solution to legal questions by shedding light on which normative factors can be used and when, in order to answer the questions. Legal methodology does not describe the rules of a certain branch of jurisprudence[112] (*de lege lata*), which latter is answered by legal dogmatics.[113]

---

**Research Tip #3.9**

The legal method contributes the first bricks to building general understanding of the legal system, its tensions, and also the art and technique of legal research.

---

The science as to the legal method consists of a theoretical and a practical part. The legal methodology encompasses the normative factors – sources of law – which can be used when deciding legal problems, and provides how these sources of law contribute to legal argumentation. The legal method depends on the situation, that is, it is used when there is a need to analyze and solve concrete problems that require answers as to what is the current law. Its application does not always give an unambiguous answer. Yet the legal method does in some situations imply alternatives. Thus, it is important to consider on what grounding a preference should be made.

Learning legal methodology is the cornerstone for studying law in Europe and doing a European Civil Law lawyer's work..

---

[111] TVARNØ *supra* note 94 at 27.

[112] In the U.S. "jurisprudence" is defined: 1. Originally (in the 18th century), the study of the first principles of the law of nature, the civil law, and the law of nations. - Also termed jurisprudentia naturalis; 2. More modernly, the study of the general or fundamental elements of a particular legal system, as opposed to its practical and concrete details. 3. The study of legal systems in general. 4. Judicial precedents considered collectively. 5. In German literature, the whole of legal knowledge. BLACK'S LAW DICTIONARY (8th ed.) (St. Paul: Minnesota, 2004).

[113] Peter Blume, JURIDISK METODELÆRE: EN INDFØRING I RETTENS OG JURAENS VERDEN [Legal Methodology: An introduction to the World of Jurisprudence and Study of Law/of law and courts] 13-15 & 18 (Copenhagen: Jurist- and Økonomforbundets Forlag [DJØF Publishing] 2004) [hereinafter BLUME].

---

**Research Tip #3.10**

Learning legal methodology contributes to and supports an understanding of legal problems, providing the individual with a critical approach to those problems and their solutions (as introduced in courses on legal dogmatics); forucs on the following five questions:[114]

1. What is the definition of a law-foundation-source ?
2. Why use a law-foundation-source ?
3. How does one use a law-foundation-source ?
4. Where are sources of law and who creates them?
5. Where does one find sources of law?

---

**Research Tip #3.11**

When solving a legal research assignment in Continental Europe, the following questions/points should be addressed:

- What is the legal problem?
- Which parts of the given facts are important?
- Which sources of law are relevant?
- Consider and analyze possible arguments pro and con.
- Provide a conclusion.

---

In general, legal rules are necessary for a society in order to show the individual how to behave and to prevent conflicts. Rules can have one or more of the following three characteristics:

- Substantive-law rules, which describe and lay down what is the standard on a certain issue;
- Procedural rules stating the process to be followed when using a particular substantive-law rule; and
- Rules providing for consequences or sanctions in case of violations.

---

[114] However, as the legal system grows more disordered, the normal legal methodology cannot always stand alone, but works more like a steppingstone for the lawyer's use of the source of law. *Idem* 14-15, 18, 64 & 75.

## 3.2.3. The Legal Method in Principle

The Legal Method is the lawyer's basic toolbox – to be employed when concrete facts are present and need to be considered and dealt with in legal terms. It is the lawyer's mission to lay down which legal rules must be used and to reach a conclusion. The method consists of many elements, not all of which necessarily have to be used every time or in the same order.

When given a set of facts and a problem, the question is how to effectively identify, consider, and address the legal issue(s) at hand.[115] Initially, one has to examine whether legal material exists.

---

**Research Tip #3.12**

In Civil Law countries, the natural starting points for examination are constitutional articles and then acts, either codes or statutes.

---

After studying the actual text of a paragraph of a code or statute, an interpretation or filling out of its text may be necessary. At this stage, the aim or intent[116] of the statute is significant. Support for ascertaining such intent can be found in the preliminary work to the statutory text. This work can include, for example, the statements given by the person who introduced the bill that became law, the minutes of negotiations in parliament, and white papers.

Then, one should look for administrative judicial precepts that are legally binding. Examples are: rules issued in the government's regulatory process or by government order; rules in the form of government or departmental circular; or, governmental instructions or guidance.

The next step, find decisions where the statute or code has been used. In Civil Law countries, there are two main types : (a) court decisions; and (b) decisions made by an administrative authority. The first will usually have

---

[115] American law students typically use the so-called IRAC (issue-rule-application-conclusion) system – both for writing memoranda on legal issues and for taking examinations. Some use IWRAC (issue-public int' law- rule-analyse-conclusion).

[116] As opposed to, in the U.S., where some U.S. judges say that legislative intent should not be considered. See Joseph L. Gerken, WHAT GOOD IS LEGISLATIVE HISTORY? JUSTICE SCALIA IN THE FEDERAL COURTS OF APPEALS (Buffalo, New York: William S. Hein & Co., Inc., 2007).

greater weight, because courts often have jurisdiction to review the decisions of administrative authorities.

Furthermore, legal literature can help to encircle the state of the law.

One must determine the legal meaning of the statute, then make an interpretation, with the aim of throwing light on or clarifying what the text of the statute stands for.

An interim conclusion should be reached at this point, concerning whether a reasonable result has been achieved or whether a re-evaluation ought to be undertaken given the circumstances. In the latter case, one should look for legal material addressing the given issue in a broader context – for instance, the aim or intent of a provision in the constitution or in an international treaty (which has been ratified and entered into force). On this basis, one can then decide whether to alter the interim conclusion.[117]

---

**Research Tip 3.13**

In order to be able to clarify which rules must be used in a certain legal system – so as to be able to determine what behavior is legal or not – one needs to acquire knowledge to assess whether the rules are appropriate and desirable.

In Europe, such information is designated by a special term of art: *"source of law.*[118]

---

However, as noted above in section 3.1.1.1. this translation into English of "retskilde" is bound to be confusing for American readers. Accordingly, "source of law" in this chapter is reformulated to "law-foundation-source."

---

[117] BLUME *supra* note 113 at Chapter 4.
[118] BLUME *supra* note 113 at 63. Americans does not talk about a "source of law" but of "sources of law".

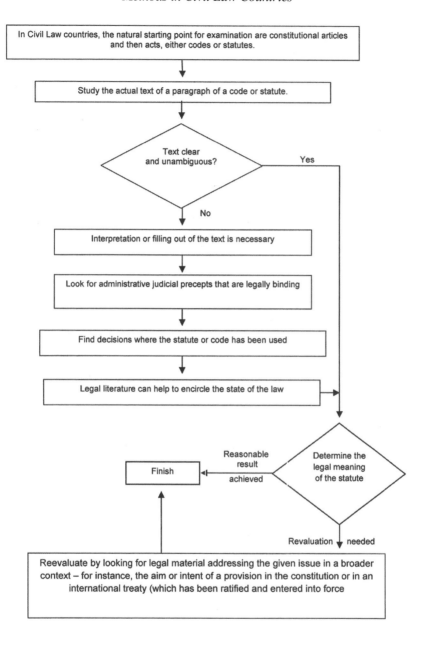

*Table 26: Research Flowchart for Civil Law*

## 3.3. The Method in Detail

Accordingly, up to this juncture in the discussion of legal research in Europe, it is clear that one needs a basic method. Whether that method is proper in turn relies on whether it relates to the law-foundation-sources and is recognized by other lawyers. The law-foundation-sources functions as legal argument, and the legal method is characterized by all the relevant arguments that are brought to light and analyzed in a reasonable and appropriate professional manner to reach an answer to a particular legal question. The application of the method is dependent upon the situation.

---

**Research Tip #3.14**

To determine whether the method has been used correctly, it is necessary to have a common understanding of:[119]

1. What a law-foundation-source is.
2. How a law-foundation-source is used.
3. Which kind of information is considered to be a law-foundation-source.

---

### 3.3.1. Law-foundation-sources

Law-foundation-sources in Civil Law countries do not describe an already-existing situation, but instead aim – as of the time they are created – to bring about change and to govern behavior.[120]

Only seldom is a single Law-foundation-source sufficient to lay down what the legal rule is. Often, fragments have to be collected from several sources of law. Thereafter, these legal arguments are harmonized and cumulated into an answer that is persuasive. The precondition is that sources of law be related to something that is subject to legal regulation.

The science on law-foundation-source carries out the orderly function of ensuring that a certain legal question always is answered in the same manner.

---

[119] BLUME *supra* note 113 at 63.
[120] BLUME *supra* note 113 at Chapter 5.

Yet, in practice, lawyers can disagree on what is the necessary or correct legal argumentation. Only seldom do lawyers disagree on whether a certain type of information is a law-foundation-source .

In Civil Law countries, there exist several types of law-foundation-sources. These types are arranged according to the way they are created, and often divided into a group of binding sources and other(s). In addition, law-foundation-sources of national or international nature may be treated differently.

---

**Research Tip #3.15**
Sources of law are divided into two main groups:

"hard law" - juridical precepts, decisions, and customary law,
&
"soft law" - preparatory works, statements by the Parliament Ombudsman, legal literature describing already existing rules or law, private source of law, and legal cultural tradition.

---

But to a certain extent, all sources are equal, as each type may influence the answer to a legal question.[121]

### 3.3.1.1. Hard (or binding) law-foundation-sources

#### 3.3.1.1.1.. Juridical precepts

A judicial precept is a set of rules, in writing, issued by an authority that has the express power to promulgate it. The value of a certain precept is determined by the status or rank of its issuing body. Principal examples are: constitutional rules, acts, codes or statutes,[122] regulations or government decrees,

---

[121] BLUME *supra* note 113 at 76. In Finland sources are divided into three groups with the following order: (1) strongly binding sources (constitution, acts, regulations, and custom); (2) weakly binding sources (preparatory legislative work and court decisions); and (3) admissible sources of law, which is not binding (jurisprudence, general legal principles, and factual arguments). See Legal order – Finland at <http://ec.europa.eu/civiljustice/legal_order/legal_order_fin_en.htm>.

[122] Acts, codes, and statutes can also be referred to as legislation.

government or departmental circulars, (ratified) treaties, and E.U. regulations and directives.

### 3.3.1.1.2. Decisions

A decision is a legal resolution or judgment of a question raised in a concrete factual context.

One group of decisions is made by the courts. In contrast to strict past practice, nowadays it is recognized that courts in Civil Law countries can "make" law to a certain extent. One exception is a case that is in the Civil Law sense classified to be a "precedence" case – see further in section 3.3.3.2 and 3.3.4.2.[123] The other exception is where an act or statute presumes or expressly permits courts to fill in gaps in legislative schemes. Thus, modern court decisions – as opposed to older ones – can today possess high value as a law-foundation-source .[124]

When legislation is old, or when many changes has occurred within a doctrinal area of law, the importance of case law increases.

However, not all case law can be used; it is only cases that constitute precedence that can be used as a law-foundation-source - see section 3.3.3.2.

The other group of decisions are made by governmental or departmental bodies. Today, such decisions have great impact on citizens' legal status. Often these decisions can be reviewed by the courts.

In those countries that do not have a special administrative court, an ombudsman's[125] statements – even though not decisions and consequently not binding on the courts – can be regarded as a substitute for an administrative court decision and thus as a law-foundation-source .[126]

---

[123] BLUME *supra* note 113 at 70.

[124] Also, the E.U. Court of Justice has through the years made new E.U. law – see below Chapter 4, section 4.1.4.

[125] See footnote 27 above.

[126] BLUME *supra* note 113 at 135.

In many judicial decisions from Europe, an American reader will not find a structure similar to the one used by most U.S. courts, namely:[127]

- The caption, which is the title of the case – such as Brown v. Board of Education or Miranda v. Arizona. In most cases, the caption reflects the last names of the two parties to the dispute. [128]

- The case citation. This consists of "the name of the court that decided the case, the law book in which the opinion was published (and therefore can be found), and also the year in which the court decided the case."

- The author of the opinion. This will be the name of the judge who authored the opinion.[129]

- The body of the opinion includes:
    - The (self-explanatory) Facts of the Case.
    - The Law of the Case: Here, the court discusses the law, including the law-foundation-source it is using to resolve the dispute before it. The basis of the court's authority can help determine the significance of its opinion. The holding of the case – if there is one – and any dicta[130] are included here as well.
    - The Disposition: This usually appears at the end of the main opinion and consists of what action the court is taking with the case. In general, a concurring opinion is an opinion by a judge who would have reached the same result as the majority, but for a different reason. Concurrences and dissents are very important. One needs to read them carefully.[131]

---

[127] ORIN S. KERR, *How to Read a Judicial Opinion: A Guide for New Law Students* (Version 2.0 - August 2005), George Washington University Law School, at <http://volokh.com/files/howtoreadv2.pdf>.

[128] Seldom given on the European continent.

[129] Seldom given on the European continent.

[130] Plural form of "*dictum,*" which is an abbreviation of the Latin phrase "obiter dictum," that means "a remark by the way." Dicta are statements in an opinion that are not actually required to resolve the case before the court.

[131] In the evolution of Common Law, a dissenting opinion may become the majority view. This reflects the reality that judicial decisions are often political decisions as well.

### 3.3.1.1.3. Customary law

Customary law[132] is ordinarily viewed as denoting customs, which have been followed generally and continuously with a sense of legal obligation. Customary law is unwritten[133] and accordingly one cannot expect it to be reported. It covers limited areas of contractual practices, land registration, and criminal law; customary law is relevant in relation to some areas of public administration and constitutional matters.[134] Because regulations provided for in written law are nowadays fairly comprehensive, custom is today rarely of any importance as a law-foundation-source .

Customary law may be recognized in case law. However, more frequently the source is found in scholarly writing or in the public legal offices that deal with the area of law in question.[135]

### *3.3.1.2. Soft Law*

The term "*soft law*"[136] covers a broad spectrum of different kinds of sources. This type of law-foundation-source is created in a more informal way. It is used in areas where there is a need for a dynamic development or evolution of law in view of continuous changes in the society. Soft law is characterized by giving advice or recommendation and thus not legally binding for the persons it relates to. They can declare / have shape of / content a custom or practice or be the forerunner for a later legal precept. This kind of source can be hard to find, as they are often not promulgated. Doctrines, commercial

---

[132] In Danish "sædvane."

[133] The term "unwritten" is used differently in the United States. There, the term covers: law that, although never enacted in the form of a statute or ordinance, has the sanction of custom and traditionally included unpublished case law. It is also termed *jus non scriptum, jus ex non scripto, lex non scripta,* and *jus moribus constitutum.* BLACK'S LAW DICTIONARY (8th ed.) (St. Paul: West, 2004).

[134]    WANDALL    *supra*    note    88.    For    the    same    in    Finland,    see <http://ec.europa.eu/civiljustice/legal_order/legal_order_fin_en.htm>.

[135] WANDALL *supra* note 88. BLUME *supra* note 113 at 49, 137, 143-144.

[136] Soft law: 1. Collectively, rules that are neither strictly binding nor completely lacking in legal significance. 2. Int'l law. Guidelines, policy declarations, or codes of conduct that set standards of conduct but are not legally binding. Black's Law Dictionary (8th ed.) (St. Paul: West, 2004).

customs, contractual provisions, and general customs can be supplementary sources of law.

### 3.3.1.2.1. Preparatory work

The purpose of preparatory or preliminary work is to state the reasons for issuing a precept and to explain the meaning behind specific parts or rules of the precept. In European Civil Law countries, it is an accepted part of the legal method to study preparatory work and include them in legal argumentation.[137]

The more recent the preparatory work, the more important it is.

The older a statute is, the less reasonable it is for a legal researcher to find support for his or her interpretation in the preparatory work to the statute, as later practice/experience likely has changed the meaning of a statute.

In addition, the more precise the text of a statute is, the less weight should be ascribed to preparatory work.

One should distinguish between preparatory work created before a bill is introduced and preparatory work established during negotiations in parliament. In practice, courts from time to time use white papers, whereas government bodies more often prefer the content of the ministers' comments to the bill.

The fact that a bill never was passed can be used in the negative as regards what the law is.[138]

### 3.3.1.2.2. Statements by the Parliamentary Ombudsman

An Ombudsman's[139] statements is not decisions and not binding on the courts. However, as a law-foundation-source such statements are considered of high authority and are adhered to by the administration. They constitute an

---

[137] In most countries of Europe, it is common practice in the preparation of any major legal reform to engage in extensive study of foreign ideas and experience. MAX RHEINSTEIN, *Comparative Law – Its Functions, Methods and Usages*, 22 ARK. L. REV. 415, 424 (1946).

[138] BLUME *supra* note 113 at 94.

[139] See footnote 27 above.

indispensable source when researching European administrative law.[140]

### 3.3.1.2.3. Legal Literature describing already Existing Rules or Law

The part of legal literature that describes the already existing rules or law (*de lege lata*) – legal dogmatics – can be used for arguments or contributions to a point of view and thereby be regarded as a law-foundation-source . However, this "source" should be limited to writings of authors who are widely acknowledged as experts. American researchers should note that legal dogmatics may be far different in use and importance than in American jurisprudence. Works of legal dogmatics in Europe will often imply a sort of production process even though nothing new is created. They contain often review and analysis of different sources of law in a particular author's paper.[141]

In Civil Law countries, legal dogmatics is divided into the following categories:

---

[140] BLUME *supra* note 113 at 135.
[141] BLUME *supra* note 113 at 151.

| | |
|---|---|
| **Private Law**<br>(Regulations between private citizens and business, including public firms) | The law of Contracts and Torts |
| | Property Right |
| | + including Law of Persons & Family law |
| | + including Consumer Rights |
| **Public Law**<br>(Regulations among public bodies and regulations between public bodies and citizens/businesses) | Constitutional law |
| | Administrative law |
| | Criminal law |
| | Law of (legal) Procedure |
| | + including Social (welfare) Law |
| | + including Environment law |
| **International Law** | Public International law |
| | E.U. law |
| | International Private law |
| | + including Maritime law |
| | + including Law of War |
| **General Topics** | Jurisprudence |
| | History of law or Legal History[142] |
| | Sociology of law |
| | Legal Informatics |
| | Legal Economy |

*Table 27: Disciplines of Legal Dogmatics[143]*

To this group of law-foundation-source also belong unofficial, published commentaries, which are written commentary on each word/paragraph of the articles of an act contributed by acknowledged scholars, civil servants, or judges.

In some European countries, court decisions may make reference to scholarly writings. However, the citation practice of European courts does not necessarily reveal the influence of academic lawyers on judicial law-making.

---

[142] Much of what is called legal history in the Civil Law tradition is baffling and inexplicable to the Common Law lawyer. He or she is used to thinking of legal history as an account of legal rules and institutions in their historical, economic, and social context. However, picking up a book on legal history in the Civil Law tradition, one is likely to find the bulk of it devoted to a discussion of schools of legal thought and of disputes between legal scholars and their followers. The protagonist or leader of this form of legal history is the legal scholar, and its subject matter is currents of thoughts about the structure and operation of the legal order, MERRYMAN *supra* note 9 at 60.

[143] BLUME *supra* note 113 at 151.

Italian courts, unlike English and German ones, do not usually make explicit reference to academic writings.[144] In Italy, a statute expressly forbids judges to make reference to scholarly works as authority in the court decisions.[145] Nevertheless, in practice, the courts sometimes do so.[146] Occasionally, Italian courts quote directly from a legal textbook or article without mentioning the author or the work.[147]

In England, in particular, appellate court references to academic literature have increased enormously.[148] These days, judges read academic articles as part of their ordinary judicial activity, and they cite them with authors' names and references.[149]

Unlike English judges, Italian judges hardly ever examine in detail the position of the legal doctrine in their judgments. In Italy, as well as in France, the expression "legal doctrine" refers to legal scholars as a collective entity.[150]

---

[144] Alexandra Braun, *Professors and Judges in Italy: It Takes Two to Tango*, 26 OXFORD JOURNAL OF LEGAL STUDIES 656, 670 (Winter 2006) [hereinafter BRAUN].

[145] "In ogni caso deve essere omessa ogni citazione di autori giuridici" ["In every case every citation of legal authors must be omitted"], Regio decreto 18 dicembre 1941, n. 1368 (Suppl. G.U. 24 dicembre 1941, n. 302), Disposizioni per l'attuazione del Codice di Procedura Civile e disposizioni transitorie [Regal decree No. 1368 of 18 Decembers 1941 (Suppl. G.U. 24 December 1941, no. 302) as Annex to the Code of Civil Procedure, Title Three, Heading Two, Section Three, Article 118, subsection 3], at <http://www.difensore.it/codici/codiceproceduracivile.htm>. See also Virgilio Andrioli, CODICE DI PROCURA CIVILE E NORME COMPLEMENTARI (Milan: Dott. A. Giuffrè Editore, 1984).

[146] The Italian Supreme Court of Cassation has acknowledged that some academic contributions in the field of leasing have been adopted by the courts. Case 5573 from Suprema Corte di Cassazione, 13 December 1989, Foro ital ano, 1990, I, 46; BRAUN, *supra* note 144 at 671 and footnote 27.

[147] Suprema Corte di Cassazione, 16 May 2000, Case no. 6323, Nuova giurisprudenza civile commentate 2001, I, 357 at 367 (in which the judges quote a passage from C.M. Bianca, Diritto civile, III, Il contratto (1984) at 238 without mentioning the author or the book); BRAUN *supra* note 144 at 671 and footnote 28.

[148] BRAUN *supra* note 144 at 668 and footnote 10.

[149] *In Re OT Computers Ltd (In Administration) Nagra v. OT Computers Ltd*, [2004] Ch 317, 332-333 para 43, [2004] EWCA Civ 653 para 43, [2004] 3 W.L.R. 88 (Court of Appeal, CA (Civ Div), May 2004 - Judge Longmore).

[150] BRAUN *supra* note 144 at 680.

### 3.3.1.2.4. Private source of law

A private law-foundation-source [151] is one that is not issued by an authorized official body, but stems from a practice followed by a group of people – a public kind of self-regulation. Examples are trade usage or private agreements.

### 3.3.1.2.5. Legal Cultural Tradition

This "source"[152] cannot be defined accurately and its basis is hard to trace. It can be described generally as using common sense in a legal argument to support the determination of whether a specific or concrete result is in accordance with the legal tradition and the values of a particular legal system. It may refer to considerations of fairness, equality, and feasibility as to societal needs.[153] It influences the decision of whether an intermediate result is reasonable and just; thus, it should be considered only as part of the last and final say on a legal issue.[154]

## 3.3.2. Use of the source of law

Another issue is to determine whether a specific law-foundation-source has to be used. This implies answering the following questions:

---

[151] In Danish "kutyme". BLUME *supra* note 113, at 137-147, 188.

[152] In Danish "Forholdets nature".

[153] Former Danish Supreme Court Judge Torben Jensen in *Domstolenes retsskabende, retsudfyldende og responderende virksomhed* [The courts' law-creating, filling out and responding activity], 1990 JOURNAL OF LAW [Ugeskrift of Retsvæsen] (UfR) [subsection] B 441.

[154] BLUME *supra* note 113 at 77. WANDALL *supra* note 88, at 4.5.

---

**Research Tip #3.16**

1. Does the source actually exist, and has it has been legally adopted?
2. Is the rule indicated in the source usable for the specific problem?
3. Is the use of the rule influenced by other sources, for example an interpretation of a court decision, is there a more appropriate rule for the issue at hand?

---

In principle, all sources of law are equal, so there is no hierarchy with some ranked higher than others. However, *hard law* sources do have priority over *soft law* ones.[155]

It is not a precondition for the use of a particular source of law that it has been published or made public – for example, a court decision has been published – unless the legal system involved has expressly made it a requirement – for example, a statute has to be publicized in a legal system's legal journal or gazette (before it can come into force). Nevertheless, it is a requirement that the source of law be trustworthy and reliable.[156]

Even if one has knowledge of all sources of law on a specific problem, it is by no means necessary that every one must be used. The requirement is simply that all *necessary* sources be used for solving the particular legal problem or question.[157]

### 3.3.3. Interpretation of the law-foundation-sources

When one has found those *law-foundation-sources* that might influence the answer to a legal question, the next step is to lay down the legal meaning of each source of law so that one can determine how each one contributes to the legal argument.[158]

---

[155] BLUME *supra* note 113 at 76.

[156] BLUME *supra* note 113 at 79-80.

[157] BLUME *supra* note 113 at 81.

[158] The general contemporary American view of statutory interpretation is that there is not a great deal to say about the subject. The American understanding of statutory interpretation still remains quite limited and a unified theory of statutory interpretation may be unattainable. The phrase "statutory interpretation" might refer to a variety of judicial actions with respect to statutes. Unfortunately, there is no consensus as to which of

For written sources of law, this implies an analysis and consideration of the text.

The aim of interpretation[159] is to find the legal purpose or meaning, which might be different from the immediate linguistic meaning.[160]

The interpretated sources compile into a "rule" or norm, which is used for legal decision-making. In the compiling process, a determination is made of how to weight each of the sources for the legal question that has to be answered. Ethical and value-based motives can sometimes exercise influence. The interpretation is done ad hoc, in relation to a concrete case (and factual context), so that it is different from case to case. The object of interpretation[161] is to reduce or remove the uncertainty of a legal rule's meaning and to preclude (or at least hinder) unreasonable results.

As explained next below, a number of interpretation methods have been developed.

---

these judicial actions are covered by the phrase "statutory interpretation," and some commentators contrast that phrase with another – "statutory construction" – to which they assign a different meaning. Other writers treat the phrases as synonymous, each phrase referring to all these judicial actions. Robert Weisberg, *The Calabresian Judicial Artist: Statutes And The New Legal Process*, 35 STAN. L. REV. 213, footnote 1 (January 1983); Daniel A. Farber, *Statutory Interpretation and Legislative Supremacy*, 78 GEO. L. J. 281 (December 1989).

[159] Interpretation, as applied to written law, is the art or process of discovering and expounding the intended signification of the language used, that is, the meaning which the authors of the law designed it to convey to others. Henry Campbell Black, HANDBOOK ON THE CONSTRUCTION AND INTERPRETATION OF THE LAWS 1 (1896).

[160] The American term "comparative interpretation" seems to have a different meaning, as the method of interpretation in the U.S. seeks to ascertain the meaning of a statute or other writing by comparing its several parts and also by comparing it as a whole with other like documents proceeding from the same source and referring to the same general subject. See BLACK'S LAW DICTIONARY (8th ed.) (St. Paul: West Publishing, 2004).

[161] This involves also the question of whether a law should be given the meaning attributed to it by the legislator at the time of enactment, or whether the statute may be treated as having a kind of independent life of its own and interpreted in the light of changing social conditions.

*3.3.3.1. Statutes*

Initially, one should note that the different interpretation[162] methods do not

[162] As for American interpretation, Stanford Law School Professor Schacter once listed the U.S. judicial resources for statutory interpretation as follows: (1) the statutory language; (2) legislative history (including committee reports, statements and other information in the Congressional Record, or other material generated in the legislative process through which the law was enacted); (3) other statutes (state or federal), or other sections of the same statute at issue in the case; (4) judicial opinions (including previous decisions by the U.S. Supreme Court or other federal or state courts); (5) canons of construction; (6) administrative materials (including federal regulations or policy statements, letters or advisory opinions written by agency officials, and agency adjudicatory decisions); (7) secondary sources (including law review and newspaper articles, treatises, other books, and policy reports); (8) dictionaries (whether general or legal); (9) "judicially-selected policy norms" (norms unified by being non-originalist and reflecting the Supreme Court Justices' own invocation of policy values that are grounded in neither the text of the statute nor the legislative history nor any other claim about intended legislative design); and (10) miscellaneous other sources (including, to a certain extent, amicus briefs filed with the Supreme Court). Jane S. Schacter, *The Confounding Common Law Originalism in Recent Supreme Court Statutory Interpretation: Implications for the Legislative History Debate and Beyond*, 51 STANF. L. R. 1, 12, 48 (1998). U.S. statutory law is the dominant source of contemporary American law, and it is the form of law that lawyers are likely to confront most often in almost any area of practice. Jane S. Schacter, *Stanford Law School – Introduction to Course: Statutory Interpretation*. However, the pattern or manner of statutory law's interpretation is disputed. Although using legislative history to help interpret unclear statutory language seems natural, the U.S. Supreme Court's actual use of legislative history is in decline. Stephen Breyer, *On the Use of Legislative History in Interpretating Statutes*, 65 S. CAL. L. REV. 845, 846 & 848 (1992). Others view the primary object of all rules for interpreting statutes to be to ascertain exactly from the words of the statute the meaning that the legislature intended. This is because government by unexpressed intent is tyrannical and it is the law that governs, not the intent of the lawgiver. Legislative history should not be used as an authoritative indication of a statute's meaning. Antonin Scalia, A MATTER OF INTERPRETATION: FEDERAL COURTS AND THE LAW: AN ESSAY 17, 29 (Princeton: Princeton University Press, 1997). See Jane S. Schacter, *Accounting for Accountability in Dynamic Statutory Interpretation and Beyond – Issues in Legal Scholarship, Dynamic Statutory Interpretation* (Berkeley: Berkeley Electronic Press, 2002): Article 5 at <http://www.bepress.com/ils/iss3/art5 >. See also Daniel A. Farber, *Statutory Interpretation and Legislative Supremacy*, 78 GEO. L. J. 281 (December 1989).

influence the determination of the meaning or use of a rule.[163]

- The most important interpretation method is the *Lex Superior Principle* – a rule at a higher level in the hierarchy is to be preferred over a rule on a lower level, that is , a legal rule issued by a lower body has to comply with rules on a higher level.[164]

- A consultative interpretation-rule for choice between rules at the same level is the *Lex Posterior Principle* – a newer statute comes before an older statute. However, there might be some reason why the older statute has not been revoked.[165]

- Another consultative interpretation-rule is the *Lex Specialis Principle* – ; there is a preference for the rule that deal with specific issue(s) of society; thus, a distinct and specific rule comes before a statute of general content.[166]

- As for rules concerning the relationship between a citizen and the public ("the state"[167]),where there are several useful rules at the same level, the rule that is in the citizen's interest or favor should be used.[168]

No guideline exists where there is a conflict between an older specific rule and a newer but more general one – or *lex posterior* contra *lex specialis*. In such situations, reasonableness, preparatory work to a statute, and legislators' intentions can be considered.

---

**Research Tip #3.17**

A U.S. student should take a course on statutory interpretation before doing research on civil law as a main issue in civil law research is interpretation

---

[163] BLUME *supra* note 113 at 164-166; Legal Order in Sweden <http://ec.europa.eu/civiljustice/legal_order/legal_order_swe_en.htm>; Legal Order in Finland at <http://ec.europa.eu/civiljustice/legal_order/legal_order_fin_en.htm>.

[164] This principle should be distinguished from the question of hierarchy between the sources of law.

[165] Or *lex posteriori derogat legi priori.*

[166] Or *lex specialis derogat legi generali.*

[167] In the European sense, see above section 3.1.1.

[168] TVARNØ *supra* note 94 at 26.

For U.S. students that has not (yet) taken a course in statutory interpretation, the following should give them an idea of what mindset a first year civil law student is put into by his legal research professor.

As for interpretation in the U.S.,[169] it can be summarized from the venerable legal encyclopedia Corpus Juris Secundum (CJS)[170] as follows:[171]
"Common law," in its broadest and most general sense, is those rules or precepts of law in any country, or that body of its jurisprudence, which is of equal application in all places, as distinguished from local laws and rules. The references in the Seventh Amendment to the Constitution of the United States, to "suits at common law, where the value in controversy shall exceed twenty dollars" and "according to the rules of the common law" mean the common law of England, as distinct from equity, admiralty and maritime jurisprudence. A like provision in a state constitution may be taken to mean the common law as modified by legislative enactment. Generally, however, "English common law" is the *lex non scripta* or unwritten law which is that

---

[169] "An act of Congress ought never to be construed to violate the law of nations [that is, public international law] if any other possible construction remains." *Murray v. charming Betsy,* 6 U.S. 64, 118, 2 Cranch 64, 2 L.Ed. 208 (U.S. Supreme Court, Feb. 1804). The reason for why judges and lawyers should divert to the principles and decisions of foreign and international law is globalization. No institution of government can afford any longer to ignore the rest of the world. One-third of U.S. gross domestic products is internationally derived. We operate today under a large array of international agreements and organizations directly impacting judicial decision-making. Globalization also represent a greater awareness of, and access to, peoples and places far different from our own. The fates of nations are more closely intertwined than ever before, and we are more acutely aware of the connections. We are already seeing internationalization of legal relations in American courts, and should see it increasingly in the future. The U.S. Supreme Court has held for more than 200 years that Acts of Congress should be construed to be consistent with international law absent clear expression to the contrary, Former Associate Justice Supreme Court Justice of the U.S. Sandra Day O'Connor, *Southern Center for International Studies, Atlanta , Georgia, October 28, 2003*

[170] CORPUS JURIS SECUNDUM: COMPLETE RESTATEMENT OF THE ENTIRE AMERICAN LAW AS DEVELOPED BY ALL REPORTED CASES (St. Paul: Thomson/West Publishing, 1936- ) (CJS) is an authoritative American legal encyclopedia that provides a clear statement of each area of law.

[171] See also, Norman J. Singer, ('Sutherland") STATUTES AND STATUTORY CONSTRUCTION (6th ed.) (St. Paul: West Group, 2006).

portion of the law of England which is based, not on legislative enactment, but on immemorial usage and the general consent of the people.[172] Decisions of a higher court, not turning on the application of statutes or constitutional principles, constitute the common law.[173]

The rules or canons of statutory construction – also termed statutory interpretation are merely aids for ascertaining legislative intent. However, such rules may be used only to remove doubt, and are never to be used to create doubt.[174]

The construction of a statute is a question for the court, and not for the jury.[175]

The process of statutory interpretation involves a reasoned search for the intention of the legislature, which begins with an examination of the language of the statute itself. However, all reasonable means will be used to arrive at the legislative intent. The court cannot attribute to the legislature an intent which is not in any way expressed in the statute. It is not the function of the court to determine and announce what, in its judgment, the statute should provide, but to ascertain, if there is ambiguity in its terms, what it does provide.[176]

As a general rule of statutory construction, the spirit or intention of a statute prevails over the letter thereof.[177] However, in some jurisdictions, intent prevails over the letter of the law;[178] the spirit and intent of legislation prevails over a literal reading of its language,[179] and the courts are not controlled by the literal meaning of the language of the statute.[180] In other jurisdictions, when the words of a law in their application to an existing situation are clear and free from all ambiguity, the letter of the law may not be disregarded under the pretext of pursuing the spirit of the statute.[181]

---

[172] 15A CORPUS JURIS SECUNDUM (CJS) Common Law 1.

[173] 15A CORPUS JURIS SECUNDUM (CJS) Common Law 3.

[174] 82 CORPUS JURIS SECUNDUM (CJS) Statutes 306.

[175] 82 CORPUS JURIS SECUNDUM (CJS) Statutes 307.

[176] 82 CORPUS JURIS SECUNDUM (CJS) Statutes 315.

[177] 82 CORPUS JURIS SECUNDUM (CJS) Statutes 317.

[178] 82 CORPUS JURIS SECUNDUM (CJS) Statutes 317, footnote 41 (referring to California, Connecticut, Maryland, Mississippi, and New Jersey).

[179] 82 CORPUS JURIS SECUNDUM (CJS) Statutes 317, footnote 42 (referring to Florida, Georgia, and Hawaii).

[180] 82 CORPUS JURIS SECUNDUM (CJS) Statutes 317, footnote 43 (referring to California, Connecticut, Illinois, Maryland, Missouri, Nebraska, and New York).

[181] 82 CORPUS JURIS SECUNDUM (CJS) Statutes 317, footnote 44 (referring to North Dakota, Pennsylvania, Arizona, California, Nebraska, North Carolina, Oregon, and Washington).

As a general rule, the courts cannot supply omissions in a statute.[182]

The general rule of statutory construction that words should be construed according to their common and approved usage does not apply to technical words and phrases that generally are considered to have a peculiar meaning. (e.g. commercial, trade, or professional terms ).[183]

The maxim *"expressio unius est exclusio alterius,"* under which the mention of one thing in a statute implies the exclusion of another, is merely an auxiliary rule of statutory construction which is not universally applicable and not conclusive. It should be applied only as a means of discovering the legislative intent which is not otherwise manifest, and should never be permitted to defeat the plainly indicated purpose of the legislature.[184]

The courts are reluctant to construe the intent of the legislature based solely on punctuation and grammatical construction, and a statute's punctuation alone is not a reliable guide in discovering its meaning.[185]

As a general rule, every word in a statute is to be given force and effect, and the courts should avoid a construction making any word surplusage.[186]

The words "or" and "and" in a statute generally are not treated as interchangeable, but they may be so treated when necessary to effectuate the obvious intention of the legislature.[187]

The presence of a comma separating a modifying clause in a statute from the clause immediately preceding it is an indication that the modifying clause was intended to modify all the preceding clauses and not only the last antecedent one.[188]

Where a statute has first been enacted in a foreign language and afterward translated into English, its history will be considered in construing it. The English text of laws enacted in Louisiana since 1812 must prevail, but the original French text prevails over an erroneous English translation of earlier laws.[189]

In construing an ambiguous statute, a court generally may consider legislative debates and reports of committees or commissions as an aid to construction,

---

[182] 82 CORPUS JURIS SECUNDUM (CJS) Statutes 320.

[183] 82 CORPUS JURIS SECUNDUM (CJS) Statutes 322.

[184] 82 CORPUS JURIS SECUNDUM (CJS) Statutes 323.

[185] 82 CORPUS JURIS SECUNDUM (CJS) Statutes 325.

[186] 82 CORPUS JURIS SECUNDUM (CJS) Statutes 327.

[187] 82 CORPUS JURIS SECUNDUM (CJS) Statutes 333.

[188] 82 CORPUS JURIS SECUNDUM (CJS) Statutes 331.

[189] 82 CORPUS JURIS SECUNDUM (CJS) Statutes 334.

however, such materials will not be considered where the language of the statute is plain and unambiguous.[190]

Statutes are to be construed in the context of the existing law, and as a part of a general and uniform system of jurisprudence.[191]

In case of ambiguity, statutes are to be construed with reference to the principles of the common law in force at the time of their passage, and statutes are not to be interpreted as effecting any change in the common law beyond that which is clearly indicated.[192]

Where a statute is ambiguous, a court generally may consult analogous statutes to determine its meaning, but the provisions of dissimilar statutes are not persuasive.[193]

Statutes adopted at the same session of the legislature generally are not to be construed as inconsistent or in conflict if it is possible to construe them otherwise.[194]

Since the more recent statute is a later expression of the legislative intent, if there is an unreconcilable conflict between two statutes, the later enactment normally will control. In such a case, the newer statute may be regarded as creating an exception to, or qualification of, the prior statute. However, where there is no clear intention to the contrary, a specific statute will not be controlled or nullified by a general one, regardless of the priority of their enactment.[195]

General and specific statutes should be read together and harmonized, if possible. However, to the event of an irreconcilable conflict between them, the specific or special statute ordinarily will prevail over the general one. Where the general act is later, the special statute will be construed as remaining an exception to the terms of the general statute, unless the more specific statute is repealed expressly or by necessary implication.[196]

Where a statute which has been construed by the courts is reenacted in substantially the same terms, the legislature is presumed to have been familiar with the judicial construction of the prior statute and to have adopted that interpretation as a part of the later act, unless a contrary intent clearly appears, or the later statute expressly provides for a different construction. The general rule that a later statute will be interpreted in accordance with a judicial con-

---

[190] 82 CORPUS JURIS SECUNDUM (CJS) Statutes 341.
[191] 82 CORPUS JURIS SECUNDUM (CJS) Statutes 391.
[192] 82 CORPUS JURIS SECUNDUM (CJS) Statutes 350.
[193] 82 CORPUS JURIS SECUNDUM (CJS) Statutes 351.
[194] 82 CORPUS JURIS SECUNDUM (CJS) Statutes 353.
[195] 82 CORPUS JURIS SECUNDUM (CJS) Statutes 354.
[196] 82 CORPUS JURIS SECUNDUM (CJS) Statutes 355.

struction of a prior statute does not apply where the later statute is unambiguous.[197]

As a general rule, however, the adoption of a statute by reference is construed as an adoption of the law as it existed at the time the adopting statute was passed. Therefore, the adopting statute normally is not affected by any subsequent modification of the statute adopted unless an intention to the contrary is clearly manifested. On the other hand, where the legislative intent to do so clearly appears, the adopting statute will include subsequent modifications of the original act.[198]

When a statute is patterned after a statute of another jurisdiction, it is appropriate to consider interpretations of the statute in the jurisdiction from which it has been borrowed.[199]

Where a state statute is virtually a verbatim copy of a statute of a sister state, the interpretation of the statute by the courts of the state where the statute was originally adopted is persuasive.[200]

The courts of the adopting state are not bound to accept the construction placed on the statute by the courts of the state from which it was adopted, and they will not do so where it would be contrary to the spirit and policy of the laws of the adopting state, or where it is regarded as unsound in principle, and against the weight of authority. Moreover, such a construction will not be applied where it is plain that the legislature adopting it had a different intention. It is the construction of the statute which prevailed in the original state at the time of its adoption by the other state that is presumed to follow the statute, and subsequent decisions have no controlling effect on the adopting state. However, such decisions may be strongly persuasive.[201]

## 3.3.3.2. Court decisions – Finding Precedential Authority

As courts in Civil Law countries do not (generally) make law,[202] court decisions have only limited value.

---

[197] 82 CORPUS JURIS SECUNDUM (CJS) Statutes 356.

[198] 82 CORPUS JURIS SECUNDUM (CJS) Statutes 357.

[199] 82 CORPUS JURIS SECUNDUM (CJS) Statutes 358.

[200] 82 CORPUS JURIS SECUNDUM (CJS) Statutes 359.

[201] 82 CORPUS JURIS SECUNDUM (CJS) Statutes 360.

[202] The French Napoleonic code expressly forbade French judges from pronouncing the law, by prohibiting judges from passing judgments exceeding the matter that was to be judged – because general rules were the domain of the law, a legislative power. In theory, then, there is no case law in France. .

> **Research Tip #3.18**
>
> As a law-foundation-source , only a decision that can be characterized as having precedential authority[203] is of real interest.[204]

In rare cases, a decision will provide a more general opinion or point of view on the legal rule(s) involved in the case.

Thus, the primary task in considering decisions from Civil Law countries is to sort out what are the precedential cases, because any other case will not have value as a *law-foundation-source*.

> **Research Tip #3.19**
>
> One has to scrutinize the background and history of a case to figure out whether the decision is regarded as having precedential value.

The crucial element or part of a court decision that is of interest when searching for precedent is the grounds of judgment (*ratio decidendi*). In a precedential case, a given ground from the court can influence a later, similar case.

Note that to become a precedential case it is not a requirement that is was decided by the highest-ranking court; thus, even a decision of a court of first instance can be a precedential authority – as long as it cannot be appealed. However, of the various court decisions, the most important as sources of law are those of the highest courts

The term "precedent" – as well as the concept of "case law," to which the term precedent is tied – means different things to different jurists in different European Civil Law legal systems. There are differences even between the

---

[203] The substantial basis for precedent is a final judgment. Peter Blume, *From Drakon to the Computer and Beyond* in NORDIC STUDIES IN INFORMATION TECHNOLOGY AND LAW 78 (Peter Blume, ed.) (Deventer, Boston: Kluwer Computer Law Series, 1991).

[204] DANISH LAW IN A EUROPEAN PERSPECTIVE (2nd ed.) (Dahl, Melchior & Tamm, eds ) (Copenhagen: DJOEF Publishing); Joseph Lookofsky, *Precedent and the Law in Denmark* - Danish National Report at the XVIIth Conference of The International Academy of Comparative Law, Utrecht 2006, at <http://www.cisg.law.pace.edu/cisg/biblio/lookofsky15.html> [hereinafter LOOKOFSKY]. BLUME *supra* note 113 at 128-130.

Scandinavian countries (Denmark, Norway, and Sweden[205]) that belong to the same Nordic Legal Family.[206]

In Denmark, the "bindingness" of any given Danish judgment – which term does not imply that the judgment has to be followed – will depend, in large measure, on the "rank" of the court, which rendered that decision, as well as on that court's relation to courts, which might be expected to "follow" it.[207] Danish courts, including the Supreme Court,[208] consider themselves bound by their own prior decisions, at least unless compelling circumstances dictate departure from established precedent. A requirement for becoming precedential is that another (judge) has considered the result and the reasoning of the prior decision to be persuasive. Sometimes, even non-Danish decisions are considered "relevant" by Danish courts, e.g., decisions rendered by the European Court of Justice and the European Court of Human Rights.[209]

In modern times, European legislators to a certain degree, in many of the statutes enacted by parliaments, reflect an intent to leave the development of many fundamental issues and doctrines up to the courts.[210] Thus, a combined law-supplementing and law-function has long been justified and recognized

---

[205] Although Finland deserves inclusion in the Nordic Legal Family in certain respects, the Finnish concept of (non-binding) precedent seems distinctly more "Civilian" than Scandinavian. See generally Aulis Arnio Tampere, *Precedent in Finland,* in INTERPRETING PRECEDENT: A COMPARATIVE STUDY (Niel MacCormick, Robert S. Summers & Arthur L. Goodhart, eds.) (Vt.: Ashgate/Dartmouth, 1999) [hereinafter MACCORMICK]. Regarding the concept of precedent in Norway and in Sweden, see generally Svein Eng, *Precedent in Norway*, and Gunnar Bergholtz, *Precedent in Sweden, idem.*

[206] LOOKOFSKY *supra* note 204.

[207] LOOKOFSKY *supra* note 204.

[208] In the Danish Supreme Court decision *Kvistgaard Jern og Metal A/S v. Carsten Tilleman Carstens*, Ugeskrift for Retsvæsen 2005. 2949, 2955 (Decision of 30 June 2005 – No. 178/2004), the Supreme Court expressly based its decision on its own prior precedents. But compare that with the "Maastricht Treaty" case, where the Supreme Court of Denmark took the unusual step of expressly distancing itself from its own prior decision on a similar question in *Helge Tagen v Statsministeren*, UfR 1973.694, (Decision of 28 July 1973), *Hanne Norum Carlsen v. Statsminister Poul Nyrup Rasmussen*, UfR 1996.1300 (Decision of 12 August 1996 – No. 272/1994).

[209] LOOKOFSKY *supra* note 204.

[210] LOOKOFSKY *supra* note 204.

as one of the Danish Supreme Court's most important tasks,[211] and without any formal restraints.[212]

A Danish judgment consists of several segments, including (in civil cases):[213]

- a presentation of the parties' respective claims;
- the parties' allegations;
- a statement of the facts of the case;
- a summary of the testimony of witnesses;
- the court's "reasoning," also referred to as the "premises," that is, the propositions upon which the court's argument is based or from which its conclusion is drawn; and, finally,
- the result.
- If the case is being heard on appeal, the judgment of the appellate court will also include a full account of the proceedings in the forum below. One reason for this is the fact that a lower court judgment, once appealed, is unlikely to be published on its own.

In all European systems that recognize judge-made law, only "similar" cases have precedential potential, so the facts of a case are obviously important for purposes of "distinguishing" the case at bar from prior decisions.

The key prospective element of a given decision is the court's reasoning (premises), that is , that part which serves to explain and legitimize the precedent-setting court's result (the *ratio decidendi* – in the U.S. called the "holding").

However, in Europe some court decisions – even by the Supreme courts – are written in such a way that the reader cannot determine the whole scope of

---

[211] Former Danish Supreme Court Judge, Torben Jensen, *Højesterets arbejdsform in Højesteret* 1661 - 1986 [The Supreme Court's Working Methods (printed in a special edition of the Danish Case Reporter in 1986] (Torben Jensen, W.E. von Eyben & Mogens Koktvedgaard, eds. (Copenhagen: Særudgave af Ugeskrift For Retsvæsen - G.E.C Gads Forlag, 1986).

[212] It is otherwise in Norway, where the Norwegian Act of 25 June 1926 (Amending the Law Relating to the Supreme Court) requires that a plenary session of the Supreme Court be convened when two or more members of an ordinary panel (of 5 justices) wish to overrule a previous decision by that Court. Svein Eng, *Precedent in Norway*, in MacCormick *supra* note 205, at 201-203.

[213] Lookofsky *supra* note 204.

a decision, because the premises are so briefly stated or formulated in such an oracle-like fashion that they provide no clear guidance beyond the decision in the given, concrete case.[214]

### 3.3.4. Relations between National Law and International / E.U. Law

*3.3.4.1. Monistic versus Dualistic Idea*

| **Research Tip #3.20** |
| --- |
| Among scholars and authorities, there exist two different approaches as to whether international law is superior or not to national law: (a) monistic; and (b) dualistic. |

Pursuant to a pure monistic concept, the national and international systems constitute a single legal system. Some monists claim international law supersedes national law. Others think the opposite.

Dualists hold that the national and the international legal systems are different, and exist in their own separate spheres. International law has no independent status in national law. It only becomes relevant when and if the national authorities decide to create national law based on international law.

Danish Law recognizes the principle of dualism and requires international legal sources to be incorporated domestically in order to have legal effect for and against its citizens. However, the last two decades have seen the recognition of international legal sources as a means of safeguarding the rights of individuals in Denmark.[215]

Finland is one of the dualist system countries in which international agreements do not become binding until they have been specifically implemented domestically. Implementing provisions are therefore analogous to national provisions of the same hierarchical rank.[216]

---

[214] Carl Torp, *I anledning af Højesterets 250-aarige Bestaaen*, in UGESKRIFT FOR RETSVÆSEN, 1911, p. 54; LOOKOFSKY *supra* note 204.

[215] WANDALL *supra* note 88.

[216] Legal Order – Finland at <http://ec.europa.eu/civiljustice/legal_order/legal_order_fin_en.htm>.

## 3.3.4.2. National law versus E.U. Law

As discussed in detail in the next chapter, one should note, that so-called Regulations from the E.U. are not to be implemented in national law; opposite so-called Directives.[217]

As for the E.U. Member States, the rules of law have different origins and values, because in each member state different authorities are empowered to adopt rules of law and the different sources of law do not all have the same status.[218]

The European Court of Justice holds that E.U. law[219] supersedes national law. However, not all Member States agree.[220]

The Danish Supreme Court has stated in the so-called "Maastricht Case" that §20 of the Danish Constitution prohibits handing over to an international organization authority to issue legislation or make decisions, if these are in conflict with provisions in the Constitution, including its list of freedoms.[221]

In the so-called "Maastricht Judgment," the German Federal Constitutional Court affirmed that the exercise of sovereign powers by the European Union "is based on authorizations from the Member States which remain sovereign and which in international matters generally act through their government ... nowhere does the Union Treaty reflect the common will of the contracting Parties to establish the Union as a distinct legal subject bearing

---

[217] On sources of EU and Danish law, see TVARNØ *supra* note 94.

[218]      Legal      order    -    General    Information <http://ec.europa.eu/civiljustice/legal_order/legal_order_gen_en.htm>.

[219] Documents with EU legislation often contain large preambles that introduce the legislation and/or express the particular legislative aims. They can be utilized when making legal arguments.

[220] In Finland, in accordance with doctrine on the supremacy of European Union law, E.U. law takes precedence over national law. Legal Order – Finland at <http://ec.europa.eu/civiljustice/legal_order/legal_order_fin_en.htm>. In Sweden, EU legislation applies to a certain extent directly in Sweden without any intermediate legislation. Legal Order – Sweden <http://ec.europa.eu/civiljustice/legal_order/legal_order_swe_en.htm>.

[221] *Hanne Norup Carlsen et. al. v. Primeminister Poul Nyrup Rasmussen*, UfR 1998.800 H at no. 9.2 (Danish Supreme Court 6 April 1998 – No. I 361/1997).

genuine competences."[222]

In contrast, the European Court of Justice has regularly held that E.U. regulations, directives, and agreements are directly, fully, and immediately binding upon E.U. Member States. In the *Costa* case, the ECJ stated,[223] "By contrast with ordinary international treaties, the EEC Treaty has created its own legal system which, on the entry into force of the Treaty, became an integral part of the legal systems of the Member States and which their courts are bound to apply ... By creating a Community of unlimited duration, having ... powers stemming from a limitation of sovereignty, or a transfer of powers from the States to the Community, the Member States have limited their sovereign rights, albeit within limited fields, and have thus created a body of law which binds both their nationals and themselves... ." The elements of the E.U. that the ECJ felt were most salient were unlimited duration, a limitation of sovereign rights, and (separately) treaty language that directly binds the Member States to follow European law.

Furthermore, the European Court of Justice has regularly held that international law – especially customary international law regarding the interpretation and effect of treaties – is binding upon the European Union and its organs. In the *Racke* case, the European Commission questioned whether international law regarding interpretation of treaties – in this case, the doctrine of "fundamental change of circumstances" – had become part of the European legal order. The ECJ emphatically stated that "the European Community must respect international law in the exercise of its powers" and "the rules of customary international law concerning the termination and suspension of treaty relations by reason of a fundamental change of circumstances are binding upon the Community institutions and form part of the Community legal order."[224]

Recently, in the *Placanica* case, the ECJ held that articles in the EC Treaty

---

[222] Judgment on the Maastricht Treaty, BVerfGE 89, 155, (Bundesverfassungsgericht, 12 October 1993).

[223] *Costa v. ENEL*, 1964 E.C.R. 585, 593 (European Court of Justice 15 July 1964 - Case 6/64).

[224] *A. Racke GmbH & Co. v. Hauptzollamt Mainz*, 1998 E.C.R. I-3655 para 45-46 (European Court of Justice , 16 June 199 - Case 162/96).

"must be interpreted as precluding national legislation."[225]

## 3.4. When to Stop

When one is performing research in a Civil Law country, one cannot stop before all sources of law have been located, reviewed, and analyzed. However, if dealing with a foreign law, this requirement is often not achievable.

| **Research Tip #3.21** |
| --- |
| It is a requirement for proper legal research in a Civil Law country always to at least have read all hard sources of law on the issue at hand. In legal research of Civil Law countries, one must be sure all hard law has been studied (including E.U. law for Member States). |

## 3.5. Conclusion / Recap

- Do not use common law / U.S. research methods on civil law research
- Find the relevant civil law research method for your country & topic
- Do not rely on the meanings & your own country's English words when researching another country
- Only rely on authorized (official) translations
- Learn about the legal family, culture, history, society & language before doing research in a foreign country
- Researching civil law requires knowledge about how to interpret text in a statute
- Only research those civil law case decisions that are regarded as precedents.

---

[225] *Criminal proceedings against Massimiliano Placanica* (Italy), [2007] 2 C.M.L.R. 25 para 64 & 71-72, [2007] ECR 00, 2007 WL 654380 (ECJ) (European Court of Justice (Grand Chamber), 6 March 2007 - Case C-338/04).

# CHAPTER 4

# European Union Resources

## 4.1. Introduction

This chapter is updated from first edition in light of the so-called Treaty of Lisbon of December 2007.

The update could have been made in either of two ways: (a) consolidate the text from first edition or (b) choose to pinpoint the changes made by the Treaty of Lisbon in a special last chaptersection and thus offer the reader the opportunity to pay particular attention to the changes that the Treaty of Lisbon provides.
I have chosen the latter alternative, as many textbooks on E.U. law have not yet been updated to give readers of such "antiquated" books notice of the changes made by the Treaty of Lisbon (of which most articles might come into force 1 January 2009).

So please, remember to check the content of the following sections 4.1-4.5 with the content of new section 4.6.

As this book is primarily aim for use in teaching courses on legal research methods, note too that the time normally allotted for such courses cannot begin to cover comprehensive teaching of European Union Law.[1]

---

[1] As of 2007, trade between U.S. & E.U. were running around €1.7 billion (~ $ 2.468 billion) per day

Right off the bat, a good book on European Union[2] "Law"[3] (written in English primarily for the U.K.) is "E.U. Law: Text, Cases and Materials".[4]

Remember that European Union 'law" is part of the law of each of the E.U. Member States, who must to a certain extent separately implement that "law" from Brussels (Bruxelles).

---

**Research Tip #4.1**

European Union "Law" should be read and studied through the law of the E.U. Member State that one is doing research on.[5]

Beware that some E.U. "law" may be not even have been "implemented into law" by a Member State (which can be sued by the European Union Commission for such failure to implement).

Secondary sources on E.U. "law" cannot be found in general but have to be searched through the particular E.U. Member State one wants to do research on.

---

The European Union[6] is unique in that it is much more than an international

---

[2] The European Union (EU) is a political and economic union of member states, located in Europe, and established by the Maastricht Treaty of 1993 upon the foundations of the pre-existing European Community.

[3] See also, Watt & Dashwood's European Union Law (5th ed)(2006 London: Thompson); Woods, Steiner & Twigg-Flesner, EU Law (9 ed.)(2006 England: Oxford University Press).

[4] Paul Craig & Grainne de Burca, EU Law: Text, Cases and Materials (4. Ed.)(Publisher: Oxford University Press, 2007 - ISBN 978-0-19-927389-8).

[5] In the context of the E.U., the term "supranational" usually refers to the institutions that exist to pursue the common E.U. interests, shared by the E.U. Member States. It also refers to the discharge of functions and exercise of powers by those institutions, transcending national boundaries, in the domains where the E.U. Member States, in the treaties, have conferred those functions and powers on them. The supranational approach is often contrasted with the intergovernmental approach that involves keeping supranational institutions, and their role, to a minimum.

[6] Dr Klaus-Dieter Borchardt, EU ABC by (EU 2000) at <http://www.europa.eu/eur-lex/en/about/abc/index.html> or <http://www.europa.eu/eur-lex/en/about/abc_en.pdf>.

organization.[7] It is not a federation like the United States. Nevertheless, to a certain extent, the E.U. has similarities in function and organization to the United States. Even so, in the E.U., there is no rule similar to the U.S. "Dormant" Commerce Clause.[8] Thus, the member states of the E.U. truly have full sovereignty.[9] However, there is also a so-called "proportionality principle" that is, European Union actions must not go beyond what is necessary to

---

[7] The E.U. is also after the Treaty of Lisbon based on two main treaties found in "European Union consolidated versions" of: Treaty on the European Union [hereinafter TEU] & Treaty on the European Communities [herinafter TEC] & Procoocols & Appendix, E.U. OJ C321 E, 29.12.2006, pp. 0001-0331, printed in Official Journal C321 E, Vol. 49, 29 December 2006 at <http://eur-lex.europa.eu/JOHtml.do?uri=OJ:C:2006:321E:SOM:EN:HTML> (visited July 2008).

[8] Even where Congress chooses not to exercise such power, States cannot regulate, even if Congress "sleeps." See Chief Justice John Marshall's dicta in *Gibbons v. Cigden*, 22 U.S. 1 (US Supreme Court 1824).

[9] However, the European Court of Justice holds that E.U. law supersedes national law. The ECJ has regularly held that EU regulations, directives and agreements are directly, fully, and immediately binding upon EU Member States. In the *Costa* case, the court stated that "[b]y contrast with ordinary international treaties, the EEC Treaty has created its own legal system which, on the entry into force of the Treaty, became an integral part of the legal systems of the Member States and which their courts are bound to apply...By creating a Community of unlimited duration, having...powers stemming from the States to the Community, the Member States have limited their sovereign rights, albeit within limited fields, and have thus created a body of law which binds both their nationals and themselves". *Costa v. ENEL* (ECJ 15 July 1964, Case 6/64), 1964 E.C.R. 585, 593. But, not all Member States agree. The Danish Supreme Court has in the so-called "Maastricht Case" stated that under §20 of the Danish Constitution an international organization is prohibited from issuing legislation or making decisions, if these are in conflict with provisions in the Danish Constitution, including its freedom rights. *Hanne Norup Carlsen et. al. v. Primeminister Poul Nyrup Rasmussen*, UfR 1998.800 H at no. 9.2 (Danish Supreme Court 6 April 1998 – No. I 361/1997). See also the so-called "Maastricht judgment" of the German Federal Constitutional Court where it affirmed that the exercise of sovereign powers by the European Union "is based on authorizations from the Member States which remain sovereign and which in international matters generally act through their government...nowhere does the Union Treaty reflect the common will of the contracting Parties to establish the Union as a distinct legal subject bearing genuine competences." Judgment on the Maastricht Treaty, BVerfGE 89, 155, (German Federal Constitutional Court, 12 October 1993).

achieve the objectives of the Treaty of Rome,[10] except that the E.U. can act in areas where member states cannot sufficiently achieve an objective but through the Community (the subsidiary principle).[11]

On 18 and 19 of October 2007, documents to a so-called "Reform Treaty" or Treaty of Lisbon[12] was approved at an informal meeting of the Heads of State and Government.[13] The treaty was signed by the Council of the European Union in Lisbon on 13 December 2007.[14] It is not as far reaching as the so-called "Constitution Treaty"[15] which was rejected by some Member States.[16] The Treaty of Lisbon will come into force on January 2009, but large parts of treaty will first take effect in 2014.[17]

[10] Or "Treaty establishing the European Economic Community" of 25 March 1957, 298 U.N.T.S. 11 and later article 5 (ex ante EC art. 3b) of Treaty of Establishing the European Community (TEC), OJ C321 E, 29.12.2006 p. 0046

[11] See TEC Article 5 (ex ante EC art. 3b), OJ C321 E, 29.12.2006 p. 0046.

[12] Table of Content on the treaty and "Information and Notices" are printed in the Official Journal of the European Union (E.U. OJ ) as C 306, Vol. 50 of 17 December 2007. Also available at <http://eur-lex.europa.eu/JOHtml.do?uri=OJ:C:2007:306:SOM:EN:HTML> (visited July 2008).

[13] See Documents approved at the Intergovernmental Conference, at the level of Heads of State and Government, of 18 October 2007 in Lisbon at <http://www.consilium.europa.eu/cms3_fo/showPage.asp?id=1317&lang=en&mode= g> (visited July 2008). In December 2007 issued as Final Act, Doc. 2007/C 306/02, OJ C306, 17.12.2007 pp. 0231-0271.

[14] Treaty of Lisbon amending the Treaty on European Union and the Treaty establishing the European Community of 13 December 2007, OJ C 307, 15.12.2007 pp. 0001—0271. Consolidated versions with Treaty of Lisbon amendments of the Treaty on European Union and the Treaty on the functioning of the European Union are published in OJ C115, 9.5.2008 pp. pp. 0001-0388 (Table of Content available at <http://eur-lex.europa.eu/JOHtml.do?uri=OJ:C:2008:115:SOM:EN:HTML> (visited July 2008)).

[15] Treaty establishing a Constitution for Europe of 29 October 2004, OJ C310, 16.12.2004 pp. 0001-0474. The treaty repealed the Treaty establishing the European Community, the Treaty of European Union, and their supplements and amendments, Art. IV-437.

[16] Table of Content on the treaty and "Information and Notices" are printed in the Official Journal of the European Union (OJ) as C310, Vol. 47 of 16 December 2004. Also available at <http://eur-lex.europa.eu/JOHtml.do?uri=OJ:C:2004:310:SOM:EN:HTML>.

[17] See Final Act, Doc. 2007/C 306/02, OJ C306, 17.12.2007 pp. 0231-0271.

Note that the Council of Europe (an international organization that is not part of the E.U., aiming to achieve greater unity among its members, which are all European democracies) and Council of the European Union (one of the legislative institutions of the E.U.) are two different institutions.[18] The European Union has been a permanent observer at the United Nations since the mid-1970s and a full participant in many major UN conferences. It is also one of the key players in the World Trade Organization (WTO).

---

**Research Tip #4.2**

American scholars who want to undertake comparative research on E.U. "law" (and Civil Law) should be careful about using legal terms,[19] even ones well-known in American legal circles, as their meanings may be quite different in Europe (and Civil Law).

---

Thus, definitions should be carefully checked before any comparison is attempted.

---

**Research Tip #4.3**

American scholars cannot use their U.S. legal research methods in researching E.U. "law" and Civil Law (see further above in Chapter 3).

---

In Europe today, Civil Law and Common Law show several signs of convergence. In the UK, statutory law increasingly overrides Common Law traditions of judicial law-making, while on the continent, legal theory increasingly acknowledges the fact and necessity of judicial precedent and law-making. Important areas of the law are unified under international treaties. British judges faithfully implement European Union law that is based primarily on Civil Law notions. The Court of Justice of the E.U. creatively applies principles from both legal worlds. But despite refreshing input from the Common Law, the dominant legal culture of the European Union and the emerging *ius*

---

[18] Council of Europe at <http://www.coe.int/> and Council of the European Union <http://europa.eu/institutions/inst/council/index_en.htm>.

[19] E.U. Glossary at <http://europa.eu/scadplus/glossary/index_en.htm>.

*commune Europaeum*[20] remain very much in the Civil Law tradition.[21]

To be able to find material on the European Union, it is important for the legal scholar to understand the different E.U. institutions and their function. Thus, the following will broadly describe the main E.U. institutions of importance for the legal scholar.

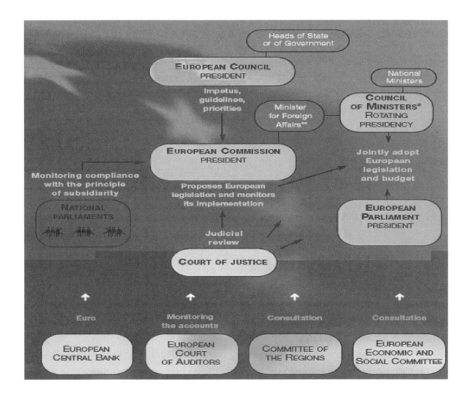

*Table 28: European Union Institutions*[22]

---

[20] See Glossary in Appendix 1.

[21] Herbert Hausmaninger, THE AUSTRIAN LEGAL SYSTEM 320 (2003 Manzsche Verlags- und Universitätsbuchhandlung).

## 4.1.1. The European Parliament

The European Parliament[23] is the only supranational institution whose members are (since 1979) democratically elected directly by the E.U.'s citizens under a system of population-based proportional representation. It represents the people of the E.U. Member States. Today, the European Parliament is firmly established as a co-legislator, has budgetary powers and exercises democratic controls over all the European institutions.

As only the E.U. Commission can initiate legislation in the E.U., the European Parliament is far from having the powers of a national parliament.

In the adoption of legislative acts, a distinction is made between the ordinary legislative procedure ("co-decision" see below), which puts the Parliament on an equal footing with the Council, and the special legislative procedures, which apply only in specific cases where Parliament has only a consultative role. On "sensitive" questions (e.g., taxation, industrial policy and agricultural policy) the European Parliament gives only an advisory opinion (the "consultation procedure"[24]). In some cases the Treaty[25] provides that consultation is obligatory, being required by the legal base, and the proposal cannot acquire the force of law unless Parliament has delivered an opinion. In this case, the Council is not empowered to take a decision alone.

Parliament can ask the Commission to present legislative proposals for laws to the Council. It plays a genuine role in creating new laws, since it examines the Commission's annual program of work and indicates which laws it would like to see introduced.

After the Commission has presented a proposal for a "legislative text," a member of the European Parliament, working in one of the parliamentary committees, draws up a report on the proposal. The parliamentary committee votes on this report and, possibly, amends it. When the text has been revised

---

[22] Source: E.U. websites (same as for all other tables in this chapter).

[23] TEC 189 (ex ante EC art. 137).

[24] TEC Article 252 (ex ante EC art. 189c). There also exists a so-called "Assent Procedure" in which the Parliament cannot make amendments, but only accept or reject.

[25] Most recently updated by the Nice Treaty of 1991, the Maastricht Treaty of 1992 and the Amsterdam Treaty of 1996. Consolidated versions of The Treaty on European Union and of The Treaty Establishing The European Community (consolidated text), Official Journal C 321E of 29 December 2006, p. 0001-0331.

and adopted in plenary, Parliament has adopted its position. This process is repeated one or more times, depending on the type of procedure and whether or not agreement is reached with the Council.

The co-decision procedure[26] was introduced by the Maastricht Treaty on European Union of 1992 (effective 1993), and was extended and made more effective by the Amsterdam Treaty of 1996. The co-decision gives the same weight to the European Parliament and the Council of the European Union on a wide range of areas (for example, transport, the environment and consumer protection). Two thirds of European laws are adopted jointly by the European Parliament and the Council. After the Commission has sent its proposal to Parliament and the Council, they consider it, and discuss it on two successive occasions. After two readings, if they cannot agree, the proposal is brought before a Conciliation Committee made up of an equal number of representatives of the Council and Parliament. Representatives of the Commission also attend the meetings of the Conciliation Committee and contribute to the discussions. When the Committee has reached agreement, the text agreed upon is sent to Parliament and the Council for a third reading, so that they can finally adopt it as a legislative text. The final agreement of the two institutions is essential if the text is to be adopted as a law. However, even if a joint text is agreed to by the Conciliation Committee, Parliament can still reject the proposed law by an absolute majority of its members.

Parliament has a power of political initiative in that it can call on the Commission to submit a proposal to the Council of the European Union.

Furthermore, the Parliament can raise questions to the Commission and Council; the Parliament can by a two-thirds vote "censure" the Commission; the Parliament can initiate lawsuits against Council or Commission for failure to act; the Parliament can veto a nomination of a Commissioner; and the Parliament has, at least to a certain extent, power over the E.U. budget.

Parliament has also appointed an Ombudsman,[27] who deals with complaints by individuals or businesses registered in the E.U. against European

---

[26] TEC Article 251 (ex ante EC art. 189 b).

[27]       The          Ombudsman's          website          is <http://www.ombudsman.europa.eu/home/en/default.htm>.

Community institutions or bodies[28] with a view to reaching an amicable solution.

Written or oral questions by members of the European Parliament (MEPs) to the Council and the Commission - as one of Parliament's means of exercising supervision - can be of high value to a researcher.

Parliament wants its work to be known and understood by the public and has provided a register that gives access to documents.[29] The European Parliament Public Register of Documents allows members of the public to carry out research into Parliament's work. It is intended to inform the public of the existence of the various documents produced by Parliament and to give access to them.

---

[28] The Ombudsman investigates complaints against the Commission, Council of European Union, Parliament, Court of Auditors, Court of Justice (except in its judicial role), European Economic and Social Committee, Committee of the Regions, European Central Bank, European Investment Bank, Europol, and any other European Community body.

[29] <http://www.europarl.europa.eu/registre/recherche/RechercheSimplifiee.cfm?langue=EN>.

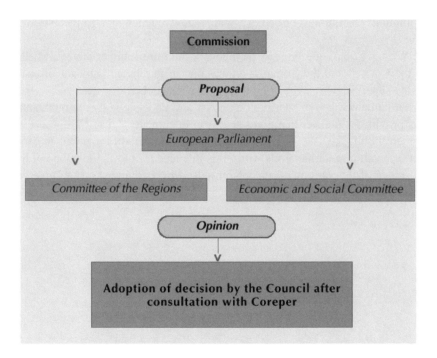

*Table 29: Consultation Procedure*

COREPER is the Committee of Permanent Representatives in the European Union. Weekly meetings are held in private. It prepares the agenda for the ministerial Council meetings and may take some procedural decisions. It oversees and coordinates the work of some 250 committees and working parties made up of civil servants from the E.U. Member States who work on issues at the technical level. It is chaired by the Presidency of the Council. There are two committees: (I) consists of deputy heads of mission from the E.U. member states in Brussels and deals largely with social and economic issues; (II) consists of heads of mission and deals largely with political, financial and foreign policy issues. Representatives of the Council Secretariat from the relevant Directorates and from the Legal Directorate are also present. There is also a special committee on agriculture.

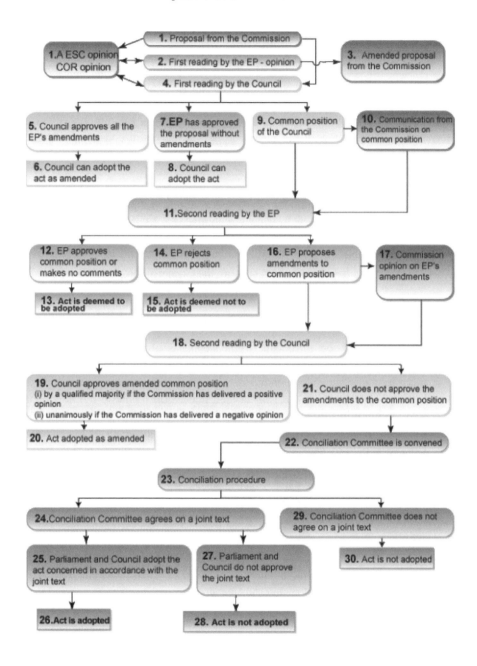

*Table 30: Co-decision Procedure*

## 4.1.2. The European Commission

The European Commission (formally the Commission of the European Communities)[30] is independent of national governments and represents the European perspective. The European Commission is the only institution empowered to initiate legislation. Furthermore, it is the union's executive branch. Together with the E.U. Courts it enforces European law.[31] On the international stage it represents the European Union, for example in the WTO.

The President of the Commission is appointed by a majority vote in the Council and the Parliament approves or rejects the proposed appointment. Then, in accord with the President appointed, the Member States appoint the 25 Commissioners. The College of Commissioners must then be endorsed as a whole by Parliament.

Parliament has the power to censure the Commission. It can force the College of Commissioners as a whole to resign.

## 4.1.3. The Council of the European Union

The Council of the European Union[32] consists of a representative of each Member State at ministerial level, authorized to commit the government of that Member State. Membership is fluid, with each government sending the minister appropriate to the subject then under consideration by the Council. The foreign minister is generally regarded as the coordinator and main representative of each government's delegation. The presidency of the European Council is held by each Member State in turn for a six month period, under a rotating system.[33]

The Council has six main responsibilities:
- Adopting European law – often jointly with the Parliament

---

[30] TEC Article 211 & 213 (ex ante EC art. 155 & 157).

[31] See "Reasoned Opinion" in glossary, Appendix 1.

[32] TEC Article 202-203 (ex ante EC art. 145-146). Consolidated version of Treaty Establishing the European Community, OJ C 321/37 of 29 December 2006.

[33] It is to be distinguished from the Council of Europe, which is a completely separate international organisation, not a European Union institution.

- Coordinating the broad economic policies of the Member States
- Concluding international agreements between the E.U. and other countries or international organizations
- Approving the E.U.'s budget together with the Parliament
- Developing the E.U.'s common foreign and security policy
- Coordinating cooperation between the national courts and police forces in criminal matters.

The Council of the European Union should be distinguished from the European Council,[34] which meets four times a year in what is informally known as the "European Summit" (E.U. summit), and is a closely related but separate body, made up of the heads of state and government of the Member States, accompanied by their foreign ministers, whose mission is to provide guidance and high level policy to the Council.

The latter council provides the necessary impetus for the development of the European Union and sets forth its general guidelines and political priorities, taking account of Parliament's recommendations. Each summit begins with a declaration by the President of the European Parliament, setting out the institution's key positions on the subjects to be addressed by the Heads of State and Government. At the end of each summit, the President of the European Council presents a report to Parliament on its outcome and launches a debate with the Members of the European Parliament.

### 4.1.4. The E.U. Courts

The E.U. courts[35] have jurisdiction to give preliminary rulings ("advisory rulings") on the interpretation of E.U. law. National courts cannot determine the validity of a European legal measure. The E.U. courts have the power to settle legal disputes between E.U. Member States, E.U. institutions, businesses, and individuals.

Only a decision made public in the language of the case is authentic, even though decisions are published in all E.U. working languages. See further

---

[34] TEU Article 4 (ex ante art. D). Consolidated version of Treaty on European Union, OJ C 321, 29.12.2006 p. 0001.
[35] TEC Article 220 (ex ante EC art. 164).

Rules of Procedure.[36]

From November 1989, the original E.C. Court, the European Court of Justice (ECJ) was augmented by a lower court, the Court of First Instance (CFI). The assistance of the CFI should to a certain extent relieve the ECJ of its caseload. The CFI is particularly responsible for actions brought by private individuals, companies, and some other organizations, as well as for cases relating to competition law. It is possible to appeal CFI decisions to the ECJ.

Decisions made by the ECJ are now numbered with a "C" for court, whereas CFI decisions are numbered with a "T" for tribunal. In the official European Court Reports, ECJ judgments have page numbers preceded by "I-," " whereas CFI judgments have page numbers preceded by "II-." Decisions are given without dissent. The CFI can be chaired by only one judge, while the ECJ has 3-5 judges in chambers or 13 judges in a Grand Chamber. There is also a lower court with appeal to the CFI, the European Union Civil Service Tribunal, for "disputes involving the European Union civil service."[37]

The judges are appointed by the E.U. Member States from among persons with a legal education.

In E.U. Court proceedings, there is a special lawyer, the "Advocate-General" (AG[38]), who participates and gives his analysis and evaluation on the case and his opinion of a proper result under European law. The AG is an institution that exists in France but not most other Civil Law countries. For an

---

[36] Rules of Procedure of the Court of Justice of the European Communities of 19 June 1991, OJ L 176, 4.7.1991, p. 0007–0032 with latest amendments in OJ L 24, 29.1.2008, p. 39–41. Consolidated version of March 2008 at <http://curia.europa.eu/en/instit/txtdocfr/txtsenvigueur/txt5.pdf> (visited July 2008).

[37] This tribunal has "first instance jurisdiction in disputes between the Communities and their servants referred to in Article 236 of the EC Treaty and Article 152 of the EAEC Treaty, including disputes between all bodies or agencies and their servants in respect of which jurisdiction is conferred on the Court of Justice." Article 1 of Annex I to Council Decision of 2 November 2004 establishing the European Union Civil Service Tribunal (2004/752/EC, Euratom), Official Journal L 333 , 09/11/2004 P. 0007 – 0011.

[38] See further, Chapter 1 on Judges and Advocates General in Rules of Procedure of the Court of Justice of the European Communities of 19 June 1991 OJ L 176 of 4 July 191 p. 0007, Consolidated version of January 2007 at <http://curia.europa.eu/en/instit/txtdocfr/txtsenvigueur/txt5.pdf>.

American scholar, the AG can to a certain extent resemble a permanent amicus curiae[39] on behalf of justice. The AG consists of eight persons appointed by E.U. Member States. The AG-opinions can definitely be of value for the legal scholar.

Through its case law, the Court of Justice has identified an obligation of administrations and national courts to apply European Community law in full within their spheres of competence and to protect the rights conferred on citizens by that law (that is, direct application of European Community law), and to display any conflicting national provision, whether prior or subsequent to the Community provision (that is, primacy of Community law over national law).

The Court of Justice has also recognized the principle of the liability of E.U. Member States for breach of Community law.

In addition, the Court of Justice also works in conjunction with the national courts, which are the ordinary courts applying European Community law. Any national court or tribunal that is called upon to decide a dispute involving Community law may, and sometimes must, submit questions to the Court of Justice for a preliminary ruling. The Court will then give an interpretation or review the legality of a rule of Community law.

Of the thousands of judgments rendered by the Court of Justice, the majority, particularly preliminary rulings, clearly have important consequences for the daily life of European citizens. Examples of some of the most important areas of Community law with which Court judgments have dealt include free movement of goods, freedom of movement of persons, freedom to provide services , equal treatment and social rights , and fundamental rights.

The procedure before the Court of Justice is as follows:

| Direct actions and appeal | | References for a preliminary ruling |
|---|---|---|
| **Written procedure** | | |
| Application | [Application for legal aid] | National court's decision to make a reference |
| Service of the application on the defendant by the Registry | Assignment of Judge-Rapporteur and Advocate General | Translation into the other official languages of the |

---

[39] "Friend of the Court".

| | | European Union |
|---|---|---|
| Notice of the action in the Official Journal of the E.U. (Series C) | | Notice of the question referred for a preliminary ruling in the Official Journal of the E.U. (Series C) |
| [Interim measures] | | |
| [Intervention] | | Notification to the parties to the proceedings, the Member States, the Community institutions, the EEA States and to the EFTA Surveillance Authority |
| Defence/Response | | |
| [Objection to admissibility] | | |
| [Reply and Rejoinder] | | |
| | | Written observations of the parties, the States and the institutions |
| The Judge-Rapporteur draws up the preliminary report ||| |
| General Meeting of the Judges and the Advocate General ||| |
| Assignment of the case to a formation ||| |
| [Measures of inquiry] ||| |
| **Oral procedure** ||| |
| [Hearing; Report of the Hearing] ||| |
| [Opinion of the Advocate General] ||| |
| Deliberation by the Judges ||| |
| **Judgment** ||| |

Notes:
Optional steps in the procedure are indicated in brackets
Cases disposed of by order do not include all the steps indicated above
Words in bold face indicate a public document

*Table 31: Procedure before the Court of Justice[40]*

Pursuant to the renumbering (or rather equivalences) of the articles of the Treaty on the European Union (TEU) and of the Treaty establishing the European Community (TEC), brought about by the Treaty of Amsterdam (1996), the Court of Justice and the Court of First Instance have introduced,

---

[40] Texts governing procedure at <http://www.curia.europa.eu/en/instit/txtdocfr/index.htm>.

with effect from May 1, 1999, a new method of citation of the articles of the TEU, TEC, European Coal and Steel community (ECSC) and Euratom Treaties. That new method is primarily designed to avoid all risk of confusion between the version of an article as it stood prior to May 1, 1999 and the version applying after that date (see Appendix 4).

The principles on which that method operates are as follows: where reference is made to an article of a treaty as it stands after May 1, 1999, the number of the article is immediately followed by two letters indicating the treaty concerned: E.U. for the Treaty on the European Union; EC for the EC Treaty; CS for the ECSC Treaty; and EA for the Euratom Treaty. Further explanation can be found at <www.curia.europa.eu/en/content/juris/index_infos.htm>.

## 4.1.5. The European Judicial Cooperation Unit

EUROJUST[41] is a newer European Union body established in 2002[42] to enhance the effectiveness of the competent authorities within E.U. Member States when they are dealing with serious cross-border and organized crime. Eurojust stimulates and improves the coordination of investigations and prosecutions and also supports the Member States in order to render their investigations and prosecutions more effective. Its mission is to enhance the development of Europe-wide cooperation in criminal justice cases. This means that Eurojust is a key interlocutor with the European institutions such as the Parliament, the Council and the Commission. It operates from The Hague in the Netherlands. Eurojust and Europol signed an agreement on close cooperation on June 9, 2004.

The College of Eurojust is composed of one member nominated by each E.U. Member State (as of 1 January 2007 27). The national members are senior, experienced prosecutors or judges; some national members are supported by deputies and assistants.

---

[41]  <http://www.eurojust.europa.eu/>  and  <http://europa.eu/agencies/pol_agencies /eurojust/index_en.htm>.

[42]  Eurojust was created by EU Council Decision 2002/187/JHA of 28 February 2002 setting up Eurojust with a view to reinforcing the fight against serious crime, OJ L 63, 6.3.2002, p. 1–13, amended by EU Council Decision 2003/659/JHA of 18 June 2003 amending Decision 2002/187/JHA setting up Eurojust with a view to reinforcing the fight against serious crime, OJ L 245, 29.9.2003, p. 44–46.

### 4.1.6. The Pillars of the European Union

The subject matter dealt with in various of the E.U. treaties is sometimes described as the "Three pillars," with the following categorization:

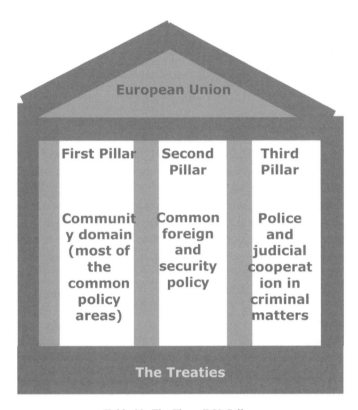

*Table 32: The Three E.U. Pillars*

The "roof" - general principles TEU Title I (art 1-7)

First pillar (the Community Law) – TEU Title II (art. 8 on the old EC Treaty) & Title IV of the (art 10 on the EURATOM Treaty). The first pillar covers:

- Customs union and a single market
- Agricultural policy
- Structural policy
- E.U. citizenship
- Education and culture
- Trans-European networks

- Consumer protection
- Health
- Research and environment
- Social policy
- Asylum policy
- External borders
- Immigration policy
- Euratom
- European Coal and Steel Community[43]

Second pillar (foreign and security policy co-operation) – TEU Title V (art 11-28). The second pillar covers:

- Cooperation, common positions and measures
- Peacekeeping
- Human rights
- Democracy
- Aid to non-member countries
- Drawing on the WEU (questions concerning the security of the E.U.)
- Disarmament
- Financial aspects of defense
- Long-term: Europe's security framework

Third pillar (police and enforcement co-operation in criminal cases ) & Closer co-operation – TEU Title VI (art 29-42) & TEU Title VII (art 43-45) Bottom – Final articles – TEU Title VIII (art 46-53) & Protocols. The pillar includes:

- Cooperation between judicial authorities in civil and criminal law
- Police cooperation
- Combating racism and xenophobia
- Fighting drugs and the arms trade
- Fighting organized crime
- Fighting terrorism
- Criminal acts against children, trafficking in human beings.

When the Treaty of Lisbon come into full force, see below section 4.6, the

---

[43] All assets and liabilities of the ECSC was transferred to the European Community on 24 July 2002. Article 1 of Protocol to the Nice Treaty, OJ C325. 24.12.2002 p. 0182.

three pillars will be merged into one single pillar. Furthermore, the "roof" will then somewhat include the Charter on basic rights.[44]

Since January 1, 2007, the E.U. has consisted of the following Member States: Austria, Belgium, Bulgaria, Cyprus, Czech Republic, Denmark, Estonia, Finland, France, Germany, Greece, Hungary, Ireland, Italy, Latvia, Lithuania, Luxembourg, Malta, Netherlands, Poland, Portugal, Romania, Slovakia, Slovenia, Spain, Sweden and the United Kingdom.[45]

---

[44] Charter of Fundamental Rights of The European Union, 2000/C 364/01, OJ C 364 18/12/2000 p. 0001-0022 or at <http://www.europarl.europa.eu/charter/pdf/text_en.pdf>. See also Commentary of The Charter of Fundamental Rights of The European Union at <http://ec.europa.eu/justice_home/doc_centre/rights/charter/docs/network_commentar y_final%20_180706.pdf>. See further below section 4.6.

[45] Candidate countries are: Croatia, former Yugoslav Republic of Macedonia, Turkey. Potential candidate countries: Albania, Montenegro, Bosnia-Herzegovina, Serbia, Republic of Kosovo. On the enlargement process, see <http://ec.europa.eu/enlargement/index_en.htm> (visited July 2008).

*Table 33: Map of The European Union (2007)*

# 4.2. Sources of E.U. law

## 4.2.1. Hard and soft Law in E.U.

---

**Research Tip #4.4**

As for E.U. avoid using (U.S.) terms as Primary and Secondary sources, but use the civil law terms "hard" and "soft" law – and as for E.U. "law"[46] the later is very hard to find/nearly non-existing.

Especially after the Treaty of Lisbon it is vital to look at national parliament's con-tributions/legislative history to E.U. "law."

---

In the European Community, the term "soft law" is also often used to de-scribe various kinds of quasi-legal instruments of the European Communi-ties: "codes of conduct," "guidelines,' "communications" etc. In the area of law of the European Communities, soft law instruments are often used to indicate how the European Commission intends to use its powers and per-form its tasks within its area of competence,[47] see for example "COM-documents."[48] The gradual process of codification beginning with soft law, that being non-mandatory or advisory principles, has been termed "creeping

---

[46]The Treaty of Lisbon has turned down the suggestion in the draft to a E.U. Constitution to use the term "law" (or code/act), see article I-6 of (the draft to the) Treaty establish-ing a Constitution for Europe, OJ C310, 16.12.2004 p. 0012.

[47] Michael G. Egge, Matteo F. Bay & Janier Ruiz Calzado, *The New EC Merger Regula-tion: A Move to Convergence, Status of Soft Law In international Law*, Antitrust Magazine, Section of Antitrust Law, AMERICAN BAR ASSOCIATION, Fall 2004 at <www.lw.com/upload/pubContent/_pdf/pub1167_1.pdf > (visited July 2008). The European Union may be somewhat ahead of the United States in recognizing the im-portance of these "soft law" regimes, Jerry L. Mashaw, *Reasoned Administration: The European Union, the United States, and the Project of Democratic Governance*, 122 THE GEORGE WASHINGTON LAW REVIEW, Vol. 76 p. 99, 122 (Nov 2007) at <http://docs.law.gwu.edu/stdg/gwlr/issues/pdf/76_1_Mashaw.pdf> (visited July 2008).

[48] COM documents: proposed legislation and other Commission communications to the Council and/or the other institutions, and their preparatory papers. Search in Eur-Lex → Preparatory acts → Commission proposals and opinions at <http://ec.europa.eu/transparency/regdoc/registre.cfm?CL=en>.

codification.[49]

## 4.2.2. E.U. "law" and Language

---

**Research Tip #4.5**

When one does research on the European Union,
the primary sources are two treaties,[50] namely on establishing the European
Community (EC[51] or TEC or (now) FTEU[52]) and on the European Union (TEU).

---

These consist in turn of the following:[53]

- European Atomic Energy Community Treaty (EURATOM)
- Treaty establishing the European Community[54] [in force]
- Treaty on European Union (TEU)[55] [in force] (originally also called the Maastricht Treaty)
- Treaty of Nice - Amending the Treaty on European Union, the Treaties Establishing the European Communities and certain related acts of 26 February 2001[56] [in force].[57]

---

[49] Klaus Peter Berger, The Principles of European Contract Law and the Concept of the "Creeping Codification" of Law, 9 EUROPEAN REVIEW OF PRIVATE LAW 21, 21 (2001).

[50] See <www.europe.eu/abc/treaties/index_en.htm>.

[51] Originally, the European Community (EC) dealt mainly with economic, social and trade matters.

[52] The Treaty of Lisbon of 2007 renames the treaty once again, now to be named the Treaty on the Functioning of the European Union (TFEU), see Presidency Conclusion's on the Brussels European Council meeting 21-22 June 2007 at <www.consilium.europa.eu/ueDocs/cms_Data/docs/pressData/en/ec/94932.pdf>.

[53] Another significant document is also the Charter of Fundamental Rights of the European Union, OJ C364, 18/12/2000 p. 0001-0022.

[54] Nice consolidated version in O.J C 325, 24.12.2002 p. 0033-0184.

[55] Nice consolidated version in OJ C325, 24.12.2002 p. 0005-0032.

[56] OJ C80, 10.3.2001 p. 0001-0087. Consolidated version in OJ C325, 24.12.2002 p. 0001-0184.

[57] An overview of the changes made by the Nice Treaty can be found in "Guide for European citizens" at <http://ec.europa.eu/comm/nice_treaty/index2_en.htm>. Other information on the treaty can be found at <http://europa.eu/scadplus/nice_treaty/index_en.htm>.

The politicians of the E.U. proposed a treaty establishing a "Constitution"[58] for Europe (TCE),[59] but it was been rejected in elections or referendums in several member-states by their citizens.

To a certain extent it is also necessary for the scholar to be aware of the founding treaties (original versions with later updating), the amending Treaties, and the accession treaties for each of the five enlargements of the E.U. that have accurred. The main history of what is now the European Union is as follows:

- 1952, 23 July – European Coal and Steel Community ("Treaty of Paris" of 1951)[60] comes into force[61]
- 1958, 1 January – Treaty establishing the European Economic Community[62] (EEC)[63] ("Treaty of Rome of 1957") & the European Atomic Energy Community Treaty (EURATOM of 1957)[64] comes into force
- 1967, 1 July - Treaty Establishing a Single Council and a Single Commission of the European Communities of 1965 (also called the "Merger Treaty")[65] comes into force[66]
- 1979 – Direct elections to European Parliament

---

[58] In reality, a treaty compiled of previous EU treaties with amendments.

[59] Official Journal C 310 of 16 December 2004 [not in force].

[60] 261 U.N.T.S. 140.

[61] It expired on 23 July 2002. All assets and liabilities of the ECSC was transferred to the European Community on 24 July 2002. Article 1 of Protocol to the Nice Treaty, OJ C325. 24.12.2002 p. 0182.

[62] With the aim to create a common market, eliminate internal trade barriers and allow free movement of factors of production.

[63] Of 25 March 1957, 298 U.N.T.S. 11. By the Maastricht Treaty of 1993, the treaty was renamed the Treaty establishing the European Community (TEC). The Treaty of Lisbon of 2007 renames the treaty once again, now to be named the Treaty on the Functioning of the European Union (TFEU), see Presidency Conclusion's on the Brussels European Council meeting 21-22 June 2007 at <www.consilium.europa.eu/ueDocs/cms_Data/docs/pressData/en/ec/94932.pdf> (visited July 2008).

[64] 261 U.N.T.S. 167.

[65] OJ 152, 13.07.1967, p 0002. Reprinted in 4 ILM 776.

[66] Provided for a Single Commission and a Single Council of the then three European Communities.

- 1987, 1 July – Single European Act of 1986[67] (SEA) (amending the Treaty of Rome to a initiate campaign for a Community without internal frontiers by 1993)[68]
- 1993, 1 November – Maastricht Treaty on European Union of 1992[69] (TEU which changed the "European Economic Community" (EEC) to the "European Community" (EC) and includes the so-called Three Pillar structure[70]) becomes operational[71]
- 1999, 1 May – Treaty of Amsterdam[72] of 1997 becomes operational & 11 Member States join using a new common currency called the EURO (€)[73]

[67] OJ L169, 29.6.1987 p. 0001. Reprinted in 25 ILM 506.

[68] With the aim to remove all frontier controls, principle of mutual recognition to product standards, open public barriers of competition to banks and insurance, remove restrictions on foreign exchange transactions and abolish restriction on cabotage (trucking). It provided for the adaptations required for the achievement of the Internal Market.

[69] OJ C 191 , 29.7.1992 p. 0001 – 0110. Reprinted in 31 ILM 247.

[70] Creating the EURO currency, common foreign and defense policy, a common citizenship and giving the European Parliament genuine power. Three pillars of the European Union: (a) the European Communities pillar; (b) the Common Foreign and Security Policy (CFSP) pillar; and (c) the Justice and Home Affairs (JHA) pillar (later named the Police and Judicial Co-operation in Criminal Matters (PJC) pillar).

[71] The Maastricht Treaty introduced new forms of co-operation between the Member State governments - for example on defence, and in the area of "justice and home affairs". By adding this inter-governmental co-operation to the existing "Community" system, the Maastricht Treaty created a new structure with three "pillars" which is political as well economic. This is the European Union (EU).

[72] The Treaty of Amsterdam made substantial changes to the Treaty on European Union, which had been signed at Maastricht in 1992. The Amsterdam Treaty meant a greater emphasis on citizenship and the rights of individuals, more democracy in the shape of increased powers for the European Parliament, a new title on employment, a Community area of freedom, security and justice, the beginnings of a common foreign and security policy (CFSP) and the reform of the institutions in the run-up to enlargement.

[73] As of June 2007, the following had shifted to the EURO (€): Andorra, Austria, Belgium, Cyprus, Finland, France (including French Guiana, Réunion, Saint-Pierre et Miquelon and Martinique), Germany, Greece, Ireland, Italy, Kosovo, Luxembourg, Malta, Monaco, Montenegro, Netherlands, Portugal, San Marino, Slovenia, Spain, and Vatican City. The Eurozone (Euro Area or Euroland) is the largest economy in the world with over 320 million people and a GDP over 2007. - Outside: Bulgaria, Czech Re-

- 2003, 1 February – Treaty of Nice[74] of 2001 becomes operational[75]
- 2005 – Dutch and French votes reject the "Treaty establishing a Constitution for Europe" of 2004 (TCE).[76]
- 2007 March - Berlin Declaration (officially the Declaration on the occasion of the 50th anniversary of the signature of the Treaty of Rome) is a non-binding European Union text signed on 25 March 2007 in Berlin (Germany)[77]
- 2009, 1 January - Treaty of Lisbon (also known as the Reform Treaty) of 13 December 2007[78]

These treaties, normal ones in the public international law sense, are the basis for relations between the present 27[79] E.U. Member States.[80]

---

public, Denmark, Estonia, U.K., Hungary, Lithuania, Latvia, Poland, Romania, Sweden, Slovakia.

[74] It dealt mostly with reforming the institutions so that the E.U. could function efficiently after its enlargement to 25 Member States. Summary of the Treaty of Nice and other information on the treaty can be found at <http://ec.europa.eu/comm/nice_treaty/index2_en.htm> and <http://europa.eu/scadplus/nice_treaty/index_en.htm>.

[75] OJ C80, 10.3.2001 p. 0001-0087. First Consolidated version in OJ C325, 24.12.2002 p. 0001-0184. Latest Consolidated version at <http://eur-lex.europa.eu/JOHtml.do?uri=OJ:C:2006:321E:SOM:EN:HTM>.

[76] OJ C310, 16.12.2004 p. 0001-0474. Index at < http://eur-lex.europa.eu/JOHtml.do?uri=OJ:C:2004:310:SOM:EN:HTML> (visited July 2008).

[77] http://www.consilium.europa.eu/ueDocs/cms_Data/docs/pressData/en/misc/93282.pdf> (English version). Other versions at < http://europa.eu/50/docs/berlin_declaration_en.pdf > or <http://www.consilium.europa.eu/cms3_applications/Applications/newsRoom/related.asp?BID=75&GRP=11617&LANG=1&cmsId=339>.

[78] Index for Consolidated (unofficial) version of EU-treaties published in E.U. Official Journal C 115, volume 51 of 9 May 2008 at <http://eur-lex.europa.eu/JOHtml.do?uri=OJ:C:2008:115:SOM:EN:HTML>. The text of the draft to the treaty can be found at <<http://www.consilium.europa.eu/uedocs/cmsUpload/cg00001re01en.pdf>> (visited July 2008).

[79] On January 1, 2007, Bulgaria and Romania joined the European Union.

[80] Consisting of more than 4,324,782 square kilometres/1,707,642 square miles, with more than 494 million people; and a GDP (nominal) 2007 (IMF) estimate of a total US$15,849 billion.

Tables to compare articles in different treaties can be found in Appendix 4 in the back of the book.

The scholar also has to be aware of the following "opt-outs" of some part of the treaties of:

United Kingdom – Social Protocol (later repealed)
Single Currency
Schengen Accord (Internal border controls over people)

Ireland - Schengen Accord

Denmark[81] - Schengen Accord & Union Citizenship[82]
The Economic and Monetary Union (EMU - Single Currency)
Defense Policy – European Secutiry and Defence Policy (ESDP)
Justice and Home Affairs (JHA)[83]

---

[81] Denmark might after a referendum in early 2009 remove some or all of its five reservations from 1992 to the Maastricht Treaty, protocols to the Treaty of Lisbon, and , see Summary of Report of 30 June 2008 on Danish Opt Outs from Danish Institute for International Studies (DIIS) at <http://www.diis.dk/graphics/Publications/Books2008/EU_udredningen_08/Preversio n/EU08_Executive_Summary%28en%29.pdf> (visited July 2008).

[82] As for the later, the reservation has no practical impact today, *idem.*

[83] Denmark later repealed its reservation on the E.U. Regulation 44/2001 of 22/12 2000 on jurisdiction and the recognition and enforcements in civil and commercial matters. OJ L 012 , 16/01/2001 P. 0001 – 0023. Denmark and the E.U. have concluded a so-called parallel treaty that causes the rules of the E.U. Regulation 44/2001 of 22/12 2000 to be used between Denmark and the other E.U. Member States. The Agreement (parallel treaty) came into force on 1 July 2007(OJ L 94, 4 April 2007, p. 70) after decision of 27 April 2006 by the Council of the European Union (OJ L120, 5 May 2006, p. 22) and decree no. 415 of 8 May 2007 from the Minister of Justice pursuant to mandate given in § 10 of Law no. 1563 of 20 December 2006 on the Brussels I Regulation ("Bruxelles I-forordning m.v.") - with the exception of the law's § 13, nr. 1 og 2. See Council Decision 2005/790/EC of 20 September 2005 on the signing, on behalf of the Community, OJ L 299, 16/11/2005 p. 0061-069, and the Agreement between the European Community and the Kingdom of Denmark on jurisdiction and the recognition and enforcement of judgments in civil and commercial matters, OJ L 299, 16/11/2005, p. 0062-0067.

European citizenship

The researcher also may find valuable information on E.U. legislation in the E.U. Parliament Documents, for example, in any question and answer sections.

Since January 1, 2007, the E.U. has had 23 official languages.[84] This fact is reason for great delays in getting new legislation into force, as new legislation cannot be published in the Official Journal before it has been translated into *all* languages. Due to lack of sufficient numbers of translators of some languages, it can take many months before a new piece of legislation can come into force. Thus, when searching for background material, one often has to go back from the time of the legislation's publication half a year or even more to find the history behind it.

When doing research on E.U. law, one must regard the law from the perspective of a Civil Law area, that is, there is no judge made law as in the U.S. (a Common Law country).

The legislation in the E.U. is made by the Council of the European Union and the Parliament in cooperation. Furthermore, the E.U. Commission does have certain rights pursuant to the treaties to make legislation and thus overrule a national Parliament-issued statute or administrative practice. All institutions and E.U. Member States are obliged to follow the judgments from the ECJ, which has the power to invalidate legislation, but not make new law even though the Court to some extent has developed general principles of law.[85]

There are different types of legislation in the E.U., among which the researcher must distinguish:[86]

- Treaties – made after negations between the E.U. Member States and only binding on a state if ratified by it.

---

[84] Decision of the Council of 18 December 2006, 2006/955/EC, amending the Rules of Procedure of the Court of Justice of the European Communities as regards the language arrangements, OJ L 386, 29.12.2006, p. 0044.

[85] Like the International Court of Justice, the European Court of Justice applies public international law. See *Opel Austria GmbH v. Council of the European Union* (E.C.J. T-115/94 1997), 1997 E.C.R. II-39 no. 90 (customary international law whose existence is recognized by the International Court of Justice is binding on the Community).

[86] See TEC Article 249 (ex ante EC art. 189).

- Regulations – which have general application, are binding in their entirety and are directly applicable in all E.U. Member States. They must be published in the Official Journal before they can come into force.
- Directives – which do not necessarily apply to all E.U. Member States. Rather than being directly applicable in those states, there is a choice of forms and methods of implementing directives into national laws. However, directives are binding on the E.U. Member States to which they are addressed as to the result to be achieved. If a directive applies to all E.U. Member States, it must be published in the Official Journal before it can come into force.
- Decisions – which are binding in their entirety upon those to whom they are addressed. Some decisions need to be published in the Official Journal before they can come into force.
- Recommendations and opinions – which have no binding force.

When reading texts of the treaties and court judgments, pre- and post-Amsterdam of 1996, one must bear in mind the following (see Appendix 5):

- In the text of the Treaty on European Union of 1992 (Maastricht):
    o provisions were identified by the letters A-S
    o The numbers were preserved for the other three treaties
- Treaty of Amsterdam of 1996:
    o EC Treaty (TEC) renumbered/equivalences from start to finish to eliminate awkward numerical oddities (e.g., Articles 104b and 130t)
    o Switch from letters to numbers in the E.U. Treaty (TEU)

## 4.2.1. Interpretation of E.U. Statutory law

As mentioned above, there are 23 official language in the European Union,[87]

---

[87] On interpretation in the E.U., see Stephen Weatherill & Paul Beaumont, E.U. LAW 184-5, 190-92,316-17 (3rd ed.) (1999 Penguin Books); Stehephen Weatherill, CASES AND MATERIALS ON EU LAW (8th ed.)(2007 Oxford Press); Paul Craig & Grainne de Burca, EU LAW – TEXT, CASES AND MATERIALS (4th ed.)(2007, Oxford Press).

of which English, French and German are "working" languages. Thus, the E.U. has 23 authoritative original versions of law,[88] as recorded in article 29 of the Rules of Procedure for the E.U. Courts (as of 15 January 2008).[89] Article 31 states "[t]he text of documents drawn up in the language of the case or in any other language authorized by the Court pursuant to Article 29 of these Rules shall be authentic."[90]

In the *Simutenkov* case, the Advocate General before the ECJ argued that the starting point is the wording of a statute, but "[i]n so doing it must be borne in mind that Community legislation is drafted in various languages and that the different language versions are all equally authentic. An interpretation of a provision of Community law thus involves a comparison of the different language versions."[91]

---

[88] However, some treaties have a different regime, e.g., the European Coal and Steel Treaty is only authentic in French. See Article 100. Nevertheless, agreement has been made that German, French, Italian and Dutch are the official and working languages. The EC and Euratom Treaties are authentic in twelve languages. See EC articles 217 & 248 and Euratom articles 190 & 225.

[89] Decision of the Council of 18 December 2006, 2006/955/EC, amending the Rules of Procedure of the Court of Justice of the European Communities as regards the language arrangements, OJ L 386, 29.12.2006, p. 0044.

[90] Rules of Procedure of the Court of Justice of the European Communities of 19 June 1991, OJ L 176, 4.7.1991, p. 0007–0032 with latest amendments in OJ L 24, 29.1.2008, p. 39–41. Consolidated version of March 2008 at <http://curia.europa.eu/en/instit/txtdocfr/txtsenvigueur/txt5.pdf> (visited July 2008).

[91] *Simutenkov v. Ministerio de Educación Y Cultura, Real Federación Española de Futbol,* [2005] 2 C.M.L.R. 11 at AG 14, [2005] ECR I-2579 at 14, 2005 WL 840128 (ECJ), [2006] All E.R. (EC) 42 (European Court of Justice (Grand Chamber) Case C-265/03 of 12 April 2005). See also, G. van Calster, *The EU's Tower of Babel – The Interpretation of the European Court of Justice of Equally Authentic Texts Drafted in More Than One Official Language,* 17 (1997) YEARBOOK OF EUROPEAN LAW 363-92 (Oxford Press 1998) [hereinafter van Galster].

---

**Research Tip #4.6**

Statutory interpretation in the E.U. is statutory interpretation without a single, authoritative text and one cannot expect different language versions of the same act or treaty always to say exactly the same thing.[92]

---

The goal for the E.U. Courts is to capture the essence of E.U. legislation. As the E.U. is a multilanguage legal regime, translation is more than a metaphor – it is a basic fact about the entire structure of the law.

---

**Research Tip #4.7**

While the ECJ does not use the translation history, the courts use comparison of the various versions of the law as an important tool.[93]

---

The ECJ looks not only at the versions written in the languages of the parties to the particular dispute before the court, but also at other versions. When a dispute is over which of two fully authentic versions of a law should prevail, the status of the statutory language is itself contested. The ECJ courts will typically not determine whether some versions reflect an error in translation. Thus, the courts will not make reference to the translation history.

The language of a statute provides privileged evidence of what the legislature intended.

---

[92] VAN GALSTER *supra* note 55 at 369.

[93] *Meico-Fell v Hauptzollamt Darmstadt*, [1991] ECR I-5569 at paras 9-10 (European Court of Justice (Sixth Chamber) Case C-273/90 of 27 November 1991 (It appears from the context in which that provision was adopted that the expression...means...that interpretation is confirmed by an examination of the other language versions, which have a clear meaning).

---

**Research Tip #4.8**

European courts are more comfortable than American courts in putting the purpose of a statute ahead of the language in the service of effectuating the legislature's will.[94]

---

In the *Schulte* case, the Advocate General before the ECJ argued that "[w]here it is difficult to interpret legislation from its wording alone, an interpretation based on purpose becomes fundamental.[95] That is the case where the provision in dispute is ambiguous."[96] Thus, the courts investigate the motivation for the legislation, including founding documents that set forth overarching legal goals, and resolve disputes in a manner that will further those goals.

In the *Promusicae* case, the Court stated that E.U. community law requires as for E.U. directives that, 'the Member States take care to rely on an interpretation of [directives] which allows a fair balance to be struck between the various fundamental rights protected by the Community legal order. Further, when implementing the measures transposing...directives, the authorities and courts of the Member States must not only interpret their national law in a manner consistent with those directives but also make sure that they do not rely on an interpretation of them which would be in conflict with those fundamental rights or with the other general principles of Community law, such as the principle of proportionality."[97]

---

[94] Lawrence M. Solan, *Statutory Interpretation in the EU: The Augustinian Approach*, BROOKLYN LAW SCHOOL, LEGAL STUDIES PAPER No. 78 page 10 (July 2007) - Available at SSRN: <http://ssrn.com/abstract=998167>.

[95] *Posthumus v Oosterwoud*, [1991] ECR I-5833 at paras 9-10 (European Court of Justice (Third Chamber) Case C-121/90 of 6 December 1991 (A comparison of the various language versions...show...That interpretation, based on the wording of the provision in question, is in conformity with its purpose).

[96] *Schulte v. Deutsche Bausparkasse Badenia AG*, [2006] 1 C.M.L.R. 11 at AG87 (Advocate General), [2005] ECR I-9215, [2006] C.E.C. 115, [2006] All E.R. (EC) 420 (European Court of Justice (Grand Chamber) Case C-350/03 of 25 October 2005).

[97] *Productores de Música de España (Promusicae) v Telefónica de España SAU* - (Reference for a preliminary ruling from the Juzgado de lo Mercantil No 5 de Madrid -

## 4.3. Where to find E.U. material

For scholars[98] who are citizens of a E.U. Member State, the following should be noted as far as access to documentation: Article 255 of the Treaty establishing the European Community states that citizens and residents of the European Union have a right of access to European Parliament, Council and Commission documents.[99]

A wealth of information about the history of Europe and its institutions since 1945 is available from European NAvigator (ENA) - an educational platform that focuses particularly on the development of a united Europe. ENA is available in English, French, German and Spanish, though some documents are available in other languages at <www.ena.lu>.[100]

Any student or scholar in the world can, from <http://eur-lex.europa.eu/en/treaties/index.htm>, access the basic legal texts on which the European Union and the European Communities are founded, plus other essential documents.[101]

---

Spain), OJ C 64, 8.3.2008, p. 0009 (E.C.J. C-275/06 (Grand Chamber), 29 January 2008).

[98] The Delegation of the European Commission to the U.S., Washington, DC, in the spring of 2007, decided to divulge itself of its entire depository collection and awarded it to the University Library System, University of Pittsburgh, currently the home of the Archive of European Integration (AEI). This depository collection begins in the early 1950s and is easily the largest EU collection in the Western Hemisphere. Over the next several years, the AEI will digitize many documents from this collection and post them on the World Wide Web. Archive of European Integration at <http://aei.pitt.edu>.

[99]         <http://www.europarl.europa.eu/parliament/public/staticDisplay.do?language= EN&id=151>.

[100] Using the site is free, although the documents are protected by copyright. ENA is developed by the CVCE (Centre Virtuel de la Connaissance sur l'Europe - Virtual Resource Centre for Knowledge about Europe), a Luxembourg-based public undertaking that is actively supported by the Ministry of Culture, Higher Education and Research.

[101] However, the Commission has proposed changes in Regulation (EC) No 1049/2001 of the European Parliament and of the Council of 30 May 2001 regarding public access to European Parliament, Council and Commission documents, OJ L145, 31.5.2001 p. 0043-0048, which pursuant to the E.U. Ombudsman would decrease access for the public, see Contribution of 2 June 2008 from the European Ombudsman to the public

From January 1, 2007, all official valid European Union websites were moved to <europa.eu>.

It should be noted that not all pages exist in the online version of the Official Journal, but only in the hardcover printed volumes.[102]

The CELEX database was closed by the end of 2006 and the information transferred to the European Union Law website, EUR-lex at <http://eur-lex.europa.eu>.

To monitor the decision-making process between the E.U. institutions, use PreLex at <http://ec.europa.eu/prelex/apcnet.cfm?CL=en>.

Summaries of E.U. legislation can be found through ScadPlus at <www.europa.eu/scadplus/scad_en.htm>.

The EUR-lex Guidelines for good results in Search by Official Journal publication[103] reference <http://www.eur-lex.europa.eu/RECH_reference_pub.do> are as follows:

- The year field takes 4 characters; the month and day fields take 2 (Example: Year 1999 Month 09 Day 12)
- Always enter the year (month and day fields are optional)
- To get the annexes to the OJ C series, enter A or E after the OJ number (Example: select the C series, then enter 123A to get an OJ with

---

hearing on the revision of Regulation 1049/2001 at <www.ombudsman.europa.eu/letters/en/20080526-1.htm> and Proposal for a Regulation of the European Parliament and of the Council regarding public access to European Parliament, Council and Commission documents, COM/2008/0229 final at <http://eur-lex.europa.eu/LexUriServ/LexUriServ.do?uri=CELEX:52008PC0229:EN:HTML>.

[102] E.g., the vital reports related to the Brussels Convention, the Lugano Convention and the E.U. Regulation 44/2001 of 22/12 2000 on jurisdiction and the recognition and enforcements in civil and commercial matters can better be found at <http://aei.pitt.edu>. For example Jenard Report no. 1 (1979), OJ C59, 5/3/1979, p. 0001-0065 at <http://aei.pitt.edu/1465/01/commercial_report_jenard_C59_79.pdf>.

[103] The Official Journal (OJ), published daily in 23 languages, consists of the L series (legislation) and the C series (information, preparatory acts and notices). The documents included in the C series are partly published only electronically. The L and C series were introduced in 1968, before which year there was a single series. Some databases used the letters B or P to distinguish this single series from series L and C. The letters B and P do not form part of the official publication reference. The Supplement S to the OJ (calls for tenders) is published in the TED database.

the reference C 123 A).

- The Supplement S to the OJ (calls for tenders) is published in the TED database (choose English in the right upper box).[104]

EUR-Lex at <http://eur-lex.europa.eu/RECH_menu.do?ihmlang=en> allows the following search:

- General search by:
  o Search terms
  o Date or time span
  o Author
  o Classification headings
  o Keyword
- Search by file category:
  o Treaties
  o Legislation
  o Preparatory acts
  o Case-law
  o Parliamentary questions
- Search by document number:
  o Natural number
  o Celex number
  o Consolidated text
- Search by publication reference;
  o Official Journal (OJ)
  o European Court Report (E.C.R.)

If one has the citation of a document, there is a website that compiles E.U. webpages - spread around the E.U.-domain - which allows one to type in and retrieve a citation at <www.geocities.com/hssphresearch/Finding_EU_Law.htm>.

---

[104] TED (Tenders Electronic Daily) is the Supplement to the Official Journal of the European Union. It contains all active notices published in the Supplement to the Official Journal (OJ S) <http://ted.europa.eu> or <http://ted.europa.eu/Exec?DataFlow=ShowPage.dfl&Template=TED/normal_search &StatLang=EN>.

### 4.3.1. Treaties

Text of the treaties can be found at <http://eur-lex.europa.eu/en/treaties
/index.htm>.

When reading texts of treaties and court judgments, pre- and post-Amsterdam, bear in mind the following (see Appendix 5):

- In the text of the Treaty on European Union (TEU) in 1992:
  - o provisions were identified by the letters A-S
  - o The numbers were preserved for the other three treaties
- Treaty of Amsterdam:
  - o EC Treaty (TEC) renumbered/equivalences from start to finish to eliminate awkward numerical oddities (e.g., Articles 104b and 130t)
  - o Switch from letters to numbers in the E.U. Treaty

Explanatory texts to the Amsterdam Treaty can be found at:

- A comprehensive Guide - <http://europa.eu/scadplus/leg/en/s50000.htm>

Explanatory texts to the Nice Treaty can be found at:

- A comprehensive Guide - <http://europa.eu/scadplus/nice_treaty/introduction_en.htm>

### 4.3.2. Regulations, Directives & Decisions:

Regulations, Directives & Decisions:

- Using the Directory of Community Legislation in Force and other acts of the Community Institutions:
  - o Vol I - Analytical Index
  - o Vol II - Chronological index and Alphabethical index
- Using the EUR-Lex database
- Community legislation in force can be found:
  - o Analytical structure (after subject matter) - <http://www.eur-lex.europa.eu/en/repert/index.htm> and archives at <http://www.eur-lex.europa.eu/en/legis/legis_archives.htm>
- Consolidated Community legislation in force (unofficial versions):
  - o Chronological Index – on year basis - <http://www.europa.eu./eur-

lex/en/consleg/chronological_index.html>
- o Search-website for consolidated legislation <http://www.eur-lex.europa.eu/RECH_consolidated.do?ihmlang= en>
- o After subject matter - <http://www.europa.eu/eur-lex/en/consleg/index.html>

## 4.3.3. Preparatory Documents (COMDocs)

Preparatory Documents (COMDocs) consist of:
- Broad policy consultative documents called "Communications", "Green Paper" and "White Paper"
- Proposals for legislation
- Reports on the implementation of policy

COMDocs can be found in:
- Paper format or on microfiche
- EUR-Lex database <http://eur-lex.europa.eu>.
- European Documents at <http://www.europa.eu/documents/index_eulaw_en.htm#eulaw >.

## 4.3.4. Official Journal

The "Official Journal" or gazette (OJ – seldom OJE) is divided into the following four parts:

| Series | Content | Comment | Citation |
|---|---|---|---|
| L | Agreed legislation | The most important part of this goes to Official Journal | OJ L 213, 7.9.1995, p 0001–0031 or OJ L213 1995 p 1 or OJ L 213, 7/9/1995 p 0001–0031 |
| C[105] | Proposed legislation, notes of ECJ judgments, information notices from the EC, EP resolutions, questions and answers | The contents of this series are varied. Information considered of public interest, but which does not fall into the categories covered by the other series, is dealt with here | OJ C 187, 24.07.1989 p 0001 or OJ C187 1989 p 1 or OJ C 187, 24/07/1989 p 0001 |
| S | Invitations to tender for public contracts | Sometimes referred to as the "supplement" | OJ S118 1995 p 0001 |
| Annex | Debates of the EP | Unlike the other series, the issue number is continuous | OJ Annex no 4-455 p 0032 |

*Table 34: E.U. Official Journal Parts*

The Supplement S to the OJ is published in the TED database (Tenders Electronic Daily).[106]

### 4.3.5. E.U. Case law

European Court decisions are available from:
- European Court Reports (ECR): the authoritative texts of ECJ opinions and judgments
- Common Market Law Reports (CMLR).

There are several types of case indexes:

---

[105] In EUR-Lex search: To get the annexes to the OJ C series, enter A or E after the OJ number. Example: select the C series, then enter 123A to get an OJ with the reference C 123 A.

[106] It contains all active notices published in the Supplement to the Official Journal (OJ S) <http://ted.europa.eu> or <http://ted.europa.eu/Exec?DataFlow=ShowPage.dfl&Template=TED/normal_search &StatLang=EN>.

- Numerical access to the case-law at <http://curia.europa.eu/en/content/juris/index.htm>. Access to the case-law by case number makes it possible to find information relating to every case brought before the Court of Justice, the Court of First Instance or the Civil Service Tribunal between 1953 and the present day. Cases are listed by number in the order in which they were lodged at the relevant Registry. Cases may also be located by party names using the "find (Ctrl+F)" function on the toolbar. Cases may be consulted by clicking on the case number.
    - o The texts of judgments and orders in cases lodged up to and including 1997 that have been published in the European Court Reports may be consulted by clicking on the case number and following the link to EUR-Lex, the interinstitutional database.
    - o Cases lodged since 1998 may be consulted by clicking on the case number and following that link to all the texts relating to the case in question, which are contained in the case-law database of this site.
    - o Cases lodged before the Court of Justice from 1953 to 1988 and since 1989.
    - o Cases lodged before the Court of First Instance: since 1989.
    - o Cases lodged before the Civil Service Tribunal : since 2005.
- Digest of Community case-law - The Répertoire de jurisprudence communautaire (only in French) at <http://curia.europa.eu/en/content/juris/index.htm>. It is a systematic collection of the summaries of the judgments and orders of the Court of Justice and of the Court of First Instance of the European Communities and the Civil Service Tribunal of the European Union delivered since their inception, presented following a layout subdivided into seven parts:
    - o the Community legal order
    - o the European Community (EC)
    - o the European Coal and Steel Community (ECSC/CS)
    - o the European Atomic Energy Community (EAEC/AE)

- o  the Brussels Convention
- o  the European Civil Service
- o  the European Union (E.U.)
- Alphabetical Table of Subject-matter - The Table alphabétique des matières (only in French) at <http://curia.europa.eu/en/content/juris/index.htm>. It lists the legal questions dealt with in the decisions of the Court of Justice and the Court of First Instance of the European Communities and the Civil Service Tribunal of the European Union and in the Opinions of the Advocates General, presented in alphabetical order.
- Annotation of judgments - The Notes de doctrine aux arrêts (only in French). It gives the references to published legal literature relating to the judgments of the Court of Justice and of the Court of First Instance of the European Communities and the Civil Service Tribunal of the European Union.
  - o  Preface
  - o  Vol. 1 : 1954 - 1988
  - o  Vol. 2 : 1989 - 2005
- Index A-Z (from 2000)  contains:
  - o  Numeric List of Cases
  - o  Alphabetic List of Parties
  - o  Vol. I:  Court of Justice (1953 - 1988)
  - o  Vol. II:  Court of Justice and Court of First Instance (since 1989)
- Notes de References des Notes de Doctrine.
  - o  The Notes de doctrine aux arrêts gives the references to published legal literature relating to the judgments of the Court of Justice and of the Court of First Instance of the European Communities and the Civil Service Tribunal of the European Union (only in French).  Index by case number to all court reports, including details of case notes in legal journals (available also online from <http://curia.europa.eu/common/recdoc/notes/index.htm>.
  - o  Preface
  - o  Vol. 1 : 1954 - 1988
  - o  Vol. 2 : 1989 - 2005
  - o  A chronological list

- Index in the final part of each years's ECR
- Index in each volume of CMLR (not annual) contains:
  - o Alphabetical table of cases
  - o Index of subject matter and community legislative provisions
  - o Treaties and regulations referred to
  - o Index of cases judicially considered
  - o Statutes cited

One can trace a court report in hardcopy in the following manner:
- If one knows the date of judgment, use the index at the back of the ECR (chronological index)
- If one only knows the case reference or the name, use the Index A-Z
- If one wants a topic search, use the annual index to ECR or the volume index to CMLR

The are several electronic sources for E.U. court decisions. Among others:
- EUR-Lex at <http;//eur-lex.europa.eu>
- Court of Justice & Court of First Instance online at <.http://curia.europa.eu/en/index.htm>
- LexisNexis
- Westlaw

## 4.3.6. Advocate-General's documentation

Opinions from the Advocate-General can be found at <http://eur-lex.europa.eu/RECH_jurisprudence.do>.[107]

## 4.3.7. E.U. Ombudsman's documentation

The E.U. Ombudsman's Reports, draft recommendations and decisions can be found at <www.europa.eu/documents/ombudsman/index_en.htm>.

## 4.3.8. Parliamentary documentation

Parliamentary documentation can be found at

---

[107]  Or  <http://eur-lex.europa.eu/SuiteJurisprudence.do?T1=V114&T3=V1&RechType= RECH_jurisprudence&Submit=Search>.

<http://www.europarl.europa.eu/>[108] or as follows:

http://www.europarl.europa.eu/guide/search/docsearch_en.htm

- Committee Reports are available in hard copy (documents) or microfiche or online from the European Parliament's website at <http://www.europarl.europa.eu/activities/archive/staticDisplay.do?language=EN&id=120>. The Reports are listed by Rapporteur.
- Resolutions can be found through the European Parliament's website, in the C series of the OJ, in EUR-Lex
- Debates (verbatim texts) are published in Annex of the OJ, which is indexed by name of MEP, subject and session.
- Parliament's questions (written questions & answers) are published in series C of the OJ and indexed in the Official Journal Index.

The European Parliament Register[109] gives access to the following official documents:

- Draft reports and opinions. Prior to the meetings of Parliament's committees, all documents on the agenda are published on Europarl. One can find them under the heading 'Meeting documents' for each committee. Access to these documents is at present possible only by date of committee meeting at <http://www.europarl.europa.eu/ committees/home_en.htm.>.
- Reports adopted in committee at <http://www.europarl.europa.eu/ plenary/default_en.htm#reports>. Search by:
  - o list of new reports
  - o rapporteur
  - o committee responsible
  - o report number
  - o PE number
  - o type of legislative procedure
  - o keywords in title or text
- Part-session minutes at <http://www.europarl.europa.eu/plenary

---

[108] Or < http://www.europarl.europa.eu/activities/archive/staticDisplay.do?language =EN&id=120 >. The European Parliament United Kingdom Office (in English) at <www.europarl.org.uk>.

[109] < http://www.europarl.europa.eu/guide/search/docsearch_en.htm >.

/default_en.htm#minutes>. A provisional version of the minutes is published prior to their approval in plenary, and is later replaced by the final version as published in the Official Journal, C series. Search by: date of sitting, or keywords(s) in title.

- Texts adopted by Parliament at <http://www.europarl.europa.eu/ plenary/default_en.htm#adop>. Opinions of Parliament, legislative resolutions, resolutions, decisions on common positions and joint texts, own-initiative resolutions, budgetary resolutions, etc. Texts published in the provisional version as approved in plenary and subsequently published in the Official Journal, C series, in their final form. Search by: date of adoption in plenary, source referred to in report, or keyword(s) in title.

- Resolutions (all resolutions since July 1994)(Rule 113 of Parliament's Rules of Procedure) and resolutions on cases of breaches of human rights, democracy and the rule of law (Rule 115). Texts published in the provisional version of 'texts adopted' as approved in plenary, and subsequently published in the Official Journal, C series, in their final form. Search by: date of adoption in plenary, reference for motion for a resolution (B6-xxxx) or keyword(s) in title.

- Written declarations (since 1999)(Rule 116) at <http://www. europarl.europa.eu/activities/expert/writtenDecl.do>. Texts published in the provisional version of 'texts adopted' at the end of the part-session at which they are adopted, and subsequently published in the Official Journal, C series, in their final form. Search by: year of distribution or date announced in plenary.

- Debates in plenary or verbatim report of proceedings and final text of debates (all debates since April 1996) at <www.europarl.europa.eu/ plenary/default_en.htm#debates>. The verbatim record of proceedings of Parliament's debates in plenary is available in the original language of the speakers and, after translation, in all the E.U.'s working languages. The original-language texts are generally published the day after the debate. Provisional translations are published at the same location approximately four weeks later. These translations are subsequently replaced by the final version, which is also published in an Annex to the Official Journal. Search by: date of sitting, speaker, or keywords(s) in heading of debate.

- Bulletins <http://www.europarl.europa.eu/bulletins/default.htm> or <http://www.europarl.europa.eu/references/bull/default_en.htm>. Presentation of the current work of Parliament and its bodies: appears monthly (except in August). A special edition is produced immediately after an E.U. summit, containing both the EP President's address to the European Council and the Presidency Conclusions.

- Parliamentary questions (since 1994/99) at <http://www.europarl .europa.eu/questions/default_en.htm>. Search by Member's name, political group, Member State of origin, question number, Official Journal number, institution to which the question is addressed, or keyword(s) in title or text..
- Rules of Procedure of the European Parliament with Index at <http://www2.europarl.europa.eu/omk/sipade2?PROG=RULES-EP&L=EN&REF=TOC>.
- Public register of the European Parliament at <http://www4. europarl.europa.eu/registre/recherche/Menu.cfm?langue=EN>
- Legislative Observatory (OEIL): European Parliament data base at <http://www.europarl.europa.eu/oeil/default.htm>.

### 4.3.9. Commission documentation

The Registers of Commission Documents (only documents produced since January 1, 2001) at <http://ec.europa.eu/transparency/index_en.htm> help to identify categories of document, related to various activities of the Commission,[110] namely:

- Green papers are discussion papers published by the Commission on a specific policy area. In some cases, they provide an impetus for subsequent legislation, at <http://www.europa.eu/documents/comm/ green_papers/index_en.htm>.
- White papers are documents containing proposals for Community action in a specific area. They sometimes follow a green paper. White papers contain an official set of proposals in specific policy areas and are used as vehicles for their development at <http://www .europa.eu/documents/comm/white_papers/index_en.htm>.
- Commission meeting at <http://ec.europa.eu/atwork/collegemeetings /index_en.htm>
- Work programme at <http://ec.europa.eu/atwork/programmes/ in-

---

[110] The European Commission Representation in the United Kingdom (in English) at <www.cec.org.uk>.

dex_en.htm>
- Register of COM, SEC and C documents at <http://ec.europa.eu/ transparency/regdoc/registre.cfm?CL=en>:[111]
  - o COM documents: proposed legislation and other Commission communications to the Council and/or the other institutions, and their preparatory papers;
  - o SEC documents: internal documents associated with the decision-making process and the general operation of Commission departments;
  - o C documents: legal acts adopted by the Commission in the exercise of its own or delegated powers.
- Register of the Committees' deliberations at <http://ec.europa.eu/ transparency/regcomitology/registre.cfm?CL=en>;
- Application of Community law <http://ec.europa.eu/community_law /index_en.htm>;
- Codecision <http://ec.europa.eu/codecision/index_en.htm>.

This register supplements the PreLex database of interinstitutional procedures <http://europa.eu/prelex/apcnet.cfm?CL=en>, which can be used to search for documents produced by the institutions in drafting Community legislation.

### 4.3.10. Council of Europe documentation

The register of the Council of the European Union has a search screen at <http://register.consilium.europa.eu/servlet/driver?typ=&page=Simple&lang =EN&cmsid=638>. The register contains references for documents produced by the Council since January 1, 1999. See also <http://www.europa.eu /documents/eu_council/index_en.htm> and <http://www.consilium.europa.eu /cms3_applications/showPage.asp?lang=EN&id=549&mode=g&name=>.

---

[111]    Help    on    document    types    can    be    found    at <http://ec.europe.eu/transparancy/regdoc/aidetypesdoc.cfm?CL=en>.

## 4.3.11. Implementing national laws

One can track the implementation and enforcement of E.U. legislation into national law country-by-country from Europe's Information Society's Thematic Portal website at <http://ec.europa.eu/information_society/policy /ecomm/implementation_enforcement/index_en.htm>.

## 4.3.12. Miscellaneous

- News: <http://europa.eu/press_room/index_en.htm >
- Statistic from Eurostat at < http://epp.eurostat.ec.europa.eu>
- EUR-Lex has:
  - o Full text of the OJ L and C series, Treaties (primary sources), Case-law, Legislation (preparatory and in force), Parliamentary Questions and Documents of public interest at <http://eur-lex.europa.eu>.
- SCADplus
  - o Contains "Summaries of legislation." Here are clear and concise summaries of E.U. legislation in all policy areas. Simply click on the subject of choice and access user-friendly explanations of legislation concerning that subject at <http://europa.eu/scadplus>.
- ECLAS - European Commission Library Catalogue
  - o Provides bibliographical references for publications, but no document delivery or copy service.
  - o In the standard version of ECLAS or in ECLAS Pro, electronic resources can be found at <http://ec.europa.eu/eclas/>; press the "Access ECLAS" button or go directly to <http:// ec.europa.eu/eclas/cgi/squery.pl?lang=en>
  - o If one only wants to search Internet Resources, press the "Internet Resource" button at <http://ec.europa.eu/eclas/> or go directly to <http://ec.europa.eu/eclas/cgi/squery.pl?lang=en &usrmode=URLs>
- The European Union's publisher
  - o Site of the official publications office of the E.U. <http://publications.europa.eu/index_en.html>.
- The Citizens Signpost Service (CSS)

    o   Aimed at E.U. citizens who encounter problems with mobility in the European Internal Market. It has an advisory service, which gives guidance and practical advice to citizens on specific problems they encounter in the E.U. and its Internal Market. The service is free. Replies are given by phone or e-mail in the language requested by the citizen (one of the 20 official languages) at <http://ec.europa.eu/citizensrights/signpost/front_end/index_en.htm>.

Many resources on the E.U. can also be found in Westlaw and LexisNexis under "European Union" material. In Westlaw, Quick Search allows one to easily retrieve material when one knows a key word, the name, the citation or the reference number.

In Westlaw:
- All European Union Materials (EU-ALL)
- European Union Legislation (EU-LEG)
- European Union Cases All (EU-CS-ALL)
- Common Market Law Reports (CML-RPTS)
- European Union Case Law (EU-CS)
- European Union Preparatory Acts (EU-ACTS)
- European Union Treaties (EU-TREATIES)
- European Union OJC Series (EU-OJCSERIES)
- European Union Parliamentary Questions (EU-QUESTIONS)
- Legal Journals Index (LJI)

In LexisNexis:
- E.U. Commission Decisions on Competition (COMDEC)
- ECJ cases (ECJ)
- E.U. Community Trademar4ks (ECTM)
- E.U. treaties (TREATY)
- E.C. Preparatory Acts; Parliamentary resolutions (PREP)
- E.U. National provisions implementing directives (NATPRV)
- E.U. Parliamentary questions (PARLQ)
- E.U. Commission legislation (LEGIS)
- E.U. law (ECLAW)
- E.U. News sources combined (ECNEWS)
- Business Guide to EU initiatives (EUINIT)

- E.U. Observer.com (EUOBSV)
- Europe Informatino Service (E.U. stories) (EISENG)
- INFO-92 (INFO92)
- RAPID (E.U. Press Releass) (RAPID)
- Tenders Electronic Daily (TED)

## 4.4. Citations

From January 1, 2007, all official European Union websites moved to <europa.eu>.

> Example in footnote:[112]
> Proposal for a Council Framework Decision on attacks against information systems COM/2002/0173 final – CNS 2002/0086 */, OJ C 203 E, 27.08.2002 p. 109 – 113.

As the E.U. has changed the numbering of several treaty articles over he last decades, it can sometimes be a good idea also to add an older citation in brackets.

> Example in footnote:
> TEC Article 252 (ex ante EC art. 189c).
> TEU Article 4 (ex ante art. D).

### 4.4.1. Official Journal

Citations for the Official Journal are:

- L, C, S: OJ <series> <issue number> <date.month.year>[113] p. <first page (four digits – fill out with zeros[114])> - <last page (four digits)>
- Annex: OJ Annex no<period-number><issue number>p<page number>

See Table 31 above in section 4.3.4.

---

[112] See remark below in footnote 114.

[113] In some E.U. publications is not used periods in the date but slash: <date/month/year>

[114] In some E.U. publications is used a period after "p" and some do not fill out with zeros.

### 4.4.2. E.U. Ombudsman

As for E.U. Ombudsman's decisions, which can be found at <www.europa.eu/documents/ombudsman/index_en.htm>, it should be noted that the citation of documents has changed as follows:

- Until 1996 - <number/dd.mm.yy>, where date is the date when the Ombudsman received the complaint.
- 1997-99 - <number/yy>, where year is only the last 2 figures of the year, and where year is the year when the Ombudsman received the complaint.
- From 2000 - <number/yyyy>, where year is the year when the Ombudsman received the complaint.

### 4.4.3. Regulations

Citation for Regulation is:

<institution>Regulations<number>/<year enacted>/<treaty as basic>of<date passed>

Note: Only for/in Regulations does the number precede the number of the act for the year of enactment. Prior to 1990, acts had a unique number. Now it is possible for a decision to have the same number as a directive.

> Example in footnotes:
> Council Regulation No 44/2001 of 22 December 2000 on jurisdiction and the recognition and enforcement of judgments in civil and commercial matters (entry into force March 1, 2002), OJ L 012, 16.1.2001 p 0001 – 0023.

### 4.4.4. Directive

Citation for Directive is:

<institution>Directive<year enacted>/<number>/<treaty as basic>of<date passed>

Note: Prior to 1990, acts had a unique number. Now it is possible for a decision to have the same number as a directive.

### 4.4.5. Court Decisions

Decisions rendered by the ECJ are numbered with a "C" for court and the CFI with a "T" for tribunal. In the official European Court Reports, ECJ judgments page numbers are preceded by "I-" and CFI judgments by "II-". Citations for case decisions from the E.U. Courts:

- Court of Justice - Citation: Case C-<number>/year <plaintiff>v<defendant>[<year>] ECR-I <page>

- Court of First Instance - Citation: Case T-<number>/year <plaintiff>v<defendant>[<year>] ECR-II <page>

> Example:
> *A. De Bloss Sprl. v. Bouyer*, 1976 E.C.R. 1497 (ECJ 14/76, 1976)
> *Ahlstrom Osakeyhtio v Commission of the European Communities* (Woodpulp case), (E.C.J. C89/85 1988), [1988] 4 C.M.L.R. 901, 1988 E.C.R. 5193

## 4.5. Reader information for Directory of Community Legislation

The preface on "Information for readers on The Directory of Community Legislation"[115] states that the directory includes not only current Community legislation, but also other instruments reflecting the activities of the European Union (E.U., ECSC, EEC, EC and Euratom), such as policy instruments and decisions taken in individual cases but of more general interest. It therefore covers:

- agreements and conventions concluded by the Communities in connection with their external relations;
- binding secondary legislation (regulations, decisions, ECSC general decisions and recommendations, EEC/EC/Euratom directives) under the Treaties establishing the European Union and the European Communities, with the exception of day-to-day administrative acts[116];
- supplementary legislation, in particular decisions of representatives of

---

[115] <http://www.eur-lex.europa.eu/en/legis/avis.htm>.

[116] Mainly acts arising from the day-to-day management of the common agricultural policy or the customs union and having a very limited period of validity, such as acts temporarily fixing various rates or amounts. For the most part, they correspond to the titles printed in light type on the contents page of the Official Journal of the European Union.

the governments of the E.U. Member States meeting within the Council;
- certain non-binding acts considered by the institutions to be important.

The Directory exists in the official languages of the European Union.

The Directory is intended purely for use as a documentation tool and the institutions do not assume any liability for its contents.

### 4.5.1. Presentation of documents

Each entry comprises: the document number of the act, its title, its bibliographical reference (in most cases the Official Journal of the European Union) and, if applicable, the document number of any amendments, with their publication reference in brackets. It also includes available consolidated versions of the basic act and its successive amendments.

> Example:
> 31977L0311
> Council Directive 77/311/EEC of 29 March 1977 on the approximation of the laws of the Member States relating to the driver-perceived noise level of wheeled agricultural or forestry tractors
> (Official Journal L 105 , 28/04/1977 P. 0001 - 0009)
>
> html
>
> Amended by 31982L0890 Replacement Article 1.2 from 21/12/1982
> Consolidated text 01977L0311-19821221
> Incorporated by 21994A0103(52)
> Implemented by 31996D0627 Implementation Article 2
> Amended by 31997L0054 Amendment Article 1.2 from 30/10/1997
> Consolidated text 01977L0311-19971030

### 4.5.2. The document number

The document number, shown in bold type above the title of the act, consists of a combination of figures and letters, the position of each having a particular meaning (see below 'Explanation of codes').

The document number enables all acts to be identified both in the body of the Directory.

The example given below is a simple, but by far the most frequent, form using 10 positions. Although the document number may theoretically extend to as many as 18 positions, there is no need for the reader to know precisely how document numbers are made up.

Example of document number:
3 1977 R 0311

3 - Documentary sector of the system (sector 3 = secondary legislation)
1977 - Year of adoption or publication of act (1977)
L - Legal form (L = directive)
0311 - Serial or other identifying number of legal act (Regulation No 0311 of the year in question)

The first number (the number 3 in the example just above) indicates the sector in the system under which the act is classified.

Also, the example shown above, the act forms part of Community secondary legislation (sector 3).

The letter, which is always in the sixth position (the letter L in the example) denotes the legal form of the act (e.g., R for regulation, D for decision, L for directive, etc.).

### 4.5.3. Title

The document number is followed by the full title of the legal act.

### 4.5.4. The publication reference

The title of the act is followed by the publication reference of the Official Journal of the European Union.

This reference consists of:
- the number of the Official Journal, preceded in the case of post-1967 instruments (when the Official Journal was divided into an 'L' and a 'C' series) by the letter for the series,
- the date of publication,
- the page number.

Example:
OJ L 105, 28.04.1977 p. 1, is interpreted as follows:

OJ - Official Journal of the European Union
L 105 - L series, No 105
28.04.1977 - date of publication
p. 1 - OJ page (page on which the text of the act begins)

### 4.5.5. References to amending acts

The publication reference of the act is followed, where appropriate, by references to subsequent acts affecting it (amending, replacing, etc.).

The act referred to is identified by its document number followed by its publication reference in brackets.

> Example:
> Amended by 31997L0054 (OJ L 277 10.10.1997 p. 24)
>
> Amended by
> 31997L0054 - Document number of amending act
> (OJ L 277 10.10.1997 p. 24) - Publication reference of amending act

## 4.5.6. References to consolidated texts

If an act and its amendments have been subject to consolidation, the Directory offers links to successive consolidated texts. The consolidated text is identified by its document number. The first part of this number is built from the document number of the basic act and identifies the consolidated family (that is, the basic act and its amendments); the second part refers to the date of effect of the last amending act.

> Example:
> Consolidated text 01997L0311- 19971030
>
> Consolidated text
> 01977L0311 - Number of the consolidated family
> 19971030 - Date of effect of the last amending act

## 4.5.7. Document retrieval

A document may be retrieved using the analytical structure.

> Example:
> Retrieval of a decision on the Combined Nomenclature.
> The relevant section entitled 'Customs tariffs', is to be found in the chapter entitled 'Customs union and free movement of goods' in the analytical structure:
> 02. Customs union and free movement of goods
> 02.20 Basic customs instruments
> 02.20.20 Customs tariffs

Acts listed in each section are arranged in ascending order of their document numbers: by sector (first figure), year, legal form (indicated by a letter) and serial or other identifying number (e.g., regulation number).

The entry for the decision in question, 597/87, is set out in the section Customs tariffs as follows:

41987D0597
87/597/ECSC: Decision of the representatives of the Governments of the Member States, meeting within the Council of 18 December 1987 on the nomenclature and rates of conventional duty for certain products and the general rules for interpreting and applying the said nomenclature and duties
(OJ L 363 23.12.1987 p. 67)

## 4.5.8. Explanation of codes

Number codes used in the document reference number, by CELEX (the database stopped at the end of 2006) documentary sector:

1 - Treaty on European Union, Treaties establishing the European Communities and Treaties amending or supplementing them.

2 - External relations of the European Communities (or of the Member States).

3 - Secondary legislation.

4 - Supplementary legislation (decisions of representatives of the Member States meeting within the Council, international conventions concluded between Member States in accordance with Treaty provisions, etc.).

0 - Consolidated documents

Sector 1 acts are not included in the Directory. However, the Accession Treaties of Denmark, Ireland and the United Kingdom of 1972, of Greece of 1979, of Spain and Portugal of 1985, of Austria, Finland and Sweden of 1994 or of the Czech Republic, Estonia, Cyprus, Latvia, Lithuania, Hungary, Malta, Poland, Slovenia and Slovakia of 2003[117] are sometimes referred to in amendment references (document numbers '11972B', '11979H', '11985I', '11994N' or '12003T').

Letter codes used in the document reference number indicate the legal form of the act:

A - Agreement, opinion

B - Budget

C - Declaration

D - Decision

E - Common foreign and security policy (CFSP) - common position, joint

---

[117] Treaty of Athens 2003 - E.U. Treaty of Accession 2003.

action, common strategy

F - Justice and home affairs (JHA) - common position, framework decision

G - Resolution

H - Recommendation

J - Non-opposition to a notified joint venture

K - ECSC Recommendation

L - Directive

M - Non-opposition to a notified concentration

O - ECB Guidelines

Q - Institutional arrangement - rules of procedure - internal agreement

R - Regulation

S - ECSC decision of general interest

X - Other document

Y - Other act (published in the 'C' series of the Official Journal)

Codes used for references to other acts

- Adopted by
- Amended by
- Completed by
- Confirmed by
- Consolidated
- Consolidated text
- Application delayed by
- Derogation in
- Application extended by
- Implemented by
- Incorporated in
- Interpreted by
- Partly suspen. by
- Partly re-est. by
- Replaced by
- See
- Suspended by

## 4.6. The changes pursuant to the Treaty of Lisbon of 2007

On December 13, 2007, a major new treaty was signed by leaders of the Member States with its purpose being to make the E.U. work more efficiently, including merging/eliminating the pillar system.[118] As with the nature of most amending treaties, the Treaty of Lisbon is not intended to be read as an autonomous text. See below section 4.6.2.

From a researcher's/scholar's point of view, the new treaty expands the area or scope of research, including the number of sources on E.U. "law"[119] and the history behind it, as Member States' national parliaments will be more involved.

### 4.6.1. Introduction

The Treaty of Lisbon (also known as the Reform Treaty) to a large extent replicates an earlier the draft to a E.U. "constitutional" treaty. However, some vital parts are not replicated in the Treaty of Lisbon, such as an official E.U. anthem, motto and an official E.U. flag.[120] Thus, politicians have had to desist from attempts at making a "federal union" and accept the facts that citizens in each European country demand preservation of their own culture and (most of their) historical inheritance and desire to remain citizens of their native countries.

As for the "languages" of the Treaty of Lisbon, Aarticle 7 states that it is "drawn up in a single original in the [23 official] languages, [and] the texts in each of these languages being equally authentic, shall be deposited in the archives of the Government of the Italian Republic, which will transmit a

---

[118] The Flexibility Clause within the Treaty of Lisbon allows for adjustments of E.U. competence within the defined parameters of the E.U. The existing clause can only be used in connection with the area of the common market. Art 352 (ex Article 308 TEC) of Consolidated TFEU, OJ C115, 9.5.2008 p. 0196.

[119] The Treaty of Lisbon rejected, in the draft E.U. Constitution, use of the term "law" (or code/act). See article I-6 of (the draft to the) Treaty establishing a Constitution for Europe, OJ C310, 16.12.2004 p. 0012.

[120] Even though a flag with a yellow star for each member state on blue background has been used publicly for years.

certified copy to each of the governments of the other signatory States."[121]

The Treaty of Lisbon once again renames what originally was called the "Treaty establishing the European Economic Community" (EEC into force on 1 January 1958)(= "Treaty of Rome" of 25 March 1957), which by the Maastricht Treaty of 1993 was renamed the "Treaty establishing the European Community" (TEC) to the "Treaty on the Functioning of the European Union" (TFEU).[122]

Thus, after the Treaty of Lisbon the two remaining major treaties are:
- the Treaty on European Union (TEU)[123]
- the Treaty on the Functioning of the European Union (TFEU)[124]

Other parts of the Treaty of Lisbon are:
- Final Provisions[125]
- Protocols[126]
- Annex with Table of Equivalences,[127] and
- Final Act of the Intergovernmental Conference,[128] including
- Declarations[129]

It cannot enter into force before having been ratified in all Member States. If this does not happen as scheduled by the end of 2008, the treaty will come into force on the first day of the month following the last ratification.[130]

A number of obstacles to the Treaty of Lisbon have risen form a negative

---

[121] OJ C306, 17.12.2007 p. 0135. Art. 55 in of consolidated TEU, OJ C115, 9.5.2008 p. 0045.

[122] Presidency Conclusion's on the Brussels European Council meeting 21-22 June 2007 at <www.consilium.europa.eu/ueDocs/cms_Data/docs/pressData/en/ec/94932.pdf> (visited July 2008).

[123] OJ C306, 17.12.2007 p. 0010-41.

[124] OJ C306, 17.12.2007 p. 0042-0133.

[125] OJ C306, 17.12.2007 p. 0134-0145.

[126] OJ C306, 17.12.2007 p. 0147-0202.

[127] OJ C306, 17.12.2007 p. 0202-0229.

[128] OJ C306, 17.12.2007 p. 0231-0271

[129] OJ C306, 17.12.2007 p. 0249-0271.

[130] Until that time, the existing Treaty of Nice will be in force. On the day the Treaty of Lisbon comes into force, the terms of office of the Secretary-General of the Council, High Representative for the Common Foreign and Security Policy, and the Deputy Secretary-General of the Council shall end.

Irish referendum of 12 June 2008,[131] but other representatives of other Member States have stated that the ratification[132] process of the Treaty of Lisbon should nevertheless be continued.[133] As of 16 July 2008, twenty-two Member States had accepted the treaty.[134]

### 4.6.2. Structure and Source of Treaties after the Treaty of Lisbon

| Main Sections in the Treaty of Lisbon[135] | | |
|---|---|---|
| Article 1(1)-(60) | changes to TEU | OJ p 0010-0042 |
| Article 2 (1)-(295) | changes to TEC | OJ p 0042-0133 |
| Article 3 | Final Provisions: Unlimited Period | OJ p 0134 |
| Article 4 | Final Provisions: About protocol no. 1 and no. 2 | OJ p 0134 |
| Article 5 | Final Provisions: Renumbering of TEU and TEC | OJ p 0134 |

---

[131] As to the results of the Irish referendum on the Treaty of Lisbon, see <http://www.referendum.ie/home/> (visited July 2008). The main concerns have been: impact on sovereignty; democratic accountability; social and public policy implications; and foreign, defense and external relations policy, including development and trade policies. A number of other issues were not directly connected to the purpose and content of the Treaty of Lisbon. See the Lisbon Reform Treaty, page 3 (Second Report from Oireachtas [Parliament of Ireland] Joint Committee on European Affairs, June 2008) at <http://euaffairs.ie/publications/Report%20on%20Lisbon%20Reform%20Treaty.doc> (visited July 2008).

[132] On the requirement in each Member State, see overview-table at <http://www.lisbon-treaty.org/wcm/index.php?option=com_content&task=view&id=689&Itemid=59> (visited July 2008).

[133] The E.U Parliament has recommended the Treaty of Lisbon, see European Parliament Committee on Constitutional Affairs' Report of 29 January 2008 on the Treaty of Lisbon, Session Doc. A6-0013/2008 at <http://www.europarl.europa.eu/sides/getDoc.do?pubRef=-//EP//NONSGML+REPORT+A6-2008-0013+0+DOC+PDF+V0//EN> (visited July 2008).

[134] Austria, Belgium, Bulgaria, Cyprus, Denmark, Estonia, Finland, France, Germany, Greece, Holland, Hungary, Slovenia, Lithuania, Latvia, Luxembourg, Malta, Poland, Portugal, Romania, Slovakia, United Kingdom. From <http://www.epha.org/a/2857> (visited 16 July 2008).

[135] OJ C306, 17.12.2007 p 0001-0271.

| Article 6 | Final Provisions: Ratification and time for coming into force | OJ p 0135 |
|---|---|---|
| Article 7 | Final Provisions: Languages and Deposit | OJ p 0135 |
| Protocols | | OJ p 0147-201 |
| Annex | tables of equivalences | OJ p 0202-229 |
| Final Act | of the Intergovernmental Conference (+ index for declarations) | OJ p 0231-0327 |
| Declarations | | OJ p 0249-271 |

The two remaining major treaties after Lisbon have the following structures:

| Treaty of European Union (TEU) | |
|---|---|
| Title I | Common Provisions |
| Title II | Democratic Principles |
| Title III | Institutions |
| Title IV | Enhanced Cooperation |
| Title V | External Actions and Common Foreign and Security Policy |
| Title VI | Final Provisions |

*Table 35: Structure in Treaty of European Union*

| Treaty on the Functioning of the European Union (TFEU) | |
|---|---|
| Part 1 | Principles |
| Part 2 | Non-discrimination and Citizenship of the Union |
| Part 3 | Union Policies and Internal Actions |
| Part 4 | Overseas Countries and Territories |
| Part 5 | External Action by the Union |
| Part 6 | Institutional and Budgetary Provisions |
| Part 7 | General and Final Provisions |

*Table 36: Structure in the Treaty on the Functioning of the European Union*

Appendix 4 in the back of the book offers tables of equivalences of articles in the treaties. Note, that the table indicates more than just a renumbering of articles.

The full text of the relevant treaty versions can be found in the Official Journal of the European Union as follows:

| E.U.-treaties Versions in Official Journal | | | |
|---|---|---|---|
| **Before Lisbon[136]** | **Lisbon Original[137]** | **After Lisbon[138]** | |
| C321 E, 29.12.2006 p. 5-36 | C306, 17.12.2007 p. 10-41 | C115, 9.5.2008 p. 13-45 | **TEU** |
| C321 E, 29.12.2006 p. 37-186 | C306, 17.12.2007 p. 42-133 | C115, 9.5.2008 p. 47-199 | **TEC / TFEU** |
| C321 E, 29.12.2006 p. 187-331 | C306, 17.12.2007 p. 134-271 | C115, 9.5.2008 p. 201-388 | **Addendums** |

*Table 37: E.U. Treaties Versions in Official Journal (Lisbon)*

### 4.6.3. E.U. Working Institutions

The following institutions working in co-operation will serve the E.U.:[139]

- The European Parliament[140] – maximum 750 members + President and no State with more than 96 members or less than a minimum 6 members – on the basis of proportion of population in each State (digressively proportional[141]).
- The European Council[142] – gives the E.U. its political direction and sets its priorities
  - It shall in the future elect its President[143] for a term of 2 ½ years (but that individual can be removed in the event of an impediment or serious misconduct). The person who is President of the

---

[136] Index-website at <http://eur-lex.europa.eu/JOHtml.do?uri=OJ:C:2006:321E:SOM:EN:HTM>.

[137] Index-website at <http://eur-lex.europa.eu/JOHtml.do?uri=OJ:C:2007:306:SOM:EN:HTML>.

[138] Index-website at <http://eur-lex.europa.eu/LexUriServ/LexUriServ.do?uri=OJ:C:2008:115:SOM:EN:HTML>.

[139] The two main E.U. advisory bodies are the Economic and Social Committee and the Committee of the Regions. Art. 300-307 of consolidated TFEU, OJ C115, 9.5.2008 p. 0177-0179.

[140] Art. 14 of consolidated TEU, OJ C115, 9.5.2008 p. 0022 and art. 223-234 of consolidated TFEU, OJ C115, 9.5.2008 p. 0149-0152.

[141] See glossary in Appendix 1.

[142] Art. 15 of consolidated TEU, OJ C115, 9.5.2008 p. 0023 and art. 235-236 of consolidated TFEU, OJ C115, 9.5.2008 p. 0152-0153.

[143] This new post has incorrectly been referred to as "President of Europe."

> European Council shall not hold a national office.[144]

- The Council[145] – the key decision-making body, along with the E.U. Parliament

  - o A Presidency of the Council - except for Foreign Affairs[146] - shall consist of pre-established groups of three Member States for a period of 18 months on the basis of equal rotation among the Member States.[147] Each member of the group shall in turn chair the Council for a six-month period.[148]

- The Commission[149] – until 1 November 2014[150] consists of one commissioner from each Member State (including its President and Vice-President/"High Representative of the Union for Foreign Affairs and Security Policy"[151])[152] at what time[153] it will be reduced to a

---

[144] Art. 15(5-6) of consolidated TEU, OJ C115, 9.5.2008 p. 0023.

[145] Art. 16 of consolidated TEU, OJ C115, 9.5.2008 p. 0024 and art. 237-243 of consolidated TFEU, OJ C115, 9.5.2008 p. 0153-0155.

[146] Art. 16(9) of consolidated TEU, OJ C115, 9.5.2008 p. 0024.

[147] Art. 1(1) of 9th Declaration concerning the European Council decision on the exercise of the Presidency of the Council, OJ C115, 9.5.2008 p. 0341.

[148] Art. 1(2) of 9th Declaration concerning the European Council decision on the exercise of the Presidency of the Council, OJ C115, 9.5.2008 p. 0341.

[149] Art. 17 of consolidated TEU, OJ C115, 9.5.2008 p. 0025 and art. 244-250 of consolidated TFEU, OJ C115, 9.5.2008 p. 0155-0157.

[150] Article 1 litra 18 ("Article 9 D, paragraph 5") of Treaty of Lisbon, OJ C306, 17.12.2007 p. 0020; Index at <http://eur-lex.europa.eu/JOHtml.do?uri=OJ:C:2007:306:SOM:EN:HTML>.

[151] The vice-President is also "High Representative of the Union for Foreign Affairs and Security Policy. Art. 18, 27 & 34 of consolidated TEU, OJ C115, 9.5.2008 p. 0026, 0032 & 0035 and art. 218(3) & 221 of consolidated TFEU, OJ C115, 9.5.2008 p. 0145 & 0147. This position merges the previous post of High Representative for the Common Foreign and Security Policy and the post of Commissioner for External Relations and European Neighborhood Policy.

[152] Art. 17(4-5) of consolidated TEU, OJ C115, 9.5.2008 p. 0025.

[153] However, article 213 of the Nice Treaty (recalled by the Treaty of Lisbon) requires the number to be reduced in 2009. See article 4, section 2 of Nice Protocol on the Enlargement of the European Union, OJ C325, 24.12.2002 p. 0166.

number of members corresponding to 2/3 of the Member States and commissioners selected on a basis of equal rotation between the Member States.

- o The only E.U. institution with the power to initiate the law on which the E.U. Parliament and Council have to take a decision.
- o Administers the budget and manages Community programs.
- o Seeks to ensure that E.U. treaties, law, rules and decisions are complied with.
- o Negotiates for the E.U. in international trade aid areas.
- o Is independent from and does not seek instructions from any government or other body.
- The Court of Justice of the European Union (ECJ) consisting of:[154]
  - o the Court of Justice.
  - o the General Court (previously the "Court of First Instance").
  - o specialized courts.[155]
- The European Central Bank (ECB[156])[157] – the central bank for the EURO (€).[158]
- The Court of Auditors.[159]

---

[154] Art. 19 of consolidated TEU, OJ C115, 9.5.2008 p. 0027 and art. 251-281 of consolidated TFEU, OJ C115, 9.5.2008 p. 0157-0167 and Protocol no. 3 on the Statute of the Court of Justice of the European Union, OJ C115, 9.5.2008 p. 0210-0229.

[155] Art. 257 of consolidated TFEU, OJ C115, 9.5.2008 p. 0160.

[156] Together with the national central banks of all E.U. Member States it constitutes the European System of Central Banks (ESCB)

[157] There is also a European Investment Bank. Art. 308-309 of consolidated TFEU, OJ C115, 9.5.2008 p. 0180 and Protocol No. 5 on the Statute of the European Investment Bank, OJ C115, 9.5.2008 p. 0251-0264.

[158] Art. 282-284 of consolidated TFEU, OJ C115, 9.5.2008 p. 0167-0168 and Protocol No. 4 on the Statute of the European System of Central Banks and of the European Central Bank, OJ C115, 9.5.2008 p. 0230-0250.

[159] An E.U. institution that acts like the auditors of a business or other organization. It monitors the E.U.'s accounts, examining the legality and regularity of the revenue and

The ECJ's jurisdiction still excludes matters of foreign policy, al though it now can review foreign policy sanction measures,[160] and can exercise jurisdiction over certain matters concerning the "Area of Freedom, Security and Justice" (AFSJ) not concerning policing and criminal cooperation.[161]

A new "emergency" procedure has been introduced into the preliminary reference system, which will require the Court of Justice to act "with the minimum of delay" when a case involves an individual in custody.[162]

The number of Advocates General has been increased from 8 to 11 and, by a political compromise, a permanent "Polish" Advocate General has been created – as is already the case for Germany, France, Italy, Spain and United Kingdom.[163]

### 4.6.4. The Legal Base for the European Union

The E.U. can only take action if it has a "legal base" in the (consolidated version of the) two treaties with amendments from the Treaty of Lisbon - which will later provide new legal bases and allow the E.U. to take action on:[164]

- Public health (such as disease prevention), in response to wider concerns affecting the safety of the general public
- Energy security

---

expenditure in the budget and ensuring sound financial management. Art. 285-287 of consolidated TFEU, OJ C115, 9.5.2008 p. 0169-0171.

[160] Art. 275 of consolidated TFEU, OJ C115, 9.5.2008 p. 0166.

[161] Art. 276 of consolidated TFEU, OJ C115, 9.5.2008 p. 0166.

[162] Art. 267, in fine, of consolidated TFEU, OJ C115, 9.5.2008 p. 0164.

[163] Declaration on Article 252 of the Treaty on the Functioning of the European Union regarding the number of Advocates-General in the Court of Justice, OJ C115, 9.5.2008 p. 0350 and Declaration ad Article 222 of the Treaty on the Functioning of the European Union on the number of Advocates-General in the Court of Justice, 18 October 2007, DS 866/07 at <http://www.consilium.europa.eu/uedocs/cmsUpload/ds00866.en07.pdf> (visited July 2008).

[164] A SUMMARY GUIDE TO THE TREATY OF LISBON (EU Reform Treaty) (National Forum on Europe)(Dublin: Government Publication Office January 2008) <www.forumoneurope.ie/eng/getFile.asp?FC_ID=338&docID=1489> (visited July 2008).

- Dealing with natural or man-made disasters
- Sport
- Space policy

No new exclusive competences have been created by the Treaty of Lisbon,[165] e.g., military capabilities remain in national hands.

In the Treaty of Lisbon, the distribution of competences in various policy areas between Member States and the Union is explicitly stated in the following three categories:

| Type of competence | **Exclusive** (full list)[166] | **Shared** (non-exhaustive list)[167] | **Complementary** (full list) |
|---|---|---|---|
| **Defini-tion** | Only the Union can adopt legally binding acts. The Member States cannot intervene unless authorized to do so by the Union, or to implement measures taken by the latter. | The Union and the Member States can adopt legally binding acts. The Member States being able to do so if the Union has not done so. | The Union can intervene only to support action by Member States (primarily through financial contributions); it may legislate but not harmonize national legislation and regulations. |
| **Subjects** | • Customs Union<br>• Establishing competition rules required for operation of the internal market<br>• Monetary policy for Member | • Internal market<br>• Social policy (for the aspects defined in the Treaty of Lisbon)<br>• Economic, social and territorial cohesion | • Protection and improvement of human health<br>• Industry<br>• Culture<br>• Tourism<br>• Education<br>• Youth<br>• Sport |

---

[165] See Presidency Conclusion's on the Brussels European Council meeting 21-22 June 2007 at <www.consilium.europa.eu/ueDocs/cms_Data/docs/pressData/en/ec/94932.pdf> (visited July 2008).

[166] In addition to these competences, the Union also has as an exclusive competence for the conclusion of international agreements when this is provided for in a legislative act of the Union, when it is necessary to enable the Union to exercise its internal competence or when it is likely to affect common rules or adversely affect their scope.

[167] Although the TFEU deals with the policies indicated in italics in this column in the article relating to shared competences, they are sectors in which Union action does not have the effect of preventing the exercise of national competences.

| | States whose currency is the euro<br>• Conservation of the biological resources of the sea under the fisheries policy<br>• Common commercial (trade) policy | • Agriculture and fisheries (excluding conservation of the biological resources of the sea)<br>• Environment<br>• Consumer protection<br>• Transport<br>• TransEuropean networks<br>• <u>Energy</u><br>• Area of freedom, security and justice<br>• Common safety concerns in the public health sphere (for the aspects defined in the Treaty of Lisbon)<br>• *Research and technological development*<br>• *Space policy*<br>• *Development cooperation* | • Vocational training<br>• <u>Civil protection</u> (disaster prevention)<br>• <u>Administrative cooperation</u> |
|---|---|---|---|

*Table 38: The Competences of the Union[168]*

## 4.6.5. National Parliaments

With the Treaty of Lisbon, national parliaments have become much more

---

[168] The TFEU also refers to the common foreign and security policy and the coordination of economic and employment policies, which, because of their specific nature, do not come under any of the three categories in this table. The areas of competence underlined in each of the columns are areas for which there are currently no specific provisions in the Treaties but in which the Union has already taken action, in particular using the provisions relating to the internal market or Article 308 TEC.

involved in the legislative process.[169] They will have the power to have a say at a very early stage, before a proposal is considered in detail by the European Parliament and the Council of Ministers.

Article 1 of Protocol No. 1 on the Role of National Parliaments in the European Union requires that draft legislative acts sent to the European Parliament and to the Council shall be forwarded to national parliaments.

The latter may send reasoned opinions[170] on whether a draft legislative act complies with the principle of subsidiarity,[171] see Protocol No. 2.[172] Thus, national parliaments have now formally been given the task of "watchdog" so that the principle of subsidiarity is respected.[173] National parliaments will have the power to block certain proposals.[174] For example, national parliaments will be able to veto measures furthering judicial cooperation in civil matters.[175]

Consolidated TEU article 12[176] states among other things that national parliaments are to contribute to the good functioning of the Union:

- by taking part in the evaluation mechanisms for the implementation of the Union policies in the area of freedom, security and justice.
- through being involved in the political monitoring of Europol and the evaluation of Eurojust's activities.

---

[169] Art. 3 in Protocol no. 1 on the role of national parliaments in the European Union. OJ C115, 9.5.2008 p. 0204.

[170] Reasoned Opinion (as for the protocol 2 of the Treaty of Lisbon on applying the principles of proportionality) - an opinion with reasons, put forward by a national parliament (or one of its Houses) that a proposal for a law, made by the Commission, is in breach of the principle of subsidiarity. In this case, a reasoned opinion is part of an "early warning system," to be operated by national parliaments.

[171] Protocol No. 1 on the Role of National Parliaments in the European Union, OJ C115, 9.5.2008, p. 0203-0205.

[172] Protocol No. 2 on the Application of the Principles of Subsidiarity and Proportionality, OJ C115, 9.5.2008, p. 206-209.

[173] Art. 12 of consolidated TEU; Protocol no. 1 on the Role of National Parliaments in the European Union; and Protocol no. 2 on the Application of the Principles of Subsidiarity and Proportionality, OJ C115, 9.5.2008 p. 0021, 0203 & 206.

[174] E.g. art. 69 & 81(3) in fine of consolidated TFEU, OJ C115, 9.5.2008 p. 0074 & 0079.

[175] Art. 85 of consolidated TFEU (art. 69 D in Treaty of Lisbon – ex ante art. 31 TEU), OJ C115, 9.5.2008 p. 0081.

[176] OJ C115, 9.5.2008 p. 0021 (art. 8c in Treaty of Lisbon).

- by being notified of applications for E.U. accession.
- by taking part in the inter-parliamentary cooperation between national parliaments and the European Parliament.

The Treaty of Lisbon contains a "Solidarity Clause" committing the Union and its Member States to act jointly in a spirit of solidarity if a Member State is the target of a terrorist attack or the victim of a natural or man-made disaster.[177]

## 4.6.6. Principles of Conferral, Subsidiarity and Propertionality

Article 5 of Consolidated TEU (see also Protocol No. 2[178]) outlines the principles of conferral, subsidiary and proportionality as follows:[179]

"(ex Article 5 TEC):
1. The limits of Union competences are governed by the principle of conferral. The use of Union competences is governed by the principles of subsidiarity and proportionality. 2. Under the *principle of conferral*, the Union shall act only within the limits of the competences conferred upon it by the Member States in the Treaties to attain the objectives set out therein. Competences not conferred upon the Union in the Treaties remain with the Member States. 3. Under the *principle of subsidiarity*, in areas which do not fall within its exclusive competence, the Union shall act only if and in so far as the objectives of the proposed action cannot be sufficiently achieved by the Member States, either at central level or at regional and local level, but can rather, by reason of the scale or effects of the proposed action, be better achieved at Union level. The institutions of the Union shall apply the principle of subsidiarity as laid down in the Protocol on the application of the principles of subsidiarity and proportionality. National Parliaments ensure compliance with the principle of subsidiarity in accordance with the procedure set out in that Protocol. 4. Under the *principle of proportionality*, the content and form of Union action shall not exceed what is necessary to achieve the objectives of the Treaties. The institutions of the Union shall apply the principle of proportionality as laid down in the Protocol on the application of the principles of subsidiarity and proportionality."

---

[177] Article 222 (= Title VII of Part V) of the consolidated version of the Treaty on the Functioning of the European Union, OJ C115, 9.5.2008 p. 0148.

[178] Lisbon Protocol No. 2 on the Application of the Principle of Subsidiarity and Proportionality, OJ C115, 9.5.2008 p. 0206-0209.

[179] OJ C115, 9.5.2008 p. 0018 (emphasis added).

The pre-Lisbon Consolidated version 2006 of article 5 of Treaty of Estab-lishing the European Community (TEC) stated:[180]

> "The Community shall act within the limits of the powers conferred upon it by this Treaty and of the objectives assigned to it therein. In areas which do not fall within its exclusive competence, the Community shall take action, in accordance with the *principle of subsidiarity*, only if and in so far as the ob-jectives of the proposed action cannot be sufficiently achieved by the Member States and can therefore, by reason of the scale or effects of the proposed ac-tion, be better achieved by the Community. Any action by the Community shall not go beyond what is necessary to achieve the objectives of this Treaty."

The principle of conferral means that the E.U. does not have general com-petences in its own right, but only those that are specifically conferred upon it by the Member States in the founding treaties and their subsequent modifica-tions. The E.U. can only act on the basis of a provision of the treaties that authorizes it to do so. In treaty terms, competence means the legal capacity or ability to legislate or to take other action. E.U. action must not exceed what is necessary to achieve the objectives of the Treaties.

The principle of subsidiarity is intended to ensure that decisions are taken as closely as possible to the citizenry and that constant checks are made as to whether action at Community level is justified in the light of the possibilities available at the national, regional or local level. The principle implies that the E.U. does not take action (in areas of shared competence) unless it is more effective than action taken at the national, regional or local level.

Protocol 2 provides national parliaments eight weeks to study European Commission legislative proposals and decide whether to send a "reasoned opinion" stating why the national parliament considers it to be incompatible with subsidiarity. National parliaments may vote to have the measure re-viewed. If one third (or one quarter, where the proposed E.U. measure con-cerns freedom, justice and security) of votes are in favor of a review, the Commission will have to review the measure and if it decides to maintain it, must give a reasoned opinion to the Union legislator as to why it considers

---

[180] OJ C321 E, 29.12.2006 p. 0046 (emphasis added).

the measure to be compatible with subsidiarity.

## 4.6.7. Legislative Procedure

With the Treaty of Lisbon, for the first time in the E.U., one million citizens from different E.U. Member States will be able to directly request that the Commission brings forward an initiative of interest to them in an area of E.U. competence.[181] A direct new source of such public participation will be the fact that legislative procedural meetings, including debates and voting, will televised.

Under the Treaty, there will be significant changes in how E.U. institutions make decisions.

The Treaty of Lisbon increases the use of qualified majority voting in the E.U. Council, and also increases involvement of the European Parliament in the legislative process through extended co-decision – making with the E.U. Council. The co-decision procedure will become the "ordinary legislative procedure" in the work of the Council and the Parliament.

In the few remaining areas - called "special legislative procedures" – the E.U. Parliament either has the right of consent to a Council measure, or vice-versa, except in the few cases where the old consultation procedure applies.[182] Decision-making procedures vary and may allow for a dominant role for either the Council of Ministers or the European Parliament. In some cases, proposals may come from sources other than the Commission. Unanimity is also allowed for in some cases.

The Treaty of Lisbon has introduced a new term: "Delegated Act."[183] Where there are non-essential elements to a legislative measure, power can be delegated to the European Commission to enact detailed measures to supplement or amend these elements. The objective, content, scope and duration of these delegations has to be defined in the original legislative measure. The Council of Ministers and the European Parliament are to supervise the use of

---

[181] Article 11(4) of Consolidated TEU, OJ C115, 9.5.2008 p. 0021.

[182] Where the Council must consult the European Parliament before voting on the Commission proposal and take its views into account. The Council is not bound by the Parliament's position but only by the obligation to consult it. Parliament must be consulted again if the Council deviates too far from the initial proposal.

[183] Art. 290 of Consolidated TFEU, OJ C115, 9.5.2008 p. 172.

this power and may also revoke any such delegation.

Annexes 2-4 of the E.U. Parliament's report on the Treaty of Lisbon list when:[184]

- qualified majority voting[185] (QMV)[186]
- ordinary legislative procedure[187]
- special legislative procedures, including some Council Acts where:
  - o Unanimity and consent of European Parliament
  - o Unanimity and consultation of European Parliament
  - o Qualified majority and consent of EP
  - o Qualified majority and consultation of EP

are required.[188]

Ireland and the United Kingdom have opted out from the change from unanimous decisions to qualified majority voting in the sector of police and judicial affairs. This decision will be reviewed in Ireland three years after the Treaty of Lisbon enters into force (if approved by public referendum). Both states will be able to opt in to these voting issues on a case-by-case basis.[189]

---

[184] REPORT ON THE TREATY OF LISBON (2007/2286(INI)) from the European Parliament's Committee on Constitutional Affairs (Rapporteurs: Richard Corbett & Íñigo Méndez de Vigo), A6-0013/2008, 29 January 2008 at <http://www.europarl.europa.eu/sides/getDoc.do?pubRef=-//EP//NONSGML+REPORT+A6-2008-0013+0+DOC+PDF+V0//EN&language=EN> (visited July 2008) [hereinafter E.U. PARL. REPORT ON LISBON].

[185] A pre-Lisbon weighted voting system (see e.g. Council Decision 2007/4/EC, OJ L1, 4.1.2007 p. 0009) will over time change to a "double-majority" system, see art. 16(3-5) of Consolidated TEU, art. 238 of Consolidated TFEU and art. 3 of Protocol no. 36 on Transitional Provisions, OJ 9.5.2008 p. 0024, 0153, 0322.

[186] The present system is so complicated that the Danish Parliament's E.U. website offers a "Majority Calculator" (in English) at < http://euo.dk/flashberegner/beregner_en.html> (visited July 2008).

[187] Article 238(1) of Consolidated TFEU states: "Where it is required to act by a simple majority, the Council shall act by a majority of its component members." OJ 9.5.2008 p. 153

[188] E.U. PARL. REPORT ON LISBON *supra* note 184.

[189] Protocol no. 36 on Transitional Provisions, OJ 9.5.2008 p. 0322.

## 4.6.8. Charter for Fundamental Rights

The Charter of Fundamental Rights of the European Union[190] lists political, social and economic rights for E.U. citizens. It is intended to make sure that European Union regulations and directives do not contradict the European Convention on Human Rights which is ratified by all E.U. Member States.

Unlike the draft of a European Constitution, the Charter of Fundamental Rights is not included in the text of the Treaty of Lisbon, which only provides a reference to the Charter. Article 6 of Consolidated TEU[191] states that the Charter has the same legal value as the E.U. Treaties, but the Charter shall not extend the competences of the Union.

The United Kingdom, as one of the two countries with a common law legal system in the E.U.[192] and a largely uncodified constitution, as well as Poland, has required a protocol to the Treaty of Lisbon, which clarifies that the Charter does not extend the rights of the courts to overturn domestic law in Britain/Poland.[193]

The Court of Justice will ensure that the Charter of Fundamental Rights is applied correctly.

---

[190] Charter of Fundamental Rights of The European Union, 2000/C 364/01, OJ C 364 18/12/2000 p. 0001-0022 or at <http://www.europarl.europa.eu/charter/pdf/text_en.pdf>. See also Commentary of The Charter of Fundamental Rights of The European Union at <http://ec.europa.eu/justice_home/doc_centre/rights/charter/docs/network_commentar y_final%20_180706.pdf>.

[191] OJ C115, 9.5.2008 p. 0019.

[192] The other is Ireland. See Anglo-American Legal Family below in Chapter 6.

[193] Protocol no. 30 on the application of the Charter of Fundamental Rigths of the European Union to Poland and to the United Kingdom, OJ C115, 9.5.2008 p. 0313; Protocol no. 8 relating to Art. 6(2) of the TEU on the accession of the Union to the European Convention on the Protection of Human Rights and Fundamental Freedoms, OJ C115, 9.5.2008 p. 0265; 1st Declaration concerning the Charter of Fundamental Rights of the European Union, OJ C115, 9.5.2008 p. 0337; 53rd Declaration by the Czech Republic on the Charter of Fundamental Rights of the European Union, OJ C115, 9.5.2008 p. 0355; 61st Declaration by the Republic of Poland on the Charter of Fundamental Rights of the European Union, OJ C115, 9.5.2008 p. 0358; 62nd Declaration by the Republic of Poland concerning the Protocol on the application of the Charter of Fundamental Rights of the European Union to Poland and to the United Kingdom, OJ C115, 9.5.2008 p. 0358.

### 4.6.9. European External Action Service

The High Representative of the Union for Foreign Affairs and Security Policy (/Vice-President) will be assisted by a joint service, the European External Action Service (EEAS)[194] that will be composed of officials from the Council, the Commission and the diplomatic services of the Member States.

At this time, it should be noted that the post of High Representative does not create new powers but streamlines E.U. external action to avoid duplication and confusion. He or she will act in foreign policy matters on the basis of decisions taken unanimously by the 27 members. He or she will complement - not replace - the foreign policy or diplomatic efforts of Member States.

### 4.6.10. Withdraw or Opt-out

The Treaty of Lisbon introduces an exit clause[195] for members wanting to withdraw from the Union. This formalizes the procedure by stating that a Member State must inform the European Council before it can terminate its membership.

Member States can have opt-outs from some policy areas. For example, regarding the area of justice and home affairs, special arrangements have been made for Denmark, Ireland and the United Kingdom.

Denmark will have to decide whether to renounce its reservations from 1992 (on the Maastricht Treaty). See mainly Lisbon Protocol No. 22 on the Position of Denmark.[196] See also Lisbon Protocol No. 16, 17, 19 and 32.[197]

---

[194] See Title V of the consolidated version of the Treaty on European Union, OJ C115, 9.5.2008 p. 0028-0041 and Part V of the consolidated version of the Treaty on the Functioning of the European Union, OJ C115, 9.5.2008 p. 0139-0148.

[195] Article 50 of consolidated TEU, OJ C115, 9.5.2008 p. 0043.

[196] Lisbon Protocol No. 22 on the Position of Denmark, OJ C115, 9.5.2008 p. 0299-0304.

[197] Lisbon Protocols No. 16 on Certain Provisions Relating to Denmark, No. 17 on Denmark, No. 19. on the Schengen Acquis Integrated into the Framework of the European Union, No. 32 on the Acquisition of Property in Denmark, OJ C115, 9.5.2008 p. 0287, 0288, 0290 and 318.

# CHAPTER 5

# Public International Law Resources

## 5.1. Introduction

As this book's primarily aim is for use in teaching courses on legal research methods in the US and in Continental Europe, this chapter should only be regarded as a very brief introduction to Public International Law.

For Latin phrases consult with Appendix 1.

For further reading on Public International Law, consider two famous European books written by Brownlie and Oppenheim.[1]

To understand the history of the sources of international law one has to keep in mind that international law developed over time.[2]

Public International Law[3] is the sum total of legal norms governing rights

---

[1] Ian Brownlie, PRINCIPLES OF INTERNATIONAL LAW (7th ed.) (Oxford University Press, 2008) & OPPENHEIM'S INTERNATIONAL LAW 23 (9th Ed.)(Eds.: Sir Robert Jennings & Sir Arthur Watts) (London and New York: Longman 1996) [hereinafter OPPENHEIM].

[2] The chief reporter of the American RESTATEMENT OF THE LAW (THIRD) - FOREIGN RELATIONS LAW OF THE UNITED STATES (American Law Institute)[hereinafter REST] has found major progress during the 21st century in international law's transition from primitive to modern. Louis Henkin, *Coda: Allegro ma non Troppo*, ASIL NEWSLETTER (Jan.-Feb. 1994), at 1.

[3] Like the International Court of Justice, the European Court of Justice applies public international law, see *Opel Austria GmbH v. Council of the European Union* (E.C.J. T-

and duties of the collectivities of the ruling classes[4] - civilized participants in international intercourse in war and peace - without which it would be virtually impossible for the participants to have steady and frequent relations.[5] It is not the rules, but a normative system that operates in a horizontal legal order. Public International Law is a process, a system of authoritative decision-making.[6] It deals with the conduct of nation-States and their relations with other States,[7] and to some extent also with their relations with individuals, business organizations, and other legal entities. In its conceptions, its specific norms and standards, and largely in practice, international law functions between States, as represented by their governments.[8]

115/94 1997), 1997 E.C.R. II-39 no. 90 (customary international law whose existence is recognized by the International Court of Justice is binding on the Community), *Ahlstrom Osakeyhtio v Commission of the European Communities* (E.C.J. C89/85 1988), [1988] 4 C.M.L.R. 901, 1988 E.C.R. 5193 no. 22-23 (Commission's decision is not contrary to the rules of public international law), and *Ahlstrom Osakeyhtio v Commission of the European Communities* (E.C.J. C89/85 1993), 1993 E.C.R I-1307 no. 30, *A.Racke GMBH & Co v. Hauptzollamt Mainz* (ECJ 16 June 1998, Case 162/96), 1998 E.C.R.-I-3655, para 45-46.

[4] As for international organizations, Judge Gros observed in his separate opinion in the WHO Agreement case that "in the absence of a super-State, each International Organization has only the competence which has been conferred on it by the States which founded it", *Interpretation of the Agreement of 25 March 1951 between WHO and Egypt*, (I.C.J., Dec 20, 1980 (No. 65), ), 1980 I.C.J. 73, 103.

[5] Thomas Jefferson wrote in support of the 1792 Declaration of the Rights of Nations: "The relationship of one nation with a foreign nation rests on natural law and moral principles as well as on recognized international law. We owe other nations a respect for their chosen form of government as we expect our own form to be respected, and we have no right to interfere in another people's choice of government or internal policy any more than they have to interfere in ours."

[6] Rosalyn Higgins, PROBLEMS & PROCESS – INTERNATIONAL LAW AND HOW WE USE IT 1 AND 267 (Clarendon Press, Oxford 1994), Rosalyn Higgins, *International Law and the Avoidance, Containment and Resolution of Disputes – General Course on Public International Law*, RECUEIL DES COURS, Vol. 230 (1991-V) page 23.

[7] In this Chapter the term "State" (that is, a nation or country or nation-state) is spelled with a capital "S" to signal the difference between a state or a region of a federal State. This pattern is also used by REST *supra* note 2.

[8] Henrik Spang-Hanssen, PUBLIC INTERNATIONAL COMPUTER NETWORK LAW ISSUES 99 (DJØF Publishing Copenhagen 2006) [hereinafter SPANG-HANSSEN-2] and Henrik

Public International Law is to be distinguished from Private International Law or Conflict of Laws,[9] which cover a certain State's rules on judicial jurisdiction and competence, foreign judgments and choice of law.[10] Private International Law is law directed to resolving controversies between private persons, natural as well as juridical, primarily in domestic litigation, arising out of situations having a significant relationship to more than one State.[11]

## 5.2. Monists versus Dualists

| Research Tip #5.1 |
|---|
| When studying Public International Law one must keep in mind from what country's perspective one is doing the research. |

This is due to the existence of two different approaches among scholars and authorities as to whether international law is superior or not to national law.

Pursuant to a pure monistic idea, the national and international systems make up one single legal system. Some monists claim international law supercedes national law. Others think the opposite.

Dualists on the other hand, hold that the national and the international legal systems are different systems, and exist in their own separate spheres. International law has no independent status in national law. It only becomes relevant if and when the national authorities decide to create national law on the basis of the international system.

Spang-Hanssen, CYBERSPACE & INTERNATIONAL LAW ON JURISDICTION 300 (DJØF Publishing, Copenhagen, 2004) [hereinafter SPANG-HANSSEN-1].

[9] SPANG-HANSSEN-1 *supra* note 8, at 206.

[10] Municipal law governs the domestic aspects of government and deals with issues between individuals, and between individuals and the administrative apparatus. The International Court of Justice, in the Case of *Barcelona Traction, Light, and Power Co, Limited* (Belgium v. Spain) (Second Phase) of February 5, 1970, 1970 I.C.J. 3, referred to the rules generally accepted by municipal legal systems, not the municipal law of a particular state.

[11] "Foreign law" is the domestic law of another national jurisdiction.

## 5.3. Sources of Public International Law

The Internet has had a dramatic impact on international legal research. In the past international law sources were difficult to identify and locate, but now many are available through websites of the United Nations, other international organizations and law schools' and university websites.

The sources of international law must not be confused with the basis of international law; the latter is to be found in the common consent of the international community. The sources of law concern the particular rules that constitute the system, and the processes by which those rules become identifiable as rules of law.[12]

The Statute for the International Court of Justice[13] (ICJ[14]) lists in Article 38 the following sources for international law:

a)  International conventions,[15] whether general or particular, establishing rules expressly recognized by the contesting States;

b)  International custom, as evidence of a general practice accepted as law;

c)  The general principles of law recognized by civilized nations;

d)  Subject to the provisions of Article 59 [no Stare Decisis Doctrine], juridical decisions and the teaching of the most highly qualified publicists[16] of the various nations, as subsidiary means for the determinations of rules of law.

The ICJ is the "Highest Court on Earth, a Bench from which there is no appeal."[17] The Court has a dual role: (A) to settle in accordance with international law the legal disputes submitted to it by States, and (B) to give advi-

---

[12] OPPENHEIM *supra* note 1 at 23.

[13]  Statute of the International Court of Justice of 26 June 1945, 156 U.N.T.S. 77, 59 Stat. 1055, T.I.A.S. No. 993 [hereinafter ICJ Statute].

[14]  Homepage <www.icj-cij.org>.

[15]  On interpretations of treaties, see especially Article 26-33 of the Vienna Convention on the Law of Treaties of 23 May 1969 (into force 27 January 1980), U.N.T.S. Vol. 1155 p. 331, also at <http://untreaty.un.org/ilc/texts/instruments/english/conventions /1_1_1969.pdf> (visited April 2007).

[16]  See below section 5.5.5.

[17]  Arthur Eyffinger, THE INTERNATIONAL COURT OF JUSTICE, 1946-1996 (Kluwer Law International, the Netherlands 1996 – ISBN 90 411 0221 3).

sory opinions on legal questions referred to it by duly authorized international organs and agencies. Pursuant to Article 59 of the ICJ Statute, a "decision of the Court has no binding force except between the parties and in respect of that particular case."

Under article 38(1)(d) of the ICJ Statute - the subsidiary category of international sources - has in recent years evolved was is called "soft law,"[18] that is, actually not law but rather agreed guidelines, commitments, joint statements, or intentions of common policies, for example resolutions adopted by the United Nations General Assembly or other multilateral bodies.[19]

---

[18] "For example, there may be an [non-binding] agreement that requests the participants harmonize their domestic laws as much as possible but does not require them to do so. There may be a provision within that requests each party to supply evidence to the other and exchange information with regard to the enforcement of competition laws, and yet leaves the ultimate implementation to the discretion of each party. In international law, this type of agreement may be referred to as a "soft law," as opposed to a "hard law," which requires contracting parties to observe the terms of an agreement," International Cooperation in the Enforcement Of Competition Policy by Mitsuo Matsushita, 468 Washington University Global Studies Law Review, Vol. 1 p. 463 at <http://law.wustl.edu/wugslr/issues/volume1/p463Matsushit a.pdf> (visited July 2008). The terminology of "soft law" remains relatively controversial because there are some international practitioners who will not even deign to accept its existence and for others, there is quite some confusion as to its status in the realm of law. However, for most international practitioners, development of soft law instruments is an accepted part of the compromises required when undertaking daily work within the international legal system, where states are often reluctant to sign up to too many commitments that might result in national resentment at over-committing to an international goal, Michael G. Egge, Matteo F. Bay & Janier Ruiz Calzado, The New EC Merger Regulation: A Move to Convergence, Status of Soft Law In international Law, Antitrust Magazine, Section of Antitrust Law, American Bar Association, Fall 2004 at <www.lw.com/upload/pubContent/_pdf/pub1167_1.pdf > (visited July 2008).

[19] SPANG-HANSSEN-1 *supra* note 8 at 229, Malcolm N.Shaw, INTERNATIONAL LAW 92 (4th ed.)(Cambridge, England: University Press 1997), Antonio Cassese, INTERNATIONAL LAW 160 (Oxford, England: Oxford University Press 2001); §103(2)(d) of REST *supra* note 2.

## 5.4. Interpretation of international instruments & Travaux Préparatoires

The main task for any of tribunal,[20] which is asked to apply or construe or interpret[21] a treaty, can be described in a single sentence: "the duty of giving effect to the expressed intention of the parties, that is, their intention as expressed in the words used by them in the light of the surrounding circumstances".[22]

Part III of the Convention on the Law of Treaties[23] contains specific rules for interpretation[24] (the rules are not regarded as codification of any custom-

---

[20] Whether an international court is obliged to fill in gaps, and to avoid pronouncing a *non liquet* ("[I]s a competent legal tribunal in the position to refuse a definite answer to a legal question (in terms of rights and duties of the parties concerned) on the basis of material gaps" in international law), is a matter of dispute. See AKEHURST'S MODERN INTRODUCTION TO INTERNATIONAL LAW 50 & 349 (8th ed.) (by Peter Malanczuk)(New York ; London : Routledge, 2002); Ige F. Dekker & Harry H.G. Post, *The Completeness of International Law and Hamlet's Dilemma, in* ON THE FOUNDATIONS AND SOURCES OF INTERNATIONAL LAW  8-30(2003, T.M.C. Asser Press, The Hague, Netherlands); Judge Rosalyn Higgin's separate opinion in *Advisory Opinion on the Legality of the Threat or Use of Nuclear Weapons* (United Nations)(International Court of Justice, Advisory opinion of 8 July 1996), 1996 I.C.J. 226, 934.

[21] On interpretation. See OPPENHEIM *supra* note 1, at 1266-1284; Ian Brownlie, PRINCIPLES OF INTERNATIONAL LAW 631-638 (5th ed.)(Oxford Press, 2002).

[22] Lord Arnold Duncan McNair, THE LAW OF TREATIES 365 (Oxford Clarendon Press 1961). See also, Rudolf Bernhardt, *Interpretation in International Law, in* ENCYCLOPEDIA OF PUBLIC INTERNATIONAL LAW 1416-1426 (Rudolf Bernhardt (Ed.), Elsevier 1995) & OPPENHEIM *supra* note 1, at 1266-128 & 423.

[23] Articles 26-38 in the Vienna Convention on the Law of Treaties of 23 May 1969 (into force 27 January 1980), U.N.T.S. Vol. 1155 p. 331, also at <http://untreaty.un.org /ilc/texts/instruments/english/conventions/1_1_1969.pdf> (visited April 2007). As of April 2007, the convention has been ratified by 108 States. The U.S. is not a party, but it signed the Convention on 24 April 1970.

[24] Treaty law is the daughter of customary international law. The interpretation of treaties takes place on the basis of customary international law and the validity of treaties is determined by customary law. Treaties per se are ineffective without the support of customary international law. There is the difference that the treaty norm remains in the form in which it is frozen into the treaty (until such time as the treaty is changed), whereas the customary norm having an independent existence of its own, can continue to develop. It is a critical advance in a situation when fast moving changes require

ary law rule, but they are rules in practice used in diplomatic circles). A "General Rule of Interpretation" is given in Article 31:

> 1. A treaty shall be interpreted in good faith in accordance with the ordinary meaning to be given to the terms of the treaty in their context and in the light of its object and purpose.
> 2. The context for the purpose of the interpretation of a treaty shall comprise, in addition to the text, including its preamble and annexes: (a) any agreement relating to the treaty which was made between all the parties in connection with the conclusion of the treaty; (b) any instrument which was made by one or more parties in connection with the conclusion of the treaty and accepted by the other parties as an instrument related to the treaty.
> 3. There shall be taken into account, together with the context: (a) any subsequent agreement between the parties regarding the interpretation of the treaty or the application of its provisions; (b) any subsequent practice in the application of the treaty which establishes the agreement of the parties regarding its interpretation; (c) any relevant rules of international law applicable in the relations between the parties.
> 4. A special meaning shall be given to a term if it is established that the parties so intended.

Articles 32 gives supplementary means of interpretation, including using preparatory works[25] as supplementary sources:

> Recourse may be had to supplementary means of interpretation, including the preparatory work of the treaty and the circumstances of its conclusion, in order to confirm the meaning resulting from the application of article 31, or to determine the meaning when the interpretation according to article 31: (a) leaves the meaning ambiguous or obscure; or (b) leads to a result which is manifestly absurd or unreasonable.

The last the rule given in Section 3 of the Convention on the Law of Treaties, "Interpretation of Treaties," Article 33, deals with interpretation of treaties authenticated in two or more languages, Article 33:

---

more adaptability and flexibility in a rule of law, I.C.J. Judge C.G. WEERAMANTRY, UNIVERSALISING INTERNATIONAL LAW 233 & 239 (Boston: Martinus Nijhoff Publishers, 2004 – ISBN 90-04-13838-2).

[25] "Travaux Préparatoires," see further below.

1. When a treaty has been authenticated in two or more languages, the text is equally authoritative in each language, unless the treaty provides or the parties agree that, in case of divergence, a particular text shall prevail.

2. A version of the treaty in a language other than one of those in which the text was authenticated shall be considered an authentic text only if the treaty so provides or the parties so agree.

3. The terms of the treaty are presumed to have the same meaning in each authentic text.

4. Except where a particular text prevails in accordance with paragraph 1, when a comparison of the authentic texts discloses a difference of meaning which the application of articles 31 and 32 does not remove, the meaning which best reconciles the texts, having regard to the object and purpose of the treaty, shall be adopted.

Black's Law Dictionary defines *Travaux Préparatoires* as: "materials used in preparing the ultimate form of an agreement or statute, and especially of an international treaty; the draft history of a treaty." The material must have been known to all parties comprehended by the main international instrument[26] (e.g., a treaty).[27] "Travaux Préparatoires" is not restricted to material set down in writing;[28] compare sections 3-4 of article 31 of the Law of Treaties.[29] However, information can only be regarded as "Travaux Préparatoires" if it has been put forward by a person who officially, in negotiations, represented a State or international organization, which later is a party to the final instrument (e.g., treaty), and – of course – this was known to the other

---

[26] Terms used for international agreements are: treaty, convention, agreement, protocol, covenant, charter, statute, act, declaration, concordat, exchange of notes, agreed minute, memorandum of agreement, memorandum of understanding and modus vivendi. Whatever their designation, all international agreements have the same legal status, except as their provisions or the circumstances of their conclusion indicate otherwise. Comment to §301 of REST *supra* note 2.

[27] Compare the main principles for all interpretations of international instruments in Part III of the Vienna Convention on Law of Treaties, *supra* note 15, and in *Young Loan Arbitration (Belgium vs. France)*, 59 INTERNATIONAL LAW REVIEW 495, 544 (1980).

[28] "The term must *normally* be restricted to material set down in writing" [authors emphasis added]. *Young Loan Arbitration (Belgium vs. France)*, 59 INTERNATIONAL LAW REVIEW 495, 544 (1980).

[29] *Supra* note 15.

parties.[30]

## 5.5. Where to find public international law?

### 5.5.1. Customary Rules of International Law

When searching to find international custom[31] as evidence of a general practice accepted as law, what is sought for, is a general recognition among States
of a certain practice as *obligatory*.

Usage versus Custom: When a custom or usage is generally established,
either between all the civilized nations in the world, or only between those of
a certain continent, as of Europe, for example, or between those who have
more frequent intercourse with each other; if that custom is in its own nature
indifferent, and further, if it be useful and reasonable, it becomes obligatory
on all the nations in question - who are considered as having given their consent to it, and are bound to observe it towards each other, as long as they have
not expressly isused a resolution that it will not be observed in the future.

But if that custom contains any thing unjust or unlawful, it is not obligatory; on the contrary, every nation is bound to relinquish it, since nothing can
oblige or authorize a State to violate the laws of nature.

The American Restatement of the Foreign Relations Law of the United

---

[30] Four Models of Publication of Travaux Preparatoires has been proposed by Jonathan
Pratter, *An Approach to Researching the Drafting History of International Agreements*
(December 2005) at <http://www.nyulawglobal.org/globalex/travaux_preparatoires.
htm>. However, only model III ("treaty-specific conference records") refers to the fact
that legally binding international instruments are always done through a conference between states or international organizations representatives. This means that although"Travaux Préparatoires" material under models I, II & IV can be found through
one of the parties' archives or websites, these models do not illustrate how international instruments are made or how the "Travaux Préparatoires" come into being or are
produced – thus they cannot be relied upon.

[31] See art. 38(b) of ICJ Statute *supra* note 13; SPANG-HANSSEN-1 *supra* note 8 at 215;
§102(1)(a) & (2) of REST *supra* note 2; STATEMENT OF PRINCIPLES APPLICABLE TO THE
FORMATION OF GENERAL CUSTOMARY INTERNATIONAL LAW as amended at the 2000
London conference (International Law Association), at <http://www.ila-
hq.org/pdf/CustomaryLaw.pdf>.

States at Section 102(2), reads "Customary international law results from a general and consistent practice of States followed by them from a sense of legal obligation." The notes to the section go on to explain that "Subsection (2), includes diplomatic acts and instructions as well as public measures and other governmental acts and official statements of policy, whether they are unilateral or undertaken in cooperation with other States ... [and for] a practice of States to become a rule of customary international law it must appear that the States follow the practice from a sense of legal obligation (opinio juris sive necessitatis); a practice that is generally followed but which States feel legally free to disregard does not contribute to customary law."

This idea is reinforced in Section 103(2)(d), discussing the evidence of a rule, and accepting as evidence "pronouncements by States that undertake to State a rule of international law, when such pronouncements are not seriously challenged by other States."

There are two Elements of Custom:
1.  Objective Element: General Practice
2.  Subjective Element: *Opinio Juris*

It is important to stress, that all elements are dependent on the circumstances of each case and situation. In the latter instance, obviously a value judgment is made by the competent decision-maker.

*Opinio juris sive necessitates* means "of the opinion that it is a necessary law." This maxim implies that an observing State must perceive a customary practice as one that it is obligated by international law to observe.

As for the objective versus subjective element, some authors have denied the importance of this psychological element. It is regarding the subjective element, again, that the ICJ has obviously had to appraise the relevant practice.

Only in exceptional cases and situations will there be created "instant" customary law. If, say, the community of all States unequivocally and without any dissent considers certain acts, which have not been known before, to be illegal, the *opinio juris* might suffice even if no practice could have yet evolved.[32]

### *5.5.1.1. Customary Norms of Different "Sanctity"*

One has to distinguish between fundamental norms versus technical and less important norms. Among fundamental norms are principles of sovereign equality of States, *pacta sunt servanda*,[33] good faith, equity.

The following are two fundamental norms in public international law:

- Ius/Jus Cogens:[34] "ones from which there can be no retreat."
- Erga Omnes:[35] "in relation to all".

#### 5.5.1.1.1. Ius/Jus Cogens

There are certain norms or rules of public international law from which there can be no derogation. These are known as *jus cogens*,[36] are *peremptory* norms that cannot be negotiated in any way, including via treaty.

Article 53 of the Vienna Convention on Treaties states, as to treaties conflicting with a peremptory norm of general international law (*ius cogens*): "A treaty is void if, at the time of its conclusion, it conflicts with a peremptory norm of general international law. For the purposes of the present Convention, a peremptory norm of general international law is a norm accepted and recognized by the international community of States as a whole as a norm from which no derogation is permitted and which can be modified only by a subsequent norm of general international law having the same character."

#### 5.5.1.1.2. Erga Omnes

Obligations erga omnes pertain to the enforceability of norms of international law; the idea appears to be that certain violations of the norms of international law are so significant that they harm the international community as a

---

[32] Other examples: acts respecting the Continental Shelf, or Economic Zones, or a multilateral treaty provision that is so general that it can gain the character of an international customary rule.

[33] See Appendix 1, Glossary.

[34] See below section 5.5.1.1.1.

[35] See below section 5.5.1.1.2.

[36] SPANG-HANSSEN-1 *supra* note 8 at 223.

whole.

The concept is controversial because it implies that individual States and the international community may be legally responsible for what occurs in the affairs of independent States.

There are two fundamental characteristics of *erga omnes*:

- Universality, in the sense that obligations erga omnes are binding on all States without exception;
- Solidarity, in the sense that every State is deemed to have a legal interest in their protection.

### 5.5.1.1.3. Differences between Jus Cogens and Erga Omnes

While *jus cogens* is a category of norm from which no derogation is permitted, *erga omnes* is but a related concept that pertains more to the rights and obligations on the part of States in the event certain rules are violated.

The *jus cogens* norms and the obligations *erga omnes* arise out of the belief that some rules or norms are so essential for the protection of fundamental interests of the international community that any breach thereof is considered to affect the international community as a whole.

The following list of differences between *erga omnes* and *jus cogens* can be set forth:

- Jus cogens develops over time;
- Erga omnes is more variable.
- Jus cogens is a rule of substance; these rules are so fundamental, that one cannot derogate from them.
- Structurally, jus cogens is a subset of erga omnes.
- Jus cogens trumps erga omnes.

Some rules identified as *erga omnes* may also be considered *ius cogens*. In brief, the relationship between the two concepts are:

- Ius Cogens: Relates to derogability
- Erga Omnes: Generality of standing

Unlike *ius cogens, erga omnes* rules may be limited to a group of States.

## 5.5.2. Treaties

A treaty[37] is a binding agreement under public international law concluded by subjects of international law, namely States and international organizations.

Treaties can be called by many names: treaties, international agreements, protocols, covenants, conventions, exchanges of letters, exchanges of notes, etc. However, all of these instruments are equally treaties, and the rules are the same, regardless of what they are called.

Treaties can be loosely compared to contracts.[38] Both are means by which willing parties assume obligations among themselves, and a party to either who fails to live up to the imposed obligations can be held legally liable for such breach.

The central principle of treaty law is expressed in the maxim *pacta sunt servanda* - "pacts must be respected".

The Vienna Convention on the Law of Treaties, article 2(1)(a), defines a treaty as: "an international agreement concluded between States in written form and governed by international law." This provision authoritatively defines "treaty" for public international law purposes.

The American Restatement (Third) of the Foreign Relations Law of the United States provides in § 301: "under customary international law oral agreements are no less binding although their terms may not be readily susceptible of proof." Comment b points out that, by any widely accepted definition, treaties are binding internationally.

In the international law hierarchy, custom has priority over treaties, but treaties may prevail over general law. The governing principles are:
- When not specified, treaty and custom have equal weight.
- General presumption: treaties are not intended to derogate from general custom.
- Lex specialis derogat generalis (specific prevails over general).

In exceptional cases, a treaty may give rise to new customary rules (or assist in their creation) "of its own impact," if it is widely adopted by States and

---

[37] See Article 38(a) ICJ Statute *supra* note 13.

[38] Judge Sir Gerald Fitzmaurice, Legal Adviser of the British Foreign Office and later Judge of the ICJ: "Treaties are not more a source of law than an ordinary private law contract."

the clear intention of the parties is to create new customary law, e.g., as in The North Sea case.[39]

Treaties can be divided into the following categories, which will be of value for the researcher:

- Law-Making Treaties (Traités-lois)
  - o Treaties which act as contracts yet resemble national statutes in content.
  - o They impose obligations on all parties to the treaty and seek to regulate the parties' behavior over a long period of time.
  - o They create law by forming an agreement upon general universal legal principles.
  - o Such treaties usually have numerous parties.
  - o Law-making treaties are often used to create general norms of conduct, and tend to be broadly applicable.
  - o However, even "law making" treaties are not enforceable against any party that does not wish to abide by the law.
- Contract Treaties (Traités-contrats)
  - o Treaties which resemble contracts - they regulate or manage a specific area of activity.
  - o These are not sources of law but merely legal transactions only applicable to the States which make the treaties and not a whole host of nations.
- Bilateral treaty
  - o A bilateral treaty is a treaty between two parties.
- Multilateral treaty
  - o A multilateral treaty is a treaty among more than two parties.
- Copies of the Bilateral and Multilateral Treaties:

---

[39] *North Sea Continental Shelf Cases* (Federal Republic of Germany vs. Denmark; Federal Republic of Germany vs. Netherlands), (International Court of Justice, Judgment of 20 February 1969), 1969 I.C.J. 3.

- o Bilateral treaties are usually written in two original copies and exchanged;
- o Multilateral treaties are written in a single original copy, which is given to a depository and then copies are distributed to the signatories;
- o Even a bilateral treaty may permit accession by other parties, and thus become a multilateral treaty after the first accession.

The dichotomy between "law-making treaties" and "contract-treaties" might not always be clear and useful from a general point of view, but the contract treaty is more likely to be nullified by war than a law-making treaty.

The background for treaties can be illustrated as follows:

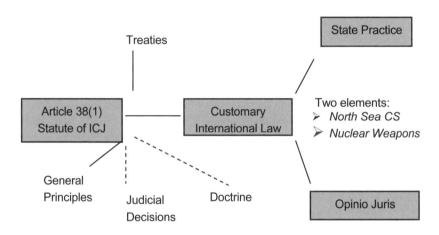

*Table 39: The background for treaties*

When a treaty "codifies" international law, it means that it collects rules and customs of international law regarding a certain topic and lists them clearly. Thus, the implication is that it is not making new law but is merely making existing customary international law into conventional international law. However, this is not entirely accurate, since codifications often will slightly modify and clarify existing customary law. The Statute of the U.N. International Law Commission defines codification as: "The more precise formulation and systematization of rules of international law in fields where there already has been extensive State practice, precedent and doctrine."

The United Nations' International Law Commission was established by the U.N. General Assembly in 1947 to promote the progressive development of international law and its codification. In doing so, the U.N. fulfilled one of the purposes in Article 13 of the U.N. Charter, which states:

1.  The General Assembly shall initiate studies and make recommendations for the purpose of:

    a)  promoting international co-operation in the political field and encouraging the progressive development of international law and its codification;

    b)  promoting international co-operation in the economic, social, cultural, educational, and health fields, an assisting in the realization of human rights and fundamental freedoms for all without distinction as to race, sex, language, or religion.

2.  The further responsibilities, functions and powers of the General Assembly with respect to matters mentioned in paragraph 1(b) above are set forth in Chapters IX and X of the U.N. Charter.

The idea is to develop international law through the restatement of existing rules or through the formulation of new rules. The Commission's work can be valuable for legal researchers because the Commission is composed of 34 members who are elected by the General Assembly for five-year terms and who serve in their individual capacities, not as representatives of their governments. Most of the Commission's work involves the preparation of drafts on topics of international law. Some topics are chosen by the Commission and others are referred to it by the General Assembly or the Economic and Social Council.

Since 1949 the Commission has submitted final drafts or reports with respect to eleven of topics or sub-topics, as follows:

- Regime of the High Seas
- Regime of territorial Waters
- Nationality, including statelessness
- Law of treaties
- Diplomatic intercourse and immunities
- Consular intercourse and immunities
- Arbitral procedure
- Succession of States in respect of treaties
- Succession of States in respect of matters other than treaties
- Jurisdictional immunities of States and their property
- State responsibility

For an example of the Commission's breadth of work on its agenda, for its fifty-fifth session in the summer of 2003, the topics were:

- Diplomatic protection

- Reservations to treaties
- Unilateral acts of States
- International liability for injurious consequences arising out of acts not prohibited by international law (international liability in case of loss from trans-boundary harm arising out of hazardous activities)
- Responsibility of international organizations
- Fragmentation of international law: difficulties arising from the diversification and expansion of international law
- Shared natural resources.

The 59th session agenda included:

- Shared Natural resources
- Respect of international organizations
- Reservations to treaties
- Effects of armed conflicts on treaties
- Obligations to extradite – expulsion of aliens.

The reports from the Commission may contain value for the researcher for interpretation of an article in a treaty, especially if the formulation of an article has not been changed subsequent to the commission's report in the final treaty text.

## 5.5.3. General Principles of Law

Article 38 (1)(c) of the Statute of the International Court of Justice[40] states the Court shall apply the general principles of law recognized by civilized nations.[41] The American Restatement[42] rightly points out that general principles, even if not incorporated or reflected in customary law or international agreement, may be invoked as supplementary rules of international law where appropriate. To avoid confusion, the researcher must make a distinction between the following principles:

- Principles generally recognized in national law
- Principles of international law
- Principles applicable in legal relations and legal logic

---

[40] See above footnote 13.

[41] SPANG-HANSSEN-1 *supra* note 8 at 226; REST *supra* note 2 at §102(1)(c) & (3).

[42] REST *supra* note 2 at § 102 (4) (on sources of international law).

General principles of municipal law are seldom used by the International Court of Justice (ICJ).

A principle of law is a general one, if it is being applied by most representative systems of municipal law. The municipal law must be internationalized. The principles must be similar, though not necessarily identical.

When a legal researcher wants to determine the content of a general principle of law he/she must use comparative law (methods).[43] Roscoe Pound, once Dean of Harvard Law School, stated: "If we…compare the authoritative techniques received in different bodies of law and the modes of applying them, this along with the established comparison of authoritative precepts and doctrines as it has gone in the past, will yield a complete, well-rounded comparative method well worthy of a place among the received methods of the science of law. Such a method is needed in the economically unifying world of today and will be needed even more as we achieve the more complete unification that will overcome the nationalism we have inherited from the sixteenth century."

### 5.5.4. Decisions of the Tribunals

Under article 38(d) of the Statute[44] of the ICJ,[45] juridical decisions of tribunals, - that is, of the ICJ itself, of arbitrations and of other tribunals and municipal courts – are only to be regarded as a subsidiary means for determinations of the rules of law. Thus, the ICJ cannot use the principle of *stare decisis*. ICJ article 59 states: "The decision of the Court has no binding force except between the parties and in respect of that particular case." However, the ICJ does refer in its decisions to its former jurisprudence in the interest of judicial constancy. Also, the ICJ has no legislative power.

The limitations in article 38 as to listed sources for the ICJ does not mean that the legal scholar should not use the international case law as a source in dissertations and theses. For example, the ICJ Fisheries and North Sea cases[46]

---

[43] See this book's Chapter 7.

[44] See above footnote 13.

[45] ICJ decisions are at <http://www.icj-cij.org/homepage/index.php>.

[46] *Fisheries Jurisdiction* (Federal Republic of Germany v. Iceland) of July 25, 1974, 1974 I.C.J. 175; *Fisheries Jurisdiction* (United Kingdom of Great Britain and Northern Ireland v. Iceland) of February 2, 1973, 1973 I.C.J. 3; *Fisheries Jurisdiction* (United

contain important considerations from different judges that, to a certain extent, reflect the evolution of international law. There are numerous collections of decisions of the international courts and arbitrate tribunals.

### 5.5.5. Writings of Publicists and Authors

Pursuant to article 38(d) of the Statute[47] of the ICJ, the teaching of the most highly qualified publicists of the various nations is to be regarded as a subsidiary means for determinations of the rules of law. However, this source is not used by the ICJ in its decisions; yet, it may be referred to in separate and dissenting ICJ opinions.

In this category of source should also be mentioned various legal research institutions:

- International Law Commission
- Institut de droit International
- International Law Association
- Hague Academy of International Law
- International Law Institute
- Restatement of the Law (Third) of the Foreign Relations Law of the United States (by the American Law Institute), especially those sections that are not stated as part of U.S. domestic law.

Among the list of persons acknowledged to belong to this source are:[48]

- Ian Brownlie, Principles of Public International Law
- M. Bedjaoui, Droit international – Bilan et perspectives
- Antonio Cassese, International Criminal Law
- Patrick Dailliere et Alain Pellet, Droit International Public
- T.O. Elias, New Horizons in International Law
- J.L. Fernandès-Flores, Derecho internacional público
- E. Jimenez de Arechaga, El derecho intercional público
- Louis Henkin (Ed.), Restatement of the Law (Third) of the Foreign

---

Kingdom of Great Britain and Northern Ireland v. Iceland) of July 25, 1974, 1974 I.C.J. 3; *North Sea Continental Shelf Cases* (Federal Republic of Germany vs. Denmark; Federal Republic of Germany vs. Netherlands) of 20 February 1969, 1969 I.C.J. 3.

[47] See above footnote 13.

[48] See further Appendix 4, Bibliography

Relations Law of the United States (by the American Law Institute); & Foreign Affairs and the United States Constitution
- Oppenheim's International Law
- Malcolm N. Shaw, International Law
- G.I. Tunkin ed., International Law – A Textbook
- W. von Vitzthum et M. Bothe, Völkerrecht

### 5.5.6. Resolutions and declarations of International Organizations

Resolutions and declarations of international organizations are not mentioned as sources in Article 38 of the ICJ. However, it appears they should be considered within the scope of the traditional sources of international law. In the future, they may be designated as a separate source category.[49]

The researcher has to be aware that different types of resolutions exist:
- Political issues
- Economic and social issues
- Legal issues
- Administrative and internal matters, like measures concerning the staff of the organization

## 5.6. Where to find material

The United Nations treaty series collection is available on online at <http://untreaty.un.org>. From 1962 onward, these have also been published in International Legal Materials (I.L.M.) by the American Society of International Law (ASIL). See also ASIL's Electronic Information System for International Law (EISIL) at <http://www.eisil.org>.[50]

General information on Public International Law can be found above in

---

[49] Ricardo Monaco, *Sources of International Law in* R. Bernhardt, ENCYCLOPEDIA OF PUBLIC INTERNATIONAL LAW, Volume Four p. 476 (2003) ( Max Planck Institute for Comparative Public Law, Elsevier 2003).

[50] See also, Guide to International Legal Research (Lexis Law Pub, June 2006 - ISBN: 978-0820575940) & Guide to International Legal Research: George Washington University International Law Review (LexisNexis, September 2003 - ISBN: 978-0327163121).

section 5.3.5. Writings of Publicists and Authors.

The leading law journals in the field of public international law are:

- American Journal on International Law (1907-)
- European Journal of international Law (1990-)
- International and Comparative Law Quarterly (1952-)
- Leiden Journal of International Law (1988-)
- Recueil des Cours (1924-) (reprints (in French and English) lectures offered each summer at the Hague Academy of International Law by leading international lawyers)
- Revue Générale de Droit Internationale Public (1984-)(in French)
- Zeitschrift für Ausländishes Öffentliches Recht und Völkerrecht (Heidelberg Journal of International Law) (1924-) (in German and English)
- British Yearbook of International Law (1921-)
- German Yearbook of International Law – Jahrbuch für Internationales Recht (1957-)
- Max Planck Yearbook of United Nations Law (1997-)
- Annuaire Français de Droit International (1955-)
- African Yearbook of International Law – Annuaire Africain de Droit International (1993-)

Various international organizations' websites that should be mentioned include:

- United Nations <www.un.org>
- International Court of Justice <www.icj-cij.org>
- International Criminal Court <www.un.org/law/icc/index.html>
- International Law Commission <www.un.org/law/ilc/index.htm>
- International Committee of the Red Cross <www.icrc.org>
- Council of Europe <www.coe.int/portalT.asp>
- European Court of Human Rights <www.echr.coe.int>
- Inter-American Court of Human Rights <www1.umn.edu/humanrts/iachr/iachr.html>
- Inter-American Commission on Human Rights <www.cidh.oas.org>
- Inter-American Court of Human Rights <www.corteidh.or.cr/index_ing.html>.

United Nations material can be found on its website <www.un.org> and legal relevant practice of the UN can be found in the official Repertory of Practice of United Nations Organs (1958-), United Nations Judicial Yearbook (1962-) and Yearbook of the United Nations (-1947-).

Material from the U.N.'s International Law Commission (ILC) can be found in the Yearbook of the International Law Commission (1949-) and at

<www. un.org/law/ilc/index.html>.

The Max Planck Institute for Comparative Public Law and International Law in Heidelberg has a very well organized web site that gives web links in a thematic order <www.mpil.de/en/LINK/epilvr.cfm>.

Yale Law School - The Avalon Project - has diplomatic documents, treaties and other documents relating to U.S. practice at <www.yale.edu/ lawweb/avalon/avalon.htm>.

Fletcher Multilaterals Project has texts of numerous international conventions - organized chronologically and thematically - as well as web links to other useful research tools at <fletcher.tufts.edu/multilaterals.html>

New York University Law Library Guide to Foreign and International Legal Databases has, under the section "Foreign databases for Jurisdiction," various web links to the national legislation and case law of many countries at <www.law.nyu.edu/library/foreign_intl/index.html>.

Antonio Cassese has published *International Law* and *International Criminal Law* at Oxford University, which publisher has created an Online Resource Centre with links to materials related to these two books. These links provide a structured way to find links to material; see <http://www.oup.com/uk/ orc/bin/9780199259397/> and <http://www.oup.com/uk/orc/bin/ 9780199259113/>.

Useful online catalogs can be found at these libraries:

- Peace Palace Library, whose catalog lists the monographs owned by the library and references every article published within one of the specialized journals that the library holds <www.ppl.nl>
- Max Planck Institute (Heidelberg) <aleph.mpg.de/aleph/fjec225vvft1q9sfvglk7g1qfrepbnsp2uak1majxu es9gvexe-02830/file/start-0>
- Max-Planck Institute - Library Catalog <www.virtual-institute.de/eindex.cfm>
- European University Institute - Library <biblio.iue.it>
- Université Paris 1 - Bibliothèque de Cujas <www-cujas.univ-paris1.fr>
- USA - Library of Congress <www.loc.gov>
- Yale Law School - Avalon Project <www.yale.edu/lawweb/avalon /avalon.htm>
- Fletcher School of Law and Diplomacy <fletcher.tufts.edu/ multilaterals.html>
- University of Chicago - International Law Database <www. lib.uchicago.edu/~llou/forintlaw.html>
- Italian National Librarian Service <opac.sbn.it>

- University of Minnesota - Human Rights Library <www1.umn.edu/humanrts/index.html>
- Peace Palace Library Catalogue <www.ppl.nl/catalogue>
- New York University Law Library Guide to Foreign and International Legal Database <www.law.nyu.edu/library/foreign_intl/index.html>
- T.M.C. Asser Instituut <www.asser.nl/vr/indxvr.htm>.

Finally, it should be noted that a great deal of material can be found in Westlaw and LexisNexis under the heading "International:"

In Westlaw:
- International law, Law reviews, Texts, and Bar Journals (INT-TP)
- International Court of Justice (INT-ICJ)
- Intenrational Criminal Tribunal for Rwanda (INT-ICTR)
- International Criminal Tribual for the Former Yougoslavia (INT-ICTY-ALL)
- International HR journal (INTLHRJ)
- International Leal Materials (ILM)
- International Commercial Arbitration (ICA-ALL)
- International Legal Material Cumulative Index (ILM-INDEX)
- International Trade Commission (FINT-ITC)
- International Trade Law and Regulation (INTTLR)
- International Treaties and Forms (INF-TF)
- International Commercial Treaties (ICA-TREATIES)
- Internet and Online Law (IOLAW)
- United Nations Commission on International Trade Law (UN-CITRAL-MODL)
- American Journal of International Law (AMJIL)
- American Society of International Law (ASIL)
- ILSA Journal of International and Comparative Law (ILSAJICL
- Index to Foreign Legal Periodicals (IFLP)
- International and Comparative Law Quarterly (ICLQ)
- Journal of International Criminal Justice (JINTCRJ)
- Journal of International Legal Studies (JILS)
- ALR International (ALRINTL)
- International Legal Materails Comulative Index (ILM-INDEX)
- Restatement of the Foreign Relations Law of the United States (REST-FOREL)

In LexisNexis:
- American Journal of International Law (AJIL)

- Internatioanl Law Review Articles (INTLR)
- International Legal Materials (ILM)
- International Trade Commission Materials (ALLITC)
- International Trade Commission Decisions (ITC)
- American Society of International Law (ASIL)
- Foreign Affairs (FORAFR)

## 5.7. Citations

As for the correct setup of citations, The New York University Journal of International Law and Politics in 2006 published a valuable Guide to Foreign and International Legal Citation (GFILC) with help from scholars in different countries,[51] which is available for free download at <http://www.law.nyu.edu /journals/jilp/Final%20GFILC%20pdf.pdf>. Given gaps in the information included in this first edition, one must expect it to be to updated.[52]

Another source for citations has been made by the Faculty at Oxford University, England,[53] which guide in the back lists citations guides for other jurisdictions.

Yet, another source for citations is the American legal citation guide known as the *Bluebook*.[54]

> Example of citation in footnotes of cases from the International Court of Justice:
> Adv. Op. Application for Review of Judgment No 158, 1973 I.C.J. 166

---

[51] The GFILC is also available in spiral-bound, paperback form by sending US$ 20 payable to "Journal of International Law and Politics" at: Circulation Department, Journal of International Law and Politics,110 West Third Street, New York NY 10012, USA. Also available for free download from <http://www.law.nyu.edu/journals/jilp/gfilc.html >.

[52] See also, MANUAL OF INTERNATIONAL AND FOREIGN LEGAL CITATION: THE GREENBOOK (Ed. Shepard Broad Law Center) (William S. Hein & Company, January 2007 - ISBN: 978-0837738307).

[53] Standard for Citation of Legal Authorities (University of Oxford, 2006) at <http://www.competition-law.ox.ac.uk/published/oscola_2006.pdf>.

[54] A UNIFORM SYSTEM OF CITATIONS ("the Bluebook"), published by the universities of Columbia, Harvard, Pennsylvania and Yale.

*Legality of the Threat or Use of Nuclear Weapons*, Advisory Opinion, 1996 I.C.J., pp. 241-242 para 29

*Nottebohm case (Liechtenstein v. Guatemala)*(Second Phase) of April 6, 1955, 1955 I.C.J. 4.

*Case concerning Military and Paramilitary Activities in and against Nicaragua (Nicaragua v. United States of America)* of June 27, 1986, 1986 I.C.J. 14, 106 para. 202

Example of citation in footnote of General Assembly resolution:
Universal Declaration of Human Rights, G.A. Res. 217A, U.N. Doc. A/810 (1948)

Example of citation in footnote of a Treaty:
Convention on the High Seas, Apr. 29, 1958, 13 U.S.T. 2312, T.I.A.S. 5200, 450 U.N.T.S. 82.
Charter of Fundamental Rights of the European Union, OJ C 364, 18/12/2000 pp. 0001-0022.

# CHAPTER 6

# Legal Families

## 6.1. Introduction

The aim of this Chapter is only to give a very broad overview of legal families.

As this book is aimed primarily at the teaching of courses on legal research methods, and as the time allotted for such courses is quite limited, comprehensive coverage of each of the legal families is not possible.

A famous book on the issue of the different legal families is K. Zweigert & H.Kötz, Introduction to Comparative Law (in English translation by Tony Weir).[1]

See also Addendum in the back of this book on the requirements for doing research in a foreign country

When studying international law and doing comparative law one should be aware of which legal family the country's law being studied belongs to.

---

[1] K. Zweigert & H.Kötz, INTRODUCTION TO COMPARATIVE LAW 145 (3rd ed.)(Tony Weir trans., Clarendon Press, Oxford 1998) [hereinafter ZWEIGERT].

---

**Research Tip #6.1**

A country's "legal family" has, among other things, a great impact on the way the law and the legal system of that country must to be interpretated.[2]

---

A legal system is an operating set of legal institutions, procedures, and rules, one for each state. National legal systems are frequently classified into families grouped pursuant to the basis of legal tradition, which is a set of deeply rooted, historically conditioned attitudes about the nature of law; about the role of law in the society and the polity; about the proper organization and operation of a legal system; and about the way law is or should be made, applied, studied, perfected, and taught. However, this does not mean that in each family there does not exist great diversity, not only in substantive rules of law, but also in their institutions and processes.[3]

In Civil Law countries, rules governing a single transaction may be placed in widely separated parts of a civil law country Code, which is abstract in language, whereas the Anglo-American follows the view that all aspects of a unitary transaction should be dealt with in the same place in the system.[4]

The factors that are crucial for the style of a legal system, or legal family are:[5]

- Its historical background and development
- Its predominant and characteristic mode of thought in legal matters
- Especially distinctive institutions
- The kind of legal sources it acknowledges and the way it handles them

---

[2] It is a well-known fact that major law firms in London and elsewhere are increasingly seeking students with specialist, regionally-focused legal knowledge (including language and cultural skills) that will equip them for a lucrative globally-oriented legal career, Werner F. Menski, COMPARATIVE LAW IN A GLOBAL CONTEXT: THE LEGAL SYSTEMS OF ASIA AND AFRICA 29 (London: Platinium, 2000).

[3] John Henry Merryman, THE CIVIL LAW TRADITION: AN INTRODUCTION TO THE LEGAL SYSTEMS OF WESTERN EUROPE AND LATIN AMERICA 1-2 (2nd ed.)(Stanford, California: Stanford University Press, 1985) [hereinafter MERRYMAN].

[4] ZWEIGERT *supra* note 1 at 145.

[5] ZWEIGERT *supra* note 1 at 68.

- Its ideology

## 6.2. A suggested division into legal families

One such division is the following:[6]
- *The Romanistic Legal Family* (France, the Benelux countries,[7] Italy, Spain and Portugal[8]) - The *Code Civile*[9] of 1804 is the heart of private law in France and the great model for the codes of private law of the whole Romanistic legal family. It is a felicitous blend of traditional legal institutions from the *droit écrit* of the South – influenced by Roman Law – and the *droit coutumier* of the North – influenced by the Germanic-Frankish customary law. It bears throughout the marks of its heritage of the pre-revolutionary law (*ancien droit*). There was never any serious discussion of a complete reception of Roman law into France – unlike Germany later on. From two royal ordinances in the 17th century came the basis for a division between private law in the narrow sense, and commercial law, which the Romanistic and Germanic legal families – except Switzerland and Italy – still recognize by having different codes, much to the surprise of Anglo-American lawyers. In France and Italy, the highest court in civil and criminal matters differs in characteristic respects from the comparable supreme courts of the Anglo-American and German legal families.[10] The French *Court of Cassation*[11] goes in for lapidary "whereas"-

---

[6] ZWEIGERT *supra* note 1 at 64. Others have divided into the following five families: Western Systems, Socialist Systems, Islamic law, Hindu Law , and Chinese Law. René David, *Traité élémentaire de droit civil comparé* 222 (1950). See also, MERRYMAN *supra* note 3 at 5.

[7] Belgium, the Netherlands, and Luxembourg.

[8] ZWEIGERT *supra* note 1 at 104

[9] or Code Napoléon [Napoleonic Code] (originally called the Code civil des Français).

[10] ZWEIGERT *supra* note 1 at 74-80 & 120.

[11] [Court of Cassation] is the main court of last resort in France. It should be pointed out that besides this Supreme Court for judicial cases (civil justice or criminal justice), France has other Supreme Courts, for example the Conseil d'État (for administrative justice), and Conseil Constitutionnel (constitutional challenges).

clauses. Legal studies in France are part of a general education.[12]

- *The Germanic Legal Family* (Germany, Austria, Croatia, Switzerland, Greece, Turkey, South Korea) - The effects of Roman law were much greater in Germany than in France and much greater than in England. Germany consisted of many small principals until 1871. As there was no common German private law, no common German courts system, and no common German fraternity of lawyers, Roman legal ideas and institutions were adopted wholesale in many parts of the country and for many areas of law.[13] The Superior German Court gives reasons which are wide-ranging and loaded with citations like a textbook, while - again - the French *Court of Cassation*[14] goes in for lapidary "whereas"-clauses. Unlike Germany, legal studies in France are part of a general education.[15]

- *The Anglo-American Legal Family* (England, and Wales, Northern Ireland, the Republic of Ireland, Scotland,[16] United States of America, Australia (both federal and individual states), New Zealand,[17] Canada (except Québec)) – The courts in the Anglo-American Legal Family can "make" law. In general, Common law demands a study of its historical origins – "the life of law has been experience." Roman law has not influenced English law (while it has affected Scottish law). Codification has never been a great thing in English law (contrary to the

---

[12] ZWEIGERT *supra* note 1 at 130-131.

[13] ZWEIGERT *supra* note 1 at 133-135.

[14] [Court of Cassation] is the main court of last resort in France, excluding cases of administrative justice, which go before the Conseil d'État.

[15] ZWEIGERT *supra* note 1 at 130-131.

[16] Scotland is often said to use the civil law system, but in fact it has a unique system that combines elements of an uncodified civil law dating back to the Corpus Juris Civilis with an element of common law long predating the Treaty of Union with England in 1707. Scottish common law differs in that the use of precedents is subject to the courts seeking to discover the principle that justifies a law, rather than to search for an example as a precedent, and that the principles of natural justice and fairness have always formed a source of Scottish Law. Other comparable pluralistic (or "mixed") legal systems operate in Quebec, Louisiana and South Africa.

[17] 1966 ENCYCLOPAEDIA OF NEW ZEALAND at <http://www.teara.govt.nz/1966/L/LegalSystem/SourcesOfLaw/en>.

United States). England has no constitution[18] (again, in contrast to the U.S.).

- *The Nordic Legal Family* (Denmark,[19] Finland,[20] Iceland,[21] Norway,[22] and Sweden[23])[24] – Nordic Legal Family law has few, if any, of the "stylistic" hallmarks of the Common Law. Roman law has played a smaller role in the legal development of the Nordic countries than in Germany. The Nordic Legal Family's laws belong to the Civil Law, but form a special legal family, alongside the Romanistic and German legal families. The political and cultural ties between these countries have always been very close, partly based on the fact that the countries for some hundred years were unified. In the 17th century, the countries each promulgated comprehensive codes unifying private law, criminal law and procedural law. In the 19th century, they began modernization of their codes, and introduced amendments were made in separate reforming laws. Furthermore, unified laws between the countries began to arise. A tendency toward conceptualism and the construction of large-scale integrated theoretical systems has never

---

[18] However, England has the so-called "Magna Carta Libertatum" ("Great Charter of Freedoms") of 1215, which led to the rule of constitutional law today. It influenced many common law and other documents, such as the United States Constitution and Bill of Rights, and is considered one of the most important legal documents in the history of democracy.

[19] Rasmus H. Wandall, RESEARCHING DANISH LAW (July 2006) at <http://www.nyulawglobal.org/globalex/Denmark.htm>.

[20] Legal order – Finland at <http://ec.europa.eu/civiljustice/legal_order/legal_order_fin_en.htm>.

[21] Rán Tryggvadóttir & Thordis Ingadóttir, RESEARCHING ICELANDIC LAW (2007) at <http://www.nyulawglobal.org/globalex/iceland.htm>.

[22] Hans Petter Graver, *The Approach to European Law in Norwegian Legal Doctrine*, in Peter Christian Müller-Graff & Erling Selvig, eds., EUROPEAN LAW IN THE GERMAN-NORWEGIAN CONTEXT: ORIGINS AND PERSPECTIVES (Berlin: Berliner Wissenschafts-Verlag GmbH, 2001- ISBN: 978-3-8305-0248-7) & at <http://www.arena.uio.no/publications/wp03_18.pdf>.

[23] Legal order – Sweden at <http://ec.europa.eu/civiljustice/legal_order/legal_order_swe_en.htm>.

[24] Usually, Scandinavia is regarded as Denmark, Norway, and Sweden. The Nordic countries are the Scandinavian ones plus Iceland and Finland.

really been followed. All the countries have a constitution and their royal families/presidents have real executive power, which power belongs to the government – a special independent branch pursuant to the countries' constitutions – along with the Parliament and the courts.

- *The Law in the Far East* (China, Japan) – Legal systems in the Far East differ fundamentally from the legal families dealt with in all western systems, where the important questions of social life should primarily be regulated by rules of objective law rather than simply by conventions or habits. Disputes are often resolved by techniques other than actions at law. Thus, in the Far East, informal means of dispute resolution are enormously important. However, China and Japan have in the last decades moved in the direction of being part of the Romano-Germanic family of law, with some elements of American law.[25]

- *Religious Legal Systems:*[26]

  o *Islamic Law:* The Shariah or Islamic law is a complex of divinely revealed rules, which a faithful Muslim must observe if he/she seeks to perform the duties of his/her religion. It does not depend on the authority of any earthly law-giver and is already existing and formulated. Only a few of the statements in the Koran (the highest source of Islamic law) constitute rules of law capable of direct application. Thus, in many cases legal consequences are not specified. In addition, there is the Sunna, which is traditionally attributed to the prophet Muhammad or to his immediate disciples.[27]

  o *Hindu Law* – It applies to all persons who are Hindu, that is, who accept the complex mass of

---

[25] Hiroshi Oda, JAPANESE LAW (Butterworths, 1992).

[26] The law of Israel is a mixed system of common law and civil law, British Mandate regulations, and, in personal matters, Jewish, Christian, and Muslim legal systems.

[27] ZWEIGERT *supra* note 1 at 303.

religious, philosophical, and social ideas com-
pendiously referred to as Hinduism. It does not
require a person to believe in a god and embraces a great variety of cults and rituals. It lacks
a clearly defined theological doctrine, but does
offer certain basic convictions of a religious or
philosophical order. The oldest "law-books" are
the smritis, which is a Sanskrit word denoting
the "remembered:" wisdom of the old priests and
scholars.[28]

---

[28] ZWEIGERT *supra* note 1 at 313.

CHAPTER 7

# Comparative Law Methods

As the future curriculum for American law schools – at least at Harvard,[1] Stanford[2] and Yale – will contain a requirement in each course to undertake comparison to other legal systems,[3] it seems appropriate for this book on legal research methods to contain a chapter on comparative law or more rightly termed, comparative (law) methods.[4] These must consist of detailed analysis as well as comparison. The process quite naturally requires study of some foreign law, after having studied the law of one's home country first.[5]

---

[1] The Harvard Law School recently announced that its first-year curriculum will reduce the number of hours spent on the traditional common-law courses and mix in three new classes: legislation and regulation, international and comparative legal studies, and problem-solving skills, ABA JOURNAL, July 2007, page 44.

[2] Stanford Law School will give law students access to the entire university and, for example, allow law students interested in intellectual property to take engineering and science classes. Law students might learn better negotiation skills at the business school or learn more nuances about the implications of a cross-border transaction by studying in the economics department. Dean Larry Kramer to ABA JOURNAL, July 2007, page 45.

[3] Compulsory jurisprudence comes too late in education and is too little. Alan Hunt, 6 *Jurisprudence, Philosophy and Legal Education – Against Foundationalism*, LEGAL STUDIES 292, 294 (November 1986).

[4] As comparative law methods deal with more than comparison, they are different from comparative jurisprudence. Consider the legal dictionary definition: "The study of the principles of legal science by the comparison of various systems of law." BLACK'S LAW DICTIONARY (8th ed.) (St. Paul: West Publishing, 2004).

[5] Max Rheinstein, *Comparative Law – Its Functions, Methods and Usages*, 22 ARK. L. REV. 415, 416 (1946) [hereinafter RHEINSTEIN].

The usefulness of comparative legal study is beyond question.[6]

Comparative legal analysis is also relevant in the E.U. framework, where comparison of different rules in the E.U. Member States often results in promulgation of rules in the form of an E.U. directive. The same applies for working out international conventions or treaties.[7]

As indicated previously, this book's primary aim is for use in teaching courses on legal research methods in the US and in Continental Europe, so this chapter should only be regarded as a very brief introduction to comparative law methods.

A famous European book (in English translation) is K. Zweigert & H.Kötz, Introduction to Comparative Law.[8] See also a number of well-regarded articles from other professors in the footnotes of this chapter.[9]

And see, the Addendum in the back of this book on the requirements for doing research in a foreign country.

---

[6] Günter Frankenberg, *Critical Comparisons: Re-Thinking Comparative Law*, 26 HARV. INT'L L. J. 411, 418 (1985) [hereinafter FRANKENBERG]. Comparative law is a tool of research and a tool of education, Otto Kahn-Freund, *On Uses and Misuses of Comparative Law*, 37 MOD. L. REV. 1 (1974) [hereinafter KAHN-FREUND II]. A man who knows no language except his own is far less able to appreciate its beauty and to understand its structure than he who can compare it with the languages of other nations, O. Kahn-Freund, *Comparative Law as an Academic Subject*, 82 THE LAW QUARTERLY REVIEW 40, 60 (1966) [hereinafter KAHN-FREUND I].

[7] Ruth Nielsen & Christian D. Tvarnø, RETSKILDER & RETSTEORIER [Source of Law & Legal Theories] 25 (1st Ed.) (Denmark, Copenhagen: Jurist- and Økonomforbundets Forlag [DJØF Publishing] 2005) [hereinafter TVARNØ] & K. Zweigert & H.Kötz, INTRODUCTION TO COMPARATIVE LAW 2 (3rd ed.) (Tony Weir trans., Clarendon Press, Oxford, 1998) [hereinafter ZWEIGERT].

[8] ZWEIGERT *supra* note 7 at 145.

[9] See also, The Oxford Handbook of Comparative law (Editor: Reiman & Zimmerman)( England: Oxford University Press 2007); Peter de Cruz, Comparative law in a Changing World (3rd ed)(London/New York: Cavendish 2007); Comparative law - A handbook (Editors: Örücü / David Nelken)( England, Oxford: Hart Publishing 2007).

## 7.1. Introduction – Not just comparison

There is no decisive definition of what comparative law or comparative (law) method is today.[10] However, comparative law is not simply a topic, but a method - or rather, it is the common name for a variety of methods of looking at law.

---

**Research Tip #7.1**

"Comparison" is quite the buzzword currently in American law schools/universities.

But, it should be used – if at all – with great caution.

A pure comparison of legal systems does not have any value or purpose, one has to figure out a *comparative method* that will work when investigating two or more countries' legal systems.

Thus, students/scholars have to know how to build a legal comparative method.

---

Comparative law has two quite distinct roots: [11]

- Legislative comparative law – when foreign laws are invoked in the process of drafting new national laws or international conventions.[12]

---

[10] Esin Örürü, *Unde Venit, Quo Tendit Comparative Law?, in* COMPARATIVE LAW IN THE 21ST CENTURY 1 (Andrew Harding and Esin Örürü (Ed.), Kluwer, 2002) [hereinafter ÖRÜRÜ].

[11] ZWEIGERT *supra* note 7 at 51.

[12] A systematic knowledge of the donor system will make a law reformer more efficient. On the European continent codification or major legislative revision normally results in the type of comparative law studies that would delight the most learned professor of that subject in the universities. Such studies are usually conducted or commissioned by officials of a country's ministry of justice. The E. U. Commission staff has performed a function somewhat similar to that of a national ministry of justice. National law makers are increasingly compelled – by the operation of the E.U. – to take into account each other's systems. At the U.S. federal level, there are no institutional arrangements or procedures for regular recourse to foreign law in the executive departments, where most bills originate. The same is true in the U.S. congressional committees. Eric Stein,

The comparative study of law can also take the form of a selective adoption of particular legal institutions or rules.[13]

- Scientific or theoretical comparative law – when the comparison of legal systems – or with other (for example, socicial or computer/technical) systems - is undertaken to improve one's legal knowledge.[14]

Comparative law offers the only way by which law can become international[15] and consequently a science.[16] The increase in cross-border activity is expanding the use and utility of comparative law, which is moving from local/region-centric to global. The internationalization of transactions, the use of the Internet, and the increasing applicability of foreign law make comparative law an indispensable tool of the legal practitioner.[17]

On the European continent, legal unity began to disappear in the 18th century as national codes were put in the place of traditional Roman law.[18] The consequence was that lawyers concentrated exclusively on their own legislation, and stopped looking over the border. Comparative law "has to put an

---

*Uses, Misuses – and Nonuses of Comparative Law*, 72 Nw. U. L. Rev. 198, 209, 210, 212 (1977-78).

[13] Rodolfo Sacco, Legal Formants, *A Dynamic Approach to Comparative Law* (Installment I of II), 39 Am. J. Comp. L. 1, 3 (1991) [hereinafter Sacco I].

[14] Comparative law remains a science as long as it acquires knowledge and regardless of whether or not the knowledge is put to any further use. Sacco I *supra* note 13 at 4 & 5.

[15] Comparative law dissolves unconsidered national prejudices, and helps to fathom the different societies and cultures of the world and to further international understanding. Zweigert *supra* note 7 at 16-25.

[16] Some claim comparative law is still not a subject in its own right, while others claim that comparative law, properly pursued, is an essentially philosophical activity. Örürü *supra* note 10 at 4 & W. Ewald, *Comparative Jurisprudence (1): What Was it Like to Try a Rat?*, 143 U. Pa. L. Rev. 1889, 2111-2112 (June 1995).

[17] P. John Kozyris, *Comparative Law in the 21st Century: New Horizons and New Technologies*, 69 Tul. L. Rev. 165-169 (1994) [hereinafter Kozyris] & Örürü *supra* note 10 at 17.

[18] All civil law systems are conglomerates of medieval European customs and the learning about Roman law that, after having been lost with the fall of the Roman Empire, was rediscovered in the 12th century. But the customs were different in different parts of Europe. Rheinstein *supra* note 5 at 417.

end to such narrow-mindedness."[19]

Comparative analysis is proper and relevant both where national rules already exist in a country, which is the starting point for the comparison with foreign law, as well as in situations where there is no existing rule in the "stepping stone country" and where foreign law thus is used as inspiration.[20] However, comparisons can also be made between different rules in a single legal system.[21] Comparison follows from a knowledge of the phenomena to be compared. One can only compare that with which one is acquainted. Knowledge of these phenomena develops by comparison.[22]

Thus, comparative law is partly comparison but mainly the analysis of the different legal systems of the world. Comparative methods have proven to be the best means available for highlighting structural regularities that would otherwise pass unobserved. It would be wrong, however, to expect comparative methods to explain the reasons for these regularities. Comparisons do not serve this purpose.[23] Thus, further analysis of where and why the differences

---

[19] ZWEIGERT *supra* note 7 at 15. Modern comparative law started in Paris in 1900 when Édouard Lambert and Raymond Saleilles suggested a common law of mankind (droit commun de l'humanité) to which comparative law was necessary. They held comparative law must resolve the accidental and divisive differences in the law of peoples at similar stages of cultural and economic development, and reduce the number of divergences in law, attributable not to the political, moral, or social qualities of the different nations, but to historical accident or to temporary or contingent circumstances. ZWEIGERT *supra* note 7 at 3.

[20] TVARNØ *supra* note 7 at 25

[21] ZWEIGERT *supra* note 7 at 2. Much of what is called legal history (or history of law) in the Civil Law tradition is baffling and inexplicable to the Common Law Lawyer who first approaches it. He/she is used to thinking of legal history as an account of legal rules and institutions in their historical, economic, and social context. However, picking up a book on legal history in the civil law tradition, he/she is likely to find the bulk of it devoted to a discussion of schools of legal thought and of disputes between legal scholars and their followers. The protagonist or leader of this form of legal history is the legal scholar, and its subject matter is currents of thoughts about the structure and operation of the legal order, John Henry Merryman, THE CIVIL LAW TRADITION: AN INTRODUCTION TO THE LEGAL SYSTEMS OF WESTERN EUROPE AND LATIN AMERICA 60 (2nd ed.) (Stanford, California: Stanford University Press, 1985).

[22] SACCO I *supra* note 13 at 5.

[23] SACCO I *supra* note 13 at 5.

exist may be appropriate.

Comparative law is a school of verity or truth, which extends and enriches the solutions. However, it is perhaps too often the story of similarities and dissimilarities[24] between legal cultures, traditions, systems, families, styles, origins, solutions and ideas.[25] Some hold that an aim for comparative law is to find the "better solution" for the time and place.[26] However, others find the "better solution" of comparative law is not worthy of being described as an academic discipline in its own right.[27] But all seem to agree that comparative law is a science with its own distinct province. Comparative law can help to illuminate the nature of legal phenomena and the relationship between law and political, moral, and other values. It can also help demonstrate the extent to which the form and substance of any legal system are not "natural," but result from the implementation of moral and political values.[28]

---

**Research Tip #7.2**

The task of the comparatist should be to cherish "difference," which involves some form of appreciation of "the other" and an a priori readiness to accept another system as valid in its own right.[29]

---

[24] Thus, the definition of comparative law in Black's Law Dictionary is somewhat wrong, as it claims: comparative law is the scholarly study of the similarities and differences between different legal systems. Actually, this is sometimes divided into three subsets: comparative legislation, comparative history of law and descriptive comparative law.

[25] FRANKENBERG *supra* note 6 at 425.

[26] ZWEIGERT *supra* note 7 at 8, 15 & TVARNØ *supra* note 7 at 25.

[27] Jonathan Hill, *Comparative Law, Law Reform and Legal Theory*, 9 OXFORD JOURNAL OF LEGAL STUDIES 101, 113 (1989) [hereinafter HILL] & Alan Watson, LEGAL TRANSPLANTS: AN APPROACH TO COMPARATIVE LAW 1-9 (University Press of Virginia, 1974) [hereinafter WATSON].

[28] HILL *supra* note 27 at 115.

[29] Werner F. Menski, COMPARATIVE LAW IN A GLOBAL CONTEXT: THE LEGAL SYSTEMS OF ASIA AND AFRICA 18 (Platinium, London 2000) [hereinafter MENSKI].

## 7.2. About the Method

---

**Research Tip #7.3**

Comparatists all over the world are perfectly unembarrassed about their adaptable methodology,[30] and see themselves as still being in an experimental stage.

---

Comparative law can scarcely be called systematic and comparatists remain appropriately eclectic.[31] Yet, modern comparative law is a critical method of legal science. Comparison has no fear of differences, however large they may be, and it measures the extent of those differences – again, be they large or small.[32]

The comparative method is the opposite of the dogmatic. The comparative method is founded upon the actual observation of the elements at work in a given legal system; whereas the dogmatic method is founded upon analytical reasoning. The comparative method examines the way in which, in various legal systems, jurists work with specific rules and general categories. The dogmatic method offers abstract definitions.[33]

---

**Research Tip #7.4**

A comparative lawyer may, and probably should, limit his field of research both in the geographical sense and as regards to subject matter.

---

But he must remain flexible and must often rely on common-sense to avoid rigorous discussion of theory and method.[34] A comparatist must set out on a voyage of discovery to find the field and yet on another voyage to find

---

[30] Sciences that have to busy themselves with their own methodology are sick sciences. Gustav Radbruch, EINFÜHRUNG IN DIE RECHTSWISSENSCHAFT 253 (12th Ed. 1969).

[31] Hiram E. Chodosh, *Comparing Comparisons: In Search Of Methodology*, 84 IOWA L. REV. 1025, 1044 & 1061(Aug 1999) [hereinafter CHODOSH], HILL *supra* note 27 at 111 & WATSON *supra* note 27 at 11.

[32] SACCO I *supra* note 13 at 7.

[33] SACCO I *supra* note 13 at 24.

[34] KAHN-FREUND I *supra* note 6 at 42 & FRANKENBERG *supra* note 6 at 417.

the tools.

When comparing closely related systems, it is usually more rewarding to explain the differences; while in two entirely unrelated systems, it is more rewarding to explain the similarities.[35]

---

**Research Tip #7.5**

It is necessary to get to know what is behind the formal legal texts and also, even more important, how these function. This requires understanding of the legal culture that produced the texts, and more broadly, the social and economic structures as well as the ethical and political values that support them.[36]

---

**Research Tip #7.6**

Laws cannot be grasped in an idealized form outside the context of the society that created them.[37]

---

A comparatist should not be limited to the staid and dry juxtaposition of the regulations of one legal system with those of another, with little or no critical analysis, for, as such, comparatists do not compare, they contrast. In Europe and North America there has been an almost irresistible tendency of comparative lawyers to translate roughly equivalent (or so it appears) concepts from two or more legal systems and then to contrast them, rather than to analyze their respective socio-legal environments and to study law and legal concepts "in context."[38]

A globally-focused study of legal systems, including the legal systems of Asia and Africa, cannot avoid taking many culture-specific, so-called "extra-legal" factors into account and therefore needs to be holistic, interdisciplinary and plurifocal in analyzing the concept of "law", for which there is no con-

---

[35] ÖRÜRÜ *supra* note 10 at 9 & Michael Bogdan, COMPARATIVE LAW 18 (1994 Kluwer).

[36] KAHN-FREUND I *supra* note 6 at 41 & 47.

[37] KOZYRIS *supra* note 17 at 168.

[38] MENSKI, *supra* note 29 at 14, Pierre Legrand, *How to Compare Now*, 16 LEGAL STUDIES 232, 234 (July 1996) [hereinafter LEGRAND]. Comparative law loses some of its utility, and most of its charm, if it reduces itself to a level of dry, formalistic, historical introductions to foreign legal systems and comparison of legal rules and institutions. KOZYRIS *supra* note 17 at 175.

sensus definition.[39] A deep understanding of law is not found in legislative texts and judicial decisions alone.[40] The range of non-legal, cultural knowledge[41] required is vastly increased when trying to make sense of Hindu law, Islamic law, African law, Chinese law or Japanese law.

Comparative law has far greater utility in substantive law than in the law of procedure, and the attempt to use foreign models of judicial organization and procedure may lead to frustration and thus be a misuse of the comparative method. One cannot take for granted that rules or institutions are transplantable. The use of the comparative method requires a knowledge not only of the foreign law, but also of its social, and above all its political, context.[42]

---

**Research Tip #7.7**

To be able to solve his/her issue, a comparatist must often investigate the history of rules and their problems.

---

He must take into account not only legislative rules, judicial decisions, the "law in the books" - and general conditions of business, customs and practices - but also in fact everything that helps to mold human conduct in the situation under consideration.[43]

---

**Research Tip #7.8**

It is wrong to believe that the first step toward comparison is to identify "the legal rule" of the countries to be compared.[44]

---

Instead of speaking of "the legal rule" of a country, one must speak of the

---

[39] MENSKI, *supra* note 29 at 51.

[40] MENSKI, *supra* note 29 at 53, LEGRAND *supra* note 38 at 235. Norwegian professor Torsten Echoff has stated: "it has never been proven that a tribe's drum-dance to solve disputes was a poorer solutions-method than what we are used to" (author's translations into English), quoted by Carl August Fleisher, RETTSKILDER OG JURIDISK METODE 256 [Source of Law and the Legal Method] (Oslo, Ad notam Gyldendal, 1998).

[41] FRANKENBERG *supra* note 6 at 411 & 414 & MENSKI, *supra* note 29 at 15.

[42] KAHN-FREUND II *supra* note 6 at 20 & 27 & SACCO I *supra* note 13 at 7-9.

[43] ZWEIGERT *supra* note 7 at 8 & 11 and SACCO I *supra* note 13 at 26.

[44] SACCO I *supra* note 13 at 21.

rules of constitutions,[45] legislatures, courts,[46] and, indeed, of the scholars[47] who formulate legal doctrine – so-called "legal formants" of which a given legal system has many.[48] The jurist concerned with the law within a single country examines all of these "legal formants" and then eliminates the complications that arise from their multiplicity to arrive at one rule. He does so by a process of interpretation. Yet this process does not guarantee that there is, in his system, only a single rule. Several interpretations will be possible and logic alone will not show that one is correct and another false.

---

**Research Tip #7.9**

Within each legal system there co-exist different "legal formants," which may or may not be in harmony with each other.[49]

---

As for court decisions, one must know not only how courts have acted but consider the influences to which judges are subject. Such influences may have a variety of origins. It is a mistake to reduce the comparative method to the study of cases. Judicial decisions have a different significance in countries where the law is based on precedent from those where it is based on statute. It is important to distinguish between the rule announced by the court and the rule it actually applied, or, as a Common Law Lawyer would say, between the court's statement of the rule and the holding of the case, that is, the facts

---

[45] No one who wishes to describe the law realistically can ignore the existence of sources other than those formerly recognized in the Constitution. Rodolfo Sacco, *Legal Formants* (Installment II of II), *A Dynamic Approach to Comparative Law*, 39 AM. J. COMP. L. 343, 344 (1991) [hereinafter SACCO II].

[46] A Common Law Lawyer – accustomed to considering judicial precedent as a main source – will find it curious that in Civil Law countries judicial decisions are not supposed to be a source of law at all. A Civil Law jurist will consult works of scholars if these faithfully describe the rule in a statute, and decisions of judges, because these are instances in which this rule has been enforced. SACCO I *supra* note 13 at 21-22.

[47] Scholarly writings, both essayistic and didactic, are a source of law, that is, they form "legal formants" of the system. SACCO II *supra* note 45 at 346. Scholarly writings were far more important in Germany between 1880 and 1900 than in France. In turn, case law has been more important in France than in Italy. SACCO I *supra* note 13 at 33.

[48] SACCO I *supra* note 13 at 22-23.

[49] SACCO I *supra* note 13 at 30 & SACCO II *supra* note 45 at 343.

on which the court arrived at a certain result.[50]

A jurist who deals with a system that is not his own often has problems of perception with legal formants that do not exist in his own system. Any account of the sources of law is incomplete unless it describes all legal formants of the system. To have a complete account, one must recognize the rules promulgated by organs of the state and enforced by its coercive power are not the only sources of law.[51]

---

**Research Tip #7.10**
Law cannot be applied unless it is interpreted.[52]

---

When law is applied, there must be an interaction between a primary source, such as statute or case precedent, and an interpretation. Interpretation is determined and disciplined by all those factors that affect the convictions of the interpreter.[53]

Comparative law can move beyond the field of evaluating differences and similarities between and among systems to become part of an interdisciplinary research, serving the scholar concerned with problems of sociology and politics. Comparative law would be a purely doctrinal study if it were to concern itself only with legal forms.[54]

Comparative legal studies serves three major purposes:[55]

- ▪ Understanding - including explanation, knowledge, legal history, jurisprudence and legal science. Disagreements over what should be compared are in part a function of divergent theoretical and practical objectives.[56]

---

[50] SACCO I *supra* note 13 at 23, 26 & 27.

[51] SACCO I *supra* note 13 at 33 & SACCO II *supra* note 45 at 344.

[52] Interpretation is guided by what the interpreter thought and felt even before he started to read and analyze the source. Josef Esser, VORVERSTÄNDNIS UND METHODENWAHL IN DER RECHTSFINDUNG: RATIONALITÄTSGRUNDLAGEN RICHTERLICHER ENTSCHEIDUNGSPRAXIS (Durchges 1972) & SACCO II *supra* note 45 at 344.

[53] SACCO II *supra* note 45 at 344-345.

[54] SACCO II *supra* note 45 at 388.

[55] CHODOSH *supra* note 31 at 1069-1070, .

[56] CHODOSH *supra* note 31 at 1074, 1090.

- Reform - including comparative judicial-decision making, and comparative legislation. A fruitful comparative law method has to do much more than set sections of codes or general legislation side-by-side.[57]
- International unification - including cross-border conflict resolution through private and public international law and international organizations.

Comparative law can be divided into:[58]

- Macrocomparison – comparing the spirit and style of different legal systems, the methods of thought and procedures they use. Research is done into methods of handling legal materials, procedures for resolving and deciding disputes, or the roles of those engaged in the law. For example, comparison of different techniques of legislation, study of the different ways of resolving conflicts adopted by different legal systems (by taking into account all actual methods of settling) disputes, and ask how effective they actually are. Thus, there is no concentration on individual concrete problems and their solutions.
- Microcomparison – a comparison that deals with specific legal institutions or problems, that is, with the rules used to solve actual problems or particular conflicts of interest. However, microcomparison may not work at all unless one takes into account the general institutional contexts in which the rules under comparison have evolved and are actually applied.

## 7.3. A Plan

A basic working-plan for a comparative (law) method is:[59]

1. As in all intellectual activity, begin with the posing of a question or the setting of a working hypothesis. Remember, that the methodology of a science is its rationale for accepting or rejecting its theories

---

[57] CHODOSH *supra* note 31 at 1075 & Roscoe Pound, *Comparative Law in Space and Time,* 4 AM. J. COMP. L. 70, 75 (1955).

[58] ZWEIGERT *supra* note 7 at 4-5.

[59] Partly from ZWEIGERT *supra* note 7 at 6.

or hypotheses.[60] Prematurely crystallized methodological rationales may do more harm than good.[61] The biggest hazard is the formulation of the problem and the choice of the criteria of relevance on the basis of which data are selected and classified for study.[62] For practical reasons, it is necessary to make a somewhat painful selection; therefore, the comparatist must make up criteria of selection.[63]

2. Next, decide the manner in which the survey-investigation will be conducted, that is, in detail describe what one intends to do (not what one hopes for, as it is premature to do that). One may have to reevaluate and re-write this as work proceeds. List which criteria are used for the selection of the material.[64]

3. Lay out the essentials of the relevant foreign law, country by country, or component by component.[65] Remember that without clarity of purpose, it is difficult to determine the content of what to report. Without specific attention to the choice of content, comparisons are vulnerable to bias and inaccuracy. One of the dangers of comparative law is the temptation to mold the data with a view to substantiating a preconceived thesis.[66] Without developed techniques of contrast and differentiation, the goal of objectivity becomes elusive.[67] Analyze each component that is to be compared in its own environment, that is, in the way a that a person educated in that environment would do it. This includes using words and terms in the way a person in such environment does. The solutions found in the different jurisdictions must be cut loose from their conceptual context and stripped of their national doctrinal overtones so that they may be seen purely in the light of their function, as an attempt to satisfy a

---

[60] Mark Blaug, THE METHODOLOGY OF ECONOMICS 47 (Cambridge University Press, 1980).

[61] CHODOSH *supra* note 31 at 1032.

[62] CHODOSH *supra* note 31 at 1053 & Sally Falk Moore, LAW AS PROCESS: AN ANTHRO-POLIGCAL APPROACH 137 (ROUTLEDGE & K. PAUL, 1978).

[63] ZWEIGERT *supra* note 7 at 42.

[64] FRANKENBERG *supra* note 6 at 430.

[65] ZWEIGERT *supra* note 7 at 43.

[66] HILL *supra* note 27 at 107 & WATSON *supra* note 27 at 12-13.

[67] CHODOSH *supra* note 31 at 1051.

particular legal need.

4.  Then use this material as a basis for critical comparison, that is, analyze by using, among other things, the methods from chapter 2 and/or 3 of this book. The comparison should be based on the idea of a logical and neutral referent. Thus, the comparatist's own legal system, culture or experience should not become the basis of and provide the conceptual framework for comparison.[68] This includes defining words and terms that are used differently in the environments to be compared.

5.  End up with a real result, that is, a critical evaluation,[69] not just a comparison-result. This could be a conclusion or conclusions about the proper policy for the law to adopt, which may involve a reinterpretation of one's own system; it could also be any other kind of result from the comparative analysis. The comparatist must be able to demonstrate and persuade the audience members of the lessons they should take away from the analysis.[70] The comparatist is in the best position to follow his/her own comparative researches with a critical evaluation – and if he/she does not, no one will.[71]

## 7.4. Advice & Comments

The basic methodological principle of all comparative law is that the problem must be stated without any reference to the concepts of one's own legal system.[72] In comparative law, always focus on the concrete problem. To ask why a foreign system has not felt the need to produce a legal solution for a particular problem may lead to interesting conclusions about it, or about one's own law.

---

[68] FRANKENBERG *supra* note 6 at 432.

[69] CHODOSH *supra* note 31 at 1052 & ZWEIGERT *supra* note 7 at 43.

[70] CHODOSH *supra* note 31 at 1086. The scholar has no other power than the one that comes from his capacity to persuade. SACCO II *supra* note 45 at 349.

[71] ZWEIGERT *supra* note 7 at 46.

[72] ZWEIGERT *supra* note 7 at 10.

---

**Research Tip #7.11**

A comparatist must avoid all limitations and restraints, especially in relation to the question of "sources of law."

---

He/she must encompass the law of the whole world - past and present, and everything that affects the law. The comparatist must make every effort to learn and remember as much as he/she can about foreign civilizations, especially those whose law has engendered the great families of legal systems.[73] Every comparatist learns that the legal system of every society faces essentially the same problems, but often solves these problems by quite different means.

The right method must largely be discovered by gradual trial and error. It is extremely doubtful whether one could draw up a logical and self-contained methodology of comparative law, which could claim to work effectively. Thus, a detailed method cannot be laid down in advance. Most probably, the science of comparative law will always remain an area where only sound judgment, common sense, and even intuition, can be of any help.

Modern comparative law is a more realistic method of legal science, which not only shows up the emptiness of legal dogmatism, but develops a new and particular system related to demands for suitable rules in life; therefore, it is functional and appropriate. Legal science in general is sick, but comparative law can cure it.[74]

When making a choice among variables, the comparatist should remember the following:

- classification
- prototypes and
- micro/macro distinctions.

Classification, or the differentiation of phenomena into categorical schemes or taxonomies, is a common tool of comparative legal studies.[75]

---

[73] ZWEIGERT *supra* note 7 at 36.

[74] ZWEIGERT *supra* note 7 at 34.

[75] Even political scientists pay deference to categories that are based on facially inconsistent differentiating criteria. Some scholars have classified legal culture families into Roman-Germanic, Common Law, socialist law, and non-Western law. Others have

Nevertehless, there are four fundamental flaws in the use of classification in comparative legal studies. First, many classifications are a starting point for comparison rather than a conclusion based on any preceding comparative study. Second, many scholars seek to justify classifications by reference to a limited number of comparative variables. Third, differentiating criteria are often poorly or inconsistently applied. Fourth, even those who object to specific classifications or to classification in general suffer from the same weaknesses they identify in the work of others.[76] A starting point should - instead of working with pre-existing categories of classification - be developing a set of classifications from independent study.[77]

The work of thoughtful comparatists illustrates the difficulties encountered in conventional classificatory systems. Without questioning the categories as starting points, many exhibit the strong tendency to search for explanations of the categories instead of selecting key differentiating features prior to making the categorization. In other words, the comparison tends to take place after the categorization rather than before. Classifications are then justified by reference to a limited number of essential variables. Differentiating criteria are often poorly or inconsistently applied.[78]

Comparative treatments of prototypes of a law, process, or institution (that are then investigated cross-nationally) may be based on a false and implicit equivalence of parochial prototypes with universals. Second, the prototypes are frequently defined too ideally and consequently may lack any real-world plausibility. Third, prototypes may also carry embedded value judgments. Fourth, similar to classification, the use of prototypes appears to be inescap-

---

been critical of this form of scholarship. CHODOSH *supra* note 31 at 1091 & endnote 302.

[76] That is, classifications tend to rely on primarily polar contrasts, e.g., black and white, without gray, or the existence or non-existence of differentiating variables. CHODOSH *supra* note 31 at 1090 & 1091 & endnote 303.

[77] "[C]lassification is a beginning rather than an end, a preliminary step 'designed to facilitate study of otherwise unwieldy bodies of information.'" "It is a prerequisite to thinking and speaking about the underlying differences and similarities among various objects." CHODOSH *supra* note 31 at 1091 & endnote 304 & Schlesinger, COMPARATIVE LAW: CASES, TEXT, MATERIALS 284-85 (6th ed.) (Foundation Press, 1998).

[78] CHODOSH *supra* note 31 at 1106-1107.

able.[79]

Both the choice of micro or macro levels of analysis and the identification of the appropriate unit of comparison pose a set of methodological concerns.[80]

By focusing on differentiation - a method of distinguishing comparative similarities and difference - one can identify six commonly-applied cross-referential[81] principles that structure the relationship between two or more concepts or the phenomena they attempt to grasp: dichotomy, overlap, relativity, interdependence, equivalence and indeterminacy.

By realizing that comparison involves three distinct, yet related, types of choice (the why, what and how), even an uneventful search for methodological rationales may open a wide array of unforeseen channels of fruitful comparative inquiry.[82]

Comparisons may be compared and differentiated[83] in part by identifying the potentially contrasting purposes that motivate them.[84] Understanding the

---

[79] CHODOSH *supra* note 31 at 1107-1109.

[80] CHODOSH *supra* note 31 at 1109.

[81] By "cross-referential" is meant the understanding of two expressions in terms of one another. This term is used instead of many alternatives, such as "opposite," "opposed," "polar," or "antithetical." Each of these alternatives assumes a significant contrast, indeed a mutual exclusivity. Cross-reference may include an equivalent relationship between two terms and is intended to be neutral as to whether the existence of two terms denotes contrast or similarity. CHODOSH *supra* note 31 at 1115-1126 and endnote 429.

[82] CHODOSH *supra* note 31 at 1130.

[83] Another set of purpose-related justification requires additional explanation, however. Purposes may be accepted or rejected in terms of their practicability. That is, one might agree with the purpose of understanding, reform, or unification, yet disagree that comparison itself can advance the objective. Therefore, to agree or disagree with an articulated purpose may depend on one's view of how well the comparison proceeds from beginning to end. CHODOSH *supra* note 31 at endnote 295.

[84] On the level of methodology, a comparison of purposes would carry an obvious risk that many comparisons could be rejected on the basis of the underlying motivations of the comparatist. Illuminating this as a point of disagreement is to be encouraged; however, transforming this into a universally applicable rationale for rejecting comparisons would be very undesirable. Developing rules that would proscribe comparisons motivated by some purposes and not others would severely limit the scope of permissible comparative inquiry. CHODOSH *supra* note 31 at endnote 296.

role of purpose in comparison necessitates a differentiation and evaluative comparison of such purposes.[85] Many disagreements can emerge from the choice of comparative variables.[86] Comparisons tend to focus on a particular subset of variables, while ignoring others. However, these comparative variable choices are infrequently explained or justified.[87]

In many comparisons, purpose, content and mode of differentiation each play a significant roles. Insufficient consideration of the complex interaction of these three features of comparison is likely to render poor results.

---

**Research Tip #7.12**

It is a good idea to check the legal dictionary of each jurisdiction to be compared.[88]

---

For example, is "code" used in the American sense (all legislation combined into one updated and compiled "act"), and if not (does "code" relate to the copying or influence of the French Code Civile?[89]), how so?

---

**Research Tip #7.13**

What in other contexts would be regarded as a good knowledge of a foreign language may not be adequate for the comparatist.[90]

---

It is not rare for a language to be combined with more than one legal language. Words do not have absolute permanent meanings. Comparatists are continually confronted with problems of translation. The question is often whether one has to use the terminology of the era of a statute's making (and, in the U.S., also of a court's decision), or replace it with modern terminology. Word and concept may be related in different ways and any theory of legal

---

[85] CHODOSH *supra* note 31 at 1089-1090.

[86] CHODOSH *supra* note 31 at 1090.

[87] This insufficiently explored problem is a critical issue in the explanation of social systems. CHODOSH *supra* note 31 at 1090 & endnote 301.

[88] For U.S. law, see Black's Law Dictionary (8th ed.)(St. Paul: West Publishing, 2004).

[89] ZWEIGERT *supra* note 7 at 85-118.

[90] WATSON *supra* note 27 at 11.

translation must consider them.[91]

To reach any sound conclusions, one must be able to establish connections between class interest and legal superstructure, legal rules and institutions.[92]

An example of a questionnaire for use in a specific comparative project is printed as Appendix 1 in Mauro Bussani & Ugu Mattei, The Common Core Approach to European Private Law Project, 3 Columbia Journal of European Journal 339, 343 (1997/98).

## 7.5. When to stop?

A comparatist should go as deep as possible into his/her chosen systems. A presumptive rule for the comparatist is that if he finds that there are great differences or indeed diametrically opposite results, he should be warned and go back to check again whether the terms in which he posed his original question were indeed purely functional, and whether he has spread the net of his researches quite wide enough.[93]

---

**Research Tip #7.14**

If there are great differences or diametrically opposite results, go back to check whether the terms in which the original question was posed were indeed purely functional, and whether the scope of the research is broad enough.

---

[91] SACCO I *supra* note 13 at 11, 12 & 14.

[92] SACCO II *supra* note 45 at 389.

[93] Zweigert *supra* note 7 at 40.

# APPENDIX

# 1. Glossary Terms & Abbreviations

See also Index below.

a fortiori - By a stronger reason. A term used in logic to denote an argument that a fact must exist because another fact exists which includes or is analogous to the first fact.

a mensa et thoro - From bed and board. Refers to a qualified divorce by which the parties are separated or live apart without affecting the marriage itself. Compare a vinculo matrimonii.

a posteriori - From the effect to the cause. A term used in logic to denote an argument which takes ascertained facts and reasons backward or inductively to show their cause.

a priori - From the cause to the effect. A term used in logic to denote an argument that takes a principle as a cause and proceeds to deduce the effects that necessarily follow.

A Uniform System of Citation, see Bluebook

a vinculo matrimonii - From the bond of matrimony. Refers to a complete and unqualified divorce. Compare a mensa et thoro.

AALL – American Association of Law Librarians.

AALS – Association of American Law Schools.

ab antique - Of an ancient date; from antiquity.

ab initi - From the beginning or inception.

accomplice - Partner in crime.

actio criminalis - Criminal act.

actor sequitur forum rei - The rule of the plaintiff having to submit to the defendant's court - plaintiff must choose the jurisdiction in which the alien is located.

actus non facit reum nisi mens sit rea - The intent and the act must both concur to constitute the crime.

actus reus - Guilty act. A wrongful deed; generally coupled with mens rea to establish criminal liability.

ad damnum - To the damage. In a complaint, the name of a clause containing a statement of a plaintiff's money loss or other damage suffered.

ad hoc - Pertaining to a particular purpose only.

ad idem - To the same effect.

ad iterim - In the meantime.

ad litem—While the lawsuit is pending.

ad satisfaciendum - To satisfy.

ad valorem - According to value.

ad vitam - For life.

addendum - Something that is added or to be added; a list or section of added material.

adjudication - A formal decree or pronouncement of judgment by a court.

ADR - Alternative Dispute Resolution

advance sheets - Paperbound pamphlets containing the most recent court decisions published in a given case reporter series. Periodically, several advance sheets are collected and published in a hard-bound version as a new case reporter volume, at which time the old advance sheets are no longer needed. The term can also apply to recent statutes or regulations. Advance sheets occur after slip laws or slip opinions but before the laws or opinions are bound in final hard copy volumes.

affidavit - A written statement of facts made under oath before someone authorized by law to administer oaths. The person making the statement is called an "affiant."

AG – Advocate-General (in the European Court of Justice).

ALA - American Library Association.

aliunde - From another place; from outside.

allegation - What a party to an action states, in a pleading, that he or she intends to prove.

amicus curiae - Friend of the court. An individual or organization who has no absolute right to appear in a lawsuit, but who is allowed by the court to offer argument to protect his or her interest or requested by the court to file a brief in the action because of a strong interest in the subject matter.

amicus curiae brief – Friend of the court brief – a brief written by an individual or group not a party to the litigation. Non parties must first ask the court for permission to file an amicus brief. Some United States Supreme Court cases will have dozens of amicus briefs submitted

Amsterdam Treaty – The Treaty on European Union of October 1997.

Amsterdam Treaty of 1996 – A treaty under the European Union.

animus - An intention; a state of mind; design; will.

animus furandi - Intention to steal.

animus testandi—Intention to make a will.

annotations - (1) The full text of a demonstrative / representative case, followed by a discussion of a significant legal trend or issue it represents; (2) In statutory research, the term is used to refer to brief summaries of court decisions interpreting and applying statutes. These summaries appear in annotated statutory compilations, after the reprinted text of individual statutes to which they relate; (3) "Annotations" is also used to refer to detailed articles, prepared and published by Lawyers Cooperative Publishing Company in its American Law Reports Annotated ("A.L.R.") series, analyzing points of law raised in selected court decisions, statutes, and administrative regulations.

answer - The pleading by which a defendant responds to a plaintiff's complaint. See complaint, pleading.

appellant - The party in an action who appeals a court's decision or judgment to a higher court. Some courts use the term "petitioner" instead of "appellant." See petitioner. Compare appellee.

appellee - The party in an action against whom an appeal is taken. The appellee is usually but not always the winner in the lower court. Further, because an appeal may involve multiple issues decided by the lower court, a given party may be an appellant with respect to some issues and an appellee with respect to others. A party's status as appellant or appellee has no necessary correlation to his or her original status as a plaintiff or defendant in the lower court. Finally, some courts use the term "respondent" instead of "appellee." Compare appellant.

assumpsit - A promise to pay to or do something for another.

aut dedere aut judicare - dedere aut judicare - The principle of "aut dedere aut judicare" is the duty of the state to extradite or to prosecute the accused; while universal jurisdiction only refers to a right of the state to prosecute the accused

automatic appeal - A criminal appeal by operation of law, directly from a trial court to the state supreme court, upon imposition of a death penalty sentence.

black letter law—A colloquial term for summary statements of fundamental and widely accepted principles of law.

Blog – web-log – essentially a journal, maintained on an Internet Website, that is periodically updated and is meant for public consumption. Typically consisting of short posts arranged in reverse chronological order. Blogs enable people to publish comments and ideas instantly for others to read.

blue book – (1) The informal designation "Bluebook" of A Uniform System of Citation, a joint publication of the law reviews of Columbia Law School, Harvard Law School, the University of Pennsylvania Law School, and Yale Law School, explaining proper citation format; (2) A book that describes the organization of federal or state government. Sometimes called black book, green book, red book or government manual.

blurb – A brief promotional notice or statement. A case blurb is a one-paragraph note for a particular legal point decided by the court.

bona fide - In good faith. (1) Made in good faith, without fraud or deceit (e.g., bona fide offer); (2) Compliant with the law (e.g., bona fide pension plan); (3) Sincere or genuine (e.g., bona fide signature). Compare mala fide.

boolean logic - A system of logic based on operators such as AND, OR, and NOT. In many search engines, search terms are linked with these Boolean operators to formulate more precise queries.

brevet - A privilege, such as a patent, granted to a private citizen by a government. In military law, a commission promoting an officer to a higher rank but without a corresponding pay increase.

brief - (1) a written document prepared by counsel to file in a legal proceeding, setting forth the pertinent facts, the applicable law, and an argument supporting counsel's position and challenging the opponent's position; (2) a summary or abstract of a court decision, usually prepared by a law student to assist in understanding the decision's significance.

briefing - A technique which serves both as an efficient means of recording notes and as an additional analytical tool.

bulletin board - A computer system used as an information source and forum for a particular interest group. The bulletin board typically holds postings made by various participants and replies to those postings from other participants, thus centrally stored

BVerfGE - Bundesverfassungsgericht (German Federal Constitutional Court).

C., see Command papers.

CALR - computer-assisted legal research.

canons – Formalized rules for construction of statutes.

capias ad satisfaciendum - A writ commanding a person to be taken and kept, so that he will appear in court on a certain day to satisfy damages or a debt.

Cartwheel – a word association technique designed to assist the creative use of indexes in law books, that is, to develop the habit of phrasing every word involved in the problem fifteen to twenty different ways.

case – (1) see action, cause of action, lawsuit; (2) a court's decision.

casebook - A compilation of extracts from instructive cases on a particular subject, usually with commentary and questions about the cases, designed as a teaching aid.

Casebook Method – An inductive system of teaching law in which students study specific cases to learn general legal principles. Professor Christopher C. Langdell introduced the technique at Harvard Law School in 1869. The casebook method is now the most widely used form of instruction in American law schools. Also termed case method; case system; Langdell method. Cf. Hornbook method.

causa mortis - In contemplation of approaching death.

cause of action - Any civil or criminal question litigated or contested before a court of justice; the basis for a lawsuit, e.g., breach of contract, trespass, assault. See also action, case, lawsuit.

caveat - Caution; warning; notice to beware.

caveat emptor - Buyer beware. A doctrine holding that purchasers buy at their own risk.

Cd., see Command papers.

cert. – see certiorari.

certiorari - To be more fully informed - An extraordinary writ (often abbreviated as "cert.") issued by an appellate court, at its discretion, directing a lower court to deliver the record in the case for review. In the United States most commonly used to refer to information (writ of certiorari) from the Supreme Court as its discretionary device to choose the cases it wishes to hear.

cestui que trust - A person who has a beneficial or equitable interest (e.g., the right to receive rents or profits) in property whose legal title is held by someone else.

cestui que vie - A person the length of whose life measures the duration of another person's estate.

cf. – "conferre" - meaning "to compare." A signal, used in connection with a citation, directing the reader's attention to an authority containing a point analogous to the point made by the person citing the authority.

CFSP – see Common Foreign and Security Policy

chattel - Movable or transferable property; especially personal property.

chose - A thing; an item of personal property.

chose in action - An item of personal property not presently in an individual's possession, but whose possession the individual has a right to recover through a legal proceeding; also refers to the right itself to bring an action for the recovery of the personal property or for some other remedy (e.g., damages for loss) with respect to the property.

citation - The title or other identification of a primary or secondary legal authority, such as a constitution, statute, court decision, or treatise. Lawyers use citations to establish or support propositions they assert in their oral and written legal arguments.

citator - A reference work used in legal research to update certain legal authorities by tracing their subsequent history and treatment, e.g., later judicial history and interpretation of reported court decisions and later judicial and legislative treatment of statutes. The title of the preeminent citator used in American legal research is Shepard's Citations.

cite - In legal research, argumentation, and writing, the term means to provide a citation; also frequently used as a shortened form of "citation." See citation.

civil - Pertaining to an appeal or original proceeding in a case that is neither criminal nor a juvenile delinquency case.

civil action - Every action other than a criminal action; an action based on a private wrong, as opposed to a crime, which is considered a wrong to the public in general. Compare criminal action.

claim - A statement or declaration of a legal right. Often used interchangeably with the term allegation. See allegation.

clean bill – a new bill, incorporating amendments to an earlier bill, which is then submitted for the earlier bill. Clean bills will be assigned a new bill number.

Cmd., see Command papers.

Cmnd., see Command papers.

code - A compilation of statutes or administrative regulations arranged by subject matter or topic.

Co-decision (E.U.) - The procedure through which the Council and the European Parliament enact most E.U. legislation. Under the Lisbon Treaty, it will form part of the Ordinary Legislative Procedure.

codicil - A supplement or addition to a will modifying, explaining, or otherwise qualifying the will in some way.

Command papers - papers submitted by the Governmental agencies to the British Parliament - are numbered and prefixed with an abbreviation of 'command' which has changed over time to allow for new sequences, as follows: C. 1870-1899; Cd. 1900-1918; Cmd. 1919-1956: Cmnd. 1956-1986; Cm. 1986- . Command Papers often cover topics on which the government intends to act, but also can include Treaties, State Papers, Policy Papers, Annual Reports, Reports of Royal Commissions, Reports of Departmental Committees, Reports of Tribunals and Commissions of Inquiry, etc. Command Papers are published by TSO (The Stationery Office - http://www.tso.org.uk/) for OPSI (The Office of Public Sector Information - http://www.opsi.gov.uk/). See guilde on British Documents at <http://guides.library.fullerton.edu/docslinks/britparlpapers.htm#COMMPAPFI NDINGAIDS>.

commissioner - A substitute judicial officer, employed by the court, who performs judicial or quasi-judicial duties assigned to him or her. A commissioner may be authorized to decide only limited pretrial issues of fact and law or to conduct complete trails. Commissioners frequently act as temporary judges.

Common Foreign and Security Policy (CFSP) (E.U.) - Following on from earlier efforts, since the early 1970s, at cooperation in the area of foreign policy, the Common Foreign and Security Policy was established as the "second pillar" in the Maastricht Treaty (1992) and developed under the Amsterdam Treaty (1997) and the Treaty of Nice (2001). The common policy exists in parallel to the separate foreign and security policies of the E.U. Member States. The Lisbon Treaty contains extensive provisions on Common Foreign and Security Policy.

common law - Principles and rules of law developed, modified, and applied by courts rather than by legislatures (which create statutory law). Common law is sometimes referred to as "judge-made law" or "case law."

Common Security and Defence Policy, see European Security and Defence Policy.

companion bill – a bill introduced in one house of Congress that is identical or very similar to a bill introduced in the other house of Congress. Since a bill must pass both houses of Congress, the introduction of companion bills can expedite the process.

complainant - The person who files a complaint; another term for "plaintiff" or "petitioner." See complaint, petitioner, plaintiff.

complaint - The pleading with which a plaintiff starts an action. In a criminal action, the complaint is called an "indictment" or "information." See pleading.

compromis - A special agreement between states to submit a particular issue either to an arbitral tribunal or to the International Court.

concurring opinion - When a court has a panel of judges ruling on a single case, a judge agreeing with the conclusions, result, or outcome stated in the opinion of the court, but disagreeing with the court's rationale, may write a separate opinion (called a "concurring opinion") agreeing with the result but stating different reasons for reaching it. Concurring opinions are not the law of the case nor binding as precedent, but they may provide a legal researcher with useful insight into the manner in which a court might interpret or apply the case in the future.

conflict of laws - see private international law.

consuetudo est servanda – All international subjects must comply with customary rules.

coram nobis - Before us. A writ of error directed to another branch of the same court.

coram non judice - A court without jurisdiction to make a particular determination.

corpus delicti - The body of a crime; the physical thing upon which a crime has been committed, e.g., the corpse of a murdered person, the burned out shell of a stolen automobile. The fact of a transgression.

corpus juris - The body of the law.

correlation table – A common characteristic of law treatises or digest is that they are occasionally revised. After revision, a correlation table will help the user find where subject matter from the older table is found in the revised edition.

Council of Europe - The Council of Europe is an intergovernmental organization, set up in 1948, which includes in its aims the protection of human rights and the promotion and awareness of Europe's cultural identity and diversity. It has a wider membership than the E.U. . Though all Member States of the E.U. are also members of the Council of Europe, the latter is a distinct organisation in its own right.

Council of Ministers / Council (E.U.) - The Council of Ministers (formally named simply the Council) is the E.U. institution in which the governments of the Member States are represented. The Council consists of one representative of each Member State at Ministerial level. The Council meets in a whole range of formations, mainly sectoral (e.g. the Ministers for Agriculture when the Council takes decisions on the Common Agricultural Policy). The President (or chair) of the Council is the Minister of the Member State currently holding the E.U. Presidency. Up to now, this was for a six-month term according to an agreed and equal rotation. The Treaty of Lisbon contains some changes in regard to the Council of Ministers. Compare with the European Council.

cour de cassation - In various countries, exist courts of cassation [court of cassation], which review and overturn previous rulings made by lower courts. They are roughly equivalent to the Supreme Court of the United States.

count - A statement or declaration of a legal right. Often used interchange-ably with the terms "allegation," "claim," and "cause of action." See allegation, claim, and cause of action.

Court of Appeal - The California court that hears (1) appeals in all noncapital cases in which a superior court has original jurisdiction and (2) appeals under other special circumstances, as prescribed by law.

criminal - pertaining to an appeal or original proceeding charging the violation of criminal law.

criminal action - A lawsuit in which the government, as prosecutor, tries to persuade a judge or jury to punish a person for violating a criminal statute.

culpa - The civil law or Roman law term employed by lawyers from non-common law countries to refer to civil fault, neglect, or negligence or lack of reasonable care.

d.b.e. - Abbreviation for de bene esse.

damages – A financial award given to a person in a lawsuit because of someone else's unlawful conduct. There are two broad categories of damages: (a) compensatory damages are awarded to repay a person for an injury or loss he or she has suffered, and (b) punitive (or exemplary) damages are imposed solely to punish someone for an injury or loss he or she inflicted on another person.

damnum absque injuria - Damage or loss that cannot be redressed by a proceeding in law.

database - A collection of information organized in such a way that users (often both people and computer programs) can quickly select desired pieces of data.

de bene esse - Conditionally; provisionally. Refers to proceedings that are allowed to stand in the interim, but which are subject to future modification, e.g., allowing a witness who may not be available for trial to testify immediately, subject to possible future re-examination and exclusion of the earlier testimony at trial if the witness becomes available.

de facto - Actually; in fact. Compare de jure.

de jure - By operation of law. Compare de facto.

de lege ferenda - Relating to the law as it should be if the rules were changed to accord with good policy.

de minimis - Minimal; trivial; so trifling as to be of no consequence in the law.

de minimis non curat lex - The law does not concern itself with trifles.

de novo - Anew; from the start.

decision - A court's or other tribunal's disposition (e.g., affirmance or reversal) of a case. Although technically different from an opinion, the two terms are often loosely used as synonyms. See and compare opinion.

dedere aut judicare – see aut dedere aut judicare.

defendant - The person defending against or denying the allegations in a complaint, indictment, or information. There can be more than one defendant in a lawsuit.

defendant in error - Another term for an appellee. See appellee.

delegated act (E.U.) - Under the proposals in the LisbonTreaty, where there are non-essential elements to a legislative measure, these laws may delegate to the European Commission the power to enact detailed measures to supplement or amend these elements. The objective, content, scope and duration of these delegations has to be defined in the original legislative measure. The Council of Ministers and the European Parliament are to supervise the use of this power and may also revoke any such delegation.

delict - A wrongful act; tort.

demurrer - A pleading stating that although the facts alleged in a complaint may be true, they are insufficient for the plaintiff to state a claim for relief and for the defendant to frame an answer.

depublished opinion - Unique to California. A Court of Appeal opinion that the Court of Appeal has certified for publication but that the California Supreme Court, acting under its constitutional power over opinion publication, directs the Reporter of Decisions not to publish in the Official Reports and that may be cited or replied upon only in limited circumstances.

détournement de pouvoir - a term of French administrative law originally, meaning abuse of administrative powers by public officials.

dicta - Plural of dictum.

dictum – see obiter dictum.

digest - An essential case-finding tool. Legal research reference works containing very brief summaries of reported court decisions, with the summaries arranged by subject matter so that all case summaries on a single point of law are collected together, regardless of the date of issuance of the individual court decisions. It is a multivolume index to the law consisting of major topic headings, thousands of subheadings, and headnotes (short summaries of legal propositions stated in published court case.

Digressively Proportional (E.U.) - This refers to a system of representation of E.U. Member States in the European Parliament, whereby the number of seats a country has is broadly proportional to the size of its population but with the ratio between the number of seats and the population size being progressively more favourable the smaller the size of a country's population.

diligentia quam in suis - The standard of care normally exercised by a particular person in the conduct of his affairs.

disposition - Termination of a proceeding. Civil dispositions before trial include transfers to another trial court, dismissals, summary judgment, and other judgments before trial. Criminal dispositions before trial include transfers to another trial court, sentences after pleas of guilty or no contest, and dismissals. Civil dispositions after trial include entry of judgment after jury trial and court trial. Criminal dispositions after trial include acquittals, grants of probation, and sentences after conviction.

dissent - When a court has a panel of judges ruling on a single case, judges disagreeing with the majority's decision may express their views in dissenting opinions, which may disagree with all or only part of the majority opinion. Dissents are not the law of the case nor binding as precedent, but they may provide legal researchers with useful summaries of competing interpretations of specific legal principles or doctrines, and help them in doing their analyses of the strengths and weaknesses of the majority decision.

dolus - The intention to inflict some harm, together with the foreseeable consequences of the intended harm.

donatio mortis causa - Gift made upon contemplation of death, and conditioned upon the occurrence of the donor's death.

double jeopardy - The principle of "ne bis in idem" (non bis in idem or non bis idem or double jeopardy)(Not twice for the same thing) - forbidding more than one trial for the same offense.

duces tecum - Bring with you. Refers to a directive instructing a person who has been summoned to appear to bring with him or her some document, piece of evidence, or other thing to be inspected. See subpoena duces tecum.

due process clause - The constitutional provision that prohibits the government from unfairly or arbitrarily depriving a person of life, liberty, or property. (There are two Due Process Clauses in the U.S. Constitution, in the 5th and 14th Amendments.)

duty - A legal obligation.

E.C. - European Community.

E.C. Treaty – The Treaty establishing the European Union (the EEC treaty with amendments of 1991).

ECHR - The European Convention on Human Rights and Fundamental Freedoms, signed in 1950 under the aegis of the Council of Europe, sets out a list of human rights, which the participating countries guarantee to respect and uphold. The Convention established, for the first time, a system of international protection for human rights offering individuals the possibility of applying to a dedicated international court – the European Court of Human Rights – for the enforcement of their rights. All Member States of the E.U. have ratified the Convention. The E.U. Lisbon Treaty envisages that the E.U., as such, would seek to join the Convention.

e.g. - Exempli gratia - meaning for example.

easement - An interest in land owned by another person, consisting of the right to use or control the land, or an area above or below it, for a specific limited purpose.

ECB – European Central Bank.

ECHR – European Court of Human Rights.

ECJ – European Court of Justice.

ECSC – European Coal and Steel Community.

ECU – European Currency Unit.

EDI – Electronic data interchange.

EEA – European Economic Area - consisting of Norway, Iceland and Liechtenstein, which participate in the E.U.'s internal market while not assuming the full responsibilities of E.U. membership. Cf. EFTA.

EEC – European Economic Community, now EC.

EFTA – European Free Trade Association (consisting of Norway, Iceland, Liechtenstein and Switzerland). Also, compare EEA.

ejusdem generic - Of the same kind, class, or nature. A rule that is some-times followed in construing the words of written documents: where general words are linked with enumerated examples of persons or things, the general words are not construed in their broadest meaning, but are construed as applying only to persons or things of the same kind, class, or nature as those specifically enumerated.

electronic agent - Computer program designed, selected, or programmed to initiate or respond to electronic messages or performances without review by an individual

e-mail - Electronic mail - the transmission of messages over networks.

EMI – European Monetary Institute.

EMS – European Monetary System.

EMU – European Monetary Union.

en banc - On the bench. Descriptive of a court session in which all judges of the court are present and participating. Refers to a session of court in which all the judges of the court (rather than a smaller panel of selected judges) participate in deciding a case.

Enjoin - To require or command someone to do, or not to do, some act. See injunction.

erga omnes – Obligations owed to the entire international community, irrespective of consent on the part of those thus affected.

ergo - Therefore.

ESCB – see European System of Central Banks.

ESDP, see European Security and Defence Policy.

et al. – "et alii" ," meaning "and others."

et seq. - Abbreviation for "et sequentia," meaning "and the following."

et ux. - Abbreviation for "et uxor." See below.

et uxor - And wife..

EURATOM – European Atomic Energy Community.

EURECA – (1) European Retrievable Carrier; (2) An early subset of the California's Registry System.

Eurojust (E.U.) - The European Judicial Co-operation Unit. A body of national prosecutors, magistrates or police officers from the Member States, established in 2002 under the Treaty of Nice to coordinate the fight against crime. The Treaty of Lisbon contains some changes in respect of Eurojust and its work.

European Council (E.U.) - The European Council is the term used to describe the institution within which the Heads of State or Government of the E.U. Member States meet regularly. It meets at least twice a year – more recently, about four times – and the President of the European Commission attends as a full member. Its functions are to give the E.U. the impetus it needs in order to develop and to define general policy guidelines and priorities. The Lisbon Treaty contains changes in regard to the European Council.

European Court of Auditors (E.U.) - The Court of Auditors is an institution that acts like the auditors of a business or other organisation. It monitors the E.U. 's accounts, examining the legality and regularity of the revenue and expenditure in the budget and ensuring sound financial management.

European Defence Agency (E.U.) - The European Defence Agency was established in 2004 to support the E.U. Member States and the E.U. Council in their effort to improve European defence capabilities in the field of crisis management, to monitor the capability commitments of Member States, and to promote harmonisation of procurement and support defence technology research.

European Security and Defence Policy (ESDP) (E.U.) - Established in 1999 at the Cologne European Council, the ESDP aims to allow the E.U. to develop its civilian and military capacities for crisis management and conflict prevention at international level, thus helping to maintain peace and international security, in accordance with the United Nations Charter. It will be renamed the Common Security and Defence Policy under the Treaty of Lisbon.

European System of Central Banks (ESCB) is made up by the European Central Bank (E.U.) and the national central banks of all E.U. Member States.

Europol - European Police Office, established under an agreement reached in 1995 and which entered into force on 1 October 1998, but only became fully operational on 1 July 1999. Europol's headquarters are in The Hague and it coordinates police co-operation throughout the E.U. in particular, agreed areas, for example in the areas of drug trafficking, clandestine immigration networks, trafficking in stolen vehicles, trafficking in human beings (including child pornography), counterfeiting currency and falsification of other means of payment, trafficking in radioactive and nuclear substances, terrorism and money-laundering. The Treaty contains some changes in respect of Europol and its work which are summarised in this document.

ex curia - Out of court.

ex injuria non oritur jus - The principle that no benefit can be received from an illegal act.

ex officio - By virtue of an office or official position.

ex parte - From the part. On or from one party only, usually without notice to or argument from the adverse party; pertaining to one party only.

ex post facto—After the fact.

ex rel.—Abbreviation for "ex relatione," meaning "upon relation of." Refers to legal proceedings commenced on behalf of the United States or an individual state, but on the instigation of an individual who has a private interest in the matter (for example, "United States ex rel. Smith v. Jones").

exempla gratia - For example (typically abbreviated as "e.g.").

expressio unius est exclusio aiterlus - A rule that is sometimes followed in construing the words of written documents: the express mention of one thing implies the exclusion of others.

expressio unius est exclusio alterius - Also termed inclusio unius est exclusio alterius; expressum facit cessare tacitum - a canon of construction holding that to express or include one thing implies the exclusion of the other, or of the alternative.

exterritorial jurisdiction - A court's ability to exercise power beyond its territorial limits.

falsus in uno, falsus in omnibus - False in one thing, false in every-thing.

federal question - In litigation, a legal issue involving the interpretation and application of the U.S. Constitution, an act of Congress, or a treaty. Jurisdiction over federal questions rests with the federal courts. 28 USCA § 1331.

felony - A criminal case alleging an offense punishable by imprisonment in a state prison or by death.

ferae naturae - Of a wild nature

fiat -Let it be done. An official proclamation.

flagrante delicto - In the very act of committing the wrong.

Flexibility Clause (E.U.) - The flexibility clause within the Lisbon Treaty, the antecedents of which go back to the Treaty of Rome, allows flexible adjustments of E.U. competence within the defined remit of the E.U. The existing clause can only be used in connection with the common market. The new clause will allow flexibility in all areas of the E.U.

fructus industriales - Fruits of one's industry or labor, e.g., cash crops produced through cultivation, such as tobacco. Compare fructus naturales.

fructus naturales—Products produced by nature alone, e.g., milk, ore. Compare fructus industriales.

fully briefed appeal - A pending appeal in which all briefs have been filed.

G.A. - General Assembly of United Nations.

GATS - General Agreement on Trade in Services.

GATT – General Agreement of Tariffs and Trade.

habeas corpus – "You have the body." A writ employed to bring a person before a court, most frequently to ensure that the party's imprisonment or detention is not illegal; refers to various writs whose object is to bring a person before a court, most commonly directing the release of a person from illegal confinement.

haec verba—See in haec verba.

headnote - A one-paragraph summary of a specific point of law decided in a case. Headnotes appear at the beginning of a case, and are usually written by the editors of the publisher of the case reporter in which the decision appears. Some times, however, the judges themselves or other court personnel will prepare these summaries.

heriditaments—Inheritable property.

hornbook – (1) A book explaining the basics of a given subject; (2) A textbook containing the rudimentary principles of an area of law. Cf. Casebook.

304

hornbook method – A method of legal instruction characterized by a straightforward presentation of legal doctrine, occasionally interspersed with questions. It predominates in the U.S. in certain fields of law, such as procedure and evidence. Cf. Socratic and Casebook methods.

i.e. – "Id est." - that is.

ibid. – see ibidem.

ibidem - At the same place, e.g., in the same book (typically abbreviated as "ibid."). See also idem.

ICC – International Criminal Court OR international chamber of commerce.

ICJ – International Court of Justice.

ICT – Information and Communication Technologies.

id est - that is (typically abbreviated as "i.e.").

id. "idem." - See below; at the same place, e.g., in the same book (typically abbreviated as "id."). In legal writing, the abbreviation for "idem" is preferred to "ibid." for referring to a previously cited reference.

IGC - Intergovernmental Conference (E.U.) - A conference composed of representatives from each E.U. Member State in which amendments to the treaties can be agreed through negotiations.

ILC – UN's International Law Commission.

in camera - In a chamber. (1) In the judge's private chambers; (2) In the courtroom with all spectators excluded.

in custodia aegis - In legal custody; in the keeping of the law.

in forma pauperis - As a pauper. Refers to permission given to a poor person to sue without paying his or her own court costs.

in haec verba - In these precise words; in the same words.

in limine - At the beginning; preliminarily.

in loco parentis - In the place of a parent.

in pals - Refers to proceedings conducted outside of court; commonly used in contradistinction to written matters or matters of record.

in pari delicto - Equally at fault.

in pari materia - Pertaining to the same subject. A rule that is sometimes followed in construing statutes: statutes dealing with the same subject matter are construed together, that is, in relation to one another, or as a whole.

in personam - Against a person. Descriptive of court actions involving or determining the rights, interests, and obligations of a person. Compare in rem.

in re - In the matter of; concerning; in regard to. The phrase is commonly used in the title of non-adversary judicial proceedings that revolve around a particular thing or person, such as a bankruptcy or guardianship proceeding (for example, "in re John Doe").

in rem - Against a thing. Descriptive of court actions involving or determining the status of a thing, and therefore the rights of persons generally with respect to that thing, such as a right to property. Commonly used to describe legal proceedings taken against a thing or piece of property (for example, a property foreclosure action), as opposed to personal actions. Compare in personam.

in rem jurisdiction (in rem) - A court's power to adjudicate the rights to a given piece of property, including the power to seize and hold it. Also termed jurisdiction in rem. Cf. personal jurisdiction; subject-matter jurisdiction.

in situ - In the original place.

in toto - Completely.

indebitatus assumpsit - An action to recover on a debt. See assumpsit.

indexable web - The publicly indexable Web is limited to those pages that are accessible by following a link from another Web page that is recognized by a search engine

indicia—Signs or indications.

indictment - A criminal complaint issued by a grand jury at the request of a prosecutor and charging a person with a crime. See complaint. Compare information.

information - A criminal complaint issued by a prosecutor (e.g., a district attorney) rather than by a grand jury, and charging a person with a crime. See complaint. Compare indictment.

information retrieval - The processes, methods, and procedures used to selectively recall recorded data from a database.

infra - Below; appearing below. Compare supra.

injunction - An order from a court requiring or commanding someone to do, or not to do, some act. See enjoin, relief, remedy.

intelligent agents – work as personal assistants in the same computer environment as the user. The object of these agents is to act in a way geared towards one certain persona and, in a manner of speaking, independently and intelligently. E.g., they sort through electronic mail according to the respective user's preferences, point out news and offers that could be of interest to the user or come up with suggestions for shopping.

inter alia - Among other things.

inter alios - Among other persons; among those who are strangers to the proceedings.

inter partes - Between or among the parties.

inter se - Among themselves.

inter vivos - Between the living. Frequently used to describe a transaction by which property is passed from one living person to another, as opposed to a transfer by will from a deceased person.

internet - a decentralized global communications network connecting millions of individual users and machines.

Internet protocol (IP) - a part of the TCP/IP suite of protocols that allows the various machines that make up the Internet to communicate with each other.

internet service provider (ISP) - an organization or company that provides access to the Internet. Examples of national-level ISPs include America Online (AOL), Earthlink, and Microsoft Network (MSN).

intra vires - Within the scope of one's powers or authority. Compare ultra vires.

intranet – A private network, within a company or organization, that serves shared applications intended for internal use only – although some may be found on the public Internet.

Ioannina Compromise of 29 March 1994 (E.U.) states that if members of the E.U. Council representing between 23 votes and 26 votes express their intention of opposing the taking of a decision by the Council by qualified majority, the Council will do all within its power, within a reasonable space of time, to reach a satisfactory solution that can be adopted by at least 68 votes out of 87. The Treaty of Nice puts an end to the Ioannina compromise. E.U. Glossary at <http://europa.eu/scadplus/glossary/ioannina_compromise_en.htm> (visited July 2008).

IP - see Internet Protocol

IP-address - An identifier for a computer or device on a TCP/IP network. Networks using the TCP/IP protocol route messages based on the IP address of the destination. The format of an IP address is a 32-bit numeric address written as four numbers separated by periods. Each number can be zero to 255 (e.g., "1.160.10.240" could be an IP address).

ipse dixit - A bare assertion that is made, but not proved.

ipso facto - In itself; by virtue of the fact itself.

IRAC – A system used by some U.S. law students to organize their answers to exam questions and to write appellate briefs. I = Issue (question), R = Rule (facts & rules), A= Application (analysis), and C = Conclusion.

ISP – see Internet Service Provider.

IT - Information technology.

ITU - International Telecommunication Union.

ius cogens – see jus cogens

ius commune Europaeum - European "common law". The phrase "the common law of the civil law systems" means those underlying laws that create a distinct legal system and are common to all its elements.

IW - Information Warfare.

j.n.o.v. - Abbreviation for "judgment non obstante veredicto," meaning "judgment notwithstanding the verdict." See non obstante veredicto.

jurisdiction - This term has two different meanings: (1) the authority of a court or other tribunal to take cognizance of a case and to render a decision in it that is legally binding on certain persons or property; and (2) a geographical territory (e.g., a state) in which a particular body of law applies.

jurisprudence – (1) The study of the fundamental elements of a legal system; (2) A system, body, or division of law.

jus cogens – or ius cogens - Peremptory norms of general international law.

key number - The name given by West Publishing Company to its digest system of indexing court decisions. West identifies thousands of narrow, separate points of law discussed in court decisions, designates those points as "sub-topics" under its broader digest topics, and then assigns a permanent "Key Number" to each subtopic. These topics, subtopics, and Key Numbers comprise the digest system West uses for indexing its case reporters. Key Numbers remain constant throughout all West digests and reporters, that is, all cases dealing with a given point of law will be summarized in West's digests under the same topic, sub-topic, and Key Number. Publishers of non-West case reporters and digests use similar indexing systems, but there the functional equivalent of a Key Number is called a "section number," or occasionally a "paragraph number."

KeyCite - Westlaw's equivalent to Shepard's/shepardize, that is a citator to determine whether a case or statute is good law and to retrieve citing references.

L.S. - See Locus Sigilli.

Langdell method – see Casebook Method.

Languages of the Treaty of Lisbon (E.U.) - This refers to the languages in which the Treaty is to be drawn up, each version being equally authentic, as set out in Article IV-10, the last article of the Lisbon Treaty.

lawsuit - A legal proceeding brought in a court in which one or more persons tries to make one or more other persons do something or stop doing something, and/or to pay damages. Other terms sometimes used interchangeably with "lawsuit" are "action," "case," and "cause of action."

Legal Base (E.U.) - In order for the E.U. to have power to act in any area, that area must have what is known as a "legal base" in the treaty structure. Any areas where the E.U. is to have such power must be recognised formally and explicitly in the legal structure of the treaties. The Treaty of Lisbon maintains all areas where there were legal bases previously and creates legal bases in some further, limited areas.

Legitimacy - This is a political concept, relating to whether, or how far, a political system or a set of political arrangements or institutions is regarded as being valid and worthy of acceptance or support by the people who are governed under such arrangements or whose lives are affected by what is done by the institutions.

Lisbon Process or Strategy (E.U.) - Launched at an E.U. summit in Lisbon, Portugal in 2000, the Lisbon Process or Strategy is a voluntary co-ordination (often referred to as the Open Method of Co-ordination) of a whole range of economic, social and sectoral policies among E.U. Member States. It aims to make the E.U. the most competitive and knowledge-based economy in the world by 2010. (Not to be confused with the Treaty of Lisbon).

lex causa – that nation's law that is used in the case at issue (Private International Law or Conflicts of Law).

lex domicilii - The law of the domicile.

lex ferenda - see de lege ferenda.

lex fori – The law of the nation in which the court dealing with the case at issue is located (Private International Law or Conflicts of Law), that is, where the suit is brought.

lex loci - The law of the place.

lex loci contractus - Either the law of the place where the contract was made, or the law by which the contract is to be governed (which may or may not be the same place) (Private International Law or Conflicts of Law).

lex loci delicti – The law in the nation, where the injury or harm has occurred or where the act has been done (Private International Law or Conflicts of Law).

lex loci solutionis – The law at the place of performance of the contract at issue (Private International Law or Conflicts of Law).

lex posterior derogate priori - A later law repeals an earlier one.

lex posterior generalis non derogate priori speciali - A later law, general in character, does not derogate from an earlier on, which is special in character.

lex rei sitae – see lex situs.

lex situs – lex rei sitae – The law in the nation where the an object or subject in the case at issue is located (Private International Law or Conflicts of Law).

lex specialis derogate generali - A special law prevails over a general law.

liability - Legally enforceable responsibility of one person to pay damages as a result of committing an injurious act or of owing an obligation or debt. See damages.

Lisbon Treaty of December 2007 (E.U.)

lis pendens - A pending lawsuit.

locus delicti - The place or, more usually, the particular state or jurisdiction in which a wrong or offense was committed.

locus sigilli—The place of the seal. The place for the seal on a written document (usually abbreviated as "LS.").

locus standi - The power to apply to a tribunal for a particular remedy; more specifically, the existence of a sufficient legal interest in the matter in issue.

logit regit actum – The law at the place determines the formality (Private International Law or Conflicts of Law).

long-arm statutes – Laws describing exterritorial jurisdiction for each state in United States.

looseleaf reporter (services) – (1) Fill a gap in the reporting of primary legal authorities by giving the most up-to-date information on case law, statutes, administrative regulations, and developing trends in the law; (2) Treatises that prove the most up-to-date information on case law, statutes, administrative regulations, and developing trends in the law.

Maastricht Treaty = The Treaty on European Union (TEU) of December 1991 [amended by the Amsterdam Treaty].

mala fide - In bad faith. Compare bona fide..

mala in se - Describes acts wrongful in themselves; unconscionable or morally wrong acts. Compare mala prohibita.

mala prohibita - Describes acts that are wrongful because prohibited by law. Compare mala in se.

malum in se - Evil in itself. A crime or act that is inherently immoral, such as murder, arson, or rape. Also termed malum per se.

malum prohibitum - Prohibited evil. An act that is a crime because it is prohibited by statute; the act itself is not necessarily immoral.

mandatory authority - See authority.

Mastricht Treaty – nick-name for the Treaty on European Union of 1992.

mens rea - Guilty mind. Criminal intent; generally coupled with actus reus to establish criminal liability.

MEP – Member of the European Parliament.

mesne - Intermediate; intervening; the middle between two extremes.

model act – Proposed laws written by the Commissioners of United State Laws and the American Law Institute, for example Model Penal Code.

modus operandi - Method of operating.

Mootness Doctrine - The principle that American courts will not decide cases in which there is no longer any actual controversy.

moral turpitude - Conduct that is contrary to justice, honesty, or morality, or that violates accepted community standards.

motion - A request made to a court asking that it do something in a lawsuit. In making a motion, a person is said to "move" the court to do something. Example: "Plaintiff moves the court to have the defendant held in contempt for refusing to answer the question."

municipal law - Municipal law governs the domestic aspects of government and deals with issues between individuals, and between individuals and the administrative apparatus.

mutatis mutandis - With the necessary changes in detail.

N.B. – see nota bene.

NCCUSL - National Conference of Commissioners on Uniform State Laws (in U.S.).

NCCUSL – National Conference of Commissioners on Uniform State Laws.

Ne bis in idem (ne bis idem) - No person should be proceeded against twice over the same matter.

ne exeat - A writ prohibiting a person from leaving the jurisdiction of the court or some other specified place.

NGO - Non-governmental organization.

Nice Treaty of 2001 - A treaty under the European Union.

nisi prius - Denotes a court of first instance; a trial court, as opposed to an appellate court.

nolle prosequi - A declaration that one is unwilling further to prosecute part or all of a case against a defendant.

nolo contendere – "I will not contend." - A plea in which a defendant in a criminal prosecution neither admits nor denies the charges, but agrees to accept punishment determined by the court. No contest.

non compos mentis - Not of sound mind or memory.

non constat – "It does not follow." - Commonly used to refer to conclusions that, although they may appear to follow, do not necessarily follow.

non obstante veredicto - Notwithstanding the verdict. Refers to a judgment entered by court order for a plaintiff or defendant, even though the jury has returned a verdict against that party.

non sequitur - Something that does not follow.

nota bene - An instruction to "note well" (frequently abbreviated as "N.B.").

nudum pactum - A promise made without legal consideration, such as a promise supported by mere good will or affection.

nulla crimen sine lege - There is no crime in the absence of (applicable) law when and where an act is committed.

nulla poena sine lege - An individual may be considered criminally responsible only for conduct which was unambiguously criminal at the time of its commission and must be sentenced in accordance with law.

nunc pro tunc - Now for then. Refers to an action having retroactive effect.

OJ – Official Journal of European Union.

obiter dicta - see obiter dictum.

obiter dictum – (1) Statements by a court in an opinion that are not necessary to the decision of the case; gratuitious or incidental commentary by a judge; (2) A statement of opinion or belief considered authoritative due to the dignity of the person making it; (3) A familiar rule; a maxim.

ODR - Online Dispute Resolutions.

OECD - Organization for Economic Cooperation and Development.

OEEC – Organization of European Economic Cooperation.

Opinion - A statement by a judge or court or other tribunal of the rationale followed in reaching the result (e.g., reversal or affirmance) in a particular case. See also concurring opinion, dissent, per curiam and plurality opinion.

original proceedings - Cases commenced in an appellate court, commonly called writ proceedings. The most common are writs of mandamus and prohibition, usually seeking an order addressed to lower court, and writs of habeas corpus, usually addressed to a person holding another in official custody.

original proceedings - Petitions for writs within the state supreme court's original jurisdiction. The most common types are mandamus and prohibition, which may relate to either civil or criminal matters, and habeas corpus.

pacta sunt servanda - The principle that agreements are binding (and are to be implemented in good faith).

parallel citation – (1) The additional, equivalent title or identification (see citation) of a single court decision's verbatim; (2) Citations to additional reporters where the text or an opinion can be found.

part material - See in pari materia.

part passu - On equal footing.

particeps criminis - A criminal accomplice; partner in crime.

party - A participant in a transaction or proceeding, e.g., party to a contract, party to a lawsuit. In a lawsuit, the most common parties are plaintiffs and defendants, although there are also other kinds of parties, such as third-party plaintiffs, third-party defendants, and intervenors.

PCIJ – Permanent Court of International Justice.

pendente lite - During the progress of a lawsuit.

per curiam - By the court. When a court sits by a panel of judges, this term is used to designate an opinion written by the whole court, rather than by one particular judge.

per diem - By the day. A charge, fee, or allowance calculated by the day.

311

per se - In and of itself; inherently.

persona non grata - A person who is considered unacceptable.

personal jurisdiction – A court's power to bring a person into its adjudicative process.

persuasive authority, see authority. A court's power to bring a person into its adjudicative process; jurisdiction over a defendant's personal rights, rather than merely over property interests. -- Also termed in personam jurisdiction; jurisdiction in personam; jurisdiction of the person; jurisdiction over the person. Cf. in rem jurisdiction.

Petersberg Tasks (E.U.) - In the Maastricht Treaty of 1992, the Member States of the E.U. undertook to enhance co-operation on international affairs through the Common Foreign and Security Policy. The Treaty of Amsterdam, 1997 reflects new priorities of humanitarian, rescue, peacekeeping and crisis management tasks – the Petersberg tasks (called after the venue in Germany where agreement on them was reached) – by incorporating these tasks into the European E.U.'s Common Foreign and Security Policy. The Lisbon Treaty extends the tasks to cover joint disarmament operations, military advice and post-conflict stabilisation.

petition - A formal written application to a government body requesting that the tribunal exercise its authority to achieve a particular effect; a complaint is an example of one kind of petition.

petition for review - A request for state supreme court review of a state court of appeal decision.

petition for review denied - An order by the state supreme court declining review of a state court of appeal decision.

petition for review granted and held - An order by the state supreme court granting review of a state court of appeal decision that will be held until a lead case addressing a related issue has been decided by the state supreme court.

petition for review granted and transferred - Any order by the state supreme court granting review of a state Court of Appeal decision but transferring review of the case to a state court of appeal without additional action by the state supreme court.

petitioner - The person who files a petition. See petition. See also appellant.

plaintiff - The person who brings a civil action by filing a complaint in a court. There can be more than one plaintiff in a lawsuit. In a criminal action, the plaintiff is called the "prosecution" or "the government."

plaintiff in error - Another term for an appellant. See appellant.

pleading - The written statement containing a party's allegations about each point or issue involved in the lawsuit. In civil actions, the principal pleadings are the complaint, filed by the plaintiff, and the answer, which is filed by the defendant and which responds to the complaint. See allegation, answer, complaint.

plurality opinion - When a court has a panel of judges ruling on a single case and no opinion of any one judge in the case obtains the agreement of the majority of judges participating, the plurality opinion is the opinion with which most of the judges on the panel agree.

pocket-parts – publishers' updating pamphlets to be inserted in a slot (a "pocket") in the cover of the hardbound volume of case digests, annotated statutes, treatises, legal encyclopediea, and ALR.

posse comitatus - The power or force of the county; the populace of a county that a sheriff may summon in certain cases to help keep the peace, make arrests, etc.

POTUS – President of the Unites States.

presentment—A statement issued by a grand jury without a prosecutor's participation and charging that a crime has been committed.

prima facie - On the face of it; at first blush. Refers to something initially presumed to be true until the appearance of some evidence to the contrary.

primary authority - See authority.

principle of conferral (E.U.) - The principle of conferral means that the E.U. does not have general competences in its own right, but only those that are specifically conferred upon it by the Member States in the founding treaties and their subsequent modifications. The E.U. can only act on the basis of a provision of the treaties that authorises it to do so. In treaty terms, competence means the legal capacity or ability to legislate or to take other action.

Principle of Loyal Cooperation (E.U.) - The principle which commits the E.U. and its individual Member States to assist each other in carrying out tasks, common or co-ordinated, which flow from the obligations they have assumed and refrain from acting in ways that would block or impede discharge of those tasks.

pro bono - For the good. Descriptive of legal services provided free of charge, especially legal services provided for the public good.

pro bono publico - For the public good.

pro forma - As a matter of form.

pro hac vice - For this one particular occasion.

proportionality (E.U.) - The principle that E.U. action must not exceed what is necessary to achieve the objectives of the Treaties.

pro se - For oneself. Descriptive of one who represents oneself in court, without the assistance of legal counsel.

pro tanto - To that extent; as far as it goes.

pro tempore - For the time being; temporarily.

profit a prendre - The right to take the fruits, or profits, from the land of another, such as the right to cut and remove timber from another's land.

pur autre vie - For or during the life of another. Denotes an estate in land which a person holds during the life-time of another designated person.

q.c.f. - Abbreviation for "quare clausum fregit." See below.

QMV, see Qualified Majority Voting.

quaere - A query; question; doubt. Frequently used to indicate that the point or statement that follows is open to question.

qualified majority voting (QMV) (E.U.) - QMV is the form of decisionmaking used for most Council of Ministers decisions. Currently, each E.U. Member State is assigned a number of votes weighted according to a scale which groups together E.U. Member States of similar population size. Under the Lisbon Treaty a new system of QMV will apply, based on a "Double Majority".

quantum meruit - The amount a person deserves as compensation for services rendered.

313

quare clausum fregit - Because he broke the close. Refers to a type of legal proceeding for trespass—specifically, "breaking a close," meaning unlawfully entering upon another person's land.

quasi-in-rem jurisdiction - Jurisdiction over a person but based on that person's interest in property located within the court's territory. Also termed jurisdiction quasi in rem.

quid pro quo - Something for something. Refers to the giving of one thing of value for another thing of value.

quo warranto - By what authority? Refers to legal proceedings undertaken to ascertain whether an officer is acting within the scope of the authority granted him by law.

ratio - ratio decidendi - The principal proposition or propositions of law determining the outcome of a case; or, the only legal consideration necessary for the decision of a particular case.

ratione materiae - By reason of the subject-matter.

ratione personae - Determined by the status and dignity of the person or entity as such.

ratione temporis - Conditioned by reference to time.

re - In regard to. Commonly used to designate legal proceedings in which there is only one party. See in re.

real property - Land and anything permanently attached to it.

real-time audio/video - Communication of either sound or images over the Internet that occurs without delay in real time, much like a telephone conversation.

reasoned opinion E.U.) - (1) The European Commission scrutinises steps taken by each Member State to implement E.U. law and, if dissatisfied, may issue what is known as a "reasoned opinion" to Member States governments. This is a sort of "early warning system" within which the Commission outlines the measures that will need to be taken in order for the E.U. Member State (s) to fully implement the E.U. law in question. Should these measures not be taken, then the Commission refers the matter to the European Court of Justice; (2) A second meaning of the term arises in the protocol of the Lisbon Treaty on applying the principles of proportionality. There, the term refers to an opinion with reasons, put forward by a national parliament (or one of its Houses) that a proposal for a law, made by the Commission, is in breach of the principle of subsidiarity. In this case, a reasoned opinion is part of an "early warning system", to be operated by national parliaments.

rebus sic stantibus - The implication of a term that the obligations of an agreement come to an end with a change of circumstances.

recall - A measure of the effectiveness of document retrieval expressed as a ratio of the total number of relevant documents in a given database (or on the Web) to the number of relevant entries or documents retrieved in response to a specific search. However, determining a search's recall can be problematic because it is often very difficult to determine the total number of relevant entries in all but very small databases. Contrast with precision.

record filed - The filing of the trial court clerk's transcripts (copies of documents filed in the case) and the reporter's transcript (the typed version of oral proceedings).

reduced to misdemeanor - Cases in which a charge original filed as a felony is disposed of as a misdemeanor.

Reform Treaty – see Lisbon Treaty

regulation - A directive issued by a government agency, pursuant to statutory authority, to implement and carry out a governmental policy or program. Unless invalidated by a court or rescinded by the agency, a regulation has the effect of law and binds those over whom the agency has regulatory power. Regulations are also referred to as "rules."

rehearing en banc – All the judges of a court sitting together to rehear a case in a panel (or more precisely, the number of judges required by local court rules "to make a full bench")

relief - Assistance or redress given to a party in a civil or criminal action when the court determines the party has a right to it. A temporary injunction is an example of the kind of relief a court has the power to grant. See, and compare with, remedy.

remand - To send back, as when an appellate court returns a case to a trial court for further proceedings.

remedy - Something that corrects a violation of civil or criminal law. Unlike relief, which can be given before, during, or after trial, a remedy is given only after an injury has been fully proved to a court. In short, a remedy is always relief, but relief is not always a remedy). Damages and permanent injunctions are two kinds of remedies in civil cases. Imprisonment, restitution, and fines are types of remedies available in criminal cases. See, and compare with, relief.

remote viewing - the capability of system administrators (whether they be IT "helpdesk" personnel or teachers in a classroom) to view what is being displayed on a given workstation or computer from their own location.

reply - A pleading sometimes made by a plaintiff in response to a defendant's answer. See pleading, answer.

reporters - Published volumes containing court decisions arranged chronologically by date of decision.

request for publication or depublication - A case in which the sole relief requested is for the state supreme court to order that a state court of appeal decision be either published or depublished.

res – Resolution; thing; object; property.

res adjudicate - A common but less preferred spelling of 'res judicata." See res judicata.

res gestae - The whole of a transaction, including all its incidental circumstances. In the law of evidence, the phrase is often used to denote one exception to the hearsay rule allowing the admission of evidence about acts and declarations surrounding the event under investigation.

res inter alios acta - A matter affecting third parties and not opposable to the legal persons between whom there is an issue.

res ipsa loquitur—The thing speaks for itself. Refers to the rebuttable presumption that a defendant who had the injury-causing instrumentality in his exclusive control must have been negligent because the accident in question would not normally have occurred without negligence in connection with the instrumentality. A tort law doctrine permitting the presumption of negligence if an accident is of a kind that ordinarily would not occur without the defendant's negligence.

res judicata - A thing adjudicated. A claim, issue, or cause of action conclusively settled by a judgment and no longer open to litigation. The principle that an issue decided by a court should not be reopened. A doctrine in civil law to the general effect that matters fully and finally adjudicated on their merits between or among parties to a lawsuit may not subsequently be re-litigated by or among those same parties, or their privies.

res nullius - An asset susceptible of acquisition but presently under the ownership or sovereignty of no legal person.

respondeat superior - Let the master answer. A doctrine in civil law by which a master (or principal) generally is liable or answerable for the wrongful acts of his servant (or agent).

respondent - A term sometimes used interchangeably with "appellee." See appellee.

restatement – Overview of law published by the American Law Institute. A leading scholar – selected as "reporter" for each legal topic – has the task to absorb all the existing case-law and extract general rules, after where a group of advisers and the reporter will formulate a text to be published as a "restatement." The task of the reporter is to lay down the law in its present positive form – not to improve or modernize it.

ripeness - (1) The circumstance existing when a case has reached, but has not passed, the point when the facts have developed sufficiently to permit an intelligent and useful decision to be made. (2) The requirement that this circumstance must exist before a court will decide a controversy. The opposite of the Mootness Doctrine.

rubric – (1) A title, category, or designation; (2) An established rule, tradition, or custom.

rule - see regulation.

sanction – 1) Official authorization; 2) A punitive or coercive measure resulting from a failure to comply with a law, rule, or court order.

scienter - To know. Guilty knowledge of the criminal, misleading, or manipulative nature of one's act or omission.

SCOTUS – Supreme court of the United States.

SEA - E.U. Single European Act of 1986

seriatim—One at a time; serially.

services of general interest (E.U.) - This is an expression in the E.U. treaties to describe telecommunications, water, postal, transport services and other infrastructure in the E.U. Member States, as well as education, health, that are widely regarded as basic necessities for a satisfactory life under modern conditions in Europe.

Session Laws – The compiled slip laws of a designated legislative session, bound together in chronological, pre-code form.

Seville Declaration (E.U.) - Solemn declarations by the Irish Government and the European Council in 2002 relating to Ireland's participation in the Common Security and Defence Policy.

Schengen Acquis - The body of legal provisions now incorporated into E.U. law and originally being two agreements concluded among European states in 1985 and 1990, which deal with the abolition of systematic border controls among the participating countries. Also termed the Schengen Agreement.

Shepard's – see shepardize.

shepardize – or Shepard's or KeyCite - To determine the subsequent history of a case, that is, has a case been overruled, modified, followed, criticized, distinguished etc., or has a statute been overruled by case law. In the early 1870's, Frank Shepard realized the necessity for tracking the discussion of principles of law in court opinions, and also tracking the history of these opinions. Thus, he devised a method for extracting this information and indexing it for the benefit of legal researchers. Today, the system is owned by LexisNexis. See also KeyCite (Westlaw)

sic - Thus; in this manner. Frequently used to indicate a mistake in an original writing being quoted.

sine die - Without assigning a date for a further meeting or hearing. Frequently used to refer to a final adjournment.

slip law – Legislative, at state and federal levels, in its first printed form; the first official text or enacted statutes. A statute published in pamphlet or single sheet form soon after its passage.

slip opinion - An individual court decision published separately from other opinions, and soon after it is rendered.

Socratic Method – A technique of philosophical discussion – and of U.S. law-school instruction – by which the questioner (a law professor) questions one or more followers (the law students), building on each answer with another question, especially an analogy incorporating the answer. The method forces law students to think through issues rationally and deductively – a skill required in the practice of common law. Also termed question-an-answer.

soft law - Refers to quasi-legal instruments which do not have any legally binding force, or whose binding force is somewhat "weaker' than the binding force of traditional law. Also, it is associated with international law. See also the book's index.

solidarity clause (E.U.) - A clause contained in the Lisbon Treaty committing the E.U. and its Member States to aid another Member State(s) if that Member State(s) is/are the victim of either a terrorist attack or natural or man-made disaster.

solvitur ambulando - "It is solved by walking," that is, the problem is solved by a practical experiment.

special legislative procedure (E.U.) - A number of areas outlined in the Lisbon Treaty lie outside the remit of the Ordinary Legislative Procedure and fall under what is described as a "Special Legislative Procedure". Decision-making procedures vary and may allow for a dominant role for either the Council of Ministers or the European Parliament. In some cases, proposals may come from sources other than the Commission. Unanimity is also allowed for in some cases.

stare decisis - To stand by things decided. The doctrine of precedent, under which a court or tribunal should follow its own previous decisions and those of other tribunals of equal or greater authority when the similar facts, regardless of whether the parties are the same, arise again in litigation - unless there is a compelling reason not to.

status quo—The existing state of things.

Stability and Growth Pact (E.U.) - An agreement introduced in the lead-up to monetary E.U. , the aim of the Stability and Growth Pact is to ensure that the E.U. Member States continued their budgetary discipline efforts once the single currency was introduced. The pact details technical arrangements on surveillance of budgetary positions as well as co-ordination of economic policies and implementation of an excessive deficit procedure, allowing the Council to penalise any participating Member State which fails to take appropriate measures to end an excessive budget deficit. In the medium term, the Member States have undertaken to pursue the objective of a balanced or nearly balanced budget.

sua sponte - On a person's or court's own motion; voluntarily; without prompting.

subpoena - Under penalty. A writ commanding a person's presence before a court or other tribunal, under threat of penalty. A court order compelling a person to appear and give testimony on a certain matter. See "subpoena duces tecum."

subpoena duces tecum - A writ, process, or order directing a person to produce or deliver certain papers or things in his possession or control.

subsidiarity (E.U.) - The principle that the European E.U. does not take action (in areas of shared competence) unless it is more effective than action taken at national, regional or local level.

sui generis - In a class by itself; the only one of its kind.

suit - See lawsuit. Also called "action."

summons - A notice delivered by a sheriff or other officer informing someone that a civil action has been commenced against him or her, and that he or she is required to appear as a defendant in court on a certain date to answer the complaint.

supranational (E.U.) - In the context of the E.U., the term usually refers to the institutions that exist to pursue the common E.U. interests, shared by the E.U. Member States. It also refers to the discharge of functions and exercise of powers by those institutions, transcending national boundaries, in the domains where the E.U. Member States, in the treaties, have conferred those functions and powers on them. The supranational approach is often contrasted with the intergovernmental approach that involves keeping supranational institutions, and their role, to a minimum.

supersedeas - Name of a writ ordering a stay in legal proceedings, such as the suspension of enforcement of a lower court judgment pending an appeal.

supra - Above; appearing above. Compare infra.

syllabus - (1) An abstract or outline of a topic or course of study. (2) a headnote. The syllabus constitutes no part of the opinion of the court but has been prepared by the reporter of decisions for the convenience of the reader.

syllogism - (1) A deductive scheme of a formal argument consisting of a major and a minor premise and a conclusion (as in "every virtue is laudable; kindness is a virtue; therefore kindness is laudable"); (2) a subtle, specious, or crafty argument; (3) deductive reasoning (Merriam-Webster Dictionary).

TCE - Treaty establishing a Constitution for Europe (not in force).

TEC – Treaty establishing the European Community.

TED (Tenders Electronic Daily) - Supplement to the Official Journal of the European Union (OJ S).

TEU – Treaty on European Union = Maastricht Treaty.

TFEU –see Treaty on the Functioning of the European Union

Thomas - Legislative information from the Library of U.S. Congress (named after Thomas Jefferson), available at <Thomas.loc.gov>.

Treaty of Athens 2003 - E.U. Treaty of Accession 2003 - Agreement between the European Union and ten countries (Czech Republic, Estonia, Cyprus, Latvia, Lithuania, Hungary, Malta, Poland, Slovenia, Slovakia), concerning these countries' accession into the E.U.

Treaty of Luxembourg 2005 - Treaty of Accession 2005 - Agreement between the member states of European Union and Bulgaria and Romania, concerning these countries' accession into the E.U.

Treaty on the Functioning of the European Union (TFEU) - The Lisbon Treaty of 2007's rename of The Treaty of Rome of 25 March 1957 = Treaty establishing the European Economic Community (EEC into force on 1 January 1958), which by the Maastricht Treaty of 1993 was renamed the Treaty establishing the European Community (TEC).

Three Pillars (of the European Union) – A categorization of the subject matters dealt with in the treaties creating the E.U.

Three Strike rule - A minimum sentence of imprisonment in a state prison for 25 years if a defendant has three or more prior felony convictions (including from another state), e.g. California Penal Code §§ 667 and 1170.12.

tort - A civil wrong for which a remedy (usually damages) may be obtained. A civil (that is, private) injury other than a breach of contract. It is different from a crime, which is considered an injury to the public even though just one person may be directly injured. A tort has three elements: (1) a legal duty that the defendant owes to the plaintiff; (2) a violation of that duty; and (3) an injury to the plaintiff resulting from that violation. Often, the same act that constitutes a tort is also a crime, and the person who commits it can be prosecuted both criminally by the government and civilly by or on behalf of the individual directly harmed. For example, if Doe deliberately shoots Roe, Doe has committed a battery that is both a tort and a crime. The government can prosecute Doe criminally, and Roe can sue Doe civilly to try to get money (that is, damages) for his injuries

tortfeasor - One who commits a tort; a wrongdoer.

travaux préparatoires - Preparatory work; preliminary drafts, minutes of conferences, and the like, relating to the conclusion of a treaty.

trial de novo - A new trial in which all the issues of fact and law are reconsidered, as if no previous trial had taken place.

U.S.C. - United States Code.

U.S.C.A. - United States Code Annotated.

U.S.C.S. – United States Code Service.

UfR – Danish case repoter using the following citation form: <"UfR" "year.page" "abbreviation in court hierarchy">: H = Supreme Court of Denmark – Højesteret - Information in English at <www.hoejesteret.dk/?id=303>; Ø = Easter Appeal Court - Østre Landsret; V = Western Appeal Court - Vestre Landsret; SH = The Maritime and Commercial Court - Sø- og Handelsretten i København; No letter = lowest Danish court (but not necessary being first instance court).

ultra vires - In excess of one's powers. Compare intra vires.

UN – United Nations.

UNCITRAL - United Nations Commission on International Trade Law.

UNCTAD - United Nations Conference on Trade and Development.

UNECE - United Nations Economic Commission for Europe.

Uniform Acts – Drafts for desirable areas for intra-American unification of law made by National Conference of Commissioners on Uniform State Laws (NCCUSL).

Uniform System of Citation, see Bluebook

USCCAN - United States Code Congressional and Administrative News - is a West Group publication that collects selected Congressional and administrative materials for publication in a single resource. USCCAN is published in monthly pamphlets that contain a cumulative subject index and cumulative Table of Laws Enacted in addition to the selected documents. Among other documents, USC-CAN. publishes the full text of new federal laws, selected committee reports from the House and Senate, signing statements, presidential proclamations, executive orders, reorganization plans, President's messages, Federal Regulations, proposed constitutional amendments, Federal court rules, and sentencing guidelines all arranged in chronological order. When published in bound volumes, the legislative history documents are placed in separate volumes apart from the rest of the materials published by USCCAN.

Uxor - Wife.

vel non - Or not; whether or not.

Vendor-neutral citation – a movement in the United States away from citing cases to bound, often commercial, reporters to citing by more a universal means (such as, for example, to title of case, docket number assigned by the court and specific paragraph number – all which remain constant regardless of publication format).

venire – To appear in court. The name of a writ summoning a jury (also called a "venire facias"). "Venire" is also used to refer to the list of names of jurors thus summoned.

venue - The proper or a possible place for the trial of a lawsuit, usually because the place has a connection with the events that have given rise to the lawsuit.

vi et armis - By force and arms.

viz. - To wit; that is to say.

voir dire—To speak the truth. A preliminary examination by a judge or lawyer to test the suitability of witnesses or prospective jurors, conducted to explore competency, conflict of interest, etc., which may be grounds for objection to their qualifications either to serve as jurors or give testimony as witnesses.

volenti non fit injuria - One who consents to injury cannot sue for damage suffered.

WIPO - World Intellectual Property organization.

writ - A written court order commanding the addressee to perform or refrain from performing a specified act, or giving authority to have it done.

WTO - World Trade Organization.

# 2. Citations and Signals for U.S. material

## CITATIONS

Citation identifies a legal authority or reference work.

The universities of Columbia, Harvard, Pennsylvania and Yale together publish the "Bluebook" ("A Uniform System of Citations"), which contains technical rules about citation form in, e.g., citing cases, statutes, administrative rules, books, legal encyclopedias and law reviews.

The Association of Legal Writing Directors has created an alternative, the ALWD Citation Manual, which contains one system for all legal documents, making no distinction between law review articles and other types of writing. The Manual has been adopted by professors at more than ninety law schools, many paralegal programs, and a number of law reviews, moot court competitions, and courts.[1]

The New York University, Journal of International Law and Politics published in 2006 a Guide to Foreign and International Legal Citation (GFILC).[2]

If one has access to Westcheck this feature should be used to check citations before delivering a dissertation (start the computer process and take a long coffee-break – if the paper is too long, divide it into parts and check each part).

The following subsections will give the most normal and relevant rules for citation in the U.S.

---

[1] <http://www.alwd.org/cm/>, The ALWD Citation Manual: A Professional System of Citation (Third Edition by Darby Dickerson - ISBN: 0735555710).

[2] The GFILC is available for free download at <http://www.law.nyu.edu/journals/jilp/gfilc.html >. The GFILC is also available in spiral-bound, paperback form by sending U.S.$ 20 payable to "Journal of International Law and Politics" to: Circulation Department, Journal of International Law and Politics, 110 West Third Street, New York NY 10012, USA.

---

**Research Tip #2.8**

REMEMBER: Under the U.S. citations system to ALSO pin-point the page referring to the quotation one makes. Thus, giving only the first page of the source is
not enough.

---

*Cases*

The standard case citation contains:

1. Name of the case
2. Published sources in which one can find the case
3. Information in parentheses indicating:
   - the year the decision was issued, and
   - when not apparent from the name of the cited re-
     porter volume,
   - the court which issued the decision; and
4. Prior or subsequent history, if any, of the case

> Example for footnotes:
> *Adam v. Saenger*, 303 U.S. 59, 62 (US 1938)
> *United States v. Layton*, 509 F.Supp 212, 216 (N.D.Cal., 1981), appeal dis-
> missed, 645 F.2d 681 (9th Cir. 1981), cert. denied, 452 U.S. 972 (US 1981).

The Bluebook specifies for each case reporter when a parallel citation
should be provided as part of a standard citation. There are several ways to
find a parallel citation if one only knows the citation of one reprint of a case:
Check the decision. If a parallel citation exists, the case caption may list it.

- Check the Table of Cases found in the case digest that summarizes
  decisions of the court that issued the decision in which one is interested. If there is a parallel citation for the decision, one will find it
  listed with the title of the decision in this table
- Check the Shepard's Citations that treat the decision in which one is
  interested. In the Shepard's table for the decision, one will normally
  find the parallel citation in parentheses as the first entry. If one does
  not find this parenthetical citation, it means (a) the parallel citation is
  contained in another volume of the same Shepard's set; (b) the parallel reprint has not been published yet; or (c) there is not / and will not
  be – a parallel reprint of the decision
- Check West's National Reporter Blue Book or (for selected states)
  West's Blue and White Books. These series of charts provide parallel
  West reporter citations for state decisions also published in official
  non-West reporters. The national edition's charts also cross-reference

parallel citations between the official U.S. Reports and West's Supreme Court Reporter.

*Statutes*

Federal statutes are cited to either:
- the United States Code (U.S.C.), which is the preferred source, or to
- the Statutes of Large (Stat.)

### Citation of the United States Code
1. Number of the Code title (each title dealing with a particular subject matter)
2. Abbreviation ("U.S.C.")
3. Statutory section number within the title
4. Date of the edition or supplement

### Citation of the Statutes of Large
1. Name of the act
2. Public law or chapter number
3. Volume number of the Statutes at Large
4. Abbreviation ("Stat.")
5. Page on which the cited statute begins
6. Year the statute was enacted

*Administrative Law*

A citation to the Code of Federal Regulations ("C.F.R.) include:
1. Number of the C.F.R. title (each title dealing with a particular subject matter)
2. Abbreviation ("C.F.R.")
3. Section number
4. Year of publication

A citation to the Federal Register ("Fed.Reg.") includes:
1. Volume number (a volume runs for the calendar year)
2. Abbreviation ("Fed.Reg.")
3. Page number on which the cited material begins
4. Year of publication

*Books*

Book citations include:
1. Volume number
2. First initial and last name of each author

3. Full main title as it appears on the title page (but not any subtitle)
4. Particular page, section, or paragraph the reader should look at (where appropriate)
5. Edition of the book (if there has been more than one edition)
6. Publication date

The Bluebook has a number of rules for citing books when the general rule does not cover the situation, such as when the book:

- is a translation
- has several editors
- has several authors

> Examples for footnotes:
> Rosalyn Higgins, PROBLEMS & PROCESS – INTERNATIONAL LAW AND HOW WE USE IT (Clarendon Press, Oxford 1994 – ISBN 0-19-876410-3)
>
> *Henrik Spang-Hanssen, Cybercrime and Jurisdiction in Denmark in* CYBER-CRIME AND JURISDICTION - A GLOBAL SURVEY (Ed. Bert-Jaap Koops & and Susan W. Brenner, 2006 T.M.C. Asser Press, The Hague – ISBN 9067042218)
>
> K. Zweigert & H.Kötz, INTRODUCTION TO COMPARATIVE LAW (3rd ed.)(Tony Weir trans., Clarendon Press, Oxford 1998)

### *Legal Encyclopedias*
Citations to the two leading U.S. national legal encyclopedias – Corpus Juris Secundum ("C.J.S.") and American Jurisprudence 2d ("Am.Jur.2d") – have the following common elements:

1. Volume number of the encyclopedia
2. Abbreviated name of the encyclopedia ("C.J.S." or "Am.Jur.2d")
3. Title of the topic in the encyclopedia
4. Section number within the topic
5. Specific page (if any) being cited within the section
6. Date of publication of the volume, as well as any pocket part for the encyclopedia if the reader is being specially referred to material in it

### *Law Reviews*
The usual citation to a law review article includes:

1. Last name of the author of the article
2. Title of the article
3. Volume number of the law review (if there is no volume number, then year of publication)

4. Abbreviated name of the law review (see the Bluebook's abbreviations list)
5. Page on which the article begins
6. Year of publication in parentheses (if not already included elsewhere in the citation)

> Examples for footnotes:
> Lawrence Lessig, *Legal Issues in Cyberspace: Hazards on the Information Superhigh-way: Reading the Constitution in Cyberspace*, 45 EMORY.L.J. 869, 899 (1996)

> Examples of articles on the www:
> Henrik Spang-Hanssen, *Hollywood Puts 3 Baltic Countries into a Second Class of E.U. or Hollywood Does Not Recognize E.U.'s Single Market (May 1, 2004)* at <www.geocities.com/hssph/articles> (last visited 24 December 2006).

## SIGNALS

Citations are frequently introduced by words called "signals." These words indicate how the writer wants one to view the cited authority in connection with the principle that the citation relates to. The signal provides a concise shorthand context for the citation.

The most common signals are:

- See generally - Indicates the cited authority provides useful background information about a given point.
- See, e.g. - Indicates that the cited authority directly supports a proposition. It further indicates that other authorities also could have been cited for the same proposition, but that no purpose would be served by citing them all because their citation would be merely duplicative.
- Cf. - Indicates that the cited authority states a proposition. Different from that stated by the person citing to the authority, but that the cited authority's proposition is sufficiently analogous to lend support.
- Contra - Indicates that the cited authority contradicts a given point.
- Id. – idem – same as just before.
- Supra – (superus) above (mentioned).
- Cert. Denied – Supreme Court denied certiorari.
- Cert. Dismissed – Supreme Court dismissed certiorari.
- Aff'd – affirmed.
- Reh'g – rehearing.

- Rev. – revised / revised.

# 3. Alphabetic – Courts in Federal Circuits[1]

| State | No | Abbrev | 1 | 2 | 3 | 4 | 5 | 6 | 7 | 8 | 9 | 10 | 11 |
|-------|-----|--------|---|---|---|---|---|---|---|---|---|----|----|
| Alabama | 22 | Ala | | | | | | | | | | | 11* |
| Alaska | 49 | Alaska | | | | | | | | | 9 | | |
| Arizona | 48 | Ariz. | | | | | | | | | 9 | | |
| Arkansas | 25 | Ark. | | | | | | | | 8 | | | |
| California | 31 | Cal. | | | | | | | | | 9 | | |
| Colorado | 38 | Colo. | | | | | | | | | | 10 | |
| Connecticut | 5 | Conn. | | 2 | | | | | | | | | |
| Delaware | 1 | Del. | | | 3 | | | | | | | | |
| District of Columbia | | D.C. | | | | | | | | | | | |
| Florida | 27 | Fla. | | | | | | | | | | | 11* |
| Georgia | 4 | Ga. | | | | | | | | | | | 11* |
| Guam | | Guam | | | | | | | | | 9 | | |
| Hawaii | 50 | Haw. | | | | | | | | | 9 | | |
| Idaho | 43 | Idaho | | | | | | | | | 9 | | |
| Illinois | 21 | Ill. | | | | | | | 7 | | | | |
| Indiana | 19 | Ind. | | | | | | | 7 | | | | |
| Iowa | 29 | Iowa | | | | | | | | 8 | | | |
| Kansas | 34 | Kan. | | | | | | | | | | 10 | |
| Kentucky | 15 | Ky. | | | | | | 6 | | | | | |
| Louisiana | 18 | La. | | | | | 5 | | | | | | |
| Maine | 23 | Me. | 1 | | | | | | | | | | |
| Maryland | 7 | Md. | | | | 4 | | | | | | | |
| Massachusetts | 6 | Mass. | 1 | | | | | | | | | | |
| Michigan | 26 | Mich. | | | | | | 6 | | | | | |
| Minnesota | 32 | Minn. | | | | | | | | 8 | | | |
| Mississippi | 20 | Miss. | | | | | 5 | | | | | | |
| Missouri | 24 | Mo. | | | | | | | | 8 | | | |
| Montana | 41 | Mont. | | | | | | | | | 9 | | |
| Nebraska | 42 | Neb. | | | | | | | | 8 | | | |
| Nevada | 36 | Nev. | | | | | | | | | 9 | | |

[1] Source: Henrik Spang-Hanssen, CYBERSPACE JURISDICTION IN THE U.S: THE INTERNATIONAL DIMENSION OF DUE PROCESS Appendix C (Complex 5/01, Norwegian Research Center For Computers and Law, Oslo University 2001). Also free downloading from website <www.geocities.com/hssph>.

| | | | 1 | 2 | 3 | 4 | 5 | 6 | 7 | 8 | 9 | 10 | 11 |
|---|---|---|---|---|---|---|---|---|---|---|---|---|---|
| New Hampshire | 9 | N.H. | 1 | | | | | | | | | | |
| New Jersey | 3 | N.J. | | | 3 | | | | | | | | |
| New Mexico | 47 | N.M. | | | | | | | | | | 10 | |
| New York | 11 | N.Y. | | 2 | | | | | | | | | |
| North Carolina | 12 | N.C. | | | | 4 | | | | | | | |
| North Dakota | 39 | N.D. | | | | | | | | 8 | | | |
| North Mariana Islands | | N.Mar.I. | | | | | | | | | 9 | | |
| Ohio | 17 | Ohio | | | | | | 6 | | | | | |
| Oklahoma | 46 | Okla. | | | | | | | | | | 10 | |
| Oregon | 33 | Or. | | | | | | | | | 9 | | |
| Pennsylvania | 2 | Pa. | | | 3 | | | | | | | | |
| Porto Rico | | P.R. | 1 | | | | | | | | | | |
| Rhode Island | 13 | R.I. | 1 | | | | | | | | | | |
| South Carolina | 8 | S.C. | | | | 4 | | | | | | | |
| South Dakota | 40 | S.D. | | | | | | | | 8 | | | |
| Tennessee | 16 | Tenn. | | | | | | 6 | | | | | |
| Texas | 28 | Tex. | | | | | 5 | | | | | | |
| Utah | 45 | Utah | | | | | | | | | | 10 | |
| Vermont | 14 | Vt. | | 2 | | | | | | | | | |
| Virginia | 10 | Va. | | | | 4 | | | | | | | |
| Virgin Islands | | V.I. | | | 3 | | | | | | | | |
| Washington | 42 | Wash. | | | | | | | | | 9 | | |
| West Virginia | 35 | W.Va. | | | | | | | | | | | |
| Wisconsin | 30 | Wis. | | | | | | | 7 | | | | |
| Wyoming | 44 | Wyo. | | | | | | | | | | 10 | |

* Until October 1, 1981 part of the 5th Circuit

# 4. Renumbering/equivalences tables of E.U. Treaties

Note that the text of articles after "renumbering" not always is the same, thus it is more correct to regard the following tables as tables of "equivalences."

## TEU - Treaty on European Union ➜ Treaty of Amsterdam

Treaty of Amsterdam amending the Treaty on European Union, the Treaties establishing the European Communities and certain related acts - Annex - Tables of equivalences referred to in article 12 of the Treaty of Amsterdam - Treaty on European Union

Official Journal C 340 , 10/11/1997 P. 0085

Previous numbering // New numbering

**TITLE I // TITLE I**
Article A // Article 1
Article B // Article 2
Article C // Article 3
Article D // Article 4
Article E // Article 5
Article F // Article 6
Article F.1 (*) // Article 7
**TITLE II // TITLE II**
Article G // Article 8
**TITLE III // TITLE III**
Article H // Article 9
**TITLE IV // TITLE IV**
Article I // Article 10
**TITLE V (***) // TITLE V**
Article J.1 // Article 11
Article J.2 // Article 12
Article J.3 // Article 13
Article J.4 // Article 14
Article J.5 // Article 15
Article J.6 // Article 16
Article J.7 // Article 17
Article J.8 // Article 18
Article J.9 // Article 19
Article J.10 // Article 20
Article J.11 // Article 21
Article J.12 // Article 22
Article J.13 // Article 23
Article J.14 // Article 24
Article J.15 // Article 25
Article J.16 // Article 26

Article J.17 // Article 27
Article J.18 // Article 28
**TITLE VI (***) // TITLE VI**
Article K.1 // Article 29
Article K.2 // Article 30
Article K.3 // Article 31
Article K.4 // Article 32
Article K.5 // Article 33
Article K.6 // Article 34
Article K.7 // Article 35
Article K.8 // Article 36
Article K.9 // Article 37
Article K.10 // Article 38
Article K.11 // Article 39
Article K.12 // Article 40
Article K.13 // Article 41
Article K.14 // Article 42
**TITLE VIa (**) // TITLE VII**
Article K.15 (*) // Article 43
Article K.16 (*) // Article 44
Article K.17 (*) // Article 45
**TITLE VII // TITLE VIII**
Article L // Article 46
Article M // Article 47
Article N // Article 48
Article O // Article 49
Article P // Article 50
Article Q // Article 51
Article R // Article 52
Article S // Article 53

(*) New Article introduced by the Treaty of Amsterdam

(**) New Title introduced by the Treaty of Amsterdam.
(***) Title restructured by the Treaty of Amsterdam.

ooo000ooo

# TEC - Treaty establishing the European Community ➜ Treaty of Amsterdam

Treaty of Amsterdam amending the Treaty on European Union, the Treaties establishing the European Communities and certain related acts - Annex - Tables of equivalences referred to in article 12 of the Treaty of Amsterdam - Treaty establishing the European Community

Official Journal C 340 , 10/11/1997 P. 0086

Previous numbering // New numbering

PART ONE // PART ONE

Article 1 // Article 1
Article 2 // Article 2
Article 3 // Article 3
Article 3a // Article 4
Article 3b // Article 5
Article 3c (*) // Article 6
Article 4 // Article 7
Article 4a // Article 8
Article 4b // Article 9
Article 5 // Article 10
Article 5a (*) // Article 11
Article 6 // Article 12
Article 6a (*) // Article 13
Article 7 (repealed) // -
Article 7a // Article 14
Article 7b (repealed) // -
Article 7c // Article 15
Article 7d (*) // Article 16

PART TWO // PART TWO
Article 8 // Article 17
Article 8a // Article 18
Article 8b // Article 19
Article 8c // Article 20
Article 8d // Article 21
Article 8e // Article 22

PART THREE // PART THREE
**TITLE I // TITLE I**
Article 9 // Article 23
Article 10 // Article 24
Article 11 (repealed) // -
CHAPTER 1 // CHAPTER 1

Section 1 (deleted) // -
Article 12 // Article 25
Article 13 (repealed) // -
Article 14 (repealed) // -
Article 15 (repealed) // -
Article 16 (repealed // -
Article 17 (repealed) // -
Section 2 (deleted) // -
Article 18 (repealed) // -
Article 19 (repealed) // -
Article 20 (repealed) // -
Article 21 (repealed) // -
Article 22 (repealed) // -
Article 23 (repealed) // -
Article 24 (repealed) // -
Article 25 (repealed) // -
Article 26 (repealed) // -
Article 27 (repealed) // -
Article 28 // Article 26
Article 29 // Article 27
CHAPTER 2 // CHAPTER 2
Article 30 // Article 28
Article 31 (repealed) // -
Article 32 (repealed) // -
Article 33 (repealed) // -
Article 34 // Article 29
Article 35 (repealed) // -
Article 36 // Article 30
Article 37 // Article 31
**TITLE II // TITLE II**
Article 38 // Article 32
Article 39 // Article 33
Article 40 // Article 34
Article 41 // Article 35
Article 42 // Article 36

Article 43 // Article 37
Article 44 (repealed) // -
Article 45 (repealed) // -
Article 46 // Article 38
Article 47 (repealed) // -

**TITLE III // TITLE III**
CHAPTER 1 // CHAPTER 1
Article 48 // Article 39
Article 49 // Article 40
Article 50 // Article 41
Article 51 // Article 42
CHAPTER 2 // CHAPTER 2
Article 52 // Article 43
Article 53 (repealed) // -
Article 54 // Article 44
Article 55 // Article 45
Article 56 // Article 46
Article 57 // Article 47
Article 58 // Article 48
CHAPTER 3 // CHAPTER 3
Article 59 // Article 49
Article 60 // Article 50
Article 61 // Article 51
Article 62 (repealed) // -
Article 63 // Article 52
Article 64 // Article 53
Article 65 // Article 54
Article 66 // Article 55
CHAPTER 4 // CHAPTER 4
Article 67 (repealed) // -
Article 68 (repealed) // -
Article 69 (repealed) // -
Article 70 (repealed) // -
Article 71 (repealed) // -
Article 72 (repealed) // -
Article 73 (repealed) // -
Article 73a (repealed) // -
Article 73b // Article 56
Article 73c // Article 57
Article 73d // Article 58
Article 73e (repealed) // -
Article 73f // Article 59
Article 73g // Article 60
Article 73h (repealed) // -

**TITLE IIIa (\*\*) // TITLE IV**
Article 73i (\*) // Article 61
Article 73j (\*) // Article 62
Article 73k (\*) // Article 63
Article 73l (\*) // Article 64
Article 73m (\*) // Article 65
Article 73n (\*) // Article 66
Article 73o (\*) // Article 67
Article 73p (\*) // Article 68
Article 73q (\*) // Article 69

**TITLE IV // TITLE V**
Article 74 // Article 70
Article 75 // Article 71
Article 76 // Article 72
Article 77 // Article 73
Article 78 // Article 74
Article 79 // Article 75
Article 80 // Article 76
Article 81 // Article 77
Article 82 // Article 78
Article 83 // Article 79
Article 84 // Article 80

**TITLE V // TITLE VI**
CHAPTER 1 // CHAPTER 1
SECTION 1 // SECTION 1
Article 85 // Article 81
Article 86 // Article 82
Article 87 // Article 83
Article 88 // Article 84
Article 89 // Article 85
Article 90 // Article 86
Section 2 (deleted) // -
Article 91 (repealed) // -
SECTION 3 // SECTION 2
Article 92 // Article 87
Article 93 // Article 88
Article 94 // Article 89
CHAPTER 2 // CHAPTER 2
Article 95 // Article 90
Article 96 // Article 91
Article 97 (repealed) // -
Article 98 // Article 92
Article 99 // Article 93
CHAPTER 3 // CHAPTER 3
Article 100 // Article 94
Article 100a // Article 95
Article 100b (repealed) // -
Article 100c (repealed) // -
Article 100d (repealed) // -
Article 101 // Article 96
Article 102 // Article 97

**TITLE VI // TITLE VII**
CHAPTER 1 // CHAPTER 1
Article 102a // Article 98
Article 103 // Article 99
Article 103a // Article 100
Article 104 // Article 101
Article 104a // Article 102
Article 104b // Article 103
Article 104c // Article 104
CHAPTER 2 // CHAPTER 2
Article 105 // Article 105
Article 105a // Article 106
Article 106 // Article 107

Article 107 // Article 108
Article 108 // Article 109
Article 108a // Article 110
Article 109 // Article 111
CHAPTER 3 // CHAPTER 3
Article 109a // Article 112
Article 109b // Article 113
Article 109c // Article 114
Article 109d // Article 115
CHAPTER 4 // CHAPTER 4
Article 109e // Article 116
Article 109f // Article 117
Article 109g // Article 118
Article 109h // Article 119
Article 109i // Article 120
Article 109j // Article 121
Article 109k // Article 122
Article 109l // Article 123
Article 109m // Article 124

**TITLE VIa (\*\*) // TITLE VIII**
Article 109n (\*) // Article 125
Article 109o (\*) // Article 126
Article 109p (\*) // Article 127
Article 109q (\*) // Article 128
Article 109r (\*) // Article 129
Article 109s (\*) // Article 130

**TITLE VII // TITLE IX**
Article 110 // Article 131
Article 111 (repealed) // -
Article 112 // Article 132
Article 113 // Article 133
Article 114 (repealed) // -
Article 115 // Article 134

**TITLE VIIa (\*\*) // TITLE X**
Article 116 (\*) // Article 135

**TITLE VIII // TITLE XI**
CHAPTER 1 (\*\*\*) // CHAPTER 1
Article 117 // Article 136
Article 118 // Article 137
Article 118a // Article 138
Article 118b // Article 139
Article 118c // Article 140
Article 119 // Article 141
Article 119a // Article 142
Article 120 // Article 143
Article 121 // Article 144
Article 122 // Article 145
CHAPTER 2 // CHAPTER 2
Article 123 // Article 146
Article 124 // Article 147
Article 125 // Article 148
CHAPTER 3 // CHAPTER 3
Article 126 // Article 149
Article 127 // Article 150

**TITLE IX // TITLE XII**
Article 128 // Article 151

**TITLE X // TITLE XIII**
Article 129 // Article 152

**TITLE XI // TITLE XIV**
Article 129a // Article 153

**TITLE XII // TITLE XV**
Article 129b // Article 154
Article 129c // Article 155
Article 129d // Article 156
TITLE XIII // TITLE XVI
Article 130 // Article 157

**TITLE XIV // TITLE XVII**
Article 130a // Article 158
Article 130b // Article 159
Article 130c // Article 160
Article 130d // Article 161
Article 130e // Article 162

**TITLE XV // TITLE XVIII**
Article 130f // Article 163
Article 130g // Article 164
Article 130h // Article 165
Article 130i // Article 166
Article 130j // Article 167
Article 130k // Article 168
Article 130l // Article 169
Article 130m // Article 170
Article 130n // Article 171
Article 130o // Article 172
Article 130p // Article 173
Article 130q (repealed) // -

**TITLE XVI // TITLE XIX**
Article 130r // Article 174
Article 130s // Article 175
Article 130t // Article 176

**TITLE XVII // TITLE XX**
Article 130u // Article 177
Article 130v // Article 178
Article 130w // Article 179
Article 130x // Article 180
Article 130y // Article 181

PART FOUR // PART FOUR
Article 131 // Article 182
Article 132 // Article 183
Article 133 // Article 184
Article 134 // Article 185
Article 135 // Article 186
Article 136 // Article 187
Article 136a // Article 188

PART FIVE // PART FIVE

**TITLE I // TITLE I**
CHAPTER 1 // CHAPTER 1
SECTION 1 // SECTION 1
Article 137 // Article 189
Article 138 // Article 190
Article 138a // Article 191
Article 138b // Article 192
Article 138c // Article 193
Article 138d // Article 194
Article 138e // Article 195
Article 139 // Article 196
Article 140 // Article 197
Article 141 // Article 198
Article 142 // Article 199
Article 143 // Article 200
Article 144 // Article 201
SECTION 2 // SECTION 2
Article 145 // Article 202
Article 146 // Article 203
Article 147 // Article 204
Article 148 // Article 205
Article 149 (repealed) // -
Article 150 // Article 206
Article 151 // Article 207
Article 152 // Article 208
Article 153 // Article 209
Article 154 // Article 210
SECTION 3 // SECTION 3
Article 155 // Article 211
Article 156 // Article 212
Article 157 // Article 213
Article 158 // Article 214
Article 159 // Article 215
Article 160 // Article 216
Article 161 // Article 217
Article 162 // Article 218
Article 163 // Article 219
SECTION 4 // SECTION 4
Article 164 // Article 220
Article 165 // Article 221
Article 166 // Article 222
Article 167 // Article 223
Article 168 // Article 224
Article 168 a // Article 225
Article 169 // Article 226
Article 170 // Article 227
Article 171 // Article 228
Article 172 // Article 229
Article 173 // Article 230
Article 174 // Article 231
Article 175 // Article 232
Article 176 // Article 233
Article 177 // Article 234
Article 178 // Article 235
Article 179 // Article 236

Article 180 // Article 237
Article 181 // Article 238
Article 182 // Article 239
Article 183 // Article 240
Article 184 // Article 241
Article 185 // Article 242
Article 186 // Article 243
Article 187 // Article 244
Article 188 // Article 245
SECTION 5 // SECTION 5
Article 188a // Article 246
Article 188b // Article 247
Article 188c // Article 248
CHAPTER 2 // CHAPTER 2
Article 189 // Article 249
Article 189a // Article 250
Article 189b // Article 251
Article 189c // Article 252
Article 190 // Article 253
Article 191 // Article 254
Article 191a (*) // Article 255
Article 192 // Article 256
CHAPTER 3 // CHAPTER 3
Article 193 // Article 257
Article 194 // Article 258
Article 195 // Article 259
Article 196 // Article 260
Article 197 // Article 261
Article 198 // Article 262
CHAPTER 4 // CHAPTER 4
Article 198a // Article 263
Article 198b // Article 264
Article 198c // Article 265
CHAPTER 5 // CHAPTER 5
Article 198d // Article 266
Article 198e // Article 267

**TITLE II // TITLE II**
Article 199 // Article 268
Article 200 (repealed) // -
Article 201 // Article 269
Article 201a // Article 270
Article 202 // Article 271
Article 203 // Article 272
Article 204 // Article 273
Article 205 // Article 274
Article 205a // Article 275
Article 206 // Article 276
Article 206a (repealed) // -
Article 207 // Article 277
Article 208 // Article 278
Article 209 // Article 279
Article 209a // Article 280

PART SIX // PART SIX
Article 210 // Article 281

Article 211 // Article 282
Article 212 (*) // Article 283
Article 213 // Article 284
Article 213a (*) // Article 285
Article 213b (*) // Article 286
Article 214 // Article 287
Article 215 // Article 288
Article 216 // Article 289
Article 217 // Article 290
Article 218 (*) // Article 291
Article 219 // Article 292
Article 220 // Article 293
Article 221 // Article 294
Article 222 // Article 295
Article 223 // Article 296
Article 224 // Article 297
Article 225 // Article 298
Article 226 (repealed) // -
Article 227 // Article 299
Article 228 // Article 300
Article 228a // Article 301
Article 229 // Article 302

Article 230 // Article 303
Article 231 // Article 304
Article 232 // Article 305
Article 233 // Article 306
Article 234 // Article 307
Article 235 // Article 308
Article 236 (*) // Article 309
Article 237 (repealed) // -
Article 238 // Article 310
Article 239 // Article 311
Article 240 // Article 312
Article 241 (repealed) // -
Article 242 (repealed) // -
Article 243 (repealed) // -
Article 244 (repealed) // -
Article 245 (repealed) // -
Article 246 (repealed) // -

FINAL PROVISIONS // FINAL PROVISIONS
Article 247 // Article 313
Article 248 // Article 314

(*) New Article introduced by the Treaty of Amsterdam.
(**) New Title introduced by the Treaty of Amsterdam.
(***) Chapter 1 restructured by the Treaty of Amsterdam.

ooo000ooo

## TCE – Treaty establishing a Constitution for Europe (not in force)

Even though the so-called European Constitution (Official Journal C310, 16/12 2004 pp. 0001-474) was never put into force, the following table of equivalences can be of use for researchers.

An * indicates new articles introduced by the Treaty Establishing a Constitution for Europe.

| The E.U. Constitution | Nice Treaty - TEU/TEC | Maastricht Treaty - TEU/TEC |
|---|---|---|
| Part I | | |
| Title I | | |
| Art. I-1 | Art. 1, 49 TEU | Art. A, O TEU |
| Art. I-2 | Art. 6(1) TEU | Art. F(1) TEU |
| Art. I-3 | Art. 2 TEU, 2 TEC | Art. B TEU, 2 TEC |
| Art. I-4 | Art. 14(2), 12 TEC | Art. 7a, 6 TEC |
| Art. I-5 | Art. 6(3), 33 TEU, 10 TEC | Art. F(1), K.5 TEU, 5 TEC |

| | | |
|---|---|---|
| Art. I-6* | | |
| Art. I-7(*) | Art. 281 TEC | Art. 210 TEC |
| Art. I-8* | | |
| Title II | | |
| Art. I-9(*) | Art. 6(2) TEU | Art. F(2) TEU |
| Art. I-10 | Art. 17 - 21 TEC | Art. 8, 8a, 8b, 8c, 8d TEC |
| Title III | | |
| Art. I-11 | Art. 5 TEC, 2 (last sentence) TEU | Art. 3b TEC, B TEU |
| Art. I-12* | | |
| Art. I-13 * | | |
| Art. I-14* | | |
| Art. I-15 | Art. 4(1) TEC | Art. 3a TEC |
| | Art. 99(1), 3(1)(i) TEC | Art. 103 TEC |
| | Art. 125 TEC | Art. 109n TEC |
| | Art. 128 TEC | Art. 109q TEC |
| | Art. 140 TEC | Art. 118c TEC |
| Art. I-16 | Art. 17, 11(2) TEU | Art. J.7, J.1 TEU |
| Art. I-17* | | |
| Art. I-18 | Art. 308 TEC | Art. 235 TEC |
| Title IV | | |
| Art. I-19 | Art. 3(1) TEU, 7(1) TEC, 5 TEU | Art. C TEU, 4(1) TEC, E TEU |
| Art. I-20 | Art. 189 TEC | Art. 137 TEC |
| | Art. 190 TEC | Art. 13 8 TEC |
| | Art. 192 TEC | Art. 13 8b TEC |
| | Art. 197 TEC | Art. 140 TEC |
| Art. I-21 | Art. 4 TEU | Art. D TEU |
| Art. I-22* | | |
| Art. I-23 | Art. 202 TEC | Art. 145 TEC |
| | Art. 203 TEC | Art. 146 TEC |
| | Art. 205(1) TEC | Art. 148 TEC |
| Art. I-24 | Art. 203 TEC | Art. 146 TEC |
| | Art. 207(1) TEC | Art. 151 TEC |
| Art. I-25 | Art. 205(2) TEC | Art. 148 TEC |
| Art. I-26 | Art. 201 TEC | Art. 144 TEC |
| | Art. 211 TEC | Art. 155 TEC |
| | Art. 213(2) TEC | Art. 157 TEC |
| | Art. 214(1) TEC | Art. 158(1) TEC |

| | | |
|---|---|---|
| | Art. 274 TEC | Art. 205 TEC |
| Art. I-27 | Art. 214(2) TEC | Art. 158 TEC |
| | Art. 217 TEC | Art. 161 TEC |
| Art. I-28* | | |
| Art. I-29(*) | Art. 220 - 224 TEC | Art. 164 - 168 TEC |
| Art. I-30 | Art. 8, 107, 105(1), 106, 108, 105(4), 212 TEC | Art. 4a, 106, 105, 105a, 107, 156 TEC |
| Art. I-31 | Art. 7, 246 - 248 TEC | Art. 4, 188a, 188b, 188c TEC |
| Art. I-32 | Art. 7(2), 257, 258, 263 TEC | Art. 4(1), 193, 194, 198a TEC |
| **Title V** | | |
| Art. I-33 | Art. 249 TEC, 13, 34 TEU | Art. 198 TEC, J.3, K.6 TEU |
| Art. I-34* | | |
| Art. I-35* | | |
| Art. I-36* | | |
| Art. I-37 | Art. 10 TEC | Art. 5 TEC |
| | Art. 202 TEC | Art. 145 TEC |
| Art. I-38 | Art. 253 TEC | Art. 190 TEC |
| Art. I-39 | Art. 254 TEC | Art. 191 |
| Art. I-40(*) | Art. 13, 16, 21, 23 TEU | Art. J.3, J.6, J.11, J.13 TEU |
| Art. I-41 | Art. 17, 21 TEU | Art. J.7, J.11 TEU |
| Art. I-42 | Art. 29 TEU, 61 TEC | Art K.1 TEU, 73i TEC |
| Art. I-43 * | | |
| Art. I-44 | Art. 27, 43 TEU | Art. J.17, K.15 TEU |
| | Art. 11 TEC | Art. 5a TEC |
| **Title VI** | | |
| Art. I-45 * | | |
| Art. I-46 | Art. 1(1) TEU | Art. A TEU |
| | Art. 6(1) TEU | Art. F TEU |
| | Art. 191 TEC | Art. 138a TEC |
| Art. I-47 * | | |
| Art. I-48 | Art. 138 TEC | Art. 118a TEC |
| | Art. 211, 212 TEC | Art. 155, 156 TEC |
| Art. I-49 | Art. 195 TEC | Art. 138e TEC |
| Art. I-50 | Art. 1 TEU | Art. A TEC |
| | Art. 255 TEC | Art. 191a TEC |
| Art. I-51 | Art. 286 TEC | Art. 213b TEC |
| Art. I-52* | | |
| **Title VII** | | |
| Art. I-53 | Art. 268, 270, 271, 280 TEC | Art. 199, 201a, 202, 209a TEC |

No
No

| | | |
|---|---|---|
| Art. I-54 | Art. 269 TEC | Art. 201 TEC |
| Art. I-55* | | |
| Art. I-56* | | |
| Title VIII | | |
| Art. I-57* | | |
| Title IX | | |
| Art. I-58 | Art. 49 TEU | Art. O TEU |
| Art. I-59 | Art. 7 TEU, 309 TEC | Art. F.1 TEU, 236 TEC |
| Art. I-60* | | |
| | | |
| **Part II** | | |
| Title I | | |
| Art. II-61 * | | |
| Art. II-62* | | |
| Art. II-63 * | | |
| Art. II-64* | | |
| Art. II-65 * | | |
| Title II | | |
| Art. II-66* | | |
| Art. II-67* | | |
| Art. II-68* | | |
| Art. II-69* | | |
| Art. II-70* | | |
| Art. II-71 * | | |
| Art. II-72* | | |
| Art. II-73 * | | |
| Art. II-74* | | |
| Art. II-75 * | | |
| Art. II-76* | | |
| Art. II-77* | | |
| Art. II-78* | | |
| Art. II-79* | | |
| Title III | | |
| Art. II-80* | | |
| Art. II-81 * | | |
| Art. II-82* | | |
| Art. II-83 * | | |
| Art. II-84* | | |

| | | |
|---|---|---|
| Art. II-86* | | |
| Title IV | | |
| Art. II-87* | | |
| Art. II-88* | | |
| Art. II-89* | | |
| Art. II-90* | | |
| Art. II-91 * | | |
| Art. II-92* | | |
| Art. II-93 * | | |
| Art. II-94* | | |
| Art. II-95 * | | |
| Art. II-96* | | |
| Art. II-97* | | |
| Art. II-98* | | |
| Title V | | |
| Art. II-99* | | |
| Art. II-100* | | |
| Art. II-101 * | | |
| Art. II-102* | | |
| Art. II-103 * | | |
| Art. II-104* | | |
| Art. II-105* | | |
| Art. II-106* | | |
| Title VI | | |
| Art. II-107* | | |
| Art. II-108* | | |
| Art. II-109* | | |
| Art. II-110* | | |
| Title VII | | |
| Art. II-111 * | | |
| Art. II-112* | | |
| Art. II-113 * | | |
| Art. II-114* | | |
| | | |
| **Part III** | | |
| Title I | | |
| Art. III-115 | Art. 3 TEU | Art. C TEU |
| Art. III-116 | Art. 3(2) TEC | Art. 3 TEC |

| | | |
|---|---|---|
| Art. III-117* | | |
| Art. III-118* | | |
| Art. III-119 | Art. 6 TEC | Art. 12 TEC |
| Art. III-120<br>Art. III-121 | Art. 153(2) TEC<br>Protocol on protection and<br>welfare of animals | Art. 129a TEC<br>Protocol on protection and<br>welfare of<br>animals |
| Art. III-122 | Art. 16 TEC | Art. 7d TEC |
| Title II | | |
| Art. III-123 | Art. 12 TEC | Art. 6 TEC |
| Art. III-124 | Art. 13 TEC | Art. 6a TEC |
| Art. III-125 | Art. 18 (2-3) TEC | Art. 8a TEC |
| Art. III-126 | Art. 19 TEC | Art. 8b TEC |
| Art. III-127 | Art. 20 TEC | Art. 8c TEC |
| Art. III-128 | Art. 21 TEC | Art. 8d TEC |
| Art. III-129 | Art. 22 TEC | Art. 8e TEC |
| Title III | | |
| Art. III-130 | Art. 14, 15 TEC | Art. 7a, 7c TEC |
| Art. III-131 | Art. 297 TEC | Art. 224 TEC |
| Art. III-132 | Art. 298 TEC | Art. 225 TEC |
| Art. III-133 | Art. 39 TEC | Art. 48 TEC |
| Art. III-134 | Art. 40 TEC | Art. 49 TEC |
| Art. III-135 | Art. 41 TEC | Art. 50 TEC |
| Art. III-136 | Art. 42 TEC | Art. 51 TEC |
| Art. III-137 | Art. 43 TEC | Art. 52 TEC |
| Art. III-138 | Art. 44 TEC | Art. 54 TEC |
| Art. III-139 | Art. 45 TEC | Art. 55 TEC |
| Art. III-140 | Art. 46 TEC | Art. 56 TEC |
| Art. III-141 | Art. 47 TEC | Art. 57 TEC |
| Art. III-142 | Art. 48 TEC | Art. 58 TEC |
| Art. III-143 | Art. 294 TEC | Art. 221 TEC |
| Art. III-144 | Art. 49 TEC | Art. 59 TEC |
| Art. III-145 | Art. 50 TEC | Art. 60 TEC |
| Art. III-146 | Art. 51 TEC | Art. 61 TEC |
| Art. III-147 | Art. 52 TEC | Art. 63 TEC |
| Art. III-148 | Art. 53 TEC | Art. 64 TEC |
| Art. III-149 | Art. 54 TEC | Art. 65 TEC |
| Art. III-150 | Art. 55 TEC | Art. 66 TEC |
| Art. III-151 | Art. 23 TEC | Art. 9 TEC |

| | Art. 24 TEC | Art. 10 TEC |
|---|---|---|
| | Art. 25 TEC | Art. 12 TEC |
| | Art. 26 TEC | Art. 28 TEC |
| | Art. 27 TEC | Art. 29 TEC |
| Art. III-152 | Art. 135 TEC | Art. 116 TEC |
| Art. III-153 | Art. 28, 29 TEC | Art. 30, 34 TEC |
| Art. III-154 | Art. 30 TEC | Art. 36 TEC |
| Art. III-155 | Art. 31 TEC | Art. 37 TEC |
| Art. III-156 | Art. 56 TEC | Art. 73b TEC |
| Art. III-157 | Art. 57 TEC | Art. 73c TEC |
| Art. III-158 | Art. 58 TEC | Art. 73d TEC |
| Art. III-159 | Art. 59 TEC | Art. 73f TEC |
| Art. III-160(*) | Art. 60 TEC | Art. 73g TEC |
| Art. III-161 | Art. 81 TEC | Art. 85 TEC |
| Art. III-162 | Art. 82 TEC | Art. 86 TEC |
| Art. III-163 | Art. 83 TEC | Art. 87 TEC |
| Art. III-164 | Art. 84 TEC | Art. 88 TEC |
| Art. III-165 | Art. 85 TEC | Art. 89 TEC |
| Art. III-166 | Art. 86 TEC | Art. 90 TEC |
| Art. III-167 | Art. 87 TEC | Art. 92 TEC |
| Art. III-168 | Art. 88 TEC | Art. 93 TEC |
| Art. III-169 | Art. 89 TEC | Art. 94 TEC |
| Art. III-170 | Art. 90 - 92 TEC | Art. 95, 96, 98 TEC |
| Art. III-171 | Art. 93 TEC | Art. 99 TEC |
| Art. III-172 | Art. 95 TEC | Art. 100a TEC |
| Art. III-173 | Art. 94 TEC | Art. 100 TEC |
| Art. III-174 | Art. 96 TEC | Art. 101 TEC |
| Art. III-175 | Art. 97 TEC | Art. 102 TEC |
| Art. III-176* | | |
| Art. III-177 | Art. 4 TEC | Art. 3a TEC |
| Art. III-178 | Art. 98 TEC | Art. 102a TEC |
| Art. III-179 | Art. 99 TEC | Art. 103 TEC |
| Art. III-180 | Art. 100 TEC | Art. 103a TEC |
| Art. III-181 | Art. 101 TEC | Art. 104 TEC |
| Art. III-182 | Art. 102 TEC | Art. 104a TEC |
| Art. III-183 | Art. 103 TEC | Art. 104b TEC |
| Art. III-184 | Art. 104 TEC | Art. 104c TEC |
| Art. III-185 | Art. 105 TEC | Art. 105 TEC |
| Art. III-186 | Art. 106 TEC | Art. 105a TEC |

| | | |
|---|---|---|
| Art. III-187 | Art. 107 TEC | Art. 106 TEC |
| Art. III-188 | Art. 108 TEC | Art. 107 TEC |
| Art. III-189 | Art. 109 TEC | Art. 108 TEC |
| Art. III-190 | Art. 110 TEC | Art. 108a TEC |
| Art. III-191 | Art. 123(4) TEC | Art. 109(l) TEC |
| Art. III-192 | Art. 114(2-4) TEC | Art. 109c (2-4) TEC |
| Art. III-193 | Art. 115 TEC | Art. 109d TEC |
| Art. III-194* | | |
| Art. III-195* | | |
| Art. III-196* | | |
| Art. III-197 | Art. 122(1), (3-5) TEC | Art 109k (1), (3-5) TEC |
| Art. III-198 | Art. 121(1-2), 122(2), 123(5) TEC | Art. 109j (1), 109k(2), 109 l (5) TEC |
| Art. III-199 | Art. 123(3), 117(2) TEC | Art. 109f (2), 109 l (3) TEC |
| Art. III-200 | Art. 124(1) TEC | Art. 109m(1) TEC |
| Art. III-201 | Art. 119 TEC | Art 109h TEC |
| Art. III-202 | Art. 120 TEC | Art. 109i TEC |
| Art. III-203 | Art. 125 TEC | Art. 109n TEC |
| Art. III-204 | Art. 126 TEC | Art. 109o TEC |
| Art. III-205 | Art. 127 TEC | Art. 109p TEC |
| Art. III-206 | Art. 128 TEC | Art. 109q TEC |
| Art. III-207 | Art. 129 TEC | Art. 109r TEC |
| Art. III-208 | Art. 130 TEC | Art. 109s TEC |
| Art. III-209 | Art. 136 TEC | Art. 117 TEC |
| Art. III-210 | Art. 137 TEC | Art. 118 TEC |
| Art. III-211 | Art. 138 TEC | Art. 118a TEC |
| Art. III-212 | Art. 139 TEC | Art. 118b TEC |
| Art. III-213 | Art. 140 TEC | Art. 118c TEC |
| Art. III-214 | Art. 141 TEC | Art. 119 TEC |
| Art. III-215 | Art. 142 TEC | Art. 119a TEC |
| Art. III-216 | Art. 143 TEC | Art. 120 TEC |
| Art. III-217 | Art. 144 TEC | Art. 121 TEC |
| Art. III-218 | Art. 145 TEC | Art. 122 TEC |
| Art. III-219 | Art. 146 - 148 TEC | Art. 123 - 125 TEC |
| Art. III-220 | Art. 158 TEC | Art. 130a TEC |
| Art. III-221 | Art. 159 TEC | Art. 130b TEC |
| Art. III-222 | Art. 160 TEC | Art. 130c TEC |
| Art. III-223 | Art. 161 TEC | Art. 130d TEC |

| | | |
|---|---|---|
| Art. III-224 | Art. 162 TEC | Art. 130e TEC |
| Art. III-225 | Art. 32(1, 2.sentence) TEC | Art. 38 TEC |
| Art. III-226 | Art. 32 TEC | Art. K.4 TEC |
| Art. III-227 | Art. 33 TEC | Art. K.5 TEC |
| Art. III-228 | Art. 34 TEC | Art. K.6 TEC |
| Art. III-229 | Art. 35 TEC | Art. K.7 TEC |
| Art. III-230 | Art. 36 TEC | Art. K.8 TEC |
| Art. III-231 | Art. 37 TEC | Art. K.9 TEC |
| Art. III-232 | Art. 38 TEC | Art. K.10 TEC |
| Art. III-233 | Art. 174 TEC | Art. 130r TEC |
| Art. III-234 | Art. 175, 176 TEC | Art. 130s, 130t TEC |
| Art. III-235 | Art. 153(1, 3-5) TEC | Art. 129a TEC |
| Art. III-236 | Art. 70, 71 TEC | Art. 74, 75 TEC |
| Art. III-237 | Art. 72 TEC | Art. 76 TEC |
| Art. III-238 | Art. 73 TEC | Art. 77 TEC |
| Art. III-239 | Art. 74 TEC | Art. 78 TEC |
| Art. III-240 | Art. 75 TEC | Art. 79 TEC |
| Art. III-241 | Art. 76 TEC | Art. 80 TEC |
| Art. III-242 | Art. 77 TEC | Art. 81 TEC |
| Art. III-243 | Art. 78 TEC | Art. 82 TEC |
| Art. III-244 | Art. 79 TEC | Art 83 TEC |
| Art. III-245 | Art. 80 TEC | Art. 84 TEC |
| Art. III-246 | Art. 154 TEC | Art. 129b TEC |
| Art. III-247 | Art. 155, 156 TEC | Art. 129c, 129d TEC |
| Art. III-248 | Art. 163 TEC | Art. 130f TEC |
| Art. III-249 | Art. 164 TEC | Art. 130g TEC |
| Art. III-250 | Art. 165 TEC | Art. 130h TEC |
| Art. III-251 | Art. 166 TEC | Art. 130i TEC |
| Art. III-252 | Art. 167 - 170, 172 (2.sentence) TEC | Art. 130j, 130k, 130l, 130m, 130o 2. TEC |
| Art. III-253 | Art. 171, 172 (1.sentence) TEC | Art. 130n, 130o TEC |
| Art. III-254* | | |
| Art. III-255 | Art. 173 TEC | Art. 173 TEC |
| Art. III-256(*) | | |
| Art. III-257 | Art. 29 TEU, 61TEC | Art. K.1 TEU, 73i TEC |
| Art. III-258* | | |
| Art. III-259* | | |

| | | |
|---|---|---|
| Art. III-260* | | |
| Art. III-261 | Art. 36 TEU | Art. K.8 TEU |
| Art. III-262 | Art. 33 TEU, 64(1) TEC | Art. K.5 TEU, 73 l(1) TEC |
| Art. III-263 | Art. 66 TEC | Art. 73n TEC |
| Art. III-264* | | |
| Art. III-265 | Art. 62 TEC | Art. 73j TEC |
| Art. III-266 | Art. 63 (points 1-2), 64(2) TEC | Art. 73k (1-2), 73 l TEC |
| Art. III-267 | Art. 63 (points 3-4) TEC | Art. 73k (3-4) TEC |
| Art. III-268* | | |
| Art. III-269 | Art. 65 TEC | Art. 73m TEC |
| Art. III-270 | Art. 31(1) (a - d) TEU | Art. K.3 TEU |
| Art. III-271(*) | Art. 31(1) (e) TEU | Art. K.3 TEU |
| Art. III-272* | | |
| Art. III-273 | Art. 31(2) TEU | Art. K.3 TEU |
| Art. III-274* | | |
| Art. III-275 | Art. 30(1) TEU | Art. K.2 TEU |
| Art. III-276 | Art. 30(2) TEU | Art. K.2 TEU |
| Art. III-277 | Art. 32 TEU | Art. K.4 TEU |
| Art. III-278 | Art. 152 TEC | Art. 129 TEC |
| Art. III-279 | Art. 157 TEC | Art. 130 TEC |
| Art. III-280 | Art. 151 TEC | Art. 128 TEC |
| Art. III-281 * | | |
| Art. III-282 | Art. 149 TEC | Art. 126 TEC |
| Art. III-283 | Art. 150 TEC | Art. 127 TEC |
| Art. III-284* | | |
| Art. III-285* | | |
| Title IV | | |
| Art. III-286 | Art. 182, 188 TEC | Art. 131, 136a TEC |
| Art. III-287 | Art. 183 TEC | Art. 132 TEC |
| Art. III-288 | Art. 184 TEC | Art. 133 TEC |
| Art. III-289 | Art. 185 TEC | Art. 134 TEC |
| Art. III-290 | Art. 186 TEC | Art. 135 TEC |
| Art. III-291 | Art. 187 TEC | Art. 136 TEC |
| Title V | | |
| Art. III-292 | Art. 3, (2. sentence), 11 TEU | Art. C, J (1) TEU |
| Art. III-293 | Art. 13 (2) TEU | Art. J.3 (1) TEU |
| Art. III-294 | Art. 11, 12 TEU | Art. J.1, J.2 TEU |

| | | |
|---|---|---|
| Art. III-295 | Art. 13 TEU | Art. J.3 TEU |
| Art. III-296 | Art. 18(1-2), 26 TEU | Art. J.8, J.16 TEU |
| Art. III-297 | Art. 14 TEU | Art. J.4 TEU |
| Art. III-298 | Art. 15 TEU | Art. J.5 TEU |
| Art. III-299 | Art. 22 TEU | Art. J.12 TEU |
| Art. III-300 | Art. 23 TUE | Art. J.13 TEU |
| Art. III-301 * | | |
| Art. III-302 | Art. 18(5) TEU | Art. J.8 TEU |
| Art. III-303 | Art. 24 TEU | Art. J.14 TEU |
| Art. III-304 | Art. 21 TEU | Art. J.11 TEU |
| Art. III-305 | Art. 19 TEU | Art. J.9 TEU |
| Art. III-306 | Art. 20 TEU | Art. J.20 TEU |
| Art. III-307 | Art. 25 TEU | Art. J.15 TEU |
| Art. III-308 | Art. 47 TEU | Art. M TEU |
| Art. III-309 | Art. 17(2) TEU | Art. J.7 TEU |
| Art. III-310* | | |
| Art. III-311 * | | |
| Art. III-312* | | |
| Art. III-313 | Art. 28(2, 5) TEU | Art. J.18 TEU |
| Art. III-314 | Art. 131 TEC | Art. 110 TEC |
| Art. III-315 | Art. 133 TEC | Art. 113 TEC |
| Art. III-316 | Art. 177 TEC | Art. 130u TEC |
| Art. III-317 | Art. 179, 181 TEC | Art. 130w, 130y TEC |
| Art. III-318 | Art. 180, 181 TEC | Art. 130x, 130 y TEC |
| Art. III-319 | Art. 181a TEC | Art. 130y TEC |
| Art. III-320* | | |
| Art. III-321 * | | |
| Art. III-322 | Art. 301 TEC | Art. 228a TEC |
| Art. III-323 | Art. 24 TEU | Art. J.14 TEU |
| | Art. 300(7) TEC | Art. 228 TEC |
| Art. III-324 | Art. 310 TEC | Art. 238 TEC |
| Art. III-325(*) | Art. 300 TEC, 24 TEU | Art. 228 TEC, J.14 TEU |
| Art. III-326 | Art. 111(1-3, 5) TEC | Art. 109 (1-3, 5) TEC |
| Art. III-327 | Art. 302 - 304 TEC | Art. 229 – 231 TEC |
| Art. III-328* | | |
| Art. III-329* | | |
| Title VI | | |
| Art. III-330 | Art. 190(4-5) TEC | Art. 253 TEC |

| | | |
|---|---|---|
| Art. III-331 | Art. 191 (point 2) TEC | Art. 138a TEC |
| Art. III-332 | Art. 192 TEC | Art. 138b TEC |
| Art. III-333 | Art. 193 TEC | Art. 138c TEC |
| Art. III-334 | Art. 194 TEC | Art. 138d TEC |
| Art. III-335 | Art. 195 TEC | Art. 138e TEC |
| Art. III-336 | Art. 196 TEC | Art. 139 TEC |
| Art. III-337 | Art. 197, 200 TEC | Art. 140, 143 TEC |
| Art. III-338 | Art. 198 TEC | Art. 141 TEC |
| Art. III-339 | Art. 199 TEC | Art. 142 TEC |
| Art. III-340 | Art. 201 TEC | Art. 144 TEC |
| Art. III-341 * | | |
| Art. III-342 | Art. 204 TEC | Art. 147 TEC |
| Art. III-343 | Art. 205(1, 3), 206 TEC | Art. 148, 150 TEC |
| Art. III-344 | Art. 207 TEC | Art. 151 TEC |
| Art. III-345 | Art. 208 TEC | Art. 152 TEC |
| Art. III-346 | Art. 209 TEC | Art. 153 TEC |
| Art. III-347 | Art. 213(2) TEC | Art. 157 (2) TEC |
| Art. III-348 | Art. 215 TEC | Art. 159 TEC |
| Art. III-349 | Art. 216 TEC | Art. 160 TEC |
| Art. III-350 | Art. 217 TEC | Art. 161 TEC |
| Art. III-351 | Art. 219 TEC | Art. 163 TEC |
| Art. III-352 | Art. 218(2), 212 TEC | Art. 156, 162 (2) TEC |
| Art. III-353 | Art. 221 TEC | Art. 165 TEC |
| Art. III-354 | Art. 222 TEC | Art. 222 TEC |
| Art. III-355 | Art. 223 TEC | Art. 167 TEC |
| Art. III-356 | Art. 224 TEC | Art. 168 TEC |
| Art. III-357* | | |
| Art. III-358 | Art. 225 TEC | Art. 168a TEC |
| Art. III-359 | Art. 220 (2. sentence), 225a TEC | Art. 164 TEC |
| Art. III-360 | Art. 226 TEC | Art. 169 TEC |
| Art. III-361 | Art. 227 TEC | Art. 170 TEC |
| Art. III-362 | Art. 228 TEC | Art. 171 TEC |
| Art. III-363 | Art. 229 TEC | Art. 172 TEC |
| Art. III-364 | Art. 229a TEC | |
| Art. III-365 | Art. 230 TEC | Art. 173 TEC |
| Art. III-366 | Art. 231 TEC | Art. 174 TEC |
| Art. III-367 | Art. 232 TEC | Art. 175 TEC |

| | | |
|---|---|---|
| Art. III-368 | Art. 233 TEC | Art. 176 TEC |
| Art. III-369 | Art. 234 TEC | Art. 177 TEC |
| Art. III-370 | Art. 235 TEC | Art. 178 TEC |
| Art. III-371 | Art. 46 e TEU | Art. L TEU |
| Art. III-372 | Art. 236 TEC | Art. 179 TEC |
| Art. III-373 | Art. 237 TEC | Art. 180 TEC |
| Art. III-374 | Art. 238 TEC | Art. 181 TEC |
| Art. III-375 | Art. 240, 292, 239 TEC | Art. 182, 183, 219 TEC |
| Art. III-376 | Art. 46 TEU | Art. L, M TEU |
| Art. III-377 | Art. 35(5) TEU | Art. K.7 TEU |
| Art. III-378 | Art. 241 TEC | Art. 184 TEC |
| Art. III-379 | Art. 242, 243 TEC | Art. 185, 186 TEC |
| Art. III-3 80 | Art. 244 TEC | Art. 244 TEC |
| Art. III-3 81 | Art. 245 TEC | Art. 245 TEC |
| Art. III-382 | Art. 112 TEC | Art. 109a TEC |
| Art. III-383 | Art. 113 TEC | Art. 109b TEC |
| Art. III-384 | Art. 248 TEC | Art. 188c TEC |
| Art. III-385 | Art. 247(2-7) TEC | Art. 188b (2-7) TEC |
| Art. III-386 | Art. 263 TEC | Art. 198a TEC |
| Art. III-387 | Art. 264 TEC | Art. 198b TEC |
| Art. III-388 | Art. 265 TEC | Art. 198c TEC |
| Art. III-389 | Art. 258 (1-2) TEC | Art. 194 TEC |
| Art. III-390 | Art. 259 TEC | Art. 195 TEC |
| Art. III-391 | Art. 260 TEC | Art. 196 TEC |
| Art. III-392 | Art. 262 TEC | Art. 198 TEC |
| Art. III-393 | Art. 266 TEC | Art. 198d TEC |
| Art. III-394 | Art. 267 TEC | Art. 198e TEC |
| Art. III-395 | Art. 250 TEC | Art. 189a TEC |
| Art. III-396 | Art. 251 TEC | Art. 189b TEC |
| Art. III-397 (*) | Art. 218(1) TEC | Art. 162(1) TEC |
| Art. III-398* | | |
| Art. III-399 | Art. 255 TEC | Art. 191a TEC |
| Art. III-400 | Art. 210, 247(8), 258 (4. sentence) TEC | Art. 154, 188b (8), 194 TEC |
| Art. III-401 | Art. 256 TEC | Art. 192 TEC |
| Art. III-402* | | |
| Art. III-403 | Art. 272(1) TEC | Art. 203 TEC |
| Art. III-404 | Art. 272 TEC | Art. 203 TEC |

| | | |
|---|---|---|
| Art. III-405 | Art. 273 TEC | Art. 204 TEC |
| Art. III-406 | Art. 271 TEC | Art. 202 TEC |
| Art. III-407 | Art. 274 TEC | Art. 205 TEC |
| Art. III-408 | Art. 275 TEC | Art. 205a TEC |
| Art. III-409 | Art. 276 TEC | Art. 206 TEC |
| Art. III-410 | Art. 277 TEC | Art. 207 TEC |
| Art. III-411 | Art. 278 TEC | Art. 208 TEC |
| Art. III-412 | Art. 279 TEC | Art. 209 TEC |
| Art. III-413 * | | |
| Art. III-414* | | |
| Art. III-415 | Art. 280 TEC | Art. 209a TEC |
| Art. III-416 | Art. 43 b, c, e, f TEU, 11(3) TEC | Art. K.15, J.1 TEU |
| Art. III-417 | Art. 43 h, 44(2, last sentence) TEU | Art. K.15, K.16 TEU |
| Art. III-418(*) | Art. 43 b TEU | Art. K.15 TEU |
| Art. III-419 | Art. 40a, 27 c TEU, 11(1-2) TEC | ** 5a TEC |
| Art. III-420 | Art. 40b, 27e TEU, 11 a TEC | |
| Art. III-421 | Art. 44a TEU | |
| Art. III-422* | | |
| Art. III-423 | Art. 45 TEU | Art. K.17 TEU |
| Title VII | | |
| Art. III-424 | Art. 299(2), (2. sentence, 3) TEC | Art. 227 TEC |
| Art. III-425 | Art. 295 TEC | Art. 222 TEC |
| Art. III-426 | Art. 282 TEC | Art. 211 TEC |
| Art. III-427 | Art. 283 TEC | Art. 212 TEC |
| Art. III-428 | Art. 284 TEC | Art. 213 TEC |
| Art. III-429 | Art. 285 TEC | Art. 213a TEC |
| Art. III-430 | Art. 287 TEC | Art. 214 TEC |
| Art. III-431 | Art. 288 TEC | Art. 215 TEC |
| Art. III-432 | Art. 289 TEC | Art. 216 TEC |
| Art. III-433 | Art. 290 TEC | Art. 217 TEC |
| Art. III-434 | Art. 291 TEC | Art. 218 TEC |
| Art. III-435 | Art. 307 TEC | Art. 234 TEC |
| Art. III-436 | Art. 296 TEC | Art. 223 TEC |
| | | |
| **Part IV** | | |

| | | |
|---|---|---|
| Art. IV-437* | | |
| Art. IV-438* | | |
| Art. IV-439* | | |
| Art. IV-440 | Art. 299(1, 3-6) TEC | Art. 227 TEC |
| Art. IV-441 | Art. 306 TEC | Art. 233 TEC |
| Art. IV-442 | Art. 311 TEC | Art. 239 TEC |
| Art. IV-443 | Art. 48 TEU | Art. 39 TEC |
| Art. IV-444* | | |
| Art. IV-445 * | | |
| Art. IV-446 | Art. 51 TEU, 312 TEC | Art. Q TEU, 240 TEC |
| Art. IV-447 | Art. 52 TEU, 313 TEC | Art. R TEU, 247 TEC |
| Art. IV-448 | Art. 53 TEU, 314 TEC | Art. S TEU, 248 TEC |

ooo000ooo

## Lisbon Treaty (info force 1 January 2009 if ratified by all Members)

Consolidated unofficial versions - with amendments from the Lisbon Treaty - on the Treaty on European Union and the Treaty on the Functioning of the European Union are the published in Official Journal of the European Union C115, 9 May 2008 pp. 0001-0360. An overview of the documents is found at <http://eur-lex.europa.eu/JOHtml.do?uri=OJ:C:2008:115:SOM:EN:HTML> (visited July 2008).

Old consolidated versions are published in OJ C321 E, 29.12.2006 p. 0001-0331.

The text of the Lisbon Treaty, with the amendment text for the two treaties, is published in OJ C06, 17.12.2007 p. 0001-0145.

The following tables of equivalences as referred to in Article 5[1] of the Treaty of Lisbon.are published in Official Journal C306, 17.12.2007 pp. 202-229.

---

[1] Article 5 paragraph 1 [US: sub- section one] states: "The articles, sections, chapters, titles and parts of the Treaty on European Union and of the Treaty establishing the European Community, as amended by this Treaty, shall be renumbered in accordance with the tables of equivalences set out in the Annex to this treaty, and which from an integral part of this Treaty."

Note, that text in "old numbering" not necessarily is the same in the Lisbon Treaty text.

A table has also been published in C115, 9 May 2008 pp. 0361-0388, however, the original centre column, which set out the intermediate numbering as used in the Lisbon Treaty, has been omitted.

*Lisbon Treaty -> Renumbering of Treaty on European Union (TEU)*

OJ C306, 17.12.2007 p. 0202-0207.

| Old Consolidated version | Lisbon Treaty text | New Consolidated version |
|---|---|---|
| Part I | | |
| Title I – COMMON PROVISIONS | Title I – COMMON PROVISIONS | Title I – COMMON PROVISIONS |
| Art. 1 | Art. 1 | Art. 1 |
| | Art. 1a | Art. 2 |
| Art. 2 | Art. 3 | Art. 3 |
| Art. 3 (repealed)[1] | | |
| | Art. 3a | Art. 4 |
| | Art 3b[2] | Art 5 |
| Art. 4 (repealed)[3] | | |
| Art. 5 (repealed)[4] | | |
| Art. 6 | Art. 6 | Art. 6 |
| Art. 7 | Art. 7 | Art. 7 |
| | Art. 7a | Art. 8 |
| Title II - PROVISIONS | Title II - PROVISIONS ON | Title II - PROVISIONS ON |

---

[1] Replaced, in substance, by Article 2 F (renumbered 7) of the Treaty on the Functioning of the European Union ("TFEU") and by Articles 9(1) and 10 A (renumbered 13(1) and 21, paragraph 3, second subparagraph) of the Treaty on European Union ("TEU").

[2] Replaces Article 5 of the Treaty establishing the European Community ("TEC").

[3] Replaced, in substance, by Article 9 B (renumbered 15).

[4] Replaced, in substance, by Article 9 paragraph (renumbered 13, paragraph 2).

| AMENDING THE TREATY ESTABLISHING THE EURO-PEAN ECONOMIC COMMU-NITY WITH A VIEW TO ES-TABLISHING THE EURO-PEAN COMMUNITY | DEMOCRATIC PRINCI-PLES | DEMOCRATIC PRINCI-PLES |
|---|---|---|
| Art. 8 (repealed)[5] | Art. 8 | Art. 9 |
| | Art. 8 A[6] | Art. 10 |
| | Art. 8 B | Art. 11 |
| | Art. 8 C | Art. 12 |
| **Title III - PROVISIONS AMENDING THE TREATY ESTABLISHING THE EURO-PEAN COAL AND STEEL COMMUNITY** | **Title III - PROVISIONS ON THE INSTITUTIONS** | **Title III - PROVISIONS ON THE INSTITUTIONS** |
| Art. 9 (repealed)[7] | Art. 9 | Art. 13 |
| | Art. 9 A[8] | Art. 14 |
| | Art. 9 B[9] | Art. 15 |
| | Art. 9 C[10] | Art. 16 |
| | Art. 9 D[11] | Art. 17 |

[5] Article 8 TEU, which was in force until the entry into force of the Treaty of Lisbon (hereinafter "current"), amended the TEC. Those amendments are incorporated into the latter Treaty and Article 8 is repealed. Its number is used to insert a new provision.

[6] Paragraph 4 replaces, in substance, the first subparagraph of Article 191 TEC.

[7] The current Article 9 TEU amended the Treaty establishing the European Coal and Steel Community. This latter expired on 23 July 2002. Article 9 is repealed and the number thereof is used to insert another provision.

[8] Paragraphs 1 and 2 replace, in substance, Article 189 TEC; paragraphs 1 to 3 replace, in substance, paragraphs 1 to 3 of Article 190 TEC; paragraph 1 replaces, in substance, the first subparagraph of Article 192 TEC; paragraph 4 replaces, in substance, the first subparagraph of Article 197 TEC.

[9] Replaces, in substance, Article 4.

[10] Paragraph 1 replaces, in substance, the first and second indents of Article 202 TEC; paragraphs 2 and 9 replace, in substance, Article 203 TEC; paragraphs 4 and 5 replace, in substance, paragraphs 2 and 4 of Article 205 TEC.

| | Art. 9 E | Art. 18 |
|---|---|---|
| | Art. 9 F[12] | Art. 19 |
| **Title IV - PROVISIONS AMENDING THE TREATY ESTABLISHING THE EUROPEAN ATOMIC ENERGY COMMUNITY** | **Title IV - PROVISIONS ON ENHANCED COOPERATION** | **Title IV - PROVISIONS ON ENHANCED COOPERATION** |
| Art. 10 (repealed)[13]<br>Art. 27 a to 27 e (replaced)<br>Art. 40 to 40 b (replaced)<br>Art. 43 to 45 (replaced) | Art. 10[14] | Art. 20 |
| **Title V - PROVISIONS ON A COMMON FOREIGN AND SECURITY POLICY** | **Title V - GENERAL PROVISIONS ON THE UNION'S EXTERNAL ACTION AND SPECIFIC PROVISIONS ON THE COMMON FOREIGN AND SECURITY POLICY** | **Title V - GENERAL PROVISIONS ON THE UNION'S EXTERNAL ACTION AND SPECIFIC PROVISIONS ON THE COMMON FOREIGN AND SECURITY POLICY** |
| | **Chapter 1 - General provisions on the Union's external action** | **Chapter 1 - General provisions on the Union's external action** |
| | Art. 10 A | Art. 21 |
| | Art. 10 B | Art. 22 |
| | **Chapter 2 - Specific provisions on the common foreign and security policy** | **Chapter 2 - Specific provisions on the common foreign and security policy** |

[11] Paragraph 1 replaces, in substance, Article 211 TEC; paragraphs 3 and 7 replace, in substance, Article 214 TEC; paragraph 6 replaces, in substance, paragraphs 1, 3 and 4 of Article 217 TEC.

[12] Replaces, in substance, Article 220 TEC; the second subparagraph of paragraph 2 replaces, in substance, the first subparagraph of Article 221 TEC.

[13] The current Article 10 TEU amended the Treaty establishing the European Atomic Energy Community. Those amendments are incorporated into the Treaty of Lisbon. Article 10 is repealed and the number thereof is used to insert another provision.

[14] Also replaces Articles 11 and 11a TEC.

|  | Section 1 - Common provisions | Section 1 - Common provisions |
| --- | --- | --- |
|  | Art. 10 C | Art. 23 |
| Art. 11 | Art. 11 | Art. 24 |
| Art. 12 | Art. 12 | Art. 25 |
| Art. 13 | Art. 12 | Art. 26 |
|  | Art. 13a | Art. 27 |
| Art. 14 | Art. 14 | Art. 28 |
| Art. 15 | Art. 15 | Art. 29 |
| Art. 22 (moved) | Art. 15a | Art. 30 |
| Art. 23 (moved) | Art. 15b | Art. 31 |
| Art. 16 | Art. 16 | Art. 32 |
| Art. 17 (moved) | Art. 28 A | Art. 42 |
| Art. 18 | Art. 18 | Art. 33 |
| Art. 19 | Art. 19 | Art. 34 |
| Art. 20 | Art. 20 | Art. 35 |
| Art. 21 | Art. 21 | Art. 36 |
| Art. 22 (moved) | Art. 15a | Art. 30 |
| Art. 23 (moved) | Art. 15b | Art. 31 |
| Art. 24 | Art. 24 | Art. 37 |
| Art. 25 | Art. 25 | Art. 38 |
|  | Art. 25a | Art. 39 |
| Art. 47 (moved) | Art. 25b | Art. 40 |
| Art. 26 (repealed) |  |  |
| Art. 27 (repealed) |  |  |
| Art. 27a (replaced)[15] | Art. 10 | Art. 20 |
| Art. 27b (replaced)[15] | Art. 10 | Art. 20 |
| Art. 27c (replaced)[15] | Art. 10 | Art. 20 |
| Art. 27d (replaced)[15] | Art. 10 | Art. 20 |
| Art. 27e (replaced)[15] | Art. 10 | Art. 20 |
| Art. 28 | Art. 28 | Art. 41 |

[15] The current Articles 27 A to 27 E, on enhanced cooperation, are also replaced by Articles 280 A to 280 I (renumbered 326 to 334) TFEU.

| | Section 2 - Provisions on the common security and defence policy | Section 2 - Provisions on the common security and defence policy |
|---|---|---|
| Art. 17 (moved) | Art. 28 A | Art. 42 |
| | Art. 28 B | Art. 43 |
| | Art. 28 C | Art. 44 |
| | Art. 28 D | Art. 45 |
| | Art. 28 E | Art. 46 |
| **Title VI - PROVISIONS ON POLICE AND JUDICIAL COOPERATION IN CRIMINAL MATTERS (repealed)**[16] | | |
| Art. 29 (replaced)[17] | | |
| Art. 30 (replaced)[18] | | |
| Art. 31 (replaced)[19] | | |
| Art. 32 (replaced)[20] | | |
| Art. 33 (replaced)[21] | | |
| Art. 34 (repealed) | | |
| Art. 35 (repealed) | | |
| Art. 36 (replaced)[22] | | |
| Art. 37 (repealed) | | |
| Art. 38 (repealed) | | |
| Art. 39 (repealed) | | |
| Art. 40 (replaced)[23] | Art. 10 | Art. 20 |

[16] The current provisions of Title VI of the TEU, on police and judicial cooperation in criminal matters, are replaced by the provisions of Chapters 1, 5 and 5 of Title IV of Part Three of the TFEU.

[17] Replaced by Article 61 (renumbered 67) TFEU.

[18] Replaced by Articles 69 F and 69 G (renumbered 87 and 88) TFEU.

[19] Replaced by Articles 69 A, 69 B and 69 D (renumbered 82, 83 and 85) TFEU.

[20] Replaced by Article 69 (renumbered 89) TFEU.

[21] Replaced by Article 61 E (renumbered 72) TFEU.

[22] Replaced by Article 61 D (renumbered 71) TFEU.

[23] The current Articles 40 to 40 B TEU, on enhanced cooperation, are also replaced by Articles 280 A to 280 I (renumbered 326 to 334) TFEU.

| | | |
|---|---|---|
| Art. 40 A (replaced)[23] | Art. 10 | Art. 20 |
| Art. 40 B (replaced)[23] | Art. 10 | Art. 20 |
| Art. 41 (repealed) | | |
| Art. 42 (repealed) | | |
| **Title VII - PROVISIONS ON ENHANCED COOPERATION (replaced)[24]** | **Title IV - PROVISIONS ON ENHANCED COOPERA-TION** | **Title IV - PROVISIONS ON ENHANCED COOPERA-TION** |
| Art. 43 (replaced)[24] | Art. 10 | Art. 20 |
| Art. 43 A (replaced)[24] | Art. 10 | Art. 20 |
| Art. 43 B (replaced)[24] | Art. 10 | Art. 20 |
| Art. 44 (replaced)[24] | Art. 10 | Art. 20 |
| Art. 44 A (replaced)[24] | Art. 10 | Art. 20 |
| Art. 45 (replaced)[24] | Art. 10 | Art. 20 |
| **Title VIII - FINAL PROVI-SIONS** | **Title VI - FINAL PROVI-SIONS** | **Title VI - FINAL PROVI-SIONS** |
| Art. 46 (repealed) | | |
| | Art. 46a | Art. 47 |
| Art. 47 (replaced) | Art. 25b | Art. 40 |
| Art. 48 | Art. 48 | Art. 48 |
| Art. 49 | Art. 49 | Art. 49 |
| | Art. 49 A | Art. 50 |
| | Art. 49 B | Art. 51 |
| | Art. 49 C | Art. 52 |
| Art. 50 (repealed) | | |
| Art. 51 | Art. 51 | Art. 53 |
| Art. 52 | Art. 52 | Art. 54 |
| Art. 53 | Art. 53 | Art. 55 |

[24] The current Articles 43 to 45 and Title VII of the TEU, on enhanced cooperation, are also replaced by Articles 280 A to 280 I (renumbered 326 to 334) TFEU.

*Lisbon Treaty -> Treaty on the Functioning of the European Union (TFEU)*

Treaty on the Functioning of the European Union (TFEU) - The Lisbon Treaty of 2007's rename of The Treaty of Rome of 25 March 1957 = Treaty establishing the European Economic Community (EEC into force on 1 January 1958), which by the Maastricht Treaty of 1993 was renamed the Treaty establishing the European Community (TEC).

OJ C306, 17.12.2007 p. 0207-0229.

| Old Consolidated version | Lisbon Treaty text | New Consolidated version |
|---|---|---|
| Part I - PRINCIPLES | Part I - PRINCIPLES | Part I - PRINCIPLES |
| Art. 1 (repealed) | | |
| | Art. 1a | Art. 1 |
| Art. 2 (repealed)[1] | | |
| | Title I - Categories and areas of union competence | Title I - Categories and areas of union competence |
| | Art. 2 A | Art. 2 |
| | Art. 2 B | Art. 3 |
| | Art. 2 C | Art. 4 |
| | Art. 2 D | Art. 5 |
| | Art. 2 E | Art. 6 |
| | Title II - Provisions having general application | Title II - Provisions having general application |
| | Art. 2 F | Art. 7 |
| Art. 3, paragraph 1 (repealed)[2] | | |
| Art. 3, paragraph | Art. 3 | Art. 8 |
| Art. 4 (moved) | Art. 97b | Art. 119 |

[1] Replaced, in substance, by Article 2 (renumbered 3) TEU.
[2] Replaced, in substance, by Articles 2 B to 2 E (renumbered 3 to 6) TFEU.

| | | |
|---|---|---|
| Art. 5 (replaced)[3] | | |
| | Art. 5a | Art. 9 |
| | Art. 5b | Art. 10 |
| Art. 6 | Art. 6 | Art. 11 |
| Art. 153, paragraph 2 (moved) | Art. 6a | Art. 12 |
| | Art. 6b[4] | Art. 13 |
| Art. 7 (repealed)[5] | | |
| Art. 8 (repealed)[6] | | |
| Art. 9 (repealed) | | |
| Art. 10 (repealed)[7] | | |
| Art. 11 (replaced)[8] | Art. 280 A to 280 I | Art. 326 to 334 |
| Art. 11 a (replaced)[32] | Art. 280 A to 280 I | Art. 326 to 334 |
| Art. 12 (repealed) | Art. 16 D | Art. 18 |
| Art. 13 (moved) | Art. 16 E | Art. 19 |
| Art. 14 (moved) | Art. 22a | Art. 26 |
| Art. 15 (moved) | Art. 22b | Art. 27 |
| Art. 16 | Art. 16 | Art. 14 |
| Art. 255 (moved) | Art. 16 A | Art. 15 |
| Art. 286 (moved) | Art. 16 B | Art. 16 |
| | Art. 16 C | Art. 17 |
| **Part II – CITIZENSHIP OF THE UNION** | **Part II - NON-DISCRIMINATION AND CITIZENSHIP OF THE UNION** | **Part II - NON-DISCRIMINATION AND CITIZENSHIP OF THE UNION** |
| Art. 12 (moved) | Art. 16 D | Art. 18 |
| Art. 13 (moved) | Art. 16 E | Art. 19 |
| Art. 17 | Art. 17 | Art. 20 |
| Art. 18 | Art. 18 | Art. 21 |

[3] Replaced, in substance, by Article 3b (renumbered 5) TEU.

[4] Insertion of the operative part of the protocol on protection and welfare of animals.

[5] Replaced, in substance, by Article 9 (renumbered 13) TEU.

[6] Replaced, in substance, by Article 9 (renumbered 13) TEU and Article 245a, paragraph 1 (renumbered 282, paragraph 1), TFEU.

[7] Replaced, in substance, by Article 3a, paragraph 3 (renumbered 4, paragraph 3), TEU.

[8] Also replaced by Article 10 (renumbered 20) TEU.

| | | |
|---|---|---|
| Art. 19 | Art. 19 | Art. 22 |
| Art. 20 | Art. 20 | Art. 23 |
| Art. 21 | Art. 21 | Art. 24 |
| Art. 22 | Art. 22 | Art. 25 |
| **Part III – COMMUNITY POLICIES** | **Part III – POLICIES AND INTERNAL ACTIONS OF THE UNION** | **Part III – POLICIES AND INTERNAL ACTIONS OF THE UNION** |
| | Title I - The internal market | Title I - The internal market |
| Art. 14 (moved) | Art. 22a | Art. 26 |
| Art. 15 (moved) | Art. 22b | Art. 27 |
| **Title I - Free movement of goods** | **Title 1a - Free movement of goods** | **Title II - Free movement of goods** |
| Art. 23 | Art. 23 | Art. 28 |
| Art. 24 | Art. 24 | Art. 29 |
| **Chapter 1 - The customs union** | **Chapter 1 - The customs union** | **Chapter 1 - The customs union** |
| Art. 25 | Art. 25 | Art. 30 |
| Art. 26 | Art. 26 | Art. 31 |
| Art. 27 | Art. 27 | Art. 32 |
| Part Three, Title X, Customs cooperation (moved) | **Chapter 1a - Customs cooperation** | **Chapter 2 - Customs co-operation** |
| Art. 135 (moved) | Art. 27a | Art. 33 |
| **Chapter 2 - Prohibition of quantitative restrictions between Member States** | **Chapter 2 - Prohibition of quantitative restrictions between Member States** | **Chapter 3 - Prohibition of quantitative restrictions between Member States** |
| Art. 28 | Art. 28 | Art. 34 |
| Art. 29 | Art. 29 | Art. 35 |
| Art. 30 | Art. 30 | Art. 36 |
| Art. 31 | Art. 31 | Art. 37 |
| **Title II - Agriculture** | **Title II - Agriculture and fisheries** | **Title III - Agriculture and fisheries** |
| Art. 32 | Art. 32 | Art. 38 |
| Art. 33 | Art. 33 | Art. 39 |
| Art. 34 | Art. 34 | Art. 40 |
| Art. 35 | Art. 35 | Art. 41 |
| Art. 36 | Art. 36 | Art. 42 |
| Art. 37 | Art. 37 | Art. 43 |
| Art. 38 | Art. 38 | Art. 44 |

| Title III - Free movement of persons, services and capital | Title III - Free movement of persons, services and capital | Title IV - Free movement of persons, services and capital |
|---|---|---|
| Chapter 1 – Workers | Chapter 1 - Workers | Chapter 1 - Workers |
| Art. 39 | Art. 39 | Art. 45 |
| Art. 40 | Art. 40 | Art. 46 |
| Art. 41 | Art. 41 | Art. 47 |
| Art. 42 | Art. 42 | Art. 48 |
| Chapter 2 - Right of establishment | Chapter 2 - Right of establishment | Chapter 2 - Right of establishment |
| Art. 43 | Art. 43 | Art. 49 |
| Art. 44 | Art. 44 | Art. 50 |
| Art. 45 | Art. 45 | Art. 51 |
| Art. 46 | Art. 46 | Art. 52 |
| Art. 47 | Art. 47 | Art. 53 |
| Art. 48 | Art. 48 | Art. 54 |
| Art. 294 (moved) | Art. 48a | Art. 55 |
| Chapter 3 – Services | Chapter 3 - Services | Chapter 3 - Services |
| Art. 49 | Art. 49 | Art. 56 |
| Art. 50 | Art. 50 | Art. 57 |
| Art. 51 | Art. 51 | Art. 58 |
| Art. 52 | Art. 52 | Art. 59 |
| Art. 53 | Art. 53 | Art. 60 |
| Art. 54 | Art. 54 | Art. 61 |
| Art. 55 | Art. 55 | Art. 62 |
| Chapter 4 - Capital and payments | Chapter 4 - Capital and payments | Chapter 4 - Capital and payments |
| Art. 56 | Art. 56 | Art. 63 |
| Art. 57 | Art. 57 | Art. 64 |
| Art. 58 | Art. 58 | Art. 65 |
| Art. 59 | Art. 59 | Art. 66 |
| Art. 60 (moved) | Art. 61 H | Art. 75 |
| Title IV - Visas, asylum, | Title IV - Area of freedom, | Title V - Area of freedom, |

| immigration and other policies related to free movement of persons | security and justice | security and justice |
|---|---|---|
| | **Chapter 1 - General provisions** | **Chapter 1 - General provisions** |
| Art. 61 | Art. 61[9] | Art. 67 |
| | Art. 61 A | Art. 68 |
| | Art. 61 B | Art. 69 |
| | Art. 61 C | Art. 70 |
| | Art. 61 D[10] | Art. 71 |
| Art. 64, paragraph 1 (replaced) | Art. 61 E[11] | Art. 72 |
| | Art. 61 F | Art. 73 |
| Art. 66 (replaced) | Art. 61 G | Art. 74 |
| Art. 60 (moved) | Art. 61 H | Art. 75 |
| | Art. 61 I | Art. 76 |
| | **Chapter 2 - Policies on border checks, asylum and immigration** | **Chapter 2 - Policies on border checks, asylum and immigration** |
| Art. 62 | Art. 62 | Art. 77 |
| Art. 63, points 1 et 2, and Art. 64, paragraph 2[12] | Art. 63 | Art. 78 |
| Art. 63, points 3 and 4 | Art. 63a | Art. 79 |
| | Art. 63b | Art. 80 |
| Article 64, paragraph 1 (replaced) | Art. 61 E | Art. 72 |
| | **Chapter 3 - Judicial cooperation in civil matters** | **Chapter 3 - Judicial cooperation in civil matters** |
| Art. 65 | Art. 65 | Art. 81 |
| Art. 66 (replaced) | Art. 61 G | Art. 74 |

[9] Also replaces the current Article 29 TEU.
[10] Also replaces the current Article 36 TEU.
[11] Also replaces the current Article 33 TEU.
[12] Points 1 and 2 of Article 63 EC are replaced by paragraphs 1 and 2 of Article 78 TFEU, and paragraph 2 / of Article 64 is replaced by paragraph 3 of Article 78 TFEU.

| | | |
|---|---|---|
| Art. 67 (repealed) | | |
| Art. 68 (repealed) | | |
| Art. 69 (repealed) | | |
| | **Chapter 4 - Judicial co-operation in criminal matters** | **Chapter 4 - Judicial cooperation in criminal matters** |
| | Art. 69 A[13] | Art. 82 |
| | Art. 69 B[13] | Art. 83 |
| | Art. 69 C | Art. 84 |
| | Art. 69 D[13] | Art. 85 |
| | Art. 69 E | Art. 86 |
| | **Chapter 5 - Police cooperation** | **Chapter 5 - Police cooperation** |
| | Art. 69 F[14] | Art. 87 |
| | Art. 69 G[14] | Art. 88 |
| | Art. 69 H[15] | Art. 89 |
| **Title V - Transport** | **Title V - Transport** | **Title VI - Transport** |
| Art. 70 | Art. 70 | Art. 90 |
| Art. 71 | Art. 71 | Art. 91 |
| Art. 72 | Art. 72 | Art. 92 |
| Art. 73 | Art. 73 | Art. 93 |
| Art. 74 | Art. 74 | Art. 94 |
| Art. 75 | Art. 75 | Art. 95 |
| Art. 76 | Art. 76 | Art. 96 |
| Art. 77 | Art. 77 | Art. 97 |
| Art. 78 | Art. 78 | Art. 98 |
| Art. 79 | Art. 79 | Art. 99 |
| Art. 80 | Art. 80 | Art. 100 |
| **Title VI - Common rules on competition, taxation and** | **Title VI - Common rules on competition, taxation** | **Title VII - Common rules on competition, taxation** |

[13] Replaces the current Article 31 TEU.
[14] Replaces the current Article 30 TEU.
[15] Replaces the current Article 32 TEU.

360

| approximation of laws | and approximation of laws | and approximation of laws |
|---|---|---|
| **Chapter 1 - Rules on competition** | **Chapter 1 - Rules on competition** | **Chapter 1 - Rules on competition** |
| **Section 1 - Rules applying to undertakings** | **Section 1 - Rules applying to undertakings** | **Section 1 - Rules applying to undertakings** |
| Art. 81 | Art. 81 | Art. 101 |
| Art. 82 | Art. 82 | Art. 102 |
| Art. 83 | Art. 83 | Art. 103 |
| Art. 84 | Art. 84 | Art. 104 |
| Art. 85 | Art. 85 | Art. 105 |
| Art. 86 | Art. 86 | Art. 106 |
| **Section 2 - Aids granted by States** | **Section 2 - Aids granted by States** | **Section 2 - Aids granted by States** |
| Art. 87 | Art. 87 | Art. 107 |
| Art. 88 | Art. 88 | Art. 108 |
| Art. 89 | Art. 89 | Art. 109 |
| **Chapter 2 - Tax provisions** | **Chapter 2 - Tax provisions** | **Chapter 2 - Tax provisions** |
| Art. 90 | Art. 90 | Art. 110 |
| Art. 91 | Art. 91 | Art. 111 |
| Art. 92 | Art. 92 | Art. 112 |
| Art. 93 | Art. 113 | Art. 113 |
| **Chapter 3 - Approximation of laws** | **Chapter 3 - Approximation of laws** | **Chapter 3 - Approximation of laws** |
| Art. 95 (moved) | Art. 94 | Art. 114 |
| Art. 94 (moved) | Art. 95 | Art. 115 |
| Art. 96 | Art. 96 | Art. 116 |
| Art. 97 | Art. 97 | Art. 117 |
|  | Art. 97a | Art. 118 |
| **Title VII - Economic and monetary policy** | **Title VII - Economic and monetary policy** | **Title VIII - Economic and monetary policy** |
| Art. 4 (moved) | Art. 97b | Art. 119 |
| **Chapter 1 - Economic policy** | **Chapter 1 - Economic policy** | **Chapter 1 - Economic policy** |
| Art. 98 | Art. 98 | Art. 120 |
| Art. 99 | Art. 99 | Art. 121 |
| Art. 100 | Art. 100 | Art. 122 |
| Art. 101 | Art. 101 | Art. 123 |

361

| | | |
|---|---|---|
| Art. 102 | Art. 102 | Art. 124 |
| Art. 103 | Art. 103 | Art. 125 |
| Art. 104 | Art. 104 | Art. 126 |
| **Chapter 2 -Monetary policy** | **Chapter 2 - Monetary policy** | **Chapter 2 - Monetary policy** |
| Art. 105 | Art. 105 | Art. 127 |
| Art. 106 | Art. 106 | Art. 128 |
| Art. 107 | Art. 107 | Art. 129 |
| Art. 108 | Art. 108 | Art. 130 |
| Art. 109 | Art. 109 | Art. 131 |
| Art. 110 | Art. 110 | Art. 132 |
| Art. 111, paragraphs 1 to 3 and 5 (moved) | Art. 188 O | Art. 219 |
| Art. 111, paragraph 4 (moved) | Art. 115 C, paragraph 1 | Art. 138 |
| | Art. 111a | Art. 133 |
| **Chapter 3 - Institutional provisions** | **Chapter 3 - Institutional provisions** | **Chapter 3 - Institutional provisions** |
| Art. 112 (moved) | Art. 245b | Art. 283 |
| Art. 113 (moved) | Art. 245c | Art. 284 |
| Art. 114 | Art. 114 | Art. 134 |
| Art. 115 | Art. 115 | Art. 135 |
| | **Chapter 3a - Provisions specific to Member States whose currency is the euro** | **Chapter 4 - Provisions specific to Member States whose currency is the euro** |
| | Art. 115 A | Art. 136 |
| | Art. 115 B | Art. 137 |
| Art. 111, paragraph 4 (moved) | Art. 115 C | Art. 138 |
| **Chapter 4 - Transitional provisions** | **Chapter 4 - Transitional provisions** | **Chapter 5 - Transitional provisions** |
| Art. 116 (repealed) | | |
| | Art. 116a | Art. 139 |
| Art. 117, paragraphs 1, 2, sixth | | |

| | | |
|---|---|---|
| indent, and 3 to 9 (repealed) | | |
| Art. 117, paragraph 2, first five indents (moved) | Art. 118a, paragraph 2 | Art. 141, paragraph 2 |
| Art. 121, paragraph 1 (moved) <br> Art. 122, paragraph 2, second sentence (moved) <br> Art. 123, paragraph 5 (moved) | Art. 117a, first paragraph[16] <br> Art. 117a, second paragraph[17] <br> Art. 117a, third paragraph[18] | Art. 140 |
| Art. 118 (repealed) | | |
| Art.123, paragraph 3 (moved) <br> Art. 117, paragraph 2, first five indents (moved) | Art. 118a, paragraph 1[19] <br> Art. 118a, paragraph 2[20] | Art. 141 |
| Art. 124, paragraph 1 (moved) | Art. 118b | Art. 142 |
| Art. 119 | Art. 119 | Art. 143 |
| Art. 120 | Art. 120 | Art. 144 |
| Art. 121, paragraph 1 (moved) | Art. 117a, paragraph 1 | Art. 140, paragraph 1 |
| Art. 121, paragraphs 2 to 4 (repealed) | | |
| Art. 122, paragraphs 1, 2, first sentence, 3, 4, 5 and 6 (repealed) | | |
| Art. 122, paragraph 2, second sentence (moved) | Art. 117a, paragraph 2, first subparagraph | Art. 140, paragraph 2, first subparagraph |
| Art. 123, paragraphs 1, 2 and 4 (repealed) | | |
| Art. 123, paragraph 3 (moved) | Art. 118a, paragraph 1 | Art. 141, paragraph 1 |

[16] Article 117a, paragraph 1 (renumbered 140, paragraph 1) takes over the wording of paragraph 1 of Article 121.

[17] Article 117a, paragraph 2 (renumbered 140, paragraph 2) takes over the second sentence of paragraph 2 of Article 122.

[18] Article 117a, paragraph (renumbered 140, paragraph 3) takes over paragraph 5 of Article 123.

[19] Article 118a, paragraph 1 (renumbered 141, paragraph 1) takes over paragraph 3 of Article 123.

[20] Article 118a, paragraph 2 (renumbered 141, paragraph 2) takes over the first five indents of paragraph 2 of Article 117.

| Art. 123, paragraph 5 (moved) | Art. 1117a, paragraph 3 | Art. 140, paragraph 3 |
|---|---|---|
| Art. 124, paragraph 1 (moved) | Art. 118b | Art. 142 |
| Art. 124, paragraph 2 (repealed) | | |
| **Title VIII – Employment** | **Title VIII - Employment** | **Title IX - Employment** |
| Art. 125 | Art. 125 | Art. 145 |
| Art. 126 | Art. 126 | Art. 146 |
| Art. 127 | Art. 127 | Art. 147 |
| Art. 128 | Art. 128 | Art. 148 |
| Art. 129 | Art. 129 | Art. 149 |
| Art. 130 | Art. 130 | Art. 150 |
| **Title IX - Common commercial policy (moved)** | Part Five, Title II, common commercial policy | Part Five, Title II, common commercial policy |
| Art. 131 (moved) | Art. 118 B | Art. 206 |
| Art. 132 (repealed) | | |
| Art. 133 (moved) | Art. 118 C | Art. 207 |
| Art. 134 (repealed) | | |
| **Title X - Customs cooperation (moved)** | Part Three, Title II, Chapter 1a, Customs cooperation | Part Three, Title II, Chapter 2, Customs cooperation |
| Art. 135 (moved) | Art. 27a | Art. 33 |
| **Title XI - Social policy, education, vocational training and youth** | **Title IX - Social policy** | **Title X - Social policy** |
| **Chapter 1 - social provisions (repealed)** | | |
| Art. 136 | Art. 136 | Art. 151 |
| | Art. 136a | Art. 152 |
| Art. 137 | Art. 137 | Art. 153 |
| Art. 138 | Art. 138 | Art. 154 |
| Art. 139 | Art. 139 | Art. 155 |
| Art. 140 | Art. 140 | Art. 156 |
| Art. 141 | Art. 141 | Art. 157 |
| Art. 142 | Art. 142 | Art. 158 |
| Art. 143 | Art. 143 | Art. 159 |
| Art. 144 | Art. 144 | Art. 160 |
| Art. 145 | Art. 145 | Art. 161 |
| **Chapter 2 - The European Social Fund** | **Title X - The European Social Fund** | **Title XI - The European Social Fund** |
| Art. 146 | Art. 146 | Art. 162 |

| | | |
|---|---|---|
| Art. 147 | Art. 147 | Art. 163 |
| Art. 148 | Art. 148 | Art. 164 |
| Chapter 3 - Education, vocational training and youth | Title XI - Education, vocational training, youth and sport | Title XII - Education, vocational training, youth and sport |
| Art. 149 | Art. 149 | Art. 165 |
| Art. 150 | Art. 150 | Art. 166 |
| Title XII – Culture | Title XII - Culture | Title XIII - Culture |
| Art. 151 | Art. 151 | Art. 167 |
| Title XIII - Public health | Title XIII - Public health | Title XIV - Public health |
| Art. 152 | Art. 152 | Art. 168 |
| Title XIV - Consumer protection | Title XIV - Consumer protection | Title XV - Consumer protection |
| Art. 153, paragraphs 1, 3, 4 and 5 | Art. 153 | Art. 169 |
| Article 153, paragraph 2 (moved) | Art. 6a | Art. 12 |
| Title XV – Trans-European networks | Title XV – Trans-European networks | Title XVI – Trans-European networks |
| Art. 154 | Art. 154 | Art. 170 |
| Art. 155 | Art. 155 | Art. 171 |
| Art. 156 | Art. 156 | Art. 172 |
| Title XVI – Industry | Title XVI - Industry | Title XVII - Industry |
| Art. 157 | Art. 157 | Art. 173 |
| Title XVII - Economic and social cohesion | Title XVII - Economic, social and territorial cohesion | Title XVIII - Economic, social and territorial cohesion |
| Art. 158 | Art. 158 | Art. 174 |
| Art. 159 | Art. 159 | Art. 175 |
| Art. 160 | Art. 160 | Art. 176 |
| Art. 161 | Art. 161 | Art. 177 |
| Art. 162 | Art. 162 | Art. 178 |
| Title XVIII - Research and technological development | Title XIII - Research and technological development and space | Title XIX - Research and technological development and space |
| Art. 163 | Art. 163 | Art. 179 |
| Art. 164 | Art. 164 | Art. 180 |
| Art. 165 | Art. 165 | Art. 181 |
| Art. 166 | Art. 166 | Art. 182 |

| | | |
|---|---|---|
| Art. 167 | Art. 167 | Art. 183 |
| Art. 168 | Art. 168 | Art. 184 |
| Art. 169 | Art. 169 | Art. 185 |
| Art. 170 | Art. 170 | Art. 186 |
| Art. 171 | Art. 171 | Art. 187 |
| Art. 172 | Art. 172 | Art. 188 |
| | Art. 172bis | Art. 189 |
| Art. 173 | Art. 173 | Art. 190 |
| **Title XIX – Environment** | **Title XIX - Environment** | **Title XX - Environment** |
| Art. 174 | Art. 174 | Art. 191 |
| Art. 175 | Art. 175 | Art. 192 |
| Art. 176 | Art. 176 | Art. 193 |
| **Title XXI – Energy** | **Title XX - Energy** | **Title XXI - Energy** |
| | Art. 176 A | Art. 194 |
| | **Title XXI - Tourism** | **Title XXII - Tourism** |
| | Art. 176 B | Art. 195 |
| | **Title XXII - Civil protection** | **Title XXIII - Civil protection** |
| | Art. 176 C | Art. 196 |
| | **Title XXIII - Administrative cooperation** | **Title XXIV - Administrative cooperation** |
| | Art. 176 D | Art. 197 |
| **Title XX - Development co-operation (moved)** | Part Five, Title III, Chapter 1, Development coopera-tion | Part Five, Title III, Chapter 1, Development cooperation |
| Art. 177 (moved) | Art. 188 D | Art. 208 |
| Art. 178 (repealed)[21] | | |
| Art. 179 (moved) | Art. 188 E | Art. 209 |
| Art. 180 (moved) | Art. 188 F | Art. 210 |
| Art. 181 (moved) | Art. 188 G | Art. 211 |
| **Title XXI - Economic, finan-** | Part Five, Title III, Chapter | Part Five, Title III, Chapter 2, |

[21] Replaced, in substance, by the second sentence of the second subparagraph of paragraph 1 of Article 188 D (renumbered 208) TFUE.

| cial and technical coopera-tion with third countries (moved) | 2, Economic, financial and technical cooperation with third countries | Economic, financial and technical cooperation with third countries |
|---|---|---|
| Art. 181 a (moved) | Art. 188 H | Art. 212 |
| **Part IV – ASSOCIATION OF THE OVERSEAS COUNTRIES AND TER-RITORIES** | **Part IV – ASSOCIA-TION OF THE OVER-SEAS COUNTRIES AND TERRITORIES** | **Part IV – ASSOCIA-TION OF THE OVER-SEAS COUNTRIES AND TERRITORIES** |
| Art. 182 | Art. 182 | Art. 198 |
| Art. 183 | Art. 183 | Art. 199 |
| Art. 184 | Art. 184 | Art. 200 |
| Art. 185 | Art. 185 | Art. 201 |
| Art. 186 | Art. 186 | Art. 202 |
| Art. 187 | Art. 187 | Art. 203 |
| Art. 188 | Art. 188 | Art. 204 |
| | **Part V - EXTERNAL ACTION BY THE UNION** | **Part V - EXTERNAL ACTION BY THE UN-ION** |
| | **Title I - General provi-sions on the union's external action** | **Title I - General provisions on the union's external action** |
| | Art. 188 A | Art. 205 |
| Part Three, Title IX, Common commercial policy (moved) | **Title II - Common com-mercial policy** | **Title II - Common com-mercial policy** |
| Art. 131 (moved) | Art. 188 B | Art. 206 |
| Art. 133 (moved) | Art. 188 C | Art. 207 |
| | **Title III - Cooperation with third countries and hu-manitarian aid** | **Title III - Cooperation with third countries and hu-manitarian aid** |
| Part Three, Title XX, Develop-ment cooperation (moved) | **Chapter 1 - development cooperation** | **Chapter 1 - development cooperation** |
| Art. 177 (moved) | Art. 188 D[22] | Art. 208 |
| Art. 179 (moved) | Art. 188 E | Art. 209 |

---

[22] The second sentence of the second subparagraph of paragraph 1 replaces, in substance, Article 178 TEC.

| | | |
|---|---|---|
| Art. 180 (moved) | Art. 188 F | Art. 210 |
| Art. 181 (moved) | Art. 188 G | Art. 211 |
| Part Three, Title XXI, Economic, financial and technical cooperation with third countries (moved) | **Chapter 2 - Economic, financial and technical cooperation with third countries** | **Chapter 2 - Economic, financial and technical cooperation with third countries** |
| Art. 181 a (moved) | Art. 188 H | Art. 212 |
| | Art. 188 I | Art. 213 |
| | **Chapter 3 - Humanitarian aid** | **Chapter 3 - Humanitarian aid** |
| | Art. 188 J | Art. 214 |
| | **Title IV - Restrictive measures** | **Title IV - Restrictive measures** |
| Art. 301 (replaced) | Art. 188 K | Art. 215 |
| | **Title V - International agreements** | **Title V - International agreements** |
| | Art. 188 L | Art. 216 |
| Art. 310 (moved) | Art. 188 M | Art. 217 |
| Art. 111, paragraphs 1 to 3 and 5 (moved) | Art. 188 N | Art. 219 |
| | **Title VI - The Union's relations with international organisations and third countries and the Union delegations** | **Title VI - The Union's relations with international organisations and third countries and the Union delegations** |
| Art. 302 to 304 (replaced) | Art. 188 P | Art. 220 |
| | Art. 188 Q | Art. 221 |
| | **Title VII - Solidarity clause** | **Title VII - Solidarity clause** |
| | Art. 188 R | Art. 222 |
| **PART V - INSTITUTIONS OF THE COMMUNITY** | **PART VI - INSTITUTIONAL AND FINANCIAL PROVISIONS** | **PART VI - INSTITUTIONAL AND FINANCIAL PROVISIONS** |
| **Title I - Institutional provisions** | **Title I - Institutional provisions** | **Title I - Institutional provisions** |
| **Chapter 1 - The institutions** | **Chapter 1 - The institutions** | **Chapter 1 - The institutions** |
| **Section 1 - The European Parliament** | **Section 1 - The European Parliament** | **Section 1 - The European Parliament** |

| | | |
|---|---|---|
| Art. 189 (repealed)[23] | | |
| Art. 190, paragraphs 1 to 3 (repealed)[24] | | |
| Art. 190, paragraphs 4 and 5 | Art. 190 | Art. 223 |
| Art. 191, first paragraph (repealed)[25] | | |
| Art. 191, second paragraph | Art. 191 | Art. 224 |
| Art. 192, first paragraph (repealed)[26] | | |
| Art. 192, second paragraph | Art. 192 | Art. 225 |
| Art. 193 | Art. 193 | Art. 226 |
| Art. 194 | Art. 194 | Art. 227 |
| Art. 195 | Art. 195 | Art. 228 |
| Art. 196 | Art. 196 | Art. 229 |
| Art. 197, first paragraph (repealed)[27] | | |
| Art. 197, second, third and fourth paragraphs | Art. 197 | Art. 230 |
| Art. 198 | Art. 198 | Art. 231 |
| Art. 199 | Art. 199 | Art. 232 |
| Art. 200 | Art. 200 | Art. 233 |
| Art. 201 | Art. 201 | Art. 234 |
| | **Section 1a - The European Council** | **Section 2 - The European Council** |
| | Art. 201a | Art. 235 |
| | Art. 201b | Art. 236 |

[23] Replaced, in substance, by Article 9 A, paragraph 1 and 2 (renumbered 14, paragraphs 1 and 2), TEU.

[24] Replaced, in substance, by Article 9 A, paragraph 1 to 3 (renumbered 14, paragraphs 1 to 3), TEU.

[25] Replaced, in substance, by Article 8 A, paragraph 4 (renumbered 11, paragraph 4), TEU.

[26] Replaced, in substance, by Article 9 A, paragraph 1 (renumbered 14, paragraph 1), TEU.

[27] Replaced, in substance, by Article 9 A, paragraph 4 (renumbered 14, paragraph 4), TEU.

| Section 2 - The Council | Section 2 - The Council | Section 3 - The Council |
|---|---|---|
| Art. 202 (repealed)[28] | | |
| Art. 203 (repealed)[29] | | |
| Art. 204 | Art. 204 | Art. 237 |
| Art. 205, paragraphs 2 and 4 (repealed)[30] | | |
| Art. 205, paragraphs 1 and 3 | Art. 205 | Art. 238 |
| Art. 206 | Art. 206 | Art. 239 |
| Art. 207 | Art. 207 | Art. 240 |
| Art. 208 | Art. 208 | Art. 241 |
| Art. 209 | Art. 208 | Art. 242 |
| Art. 210 | Art. 210 | Art. 243 |
| **Section 3 - The Commission** | **Section 3 - The Commission** | **Section 4 - The Commission** |
| Art. 211 (repealed)[31] | | |
| | Art. 211a | Art. 244 |
| Art. 212 (moved) | Art. 218, paragraph 2 | Art. 249, paragraph 2 |
| Art. 213 | Art. 213 | Art. 245 |
| Art. 214 (repealed)[32] | | |
| Art. 215 | Art. 215 | Art. 246 |
| Art. 216 | Art. 216 | Art. 247 |
| Art. 217, paragraphs 1, 3 and 4 (repealed)[33] | | |
| Art. 217 | Art. 217 | Art. 248 |

[28] Replaced, in substance, by Article 9 C, paragraph 1 (renumbered 16, paragraph 1), TEU and by Articles 249 B and 249 C (renumbered 290 and 291), TFEU.

[29] Replaced, in substance, by Article 9 C, paragraphs 2 and 9 (renumbered 16, paragraphs 2 and 9,) TEU.

[30] Replaced, in substance, by Article 9 C, paragraphs 4 and 5 (renumbered 16, paragraphs 4 and 5), TEU.

[31] Replaced, in substance, by Article 9 D, paragraph 1 (renumbered 17, paragraph 1), TEU.

[32] Replaced, in substance, by Article 9 D, paragraph 3 and 7 (renumbered 17, paragraphs 3 and 7), TEU.

[33] Replaced, in substance, by Article 9 D, paragraph 6 (renumbered 17, paragraph 6), TEU.

| | | |
|---|---|---|
| Art. 218, paragraph 1 (re-pealed)[34] | | |
| Art. 218, paragraph 2 | Art. 218 | Art. 249 |
| Art. 219 | Art. 219 | Art. 250 |
| **Section 4 - The Court of Justice** | **Section 4 - The Court of Justice of the European Union** | **Section 5 - The Court of Justice of the European Union** |
| Art. 220 (repealed)[35] | | |
| Art. 221, first paragraph (re-pealed)[36] | | |
| Art. 221, second and third paragraphs | Art. 221 | Art. 251 |
| Art. 222 | Art. 222 | Art. 252 |
| Art. 223 | Art. 223 | Art. 253 |
| Art. 224[37] | Art. 224 | Art. 254 |
| | Art. 224a | Art. 255 |
| Art. 225 | Art. 225 | Art. 256 |
| Art. 225 a | Art. 225a | Art. 257 |
| Art. 226 | Art. 226 | Art. 258 |
| Art. 227 | Art. 227 | Art. 259 |
| Art. 228 | Art. 228 | Art. 260 |
| Art. 229 | Art. 229 | Art. 261 |
| Art.229 a | Art. 229a | Art. 262 |
| Art. 230 | Art. 230 | Art. 263 |
| Art. 231 | Art. 231 | Art. 264 |
| Art. 232 | Art. 232 | Art. 265 |
| Art. 233 | Art. 233 | Art. 266 |

[34] Replaced, in substance, by Article 252a (renumbered 295), TFEU.

[35] Replaced, in substance, by Article 9 F (renumbered 19), TEU.

[36] Replaced, in substance, by Article 9 F, paragraph 2, first subparagraph (renumbered 19, paragraph 2, first subparagraph), TEU.

[37] The first sentence of the first subparagraph is replaced, in substance, by Article 9 F, paragraph, second subparagraph (renumbered 19, paragraph 2, second subparagraph), TEU.

| | | |
|---|---|---|
| Art. 234 | Art. 234 | Art. 267 |
| Art. 235 | Art. 235 | Art. 268 |
| | Art. 235a | Art. 269 |
| Art. 236 | Art. 236 | Art. 270 |
| Art. 237 | Art. 237 | Art. 271 |
| Art. 238 | Art. 238 | Art. 272 |
| Art. 239 | Art. 239 | Art. 273 |
| Art. 240 | Art. 240 | Art. 274 |
| | Art. 240a | Art. 275 |
| | Art. 240b | Art. 276 |
| Art. 241 | Art. 241 | Art. 277 |
| Art. 242 | Art. 242 | Art. 278 |
| Art. 243 | Art. 243 | Art. 279 |
| Art. 244 | Art. 244 | Art. 280 |
| Art. 245 | Art. 245 | Art. 281 |
| | **Section 4a - The European Central Bank** | **Section 6 - The European Central Bank** |
| | Art. 245a | Art. 282 |
| Art. 112 (moved) | Art. 245b | Art. 283 |
| Art. 113 (moved) | Art. 245c | Art. 284 |
| **Section 5 - The Court of Auditors** | **Section 5 - The Court of Auditors** | **Section 7 - The Court of Auditors** |
| Art. 246 | Art. 246 | Art. 285 |
| Art. 247 | Art. 247 | Art. 286 |
| Art. 248 | Art. 248 | Art. 287 |
| **Chapter 2 - Provisions common to several institutions** | **Chapter 2 - Legal acts of the Union, adoption procedures and other provisions** | **Chapter 2 - Legal acts of the Union, adoption procedures and other provisions** |
| | **Section 1 - The legal acts of the Union** | **Section 1 - The legal acts of the Union** |
| Art. 249 | Art. 249 | Art. 288 |
| | Art. 249 A | Art. 289 |

| | | |
|---|---|---|
| | Art. 249 B[38] | Art. 290 |
| | Art. 249 C[38] | Art. 291 |
| | Art. 249 D | Art. 292 |
| | **Section 2 - Procedures for the adoption of acts and other provisions** | **Section 2 - Procedures for the adoption of acts and other provisions** |
| Art. 250 | Art. 250 | Art. 293 |
| Art. 251 | Art. 251 | Art. 294 |
| Art. 252 (repealed) | | |
| | Art. 252a | Art. 295 |
| Art. 253 | Art. 253 | Art. 296 |
| Art. 254 | Art. 254 | Art. 297 |
| | Art. 254a | Art. 298 |
| Art. 255 (moved) | Art. 16 A | Art. 15 |
| Art. 256 | Art. 256 | Art. 299 |
| | **Chapter 3 - The Union's advisory bodies** | **Chapter 3 - The Union's advisory bodies** |
| | Art. 256a | Art. 300 |
| **Chapter 3 - The Economic and Social Committee** | **Section 1 - The Economic and Social Committee** | **Section 1 - The Economic and Social Committee** |
| Art. 257 (repealed)[39] | | |
| Art. 258, first, second and fourth paragraphs[40] | Art. 258 | Art. 301 |
| Art. 258, third paragraph (repealed)[40] | | |
| Art. 259 | Art. 259 | Art. 302 |
| Art. 260 | Art. 260 | Art. 303 |
| Art. 261 (repealed) | | |
| Art. 262 | Art. 262 | Art. 304 |

[38] Replaces, in substance, the third indent of Article 202 TEC.
[39] Replaced, in substance, by Article 256a, paragraph 2 (renumbered 300, paragraph 2), TFEU.
[40] Replaced, in substance, by Article 256a, paragraph 4 (renumbered 300, paragraph 4), TFEU.

| Chapter 4 - The Committee of the Regions | Section 2 - The Committee of the Regions | Section 2 - The Committee of the Regions |
|---|---|---|
| Art. 263, first and fifth paragraphs (repealed)[41] | | |
| Art. 263, second to fourth paragraphs | Art. 263 | Art. 305 |
| Art. 264 | Art. 264 | Art. 306 |
| Art. 265 | Art. 265 | Art. 307 |
| Chapter 5 - The European Investment Bank | Chapter 4 - The European Investment Bank | Chapter 4 - The European Investment Bank |
| Art. 266 | Art. 266 | Art. 308 |
| Art. 267 | Art. 267 | Art. 309 |
| Title II - Financial provisions | Title II - Financial provisions | Title II - Financial provisions |
| Art. 268 | Art. 268 | Art. 310 |
| | Chapter 1 - The Union's own resources | Chapter 1 - The Union's own resources |
| Art. 269 | Art. 269 | Art. 311 |
| Art. 270 (repealed)[42] | | |
| | Chapter 2 - The multiannual financial framework | Chapter 2 - The multiannual financial framework |
| | Art. 270a | Art. 312 |
| | Chapter 3 - The Union's annual budget | Chapter 3 - The Union's annual budget |
| Art. 272, paragraph 1 (moved) | Art. 270b | Art. 313 |
| Art. 271 (moved) | Art. 273a | Art. 316 |
| Art. 272, paragraph 1 (moved) | Art. 270b | Art. 313 |
| Art. 272, paragraph 2 to 10 | Art. 272 | Art. 314 |
| Art. 273 | Art. 273 | Art. 315 |
| Art. 271 (moved) | Art. 273a | Art. 316 |

[41] Replaced, in substance, by Article 256a, paragraph 3 and 4 (renumbered 300, paragraphs 3 and 4), TFEU.
[42] Replaced, in substance, by Article 268, paragraph 4 (renumbered 310, paragraph 4), TFEU.

| | Chapter 4 - Implementation of the budget and discharge | Chapter 4 - Implementation of the budget and discharge |
|---|---|---|
| Art. 274 | Art. 274 | Art. 317 |
| Art. 275 | Art. 275 | Art. 318 |
| Art. 276 | Art. 276 | Art. 319 |
| | **Chapter 5 - Common provisions** | **Chapter 5 - Common provisions** |
| Art. 277 | Art. 277 | Art. 320 |
| Art. 278 | Art. 278 | Art. 321 |
| Art. 279 | Art. 279 | Art. 322 |
| | Art. 279a | Art. 323 |
| | Art. 279b | Art. 324 |
| | **Chapter 6 - Combating fraud** | **Chapter 6 - Combating fraud** |
| Art. 280 | Art. 280 | Art. 325 |
| | **Title III - Enhanced cooperation** | **Title III - Enhanced cooperation** |
| Art. 11 and 11a (replaced) | Art. 280 A[43] | Art. 326 |
| Art. 11 and 11a (replaced) | Art. 280 B[43] | Art. 327 |
| Art. 11 and 11a (replaced) | Art. 280 C[43] | Art. 328 |
| Art. 11 and 11a (replaced) | Art. 280 D[43] | Art. 329 |
| Art. 11 and 11a (replaced) | Art. 280 E[43] | Art. 330 |
| Art. 11 and 11a (replaced) | Art. 280 F[43] | Art. 331 |
| Art. 11 and 11a (replaced) | Art. 280 G[3] | Art. 332 |
| Art. 11 and 11a (replaced) | Art. 280 H[43] | Art. 333 |
| Art. 11 and 11a (replaced) | Art. 280 I[43] | Art. 334 |
| **PART VI - GENERAL AND FINAL PROVISIONS** | **PART VII - GENERAL AND FINAL PROVISIONS** | **PART VII - GENERAL AND FINAL PROVISIONS** |
| Art. 281 (repealed)[44] | | |

[43] Also replaces the current Articles 27 A to 27 E, 40 to 40 B, and 43 to 45 TEU.

[44] Replaced, in substance, by Article 49 C (renumbered 52), TEU [consolidated table-version states renumbered 47].

| Art. 282 | Art. 282 | Art. 335 |
|---|---|---|
| Art. 283 | Art. 283 | Art. 336 |
| Art. 284 | Art. 284 | Art. 337 |
| Art. 285 | Art. 285 | Art. 338 |
| Art. 286 (replaced) | Art. 16 B | Art. 16 |
| Art. 287 | Art. 287 | Art. 339 |
| Art. 288 | Art. 288 | Art. 340 |
| Art. 289 | Art. 289 | Art. 341 |
| Art. 290 | Art. 290 | Art. 342 |
| Art. 291 | Art. 291 | Art. 343 |
| Art. 292 | Art. 292 | Art. 344 |
| Art. 293 (repealed) | | |
| Art. 294 (moved) | Art. 48a | Art. 55 |
| Art. 295 | Art. 295 | Art. 345 |
| Art. 296 | Art. 296 | Art. 346 |
| Art. 297 | Art. 297 | Art. 347 |
| Art. 298 | Art. 298 | Art. 348 |
| Art. 299, paragraph 1 (repealed)[45] | | |
| Art. 299, paragraph 2, second, third and fourth subparagraphs | Art. 299 | Art. 349 |
| Art. 299, paragraph 2, first subparagraph, and paragraphs 3 to 6 (moved) | Art. 311a | Art. 355 |
| Art. 300 (replaced) | Art. 188 N | Art. 218 |
| Art. 301 (replaced) | Art. 188 K | Art. 215 |
| Art. 302 (replaced) | Art. 188 P | Art. 220 |
| Art. 303 (replaced) | Art. 188 P | Art. 220 |
| Art. 304 (replaced) | Art. 188 P | Art. 220 |
| Art. 305 (replaced) | | |
| Art. 306 | Art. 306 | Art. 350 |
| Art. 307 | Art. 307 | Art. 351 |

[45] Replaced, in substance, by Article 49 C (renumbered 52), TEU.

| | | |
|---|---|---|
| Art. 308 | Art. 308 | Art. 352 |
| | Art. 308a | Art. 353 |
| Art. 309 | Art. 309 | Art. 354 |
| Art. 310 (moved) | Art. 188 M | Art. 217 |
| Art. 311 (repealed)[46] | | |
| Art. 299, paragraph 2, first subparagraph, and paragraphs 3 to 6 (moved) | Art. 311a | Art. 355 |
| Art. 312 | Art. 312 | Art. 356 |
| **Final Provisions** | | |
| Art. 313 | Art. 313 | Art. 357 |
| | Art. 313a | Art. 358 |
| Art. 314 (repealed)[47] | | |

[46] Replaced, in substance by Article 49 B (renumbered 51), TEU.
[47] Replaced, in substance by Article 53 (renumbered 55) TEU.

## 5. Some Popular Databases in Westlaw

In Westlaw, the main division of categories is into the following, from choosing online the menu View Westlaw Directory:

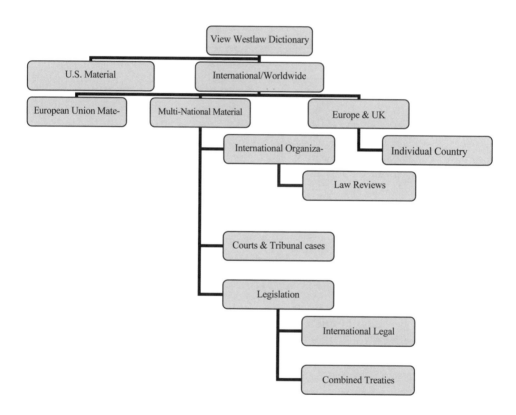

*Table 40: Westlaw Database Overview*

## Some Popular Databases in Westlaw

| Subject | Database Identifier |
|---|---|
| All Federal & State cases (U.S.) | ALLCASES |
| UK-cases | UK-CASELOC |
| European Reports All | EU-RPTS-ALL |
| European Union Cases All | EU-CS-ALL |
| Common Market Law Reports (EU) | CML-RPTS |
| Federal Communications – Cases (U.S.) | FCOM-CS |
| Intellectual Property cases | FIP-CS |
| All Law Reports (U.S.) | All-RPTS |
| International Court of Justice | INT-ICJ |
| International Criminal Tribunal for Rwanda | INT-ICTR |
| International Criminal Tribunal for the Former Yugoslavia | INT-ICTY-ALL |
| International Commercial Arbitration | ICA-ALL |
| WTO & GATT Panel decisions | WTO-DEC |
| | |
| Text & Periodicals (U.S.) | TP-ALL |
| Journal & Law Review (U.S.) | JLR |
| Text & Treatises (U.S.) | TEXTS |
| American Law Reports (U.S.) | ALR |
| American Jurisprudence 2d (U.S.) | AMJUR |
| Restatement (U.S.) | REST |
| American Journal of Comparative Law (U.S.) | AMJCL |
| Communications Law Reviews, Texts & Bar Journals (U.S.) | COM-TP |
| Intellectual Property - Reviews, Texts & Bar Journals (U.S.) | IP-TP |
| Legislation cases (Text & Periodicals) (U.S.) | LTG-TP |
| American Journal of Comparative Law (U.S.) | AMJCL |
| Communications Law Reviews, Texts & Bar Journals (U.S.) | COM-TP |
| Intellectual Property - Reviews, Texts & Bar Journals (U.S.) | IP-TP |

| | |
|---|---|
| Legislation cases (Text & Periodicals) (U.S.) | LTG-TP |
| | |
| World Journals and Law Review | WORLD-JLR |
| International Law, Law reviews, Texts, and Bar journals | INT-TP |
| International HR journal | INTLHRJ |
| International Legal Material | ILM |
| International Legal Material Cumulative Index | ILM-INDX |
| International Trade Commission | FINT-ITC |
| International Trade Law and Regulation | INTTLR |
| U.N. Commission on International Trade Law – Model laws | UNITRAL-MODL |
| American Journal of International Law | AMJIL |
| American Society of International Law | ASIL |
| ILSA Journal of International and Comparative Law | ILSAJICL |
| International and Comparative Law Quarterly | ICLQ |
| Journal of International Criminal Justice | JINTCRJ |
| Journal of International Legal Studies | JILS |
| ALR International | ALRINTL |
| Restatement of the Foreign Relations Law of the United States | REST-FOREL |
| Index to Foreign Legal Periodicals | IFLP |
| | |
| United Kingdom law Reviews | UK-JLR |
| | |
| European Law Review | EURLR |
| Columbia Journal of European Law | CLMJEURL |
| European Competition Law Review | ECLR |
| European Intellectual Property Review | EIPR |
| | |
| All European Union Materials | EU-ALL |
| European Union Commission legislation | EU-LEG |

## Some Popular Databases in Westlaw

| | |
|---|---|
| European Union Treaties | EU-TREATIES |
| European Union Preparatory Acts | EU-ACTS |
| European Parliamentary questions | EU-QUESTIONS |
| European Union OJC Series | EU-OJCSERIES |
| Tenders Electronic Daily | TENDERDLY |
| European Union Community Trademark | EC-TM |
| Legal Journals Index | LJI |
| | |
| State Statutes Annotated (U.S.) | ST-ANN-ALL |
| | |
| Combined Treaties | CMB-TREATIES |
| International Treaties and Forms | INT-TF |
| International Commercial Arbitration Treaties | ICA-TREATIES |
| | |
| Internet and Online Law | IOLAW |

# 6. Bibliography

A Summary Guide to the Treaty of Lisbon (EU Reform Treaty) (National Forum on Europe)(Dublin: Government Publication Office January 2008) <www.forumoneurope.ie/eng/getFile.asp?FC_ID=338&docID=1489> (visited July 2008)

A Uniform System Of Citations ("The Bluebook"), (18th ed.) (Cambridge, MA: Harvard Law Review Assn, 2005)

Abramson, Jill & John Kennedy And Ellen Joan Pollock, Inside The West Empire, The American Lawyer (October 1983), P. 90

Akehurst's Modern Introduction To International Law (8th ed.) (By Peter Malanczuk)(New York ; London : Routledge, 2002 - ISBN 0415243556)

ALWD Citation Manual: A Professional System of Citation (3rd ed. by Darby Dickerson, Association of Legal Writing Directors (ALWD)) (Aspen Publishers, 2003 - ISBN: 0735536406)

Andrioli, Virgilio, Codice Di Procura Civile E Norme Complementari (Milan: Dott. A. Giuffrè Editore, 1984 – ISBN 88-14-00110-3).

Armstrong, J.D.S. & Christopher A. Knott, Where the Law is: An Introduction to Advanced Legal Research (2nd ed.) (St. Paul: Thompson West, 2006 – ISBN 10-314-16296-8)

Ansay, TuRul & Atilla Harmathy (Eds.), Introduction To Hungarian Law (Kluwer Law International, 1998 - ISBN 978-9041110664)

Barnes, Adversarial Legalism, The Rise Of Judicial Policymaking, And The Separation Of Powers Doctrine, In Making Policy, Making Law: An Interbranch Perspective (Miller & Barnes, Eds.)(Washington, D.C.: Georgetown University Press, 2004 – ISBN 1589010256)

Bedjaoui, M. , Droit International – Bilan Et Perspectives, Pédone/Unesco, 2 Vol., 1991 (Éd. Anglaise, Nijhoff/Unesco, Dordrecht, 1992)

Berger, Klaus Peter, The Principles of European Contract Law and the Concept of the "Creeping Codification" of Law, 9 European Review Of Private Law 21 (Kluwer Law International 2001)

Bergholtz, Gunnar, Precedent In Sweden In Interpreting Precedent: A Comparative Study (Niel Maccormick, Robert S. Summers & Arthur L. Goodhart, Eds.) (Vt.: Ashgate/Dartmouth, 1999 - ISBN: 9781855216860)

Bernhardt, Rudolf, Interpretation In International Law, In Encyclo-Pedia Of Public International Law (Rudolf Bernhardt (Ed.), Elsevier 1995 – ISBN 0-444-86245-5)

Berring, Robert C. & Elizabeth A. Edinger, Finding the Law (12th ed.) (St, Paul, Minn: Thomson/West, 2005 – 9870314145796)

Berring, Robert C. & Elizabeth A. Edinger, Legal research survival Manual (St. Paul, MN: Thomson/West, 2002 – 9870314264008)

Berring, Robert C. & Mike Jacobstein, Truly A Giant, 97 Law Library Journal 633 (2005).

Black, Henry Campbell, Handbook On The Construction And Interpretation Of The Laws (1896).

Black's Law Dictionary (8th ed.) (St. Paul: West Publishing, 2004).

Blaug, Mark, The Methodology Of Economics (Cambridge University Press, 1980 - ISBN 0521222885).

Bluebook – See A Uniform System Of Citations.

Blume, Peter, From Drakon To The Computer And Beyond In Nordic Studies In Information Technology And Law (Peter Blume, Ed.) (Deventer, Boston: Kluwer Computer Law Series, 1991– ISBN 90-6544-5064).

Blume, Peter, Juridisk Metodelære: En Indføring I Rettens Og Juraens Verden [Legal Methodology: An Introduction To The World Of Jurisprudence And Study Of Law/Of Law And Courts] (Copenhagen: Jurist- og Økonomforbundets Forlag [DJØF Publishing] 2004 – ISBN 87-574-1062-3)

Bogdan, Michael, Comparative Law (1994 Kluwer – ISBN -10: 9065448616)

Bogdan, Michael (Ed.), Swedish Law in the New Millennium (Stockholm: Norstedts Juridik, 2000 - ISBN 91-39-00628-X)

Bocken, Hubert & Walter de Bondt, Introduction to Belgian Law (Kluwer Law International, 2000 - ISBN-13: 978-9041114563)

Borchardt, Klaus-Dieter, E.U. ABC By (Eu 2000) At <Http://Www.Europa.Eu/Eur-Lex/En/About/Abc/Index.Html> Or <Http://Www.Europa.Eu/Eur-Lex/En/About/Abc_En.Pdf>.

Braun, Alexandra, Professors And Judges In Italy: It Takes Two To Tango, 26 Oxford Journal Of Legal Studies 656 (Winter 2006)

Breyer, Stephen, On The Use Of Legislative History In Interpretating Statutes, 65 Southern California Law Review 845 (1992).

Brownlie, Ian, Principles Of International Law (5th ed.) (Oxford Press, 2002 – ISBN 0-19-876298-4).

Brownlie, Ian, Principles Of International Law (7th ed.) (Oxford University Press, 2008 – ISBN 978-0199217700)

Brudney, James J., Liberal Justices' Reliance On Legislative History: Principle, Strategy, And The Scalia Effect, Ohio State Public Law Working Paper No. 95, Center For Interdisciplinary Law And Policy Studies Working Paper Series No. 64

Buergenthal, Thomas, Public International Law In A Nutshell (3$^{rd}$ Ed West Group 2002)

Burnham, William, Introduction to the Law and Legal System of The United States (West Group, 2006 – ISBN 0-314-25393-9)

Cabrero, Olga, Guide To Legal Research In Spain (Feb. 2005) at <http://www.llrx.com/features/spain.htm >.

Cassese, Antonio, International Law (2$^{st}$ ed.) (Oxford University Press, 20005 – ISBN 978-0199259397)

Cassese, Antonio, International Criminal Law (1$^{st}$ ed.) (Oxford University Press, 2003 – ISBN 0-19-925911-9)

Chodosh, Hiram E., Comparing Comparisons: In Search Of Methodology, 84 Iowa Law Review 1025 (Aug, 1999)

Chorus, Jeroen M.J., Piet-Hein. M. Gerver & Ewoud H. Hondius (Eds.), Introduction To Dutch Law (Editors: ) (4th Ed.) (Kluwer Law International, 2007 - ISBN 978-9041122698)

Civil Law Dictionary With Civil Law Glossary And Common Law Glossary at <http://civillawdictionary.pbwiki.com>.

Clark, David S. & Tugrul Ansay, Introduction to the Law of the United States (2$^{nd}$ ed.) (The Hague/New York: Kluwer Law International, 2002 – ISBN 9879041117489)

Cohen, Morris L & Kent C. Olson, Legal Research (8$^{th}$ Ed.)(Thomson West, 2000 - West Nutshell Series – ISBN 0-314-14707-1)

Comparative law - A handbook (Editors: Örücü / David Nelken)(2007 England, Oxford: Hart Publishing - ISBN 978-1-84113-596-0)

Congressional Quarterly's Federal Regulatory Directory (Washington D.C.: Congressional Quarterly Inc., 1979/80 - - ISSN 0195-749X)

Corpus Juris Secundum: Complete Restatement Of The Entire American Law As Developed By All Reported Cases (St. Paul: Thomson/West Publishing, 1936- )

Cottin, Stéphane & Jérôme Rabenou, Researching French Law (May 2005 With Update May 2007) at <http://www.llrx.com/features/french.htm>.

Craig, Paul & Grainne De Burca, Eu Law – Text, Cases And Materials (4$^{th}$ Ed.)(Clarendon Press, Oxford Press 2007 – ISBN 978-0-19-927389-8)

Dailliere, Patrick, Et Alain Pellet, Droit International Public, Librairie Générale De Droit Et De Jurisprudence, E.J.A., Paris, 1999 (ISBN 2-275-01588-4)

Danish Law In A European Perspective (2nd Ed.) (Dahl, Melchior & Tamm, Eds ) (Copenhagen: DJOEF Publishing - ISBN 978-8760703553)

David, René, Traité Élémentaire De Droit Civil Comparé (1950)

# Bibliography

de Arechaga, E. Jimenez, El Derecho Intercional Público (Tecnos, Madrid, 1980)

de Cruz, Peter, Comparative law in a Changing World (3rd ed)(2007 London/New York: Cavendish - ISBN 978-1-85941-936-6)

Dekker, Ige F. & Harry H.G. Post, The Completeness Of International Law And Hamlet's Dilemma, In On The Foundations And Sources Of International Law (T.M.C. Asser Press, The Hague, 2003 – ISBN 90-6704-158-0)

Dessemontet, Francois & Tugrul Ansay (Eds.), Introduction To Swiss Law (Editors: ) (3rd Ed.) (Kluwer Law International, 2004 - ISBN 978-9041122605)

Egge, Michael G., Matteo F. Bay & Janier Ruiz Calzado, The New EC Merger Regulation: A Move to Convergence, Status of Soft Law In international Law, Antitrust Magazine, Section of Antitrust Law, American Bar Association, Fall 2004 at <www.lw.com/upload/pubContent/_pdf/pub1167_1.pdf > (visited July 2008)

Elias, T.O., New Horizons In International Law, Sijthoff Et Noordhoff (Alphen, 1979)

Eng, Svein, Precedent In Norway,In Interpreting Precedent: A Comparative Study (Niel Maccormick, Robert S. Summers & Arthur L. Goodhart, Eds.) (Vt.: Ashgate/Dartmouth, 1999 - ISBN: 9781855216860)

Esser, Josef, Vorverständnis Und Methodenwahl In Der Rechtsfindung: Rationalitätsgrundlagen Richterlicher Entscheidungs-Praxis (Durchges, 1972 - ISBN: 3807260013)

Evald, Jens, Retskilderne Og Den Juridiske Metode [Source Of Law And The Legal Method] (2nd. Ed.) (Copenhagen: DJØF Publishing, 2000 - ISBN 978-87-574-6493-1k).

Ewald, W., Comparative Jurisprudence (1): What Was It Like To Try A Rat?, 143 University of Pennsylvania Law Review 1889 (June 1995).

Eyffinger, Arthur, The International Court Of Justice, 1946-1996 (Kluwer Law International, The Netherlands 1996 – ISBN 90 411 0221 3).

Fameli, Elio & Fiorenza Socci, Guide To Italian Legal Research And Resources On The Web (Translated By Deirdre Exell Pirro) (March 2005 With June 2006 Update), at <http://www.nyulawglobal.org/globalex/italy.htm>

Farber, Daniel A. , Statutory Interpretation And Legislative Supremacy, 78 Georgetown Law Journal 281 (December 1989).

Farber, Daniel A., Statutory Interpretation And Legislative Supremacy, 78 Georgetown Law Journal 281 (December 1989).

Federalists Papers (Ed. By Isaac Kramnick) (Harmondsworth, Middlesex, England: Penguin, 1987 – ISBN 0140444955)

Fernandès-Flores, J.L., Derecho Internacional Público, Eds, De Derecho Reunidas (Madrid, T.I, 1980)

# Bibliography

Fleisher, Carl August, Rettskilder Og Juridisk Metode [Source Of Law And The Legal Method] (Oslo, Ad Notam Gyldendal, 1998 – ISBN 82-417-0954-4)

Fogel, Paul D. & David J. De Jesus, Unpublished Opinions, Forum Column, Daily Journal, December 20, 2006

Fox, Elyse H., The legal research dictionary: From advance sheets to pocket parts (2nd ed.) (Chapel Hill, N.C.: Legal Information Services, 2006 – 9780941991025)

Frank, Jerome, Law And The Modern Mind (New York: Brentano's, 1930).

Frankenberg, Günter, Critical Comparisons: Re-Thinking Comparative Law, 26 Harvard International Law Journal 411 (1985)

Frankfurter, Felix, Some Reflections On Reading Of Statutes, 47 Columbia Law Review 527 (May 1947)

Frankowski, Stanislaw & Adam Bodnar (Eds.), Introduction to Polish Law (Editors: ) (Kluwer Law International, 2005 - ISBN 978-9041123312)

Galanter, Marc, The Vanishing Trial, Vol. 10, No.4, Dispute Resolution Magazine 3 (Summer 2004)

Garner, Bryan A., A dictionary of modern legal usage (New York: Oxford University Press, 1995 – ISBN 9870195077698)

Gerken, Joseph L., What Good Is Legislative History? Justice Scalia In The Federal Courts Of Appeals (Buffalo, New York: William S. Hein & Co., Inc., 2007 - ISBN 9780837732329).

GFILC, See Guide To Foreign And International Legal Citation

Gleerup, Anne, Ulla Rosenkjær, Leif Rørbæk, An introduction to Danish law (2nd Ed.) (Denmark: Drammelstrupgaard, 2008 - ISBN 978-87-988688-3-5)

Graver, Hans Petter, The Approach To European Law In Norwegian Legal Doctrine, In Peter Christian Müller-Graff & Erling Selvig, Eds., European Law In The German-Norwegian Context: Origins And Perspectives (Berlin: Berliner Wissenschafts-Verlag Gmbh, 2001- ISBN: 978-3-8305-0248-7) & at <http://www.arena.uio.no/publications/wp03_18.pdf>

Griswold, Erwin N., The Harvard Law Review – Glimpses Of Its History As Seen By An Aficionado, Harvard Law Review: Centennial Album 1 (1987) at <http://www.harvardlawreview.org/centennial.shtml>

Guide To Foreign And International Legal Citation (GFILC) (New York University, Journal Of International Law And Politics, 2006). Free download at <http://www.law.nyu.edu/journals/jilp/final%20gfilc%20pdf.pdf>. (Also Available In Spiral-Bound, Paperback Form by sending U.S.$ 20 payable to: Circulation Department, Journal Of International Law And Politics,110 West Third Street, New York, NY 10012, USA)

Guide to International Legal Research (Lexis Law Pub, June 2006 - ISBN: 978-0820575940)

Guide To International Legal Research (2006 Ed.) (The George Washington University Law School International Law Review, LexisNexis - ISBN: 0820574872)

Hausmaninger, Herbert , The Austrian Legal System (Manzsche Verlags- Und Universitätsbuchhandlung, 2003 – ISBN 3-214-00289-9)

Hazelton, Penny A., Specialized Legal Research, (Gaithersburg: Aspen Law & Business, 1987 – ISBN 9780316136259)

Henkin, Louis (Ed), Restatement (Third) Of Foreign Relation Law (St. Paul: American Law Institute, 1987)

Henkin, Louis, Coda: Allegro Ma Non Troppo, American Society Of International Law Newsletter (Jan.-Feb. 1994) 1.

Henkin, Louis, Foreign Affairs And The United States Constitution

Higgins, Rosalyn, International Law And The Avoidance, Containment And Resolution Of Disputes – General Course On Public International Law, Recueil Des Cours, Vol. 230 (1991-V) page 23.

Higgins, Rosalyn, Problems & Process – International Law And How We Use It (Clarendon Press, Oxford 1994 – ISBN 0-19-876410-3)

Hill, Jonathan, Comparative Law, Law Reform And Legal Theory, 9 Oxford Journal Of Legal Studies 101 (1989)

Hornby, D. Brock, The Business Of The U.S. District Courts, 10 Green Bag 2d 453 (Summer 2007)

Hunt, Alan, Vol. 6 No 3 Jurisprudence, Philosophy And Legal Education – Against Foundationalism, Legal Studies 292 (November 1986)

Jacobstein, J. Myron & Roy M. Mersky, Fundamentals Of Legal Research 1-2 (5th Ed.) (Westbury, N.Y. : Foundation Press, 1990 - ISBN 9780882777948).

Jensen, Torben, Højesterets Arbejdsform In Højesteret 1661 - 1986 [The Supreme Court's Working Methods (Printed In A Special Edition Of The Danish Case Reporter In 1986] (Torben Jensen, W.E. Von Eyben & Mogens Koktvedgaard, Eds. (Copenhagen: Særudgave Af Ugeskrift For Retsvæsen - G.E.C Gads Forlag, 1986).

Jensen, Torben, Domstolenes Retsskabende, Retsudfyldende Og Responderende Virksomhed [The Courts' Law-Creating, Filling Out And Responding Activity], 1990 Journal Of Law [Ugeskrift Of Retsvæsen] (UfR) [Subsection] B 441

Kahn-Freund, Otto Comparative Law As An Academic Subject, 82 The Law Quarterly Review 40 (1966)

Kahn-Freund, Otto, On Uses And Misuses Of Comparative Law, 37 Modern Law Review

1 (1974)

Kerameus, Konstantinos D. & Phaedon J. Kozyris (Eds.), Introduction to Greek Law (Editors: ) (3rd Ed.) (Kluwer Law International, 2008 - ISBN 978-9041125408)

Kerr, Orin S., How To Read A Judicial Opinion: A Guide For New Law Students (Version 2.0 - August 2005), George Washington University Law School, at <http://volokh.com/files/howtoreadv2.pdf>

Kozyris, P. John, Comparative Law In The 21st Century: New Horizons And New Technologies, 69 Tulane Law Review 165 (1994)

Kunz, Christina L. (et. Al.), The Process of Legal Research (6 ed., New York : Aspen Publishers, 2004. - ISBN: 978-0-735536661 (alk. paper) - ISBN: 9780735540408 (teacher's manual))

Legrand, Pierre, How To Compare Now, Vol. 16, No. 2, Legal Studies 232 (July 1996)

Lena, Jeffrey S. & Ugo Mattei (Eds.), Introduction to Italian law (Hague/London/New York: Kluwer Law International 2002 - ISBN: 978-9041117076)

Llewellyn, Karl & Karl N. Llewellyn, Jurisprudence : Realism In Theory And Practice (Chicago: University Of Chicago Press, 1962)

Lookofsky, Joseph, Precedent And The Law In Denmark - Danish National Report At The XVII'th Conference Of The International Academy Of Comparative Law, Utrecht 2006, at <Http://www.cisg.law.pace.edu/cisg/biblio/lookofsky15.html>

Maccormick, Niel & Robert S. Summers & Arthur L. Goodhart, Interpreting Precedent: A Comparative Study (Eds.) (Vt.: Ashgate/Dartmouth, 1999 - ISBN: 9781855216860)

Manual of International and Foreign Citation: The Greenbook (Ed. Shepard Broad Law Center) (William S. Hein & Company, January 2007 - ISBN: 978-0837738307)

Manz, William H., Guide To State Legislative And Administrative Materials (2002 Ed.) (Buffalo, New York: William S. Hein, 2002 – ISBN 0837701562)

Mashaw, Jerry L., Reasoned Administration: The EuropeanUnion, the United States, and the Project of Democratic Governance, 122 The George Washington Law Review, Vol. 76 p. 99 (Nov 2007) at <http://docs.law.gwu.edu/stdg/gwlr/issues/pdf/76_1_Mashaw.pdf> (visited July 2008)

McDermott, James A., Recommended Law Books (Chicago, Ill.: Committee on Business Law Libraries, Section of Corporation, Banking and Business Law, American Bar Association, 1986 – ISBN 9780897072397)

McGill, Canadian Guide to Uniform Legal Citation, (6 Ed.) (Thomson Carswell, - ISBN: 0-459-24394-2)

McKinney, Ruth Ann, Legal Research: A practical guide and self-instructional workbook (St. Paul, Minn: Thomsom/West, 2003)

McKinney, Ruth Ann, Reading like a lawyer: Time-saving strategies for reading law like an expert (Durham, N.C.: Carolina Academic Press, 2005 – ISBN 9781594600326)

Mcnair, Lord Arnold Duncan, The Law Of Treaties (Oxford Clarendon Press 1961).

Menski, Werner F., Comparative Law In A Global Context: The Legal Systems Of Asia And Africa (Platinium, London 2000 – ISBN 0-9535728-1-1).

Merryman, John Henry, The Civil Law Tradition: An Introduction To The Legal Systems Of Western Europe And Latin America (2nd Ed.)(Stanford University Press , 2001)

Michaels, Ralf & Nils Jansen, Private Law And The State: Comparative Perceptions And Historical Observations, In Rabels Zeitschrift Für Ausländisches Und Internatio-Nales Privatrecht, Vol. 71, No. 2, 2007 P. 32

Michaels, Ralf & Nils Jansen, Private Law Beyond The State? Europeanization, Globaliza-tion, Privatization, 54 American Journal Of Comparative Law 843 (Fall 2006)

Monaco, Ricardo, Sources Of International Law in R. Bernhardt, Encyclopedia Of Public International Law, Volume Four (2003) (Max Planck Institute For Comparative Public Law, Elsevier 2003 – ISBN 0-444-86247-1)

Moore, Sally Falk, Law As Process: An Anthropological Approach (Routledge & K. Paul, 1978 - ISBN: 0710087586)

Nedzel, Nadia E., Legal Reasoning, Research, and Writing for International Graduate Students (2nd Ed.)(Aspen Publishers Inc., 2008 - ISBN-13: 978-0735569539)

Neacşu, Dana, Google, Legal Citations, And Electronic Fickleness: Legal Scholarship In The Digital Environment at 1 (Social Science Research Network, June 2007). Available at SSRN: <http://ssrn.com/abstract=991190>.

Nedzel, Nadia E., Legal Reasoning, Research, and Writing for International Graduate Students (Aspen Publishers, 2004 - ISBN: 978-0735535190)

Nielsen, Ruth & Christian D. Tvarnø, Retskilder & Retsteorier [Source Of Law & Legal Theories] (1st Ed.) (Copenhagen: Jurist- og Økonomforbundets Forlag [DJØF Publish-ing], 2005 – ISBN 87-574-1199-9)

Oda, Hiroshi, Japanese Law (Butterworths, 1992 - ISBN 040666921x).

Oppenheim's International Law (Sir Robert Jennings & Sir Arthur Watts Eds.) (9th ed.) (London & New York: Longman, 1996 – ISBN 0582302455).

Örürü, Esin, Unde Venit, Quo Tendit Comparative Law?, In Comparative Law In The 21st Century (Andrew Harding And Esin Örürü (Ed.), Kluwer 2002 – ISBN 90-411-9875-X)

Oxford Standard for Citation of Legal Authorities (University of Oxford, 2006) at <http://www.competition-law.ox.ac.uk/published/oscola_2006.pdf>.

Pascal, Robert A., Louisiana Civil Law And Its Study, 60 Louisiana Law Review 1 (Fall

1999)

Picard, E. & G Berman (Eds.), Introduction To French Law (Editors: n) (Kluwer Law International, 2008 - ISBN 978-9041124661)

Posner, Richard A., Against The Law Reviews:Welcome To The World Where Inexperi- Enced Editors Make Articles About The Wrong Topics Worse, 2004 (Dec) Legal Af- Fairs 57

Pound, Roscoe, Comparative Law In Space And Time, 4 American Journal Of Compara- tive Law 70 (1955).

Pratter, Jonathan, An Approach To Researching The Drafting History Of International Agreements            (December            2005)            At <http://www.nyulawglobal.org/globalex/travaux_preparatoires. htm>.

Price, Miles O. And Harry Bitner, Effective Legal Research: A Practical Manual Of Law Books And Their Use (New York: Prentice Hall, 1953).

Prince, Mary Miles, Bieber's dictionary of legal Abbreviations: A reference guide for attorneys, legal secretaries, paralegals, and law students (Buffalo, New York: W.S. Hein, 2001)

Radbruch, Gustav, Einführung In Die Rechtswissenschaft (12<sup>th</sup> ed. 1969)

Reiman, Mathais (Ed. Reinhard Zimmermann), The Oxford Handbook Of Comparative Law (Oxford University Press 2006 – ISBN 978-0-19-929606-4)

Report on the Treaty of Lisbon (2007/2286(INI)) from the European Parliament's Commit- tee on Constitutional Affairs (Rapporteurs: Richard Corbett & Íñigo Méndez de Vigo), A6-0013/2008,            29            January            2008            at <http://www.europarl.europa.eu/sides/getDoc.do?pubRef=- //EP//NONSGML+REPORT+A6-2008-0013+0+DOC+PDF+V0//EN&language=EN> (visited July 2008)

Restatement of Foreign Relations Law Of The United States (Third) (American Law Institute)

Rheinstein, Max, Comparative Law – Its Functions, Methods And Usages, 22 Arkansas Law Review 415 (Fall 1968)

Rumbauer, Marjorie Dick, Legal Problem Solving: Analysis, research and writing (5 ed., St. Paul, Minn. : West Pub. Co., 1991 - ISBN: 978-0-314842435)

Sacco, Rodolfo, Legal Formant:, A Dynamic Approach To Comparative Law (Installment II of II), 39 The American Journal Of Comparative Law 343 (Spring 1991)

Sacco, Rodolfo, Legal Formants, A Dynamic Approach To Comparative Law (Installment I of II), 39 The American Journal Of Comparative Law 1 (1991)

Scalia, Antonin, A Matter Of Interpretation: Federal Courts And The Law: An Essay

(Princeton: Princeton University Press, 1997 - ISBN 0691026300).

Schacter, Jane S., Accounting For Accountability In Dynamic Statutory Interpretation And Beyond – Issues In Legal Scholarship, Dynamic Statutory Interpretation (Berkeley: Berkeley Electronic Press, 2002): Article 5 at <http://www.bepress.com/ils/iss3/art5 >

Schacter, Jane S., The Confounding Common Law Originalism In Recent Supreme Court Statutory Interpretation: Implications For The Legislative History Debate And Beyond, 51 Stanford Law Review 1 (1998).

Schlesinger, Comparative Law: Cases, Text, Materials (6th ed.) (Foundation Press, 1998 - ISBN 1566624584)

Shapira, Amos & Keren C. Dewitt-Arar (Eds.), Introduction To The Law Of Israel (Editors: ) (Kluwer Law International, 1995 - ISBN 978-9065448354)

Sharpiro, Fred R., The Oxford dictionary of American legal quotations (New York: Oxford University Press, 1993 – ISBN 9780195058598)

Sharpiro, Fred R., The Yale Book of Quotations (New Haven: Yale University Press, 2006 – ISBN 9780300107982)

Shaw, Malcolm N., International Law (4th Ed.)(Cambridge University Press – ISBN 0521576679)

Singer, Norman J. ('Sutherland") Statutes And Statutory Construction (6th Ed.) (St. Paul: West Group, 2006)

Slapper, Gary, The English Legal System (9 Ed.) (Routledge Cavendish, 2008 - ISBN-13: 978-0415459549)

Solan, Lawrence M., Statutory Interpretation In The Eu: The Augustinian Approach, Brooklyn Law School, Legal Studies Paper No. 78 Page 10 (July 2007) - Available at SSRN: <http://ssrn.com/abstract=998167>.

Solomon, Andrew T., Making Unpublished Opinions Precedential: A Recipe for Ethical Problems & Legal Malpractice?, 26 Mississippi College Law Review 185 (2007)

Spang-Hanssen, Henrik, Cyberspace & International Law On Jurisdiction - Possibilities Of Dividing Cyberspace Into Jurisdictions With Help Of Filters And Firewall Software (Djøf Publishing, Copenhagen, 2004 - ISBN 87-574-0890-1).

Spang-Hanssen, Henrik, Cyberspace Jurisdiction In The U.S: The International Dimension Of Due Process (Complex 5/01, Norwegian Research Center For Computers And Law, Oslo University 2001 - ISBN 82-7226-046-8), Also Free Downloading From Research Website <Www.Geocities.Com/Hssph>.

Spang-Hanssen, Henrik, Public International Computer Network Law Issues (Djøf Publishing Copenhagen, 2006 - ISBN 87-574-1486-6)

# Bibliography

Statsky, William P.,, Legal Research and Writing: Some Starting Points (5th ed. Albany, NY : West Legal Studies, 1998 - ISBN 978-0-314129017)

Stein, Eric, Uses, Misuses – And Nonuses Of Comparative Law, 72 Northwestern University Law Review 198 (1977-78)

Sutherland Statutes And Statutory Construction, See Under Singer, Norman J.

Tampere, Aulis Arnio, Precedent In Finland, In Interpreting Precedent: A Comparative Study (Niel Maccormick, Robert S. Summers & Arthur L. Goodhart, Eds.) (Vt.: Ashgate/Dartmouth, 1999 - ISBN: 9781855216860)

The Oxford Handbook of Comparative law (Editor: Reiman & Zimmerman)(2007 England: Oxford University Press - ISBN 978-0-19-953545-3)

Torp, Carl, I Anledning Af Højesterets 250-Aarige Bestaaen, In Ugeskrift For Rets-Væsen, 1911, P. 54

Tryggvadóttir, Rán & Thordis Ingadóttir, Researching Icelandic Law (2007) at <http://www.nyulawglobal.org/globalex/iceland.htm>.

Tunkin , G.I., (Ed)., International Law – A Textbook, (Progress Publ, Moscow, 1986)

Tvarnø, Christian D. & Ruth Nielsen, Retskilder & Retsteorier [Source Of Law & Legal Theories] (1st ed.) (Copenhagen: Jurist- and Økonomforbundets Forlag [Djøf Publishing], 2005 – ISBN 87-574-1199-9)

Van Calster, G., The Eu's Tower Of Babel – The Interpretation Of The European Court Of Justice Of Equally Authentic Texts Drafted In More Than One Official Language, 17 (1997) Yearbook Of European Law 363 (Oxford Press 1998 – ISBN 0-19-826883-1)

Von Vitzthum, W., Et M. Bothe, Völkerrecht (De Gruyter, Berlin, 1997)

Wandall, Rasmus H., Researching Danish Law (July 2006) at <http://www.nyulawglobal.org/globalex/denmark.htm>.

Watson, Alan, Legal Trans-Plants: An Approach To Comparative Law (University Press Of Virginia, 1974 - ISBN 0813905761)

Watt & Dashwood's European Union Law (5th ed)(2006 London: Thompson ISBN 978-00421-92560-1)

Wayne, Erika V. & J. Paul Lomio, Book Lovers Beware: A Survey Of Online Re-Search Habits Of Stanford Law Students (Robert Crown Law Library Legal Research Paper Series, Research Paper No. 2) (2005)

Weatherill, Stehephen, Cases And Materials On Eu Law (8th ed.)(2007 Oxford Press – ISBN 978-0-19-921401-3)

Weatherill, Stephen & Paul Beaumont, E.U. Law (3rd Ed.)(Penguin Books, 1999)

Weber, Max, Wirtschaft Und Gesellschaft; Grundriss Der Verstehenden Sozi-Ologie. Mit Einem Anhang; Die Rationalen Und Soziologischen Grundlagen Der Musik (4 Ed. Ew

Hrsg. Aufl., Besorgt Von Johannes Winckelmann, Tübingen 1956); Guenther Roth & Claus Wittich, Eds. Max Weber, Economy And Society: An Out-Line Of Interpretive Sociology, (Trans. Ephraim Fischoff [And Others], New York: Bedminster Press, 1968).

Weisberg, Robert, The Calabresian Judicial Artist: Statutes And The New Legal Process, 35 Stanford Law Review 213 (January 1983)

Woods, Steiner & Twigg-Flesner, EU Law (9 ed.)(2006 England: Oxford University Press - ISBN 978-0-19-927959-3)

Wren, Christopher G. & Jill Robinson Wren, The Legal Research Manual – A Game Plan For Legal Research And Analysis (2$^{nd}$ ed.) (Adams & Ambrose Publishing, 1988 – ISBN 0-916951-16-2)

Zekoll, Joachim & Mathias Reimann (Eds.), Introduction to German Law (Editors: ) (2nd Ed.) (Kluwer Law International, 2005 - ISBN-13: 978-9041122612)

Zweigert, K. & H.Kötz, Introduction To Comparative Law (3$^{rd}$ ed.) (Tony Weir Trans., Clarendon Press, Oxford, 1998 – ISBN 0-19-826859-9)

# 7. Tables

## Tables

# 8. Index

## §

## A

## B

## C

# O

# P

# Q

# R

## S

# The Modern Law Schools'
# *Uriaspost* – the Post of Danger

by
**Henrik Spang-Hanssen**

\*\*\*\*\*\*\*\*\*\*\*\*

This is an addendum or " teacher's manual" to the **civil law part** of the book:

LEGAL RESEARCH METHODS IN THE US & EUROPE
Second Edition

and its corresponding website at <**www.geocities.com/legalrm**>

© 2008 Henrik Spang-Hanssen – Independent Senior Researcher

E-mail: hssph@yahoo.com
Research website: www.geocities.com/hssph
SSRN author: http://ssrn.com/author=943044

# The Modern Law Schools' *Uriaspost* – the Post of Danger

## 1. Introduction

In Second Samuel 11, King David puts one of his officers, Uriah, in a very dangerous position so as to achieve an objective. Modern law schools have decided to teach their students law beyond their national borders and thus put teachers in a somewhat similar position to Uriah as far as trying to teach the law (i.e., civil law) of, for example, a country in continental Europe.

> The American law graduate will find that at least two years is necessary for studying abroad in Europe effectively, and that "the first year is likely to be wasted."
>
> The organization of legal studies in Europe is "so different" from what it is in the U.S. that "an American student is likely to be lost unless he is individually guided."
>
> Max Rheinstein, *Comparative Law – Its Functions, Methods and Usages*, 22 ARK. L. REV. 415, 424-25 (Fall 1968).

Civil law is today the dominant legal tradition in (see BOOK[1] page 102):

- Continental Europe
- All of Central and South America
- Many parts of Africa
- Many parts of Asia
- American State of Louisiana
- American Territory of Puerto Rico
- Canadian Province of Quebec
- Scotland
- Israel

This document, will try, from a continental European point of view, to provide a guide to American teachers and students as to what one should keep in mind before deciding to and then teaching/studying legal research (or using a comparative method) for the law of a country on the European continent.

To a very large extent, this is the same drill for a European wanting to do research on the law of another European country. Thus, an American is not specially disadvantaged but may not, as the Europeans, have been brought up realizing the difficulties lying ahead – or anticipating the kind of shock that can be felt.

Continental Europe consists of 47 countries (25 are in the European Union), of which none uses English as its legal language. The E.U.'s homepage must use the following language translations for its gateways:

---

[1] "BOOK" means: J. PAUL LOMIO & HENRIK SPANG-HANSSEN, LEGAL RESEARCH METHODS IN THE U.S. AND EUROPE (2nd Edition) (DJØF Publishing, Copenhagen 2009). **Table of Contents & Index of the BOOK** are given at the book's corresponding website < >.

| | |
|---|---|
| bg | Портал на Европейския съюз |
| cs | Portál Evropské unie |
| da | Internetportalen til EU |
| de | Das Portal der Europäischen Union |
| et | Euroopa Liidu portaal |
| el | Η δικτυακή πύλη της Ευρωπαϊκής Ένωσης |
| en | Gateway to the European Union |
| es | El portal de la Unión Europea |
| fr | Le portail de l'Union européenne |
| ga | Tairseach an Aontais Eorpaigh |
| it | Il portale dell'Unione europea |
| lv | Eiropas Savienības portāls |
| lt | Europos Sajungos portalas |
| hu | Az Európai Unió portálja |
| mt | Il-portal ta' l-Unjoni Ewropea |
| nl | De portaalsite van de Europese Unie |
| pl | Portal Unii Europejskiej |
| pt | O portal da União Europeia |
| ro | Portalul Uniunii Europene |
| sk | Portál Európskej únie |
| sl | Portal Evropske unije |
| fi | Euroopan unionin portaali |
| sv | EU:s webbportal |

## 2. The first heavy task

To be able to figure out how to do legal research or study the law of a (foreign) European continental country first of all requires that one knows and can read the language of the particular country to be investigated. Europeans learn one to three foreign languages in school.

Thus, language skills are the first and most vital decision maker. If one cannot read the law of a foreign country, it may be next to impossible to do any decent legal research.

---

**Tip #1**

On the basis of the foreign languages you can read, decide on a country using that language as its official language for its law.

---

Language constitutes a very heavy barrier for studying the law of a (foreign) European continental country, as only a micro-percentage is ever translated into, for example, English.

> ## Tip #2
>
> As for the text of legislation and court decisions, *et cetera*, only use translation(s) made by officially authorized translators.
>
> European courts and governments will never rely on non-authorized translations; thus, carefully check who did the translating.
>
> It is wrong - and out of proper context - to teach legal research on the basis of non-authorized translations, as it gives students the impression they can always use such material.

Even for Member States of the European Union one can not expect, for example, the English version to be a true translation of the twenty-three other language-versions; each translation to a certain degree reflects the law of the country that uses that particular language.

Thus, an English version can differ from a Danish or Swedish version - and even though those two countries are said to belong to the same (Nordic) legal family, their versions will also differ. Therefore, even for E.U. law, one must not try to circumvent the law of a certain E.U. country by using the English version. It is necessary to pay attention to the particular E.U. (language) law version of the country to be investigated.

The European Union website "Translation and Drafting Aids in the European Union Languages" at <http://ec.europa.eu/translation/index_en.htm> contains links to the following Multilingual resources:

- E.U. Terminology
- Europa Glossary
- Eurovoc Thesaurus
- Acronyms & Abbreviations
- Drafting Guides
- Interinstitutional Style Guide
- Language Aids for E.U. Translations
- Europa Languages and Europe

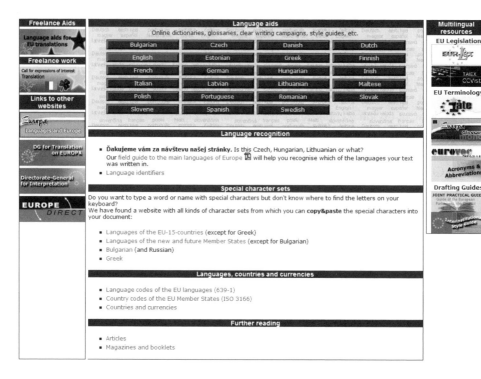

Beyond knowing the language, a researcher also must know something about the history of the country, its culture and society. Without such background knowledge, it is nearly impossible to understand the basis for the country's law. The CIA World Factbook (https://www.cia.gov/library/publications/the-world-factbook/ index.html) and Wikipedia.org both provide helpful initial information on different countries.

---

**Tip #3**
Choose the law of a country about which you know something as to its history, culture and society.

---

## 3. The second heavy task

If one can read several foreign languages, one should determine which legal family one prefers to investigate. If one has previously researched a legal family, it will obviously not require as much preparation to investigate the law of another country belonging to the same legal family.

On the other hand, if one wants to get a broader view of the law of different continental European countries, it can be more productive to choose the law belonging to another legal family (provided that one can still read the language, and knows something of the history, culture, *et cetera* of that country).

One way of dividing countries into legal families (see BOOK chapter 6) is:

- Romanistic Legal Family (France, the Benelux countries, Italy, Spain and Portugal)
- Germanic Legal Family (Germany, Austria, Croatia, Switzerland, Greece, Turkey, South Korea)
- Nordic Legal Family (Denmark, Finland, Iceland, Norway, and Sweden )
- Anglo-American Legal Family (England, and Wales, Northern Ireland, United States of America, Australia, Canada (except Québec))
- Law in the Far East (China, Japan)
- Religious Legal Systems (A. Islamic Law, B. Hindu Law)

| Tip #4 |
|---|
| Choose a country whose law belongs to a legal family that one prefers (and knows something about). |

In turning to a new legal family, it can naturally be helpful to do a little research into it and its cultural background, *et cetera* [see BOOK chapter 6].

## 4. The third heavy task

If one is brought up with common law and wants to study civil law, one should at a very minimum learn by heart the content of table 1 in Chapter One of BOOK.

And, an American should - before investigation of any law of continental Europe - also have read section 3.1 of BOOK, and especially beware of the difference in terms mentioned in section 3.1.1.1.

| Tip #5 |
|---|
| Be fully aware of the difference between common law and civil law. Also, note that the same English words and terms can be used – and understood - differently in the U.S. and in continental Europe. |

## 5. The fourth heavy task

Nearly every country in continental Europe has its own way of doing legal research. Thus, one must study the chosen country's special methods, which can often best be achieved by reading a guide or textbook authored by a native.

Note that teaching legal research is quite different in the U.S. and in Europe, as the aims of the courses are different [see BOOK page 109].

---

**Tip #6**

Often, useful guides on how to do legal research in a certain country, written by natives, can be found in English; for example, at Globalex
<http://www.nyulawglobal.org/globalex/>.

---

## 6. Comparative Method or nothing

Because a pure comparison of legal systems does not have any value or purpose, one has to figure out a comparative method that will work when investigating two or more countries' legal systems (see BOOK chapter 7, especially section 7.3 about "A Plan" for making a comparative method).

Pure comparison is without value since the same words/terms can have different meanings or be used differently in the legal systems (and their societies/cultures). Furthermore, even the legal systems and institutions of closely situated/related European countries can present great differences. Hence, the crucial importance of developing a method to compare the chosen legal systems.

An alternative is to decide not to make any comparisons at all, and try to forget anything one has learned about one's own legal system. This is like starting out on an "adventure" into a foreign legal system with a totally fresh mind (akin to having learned to walk and then abandoned that form of locomotion to figure out how to fly or swim!).

---

**Tip #7**
Decide whether to develop a comparative method.
Or, alternatively, not to make any comparisons at all.

Thus, students/scholars have to know how to build a legal comparative method.

The word "comparison" should not be used.

---

# 7. "Getting into the country"

When the above mentioned steps are taken, one is ready to begin the real task of investigating the law of the foreign country and its legal research methods.

The following will try to be a (further) manual for the topic of legal research, especially for Americans.

It will deal primarily with where to find the law, as any comprehensive introduction to a civil law country's specific "legal research methods" is beyond the scope of this document. As for the latter, an overall introduction is given in BOOK chapter 3.

One should not forget that in continental Europe case law is, overall, not important. Thus, searching for or studying case law should be the very last item on the agenda – and only if there is time for it.

---

**Tip #8**

Teaching on how to find the law (in the U.S.: legal research) is not a normal course of study in civil law countries;
it is rare that one will find texts or hornbooks similar to those in the U.S.

In civil law countries, books on "legal research" will deal with what *is* law (*law-foundation-sources*[2]) and how statutes are interpretated.

---

Thus, in civil law countries it is more or less all about statutes.

---

**Tip #9**

Do not waist time on the case law of civil law countries.
Instead, spend time on acts and statutes - and their interpretation.

---

## 7.1. The country's structure

A basic requirement for doing legal research on a particular country in continental Europe is to know:

- The Constitution – and thereby the structure between:

---

[2] See definition in BOOK page 107.

- o Parliament
- o Government (N.B. the term is used differently in the U.S.)
- o President / Majesty, and
- o Courts
  - What the powers are for each of the above mentioned institutions
  - How statutes are interpreted
  - How the country's law in its entirety is divided into parts [see BOOK research Tip #3.4, page 106-107 & table 27]
  - What is *hard law* and what is regarded as *soft law*

Some guidance can be found at the ECJ's (CVRIA) website on "European Union Law in Europe" (English version) at <http://curia.europa.eu/en/content/outils/liens/index.htm>, which gives information about:

- National and international case law → Case-law (national and international):
  - o Database of case-law of the courts and tribunals of the Member States in the field of Community law (English) (French)
  - o Synthesis of the principal decisions of national courts and tribunals (extract from the Annual Report of the European Commission on monitoring the application of Community law)
- National and international legal sites → Institutional and Legal Internet Sites:

**Institutional and Legal Internet Sites**

*Select a country :*

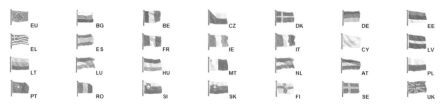

The legal order for several Member States of the E.U. is also given (English version)                                                                        at
<<u>www.ec.europa.eu/civiljustice/legal_order/legal_order_gen_en.htm</u>>:

Do not waist time on the issue of citation format, as in continental Europe there is no official pattern to citations (see BOOK section 3.1.8).

Moreover, civil law countries do not require Shepardizing (that is, using a legal citator to check the currency) of case law because judicial precedent is not important and because a newer statute on the same subject always will overrule an older one (see BOOK 114).

No civil law countries have anything like the United States Code (U.S.C.) (see BOOK section 3.1.4).

The term "code" in continental Europe is used as a synonym for an act or a law (see BOOK page 113).

## 7.2. Online searching

American students, who are taught about and how to use online legal databases such as Westlaw and LexisNexis, sometimes are not aware of databases on foreign law.

As for European Union law, information is often hard to find since the E.U. search-systems are not integrated into a convenient system.

Legal research courses should alert students as to how to go about finding foreign law.

However, the main obstacle is language. If a student cannot read the foreign country's official language, then he/she can perform little if any research or study on that civil law country. This is due to the fact that a civil law lawyer or student will begin searching for the act(s) or statute(s) that deal(s) with the particular issue surveyed; next read the text of such law; and thereafter search for commentary. Case decisions should only be searched if mentioned as important (a "precedent case") in the previously mentioned material. Beyond this, in civil law countries it is only to a small extent possible to search electronically for legal material; hence, the investigation has to be done "through" library shelves, which – depending on the library's collection - might not contain the investigated country's material. If online systems do exist, then it will again be necessary to be able to read the foreign country's language (and sometimes costly subscriptions are required).

## 7.2.1. Westlaw databases

Students should be aware of the special International Directory offered by Westlaw. It gives access to some foreign information in English, but not much from continental Europe.

Also, see the list of some popular databases in Westlaw in BOOK Appendix 5.

## International Directory

Search the Westlaw Directory:

[_____] [Search]

**Westlaw International Subscriptions**
General, Regional, Topical, News, ...

**Australian Materials**
Cases, Topical, ...

**Canadian Materials**
Cases, Legislation, ...

**European Union Materials**
Cases, Legislation, ...

**United Kingdom Materials**
Cases, Legislation, Topical, ...

**Hong Kong**
Civil Procedure (Hong Kong White Book), Cases, Legislation, ...

**U.S. Federal Materials**
Cases, Statutes, Admin. Mat'l, Rules, ALR International, ...

**International/Worldwide Materials**
N. America, EU, UK, Asia Pacific, ...

**Law Reviews and Journals**
World Journals and Law Reviews, ...

**International Practice Areas**
International Commercial Arbitration, ...

**Business & News**
News, Companies, People, Industries, ...

Also, see the Corresponding website for BOOK <www.geocities.com/legalrm>.

Westlaw's special overview site for European Union material is actually quite good and searching - when available - through Westlaw is often easier than through the E.U.'s own website.

---

**Welcome to European Union Research**

**Select Database(s)**

☐ All
☐ European Union Legislation (EU-LEG) ⓘ
☐ European Union Cases All (EU-CS-ALL) ⓘ
☐ European Union Preparatory Acts (EU-ACTS) ⓘ
☐ European Union Treaties (EU-TREATIES) ⓘ
☐ European Union OJC Series (EU-OJCSERIES) ⓘ
☐ European Union Parliamentary Questions (EU-QUESTIONS) ⓘ

**Terms and Connectors** | **Natural Language**

Search: [                              ] **Search Westlaw**

[ Recent Searches & Locates ▾ ]

Dates: [ Unrestricted ▾ ]

**Add Connectors or Expanders** Help

| & | AND | /s | In same sentence |
| space | OR | +s | Preceding within sentence |
| " " | Phrase | /p | In same paragraph |
| % | But not | +p | Preceding within paragraph |
| ! | Root expander | /n | Within n terms of |
| * | Universal character | +n | Preceding within n terms of |

## 7.2.2. European Union websites

The European Union's website (http://europa.eu/) is not always easy to figure out. Frequently, it seems, one has to search through various sub-pages to find material one wants.

There are two webpages that in general give access to the most common information needed. One is an index to most of the institutions in the E.U.; the other is an index to most of the E.U. sub-webpages that in turn provide access to E.U. documents.

These are the two pages in English (http://europa.eu/index_en.htm) (see above under section One, other alternative languages):

---

**ACTIVITIES** | **INSTITUTIONS** | **DOCUMENTS** | **SERVICES**

## HOW THE EUROPEAN UNION WORKS
### A CITIZEN'S GUIDE TO THE EU INSTITUTIONS

**Institutions**

- European Parliament
- Council of the European Union
  - Presidency
- European Commission
- Court of Justice of the European Communities
- European Court of Auditors
- European Ombudsman
- European Data Protection Supervisor

**Financial bodies**

- European Central Bank
- European Investment Bank
  - European Investment Fund

**Advisory bodies**

- European Economic and Social Committee
- Committee of the Regions

**Interinstitutional bodies**

- Office for Official Publications of the European Communities
- European Personnel Selection Office
- European Administrative School

**Decentralised bodies of the European Union (agencies)**

- Community agencies
- Common Foreign and Security Policy
- Police and Judicial Cooperation in criminal matters
- Executive agencies

---

**ACTIVITIES** | **INSTITUTIONS** | **DOCUMENTS** | **SERVICES**

## WHERE TO FIND EU DOCUMENTS - AN ONLINE LIBRARY

**European law**

- EUR-LEX, the portal to European Union law
- ŒIL, the Legislative Observatory
- Pre-Lex, monitoring of the decision-making process between institutions
- Case law
- Summaries of legislation

**Documents common to all the institutions**

- EU Bookshop
- Bulletin of the European Union
- General Report on the Activities of the European Union
  - One year of Europe
- Historical Archives of the European Union
- Glossary

**Documents of individual institutions**

- Document registers
- European Parliament
- Council of the European Union
  - European Council
- European Commission
- Court of Justice and Court of First Instance
- Court of Auditors
- European Ombudsman
- European Data Protection Supervisor
- European Central Bank
- European Investment Bank
- European Economic and Social Committee
- Committee of the Regions

---

Also, to gain an overview on Finding E.U. Law see the content at <www.geocities.com/hssphresearch/Finding_EU_Law. htm>.

On each of these webpages, one can choose another language and thereby find the vocabulary of E.U. institutions as used by the different Member States of the E.U.

Note that the second page provides a link to a "Glossary" (in different languages). A search in the English-language glossary will show that in the U.S. words/terms sometimes are used differently than in the E.U.

Also, see the corresponding website for BOOK <www.geocities.com/legalrm>.

E.U. teaching material[3] can be found at <http://europa.eu/geninfo/info/guide/index_en.htm>, which site, among others, gives a link to audiovisual material <http://ec.europa.eu/avservices/home/index_en.cfm> and EUtube <http://youtube.com/eutube>. See also E.U. television news service on the Internet at <http://ec.europa.eu/avservices/ebs/schedule.cfm>.[4]

## 8. Miscellaneous

Overall, it seems that teaching on civil law generally must remain quite superficial, as it is more than likely that a university's or other law library will not contain sufficient foreign legal source material to enable the legal research a native would do. Furthermore, for language reasons, students will not be able to perform legal research as a native would. Third, as the bases of civil law will be statutes, legal research in civil law countries will have to be done fundamentally differently from how it is done in the United States[5] – concentrating on what statutes say and how they are to be interpreted.

---

[3] On the Treaty of Lisbon see BOOK section 4.6 and Report on the Treaty of Lisbon(2007/2286(INI)) from the European Parliament's Committee on Constitutional Affairs (Rapporteurs: Richard Corbett & Íñigo Méndez de Vigo), A6-0013/2008, 29 January 2008 at <http://www.europarl.europa.eu/sides/getDoc.do?pubRef=-//EP//NONSGML+REPORT+A6-2008-0013+0+DOC+PDF+V0//EN&language=EN> (visited July 2008); Treaty of Lisbon at a glance at <http://europa.eu/lisbon_treaty/glance/index_en.htm>; Treaty of Lisbon – Questions and answers at <http://europa.eu/lisbon_treaty/faq/index_en.htm> (both visited July 2008).

[4] Material for beginners: How the European Union Works: Your Guide to the EU Institutions (European Commission, 2007 - ISBN 92-79-03653-X) at <ec.europa.eu/publications/booklets/eu_glance/68/en.pdf> and Europe in 12 Lessons at <http://europa.eu/abc/12lessons/>.

[5] Conversely, it is a huge error that European universities (and Westlaw and LexisNexis outside the U.S.) do not offer students courses on how to do American legal research, including how to use Westlaw and LexisNexis as tools for doing legal research. European students are not taught the significance of, for example, using Shepard's

Thus, courses on legal research of foreign civil law countries should focus on: what legal family the particular country belongs to; the institutions existing under the investigated country's constitution and their respective powers; which instruments (acts, rules, decrees, *et cetera*) each institution can issue; if possible, where the sources can be found in publications (in a library) and/or online; and studying a guide on legal research for the particular civil law country.

If an investigated country is a Member State of the European Union, it is obvious that the different E.U. institutions and the Union's different legal instruments (regulations, directives, *et cetera*) and how to find them, will influence/have an effect on the investigated country's law.

Beyond that, a course on legal research in civil law countries should include teaching of the general issues mentioned in BOOK chapter 3, including the basic rules for interpretation (BOOK pages 150-153).

After some time teaching the basics on civil law, it may be appropriate to let students divide into groups and investigate one or several civil law countries' official websites and then culminate with either a paper or a presentation on what is the legal language of the investigated country(ies); how the particular civil law country(ies) work(s); what a legal research guide for the country(ies) communicate(s) about sources and interpretation(s), *et ceterea*; and where to find source material (in print or online).

## 9. Conclusion

Law schools that have chosen to offer cross-border law courses should appreciate the great efforts teachers in today's legal research classes will have to expend in preparation for such courses. And if they do not succeed to the degree students expect, law schools should still acknowledge that the teachers have been given a *Uriaspost* and be satisfied that they have at least survived the struggle.

---

Citations (in LexisNexis) or KeyCite (in Westlaw). In Europe, Westlaw and Lexis are in general used (by librarians, professors and students) in the same way Americans use products such as HeinOnline to retrieve documents, that is, simply as library indexes. Moreover, it appears Westlaw and LexisNexis do not seem to be interested in offering outside the U.S. courses that are offered to students/scholars in the U.S. Thus, American law schools should perhaps feel an obligation to teach visiting scholars and foreign students about how to do legal research in the United States and about differences from the legal research methods used in civil law countries.

The time may well have come when American law schools should realize that they need the assistance of scholars brought up in civil law countries[6] – just as European universities nowadays routinely invite or hire foreign continental European and American scholars to come and give lectures or advise students and colleagues on their native law. Arguably, today's law faculties should at least include one full time scholar brought up in a civil law country – or maybe even one from each legal family. Otherwise, it seems fair to conclude that the faculty cannot truly fulfill their modern "transnational" commitment to students.

## 10. Sample Syllabus

| Class | Topic | Reading Assignment | Other Assignments |
|---|---|---|---|
| 1 | Basic differences between common law and civil law<br><br>Legal families | Book chapter 1<br><br>Book chapter 6 | Consider the reading with the country wizard given in Appendix A and prepare for discussion on the differences between the U.S. and a country in continental Europe |
| 2 | How to create a comparative method | Book chapter 7 | |
| 3 | Civil law basics for Americans<br><br>Legal science and legal philosophy in civil law countries | Book section 3.1 until subsection 3.1.6.<br><br>Book subsection 3.1.7 | |
| 4 | Citations<br><br>Introduction to legal research in civil law countries | Book subsection 3.1.8.<br><br>Book subsection 3.2.1. | |

---

[6] Such professors should, of course, be hired with the minimum condition that they assist the law schools' students in researching and writing papers concerning basic civil law legal methods.

|   | Legal methodology | Book subsection 3.2.2. |   |
|---|---|---|---|
|   | The legal method in principle | Book subsection 3.2.3 |   |
| 5 | The method in detail | Book section 3.3 until subsection 3.3.2 |   |
| 6 | Use of the source of law | Book subsection 3.3.2. | Exercises: Fill out the fields in Appendix B |
|   | Interpretation of the law-foundation-sources | Book subsection 3.3.3. |   |
| 7 | Relations between national law and International / E.U. law | Book subsection 3.3.4 |   |
| 8 | European Union resources[7] | Book section 4.1[8] | Exercise C |
| 9 | Sources of E.U. law | Book section 4.2[9] | Exercise D |
|   | Where to find E.U. material Inclusive online websites | Book section 4.3[10] |   |
| 10 | Student presentations |   |   |

## 11. Examples of exercises

Some suggestions to teachers of exercises are given below in Appendixes A-E.

---

[7] Some E.U. secondary education teaching material can be found at <www.eurunion.org/infores/teaching/secondary.htm> (visited July 2008).
[8] Remember to compare with content in section 4.6.
[9] Remember to compare with content in section 4.6.
[10] Remember to compare with content in section 4.6.

## Appendix A - Default scenario: continental European civil law country

The following facts can be regarded as the default scenario when doing research on a continental European civil law country.

They should give Americans some insight into how the continental European countries work in essence.

Regard the remainder of this appendix as a continental European civil law "wizard:"

Based on the country's constitution, the power in the country is divided into the following three branches:

- The Executive power, which branch consists of:
  - The head of the country, who is a constitutional king/queen, which means he/she is not an absolute monarch
  - A government or cabinet led by a Prime Minister
- The Legislative power
- The Judicial power

- For Members of the European Union: the E.U. institutions have some impact on each country.
  But basically, the E.U. only has the powers that each Member State has handed over to it directly (as most recently "updated" by the Lisbon Treaty of December 2007).

The **Legislative power** is in the Parliament, whose members are elected by a direct vote of the country's citizens. It is the only power to enact law/statutes. The Parliament can by a majority vote declare its mistrust in the government but cannot dissolve the government/cabinet. In such case of declared mistrust, a new government has to be composed, but new public elections will not be held unless the Prime Minister decides they should be.

Bills are introduced either by a Member of Parliament or by a cabinet minister. If an introduced bill obtains the support of a majority (normally 50 %) of the Members of Parliament it is then sent to a committee that studies the bill and makes recommendations. The bill – with suggested amendments – is thereafter read a second time in Parliament. If it continues to receive majority support, it will go to further negotiations in the committee, or go straight to a third and final vote in Parliament. If supported by a majority at this point, the bill in its final text will become law.

All bills and negotiations on the floor of Parliament will be printed in the Parliament's Records.

The statute or act that results will be signed by the responsible minister and the king/queen and enter into force either when published in the Official Journal or later, at a special date stated in its text.

The **Judicial power** cannot declare laws/statutes (made by Parliament) unconstitutional. Judges are appointed by the government and can only be removed through an impeachment process. Each judge has to retire at the age of 65.

The court system consists of district courts, appeal courts and a Supreme Court.

All court decisions can be appealed to a higher level court, but they can only be appealed once again upon permission of a special independent committee, whose members are appointed by Parliament.

Court decisions can not be remanded and returned to a lower court. The *stare decisis* doctrine is not used. The courts' task is to use – not make - the law and they can only interpret (fill in gaps) in a statute's text to a very small (and narrow) degree.

A commercial publisher will, upon subscription, publish those court decisions that the publisher's advisory board recommends should be published. Every citizen can, by paying a handling fee, obtain a copy of a decision from the court that issued the decision.

**The government/cabinet** is set up in the following way: After a four-year term – or after decision by the Prime Minister – a public election will be held with all seats of the Parliament on the ballot. All citizens have the right to vote, and an election place cannot close before all citizens have had a chance to vote. Every vote has to be counted. A special commission of the country oversees the election.

After it has been established which persons have been elected to the Parliament and how many member seats each party has won, each party's leader will inform the king/queen as to whom the party suggests should lead the negotiations for drawing up a government/cabinet. After holding meetings, the person appointed by the king/queen as negotiator will announce which person he/she suggests should form the government/cabinet.

This latter person will then negotiate with others and decide what should be the political program for the government/cabinet and then seek to obtain the support of a majority of the elected Members of Parliament.

If majority support is achieved, the person will inform the king/queen that a government/cabinet has been set up and how the group of responsible individuals of the government/cabinet (the ministers) have distributed tasks/responsibilities between themselves. The king/queen will appoint the cabinet including the person chosen to be Prime Minister.

The ministers (in the U.S.: cabinet "secretaries") will thereafter initiate bills for Parliament and run their individual ministries. Often ministers are also elected members of the Parliament.

The ministers can issue decrees/rules pursuant to delegated powers given by Parliament through acts/statutes.

The police and prison system, and the administrative parts of the court system, fall under the Minister of Justice, who also (sometimes with Parliament's participation) issues court rules.

**Cities, towns and local communities** are run by elected mayors together with elected councils. They fall under the supervision of the government/cabinet (and Parliament).

## Appendix B – Sample country datasheet

Choose a country on continental Europe, search the Internet and fill out the form below.

Country: _____

Official Language: _____

Belong to Legal Family: _____

| Word in English | Word in official language (for example in German: Verfassung = Constitution) | Official Website |
|---|---|---|
| Constitution | | |
| Parliament | | |
| Bills | | |
| Parliament Reporter | | |
| New law / acts | | |
| Government | | |
| President / Majesty | | |

| Courts | | |
|---|---|---|
| Supreme Court | | |
| Case Reporter | | |
| Legal Law Review | | |
| | | |

# Appendix C – Statutory interpretation example

In 1848, due to the many horse carriages in the cities and towns, the Parliament of country A decided that the traffic direction should be on the right-hand side of the road. The rule became a statute in a new act named the Traffic Direction Act.

In 1920, a white paper on the traffic situation showed three quarters of the automobiles in country A were produced and imported from the United Kingdom (where traffic stays to the left side of the road). Thus, these imported cars all had steering wheels on their right-hand side. Hence, the paper concluded that it would be safer if the traffic direction was changed to the left side of the road. This suggestion became a statute in the Road Act, which contains, among other things, rules on road conditions and snow clearance. However, by an inadvertent error, the statute in the Traffic Direction Act was not revoked.

Using the rules of interpretation, discuss which side – left or right - would be correct for traffic direction, and upon which rule the interpretation is based?

In 1970, country A became a Member State of the European Union in which there already existed a Council Regulation on Traffic of 25 December 1968 stating that the driving direction in the European Union is the right-hand side of the road, as most cars in the Union have the steering wheel on their left side.

Using the rules of interpretation, discuss which side would be correct for traffic direction, and upon which rule the interpretation is based?

## Appendix D – Various exercises

In the European Union regime:

Discuss the differences between:

- Council Regulation EC/44/2001 of 22 December 2000 on Jurisdiction and the recognition and enforcement of judgments in civil and commercial matters, published in O.J. L 012 – 16/01/2001 P.0001-0023

and

- Brussels Convention on Jurisdiction and Enforcement of Judgments in Civil and Commercial Matters of 27 September 1968, published in O.J. L 299, 31/12/1972 p. 0032-0042

(Students should, of course, by themselves find these instruments online in the European Union Official Journal.)

Which of the two above instruments is the valid one?

What does "Curia" (CVRIA) stand for? (What E.U. institution does the term cover?)

Who publish documents with the term "COM" in the journal number / record number?

What is EUR-Lex?

What is the difference between the Council of Europe and the Council of the European Union - and what are their respective homepages?

## Appendix E – Terminology exercises

- Explore what terms a foreign country in Europe uses as compared to U.S. terms like "act," "section," "paragraph," and "subsection."

- What does "litra" or "litera" mean in a European statute?

- Try to find words/terms that differ from U.S. legal terms (for example, from Black's Law Dictionary) on the E.U. Glossary (http://europa.eu/index_en.htm → under the tab "Documents")

- Find a Legal Research Guide for a chosen country and present highlights on that country's law to others.

- In the E.U., what is a "Statement of reasons"? [Use: Codecision Glossary at <http://ec.europa.eu/codecision/stepbystep/glossary_en.htm>].

- In the E.U., what does "Adoption and implementation of the acquis" mean? [Use: Enlargement Glossary at <http://ec.europa.eu/enlargement/glossary/index_en.htm>].

- In the E.U., is the "Exequatur" procedure used between the E.U. Member States? [Use: European Judicial Network in Civil and Commercial Matters Glossary at <http://ec.europa.eu/civiljustice/glossary/glossary_en.htm>]

- In the E.U., what does "GFP" stand for and mean? [Use: Environmental Glossary at <http://glossary.eea.europa.eu/EEAGlossary/>].

- In the E.U., what does "COM" mean? [Use: Information Society Glossary at <http://ec.europa.eu/information_society/tl/help/glossary/index_en.htm>].

- In the E.U., what does "Copenhagen criteria" mean? [Use: Justice and Home Affairs glossary at

<http://ec.europa.eu/justice_home/glossary/glossary_welcome
_en.htm>].

# Backlist

DJØF Publishing
www.djoef-forlag.dk

**Art and Law**
The copyright Debat
By Morten Rosenmeier & Stina Theilmann (eds.) – 1. ed. 2005
ISBN 978-87-574-1298-7

**Changing international Law to Meet New Challenges**
Interpretation, Modification and the Use of Force
By Andreas Laursen – 1. ed. 2006
ISBN 978-87-574-1529-2

**Crime, Punishment and Justice**
Selected articles from a Scholarly Career
By Ulla V. Bondesen – 1. ed. 2007
ISBN 978-87-574-1763-0

**Cyberspace & International Law on Jurisdiction**
By Henrik Spang-Hanssen – 1. ed. 2004
ISBN 978-87-574-0890-4

**Danish Arbitration Act 2005**
By Ketilbjørn Hertz – 1. ed. 2005
ISBN 978-87-574-1427-1

**Free Movement in the European Union**
By Morten Broberg & Nina Holst-Christensen – 3. ed. 2007
ISBN 978-87-574-1566-7

**Gender Equality in European Contract Law**
By Ruth Nielsen – 1. ed. 2004
ISBN 978-87-574-0687-0

**Is the Sui Generis Rights a Failed Experiment?**
A legal and Theoretical Exploration of How to Regulate Unoriginal Database Contents
By Robin Elisabeth Herr – 1. ed. 2008
ISBN 978-87-574-1881-1

**Judicial Accommodation of Human Rights in the European Union**
By Ane Maria Røddik Christensen – 1. ed. 2007
ISBN 978-87-574-1689-3

**Law and Learning in the Middle Ages**
Proceedings of the Second Carlsberg Academy Conference on Medieval Legal history
By Mia Münster-Swendsen & Helle Vogt (eds.) – 1. ed. 2006
ISBN 978-87-574-1437-0

**Law and Power in the Middle Ages**
Proceedings of the Fourth Carlsberg Academy Conference of Medieval Legal history.
By Per Andersen, Mia Münster-Swendsen & Helle Vogts (eds.) – 1. ed. 2008
ISBN 978-87-574-1884-2

**Law and Religion in Multicultural Societies**
By Rubya Mehdi, Hanne Petersen, Erik Reenberg Sand & Gordon R. Woodman (eds.), 1. ed. 2008
ISBN 978-87-574-1843-9

**Law before Gratian**
Law in Western Europe c. 500-1100
Proceedings of the third Carlsberg Academy Conference on Medieval Legal history
By Per Andersen, Mia Münster-Swendsen & Helle Vogt (eds.) – 1. ed. 2007
ISBN 978-87-574-1647-3

**Mediation**
– a non-model
By Vibeke Vindeløv – 1. ed. 2007
ISBN 978-87-574-1479-3

**Mediation**
Six ways in seven days
By Hans Boserup – 1. ed. 2007
ISBN 978-87-574-1755-5

**Regulating competition in the EU**
By Bent Iversen, Pernille Wegener Jessen. Bent Ole Gram Mortensen, Michael Steinicke & Karsten Engsig Sørensen (eds.) – 1. ed. 2008
ISBN 978-87-574-1697-8

**Retfærd**
**Piere Bourdieu: From Law to Legal Field**
By Ole Hammerslev (ed.) – 1. ed. 2006
ISBN 978-87-7318-677-0

**The Principal Danish Criminal Act**
The criminal Code, The Corrections Act, The Administration of Justice Act
By Vagn Greve, Gitte Høyer, Malene Freese Jensen & Martin Spencer – 3. ed. 2006
ISBN 978-87-574-1334-2

**The New EU Public Procurement Directive**
By Ruth Nielsen & Steen Treumer (eds.) – 1. ed. 2005
ISBN 978-87-574-1244-4

**Public international Computer Network Law Issues**
By Henrik Spang-Hanssen – 1. ed. 2006
ISBN 978-87-574-1486-8

**Public Procurement Law**
– the EU directive on public contracts
By Simon Evers Hjelmborg, Peter Stig Jakobsen & Sune Troels Poulsen – 1. ed. 2006
ISBN 978-87-574-1408-0

**The Services Directive**
– Consequences for the Welfare State and the European Social Model
By Ulla Neergaard, Ruth Nielsen & Lynn Rosberry (eds.) – 1. ed. 2008
ISBN 978-87-574-1806-4

**Yearbook for Nordic Tax Research**
Taxation of Pensions
By Robert Påhlsson (ed.) – 1. ed. 2007
ISBN 978-87-574-1774-6

**Yearbook of Nordic Tax Research 2008**
Taxcation of Capital and wage Income: Towards separated or more Integrated Personal Tax Systems?
By Robert Påhlsson (ed.) – 1. ed. 2008
ISBN 978-87-574-1872-9